P9-COP-641

CHILDREN OF GRACE
THE NEZ PERCE WAR OF 1877

BRUCE HAMPTON

UNIVERSITY OF NEBRASKA PRESS
LINCOLN AND LONDON

⊗

First Nebraska paperback printing: 2002

Library of Congress Cataloging-in-Publication Data
Hampton, Bruce.
Children of grace: the Nez Perce War of 1877 / Bruce Hampton.
p.   cm.
Originally published: New York: H. Holt, 1994.
Includes bibliographical references and index.
ISBN 0-8032-7334-7 (pbk.: alk. paper)
1. Nez Percâ Indians—Wars, 1977.   I. Title.
E83.877 .H36   2002
978.8′2—dc21
2002020312

CHILDREN OF GRACE

In thinking about American Indian history,
it has become essential to follow the
policy of cautious street crossers:
Remember to look both ways.
—Patricia Nelson Limerick, *The Legacy of Conquest* (1987)

1

*I*t was midday nearly halfway through *hillal,* the season of melting mountain snow and rising rivers—called by whites the
month of June—when three Nez Perce warriors halted their horses
along the pine-covered ridge and looked over the Idaho prairie
below.

Two of the three young men were riding together on a single
horse, and whites later would recall their surprise at the poor condition of both mounts. They had not come far that day, only from the
ancient campsite called Tepahlewam, one that had been used each
summer for generations, perhaps millennia. Some six hundred or
more Nez Perce had been camped there since early June, more than
two-thirds women, children, and elderly men.

This summer was different, for their people had brought nearly
all their possessions with them. Tepahlewam, as well as the surrounding land they inhabited during other seasons of the year, was
no longer theirs. Before the end of the coming day, June 14, 1877,
whites had demanded that they stand within the boundaries of the
Indian reservation to the north, joining other Nez Perce bands already there. If they did not come willingly, the one-armed general

they called Cut Arm had said they would be forced by "bullets or bayonets."

During the previous two weeks, women dug the roots of camas and kouse while men raced horses and sat around talking about what was happening to themselves, their land, their dignity. Much of the talk had been melancholy, but it was also prideful and brimming with hatred toward whites. The reservation boundaries seemed capricious and unjust, forced upon them by a treaty they had never agreed to, allowing them only a fraction of the land originally promised. Moreover, the deadline, which only gave them a month to remove to the reservation, had cost them hundreds of cattle and horses they had been unable to herd across the swollen spring rivers. Settlers and miners had overrun their land, had cheated, robbed, and even sometimes killed their friends and relatives. Not once, the Nez Perce claimed, had they taken up a weapon in anger against a white man.[1]

Allalimya Takanin, known to whites as Looking Glass, a sympathetic tribesman from a village whose lands were unaffected by the decree, warned the other headmen to keep their young warriors in check. Although he returned to his village on June 10, Looking Glass continued to worry. In the following days, he would send three different emissaries to Tepahlewam cautioning the other chiefs to quiet those advocating vengeance.

The three youths riding the two horses were members of White Bird's band and all were related. Sarpsis Ilppilp was the cousin of Wahlitits, and behind Wahlitits rode his seventeen-year-old nephew, Swan Necklace. After so much time it is impossible to know precisely what happened earlier that day, but it is believed that Wahlitits and Sarpsis Ilppilp had ridden together in a traditional parade ceremony, called *tel-lik-leen*. In passing through the village, their horse stepped on a piece of canvas covered with drying kouse roots.

The owner shouted at Wahlitits, "See what you do! Playing brave you ride over my woman's hard-worked food! If you are so brave, why don't you go kill the white man who killed your father?" Those present who would survive the coming war recalled that Wahlitits replied bitterly, "You will be sorry for your words."[2]

Wahlitits's father had been killed two years before by a white man named Larry Ott. When Ott built a fence around a piece of property that formerly had been used as a campground by the Nez Perce, the Indian objected and a heated argument ensued. One account says Wahlitits's father threw a rock that hit Ott and knocked him to the ground. Others say the old man merely shook a blanket at Ott's horse. In any event, Ott retaliated by shooting the chief, who died a few days later. A grand jury convened but discharged the case because Indian witnesses refused to be sworn, saying that "they do not believe in a God, that the earth made them, and that they could tell the truth without holding up their hand."[3]

Now, stung by the taunt, Wahlitits collected Sarpsis Ilppilp, and with Swan Necklace along as horse holder, began riding south along the Salmon River to the home of Larry Ott.

Winding down the steep trail into White Bird Creek, the three youths stopped at Harry Mason's store. They wanted to trade a horse for a rifle, but Mason declined. The shopkeeper had administered a whipping to two Nez Perce earlier that spring, and although a council of arbitration had ruled in his favor, Mason was uneasy. While the men dickered, Mason kept his hand on a revolver under the counter.

Crossing the Salmon River, the three riders arrived at Ott's ranch about six miles upriver. He was not at home. After waiting several hours, they grew impatient and continued upriver to the home of Richard Devine, a retired English sailor. Devine had allegedly murdered a crippled Indian years before and was known for his cruelty to the Nez Perce.

Leaving Swan Necklace with the horses, Sarpsis Ilppilp and Wahlitits entered the cabin and found the fifty-two-year-old prospector alone in bed. Overpowering him, they killed Devine with his own rifle. Then they started back downriver, arriving early the next morning at Henry Elfers's homestead. Elfers had not done the Nez Perce great harm, but some claimed that he had set his dogs on defenseless Indians in the past, and he had been on the council that had acquitted Harry Mason that spring. Now the Indians shot and killed Elfers and two hired hands, stole his gun and several horses, then continued on to White Bird Creek.

Soon the warriors met Samuel Benedict, who was out looking for lost cows. Sarpsis Ilppilp knew the man well. Two years before,

Benedict had unloaded a shotgun full of buckshot at him when he and several other Nez Perce had visited Benedict's store demanding liquor. Injured in the head, Sarpsis Ilppilp eventually recovered. He now raised his rifle and shot Benedict, who fell to the ground, wounded in both thighs. He lay still, feigning death, and the three youths hurried back to Tepahlewam.

There, people streamed around them shouting approval, and some warriors immediately prepared for battle. Led by Sarpsis Ilppilp's father, Yellow Bull, the group was mostly composed of young men from White Bird's band. Heinmot Tooyalakekt—known to whites as Chief Joseph—and his brother Ollokot, both of the Wallowa band and longtime advocates of peace, were across the Salmon River butchering cattle they had left behind earlier.

After the warriors departed, the headmen in camp went into council. Some thought war inevitable while others cautioned restraint. At the end, they decided to wait and see how the whites reacted. Meanwhile, they determined that Tepahlewam was unsafe and prepared to break camp the next day. When Joseph and Ollokot returned the following morning, they pleaded with the others to remain, saying they would "make some kind of peace" with the whites. But the mood was one of mistrust, for the Nez Perce knew that seldom did whites discern between actions of individual Indians and those of an entire band. Although only one of the men who joined Yellow Bull's raiders was from the Wallowa band, Joseph remarked later that he could "hardly go back," knowing that whites would say "that my young men have killed the white men."[4] Adding to Joseph's reluctance to move was the fact that his wife had just given birth to a daughter the day before.

Late that night, however, unknown assailants fired several shots through the remaining tipis, frightening the occupants but injuring no one. In the morning, the Wallowas broke camp and hurried to join the other bands.

Shortly after noon on June 14, Yellow Bull and the raiders approached Jack Manuel's ranch on White Bird Creek. Earlier, Manuel's nearby neighbor, seventy-four-year-old James Baker, had brought news of the outbreak. Baker wanted to go to Mount Idaho, but Manuel convinced him that it was safer to remain at his ranch.

Baker went home, only to return an hour later, this time with Patrick Brice, a forty-year-old prospector passing through on his way to the settlements. The men conferred, and Baker and Brice soon departed to warn settlers at Mount Idaho. They had gone only a short distance, however, when they saw Indians approaching and quickly turned back.

Instead of staying at Manuel's ranch, the men decided to go immediately to Baker's ranch, about a mile away, believing its stone cellar more defensible than the Manuel homestead. Brice and Manuel's father-in-law, George Popham, volunteered to stay behind and lock the doors while Baker, Manuel and his wife, Jennet, and their two children, six-year-old Maggie and her eleven-month-old brother, started for Baker's ranch. They had only gone a short distance when about twenty warriors attacked. Baker fell first and, as Maggie later recalled, raised himself up off the ground only long enough to say what sounds like a subtitle in a silent Western: "Goodbye, Jack, they've got me!"[5] Manuel was hit by an arrow in the back of his neck and fell off his horse when another warrior took aim with a rifle and shot him through the hip. As he tumbled down the hill into the brush, the warriors left him for dead. Riding behind her father, Maggie suffered two arrow wounds, one in the upper arm and another in the back of her head. As she fell from the horse, she broke her arm just above the wrist.

In the confusion, Jennet Manuel—small, thin, and said to be adorned with blond hair reaching almost to her feet—gathered her children and began running back to the house. The Nez Perce followed close behind, gaining on her when she left the road. As Brice watched from the house, a warrior chased her until she fell over a rock, injuring both her knee and her son whom she was carrying. There Brice claims the man caught her and, in the only proper printed language of the day, "accomplished his desires."[6]

From outside the house, the warriors indicated to Popham and Brice that they would not be harmed if they gave up their weapons. After a few tense moments, the men handed over a rifle and a shotgun, and true to their word, the warriors departed. Jennet Manuel went into the house to care for her children's wounds, while the men, having been told by the Indians that others might not be so merciful, took to the brush outside. Sometime that night, Brice and Popham became separated when they heard more warriors approaching along the trail. The next morning Brice found Maggie in a thicket close to the house; her whimperings had drawn him to her. He wrapped her in a blanket and gave her water, but the little girl was in deep shock, needing food and medical attention. Maggie told Brice that the night before an Indian had entered the house, stabbing her mother to death and killing her baby brother. Brice hid with the little girl that day and the next, then finally decided he had to seek help or watch her die.

Accompanied by Maggie, shoeless and wearing only a nightgown, an unarmed Brice walked out of the willows toward a nearby group of warriors and asked for permission to leave. He said he wanted nothing to do with their fight with the whites, that all he wanted was to take the little girl to safety at Camas Prairie. Some wanted to kill him, but one warrior interceded, demanding to know if the men were willing to care for the child once the white man was dead. When all fell silent, Brice picked up Maggie and started for Mount Idaho. But before he left, he entered the Manuel house to look for Jennet Manuel and her baby son. Brice found no sign of them.

Sunday night Brice and Maggie climbed the hill between White Bird Creek and Camas Prairie. Several miles beyond, they reached an abandoned ranch that earlier had been looted by a war party. Finding some stale bread and salted pork, the two "fared sumptuously." Then Brice fashioned an empty dry-goods box into a seat, Maggie scrambled on, and Brice strapped the box to his back. The next evening they walked into Mount Idaho to an astonished welcome.[7]

But what happened to Jennet Manuel and her baby son? Why had Brice not found their bodies in the house? Throughout her long life, Maggie Manuel continued to hold to her original story, going so far as to accuse Chief Joseph of being the man who had stabbed her mother in the breast with a knife and then killed her baby brother, leaving them both lying in a pool of blood. As she stood barefoot over their corpses, Maggie recalled, "the blood oozed between my toes."[8] In shock and suffering from her own wounds, she wandered outside and hid in the willows until Brice found her. The same day

Maggie and Brice made their escape, the Nez Perce burned the Manuel house.

Local newspapers made much of this, declaring Jennet Manuel was "ravaged and then burned at the stake." Several men later sifted through the ashes but failed to find any human bones. One investigator discovered a pair of earrings she had been wearing, some taking it as proof that the woman and her son perished in the flames. A settler at Slate Creek later wrote that he overheard an Indian say that they had been killed by a drunken warrior. Whether they died from wounds or fire, Jennet Manuel and her son were never seen again.[9]

A few miles downstream from the Manuels, a fiery redheaded Isabella Benedict watched her wounded husband ride into the yard outside their house the morning of June 14. As she ran to help him, he slipped painfully off his horse and lay on the ground, bleeding profusely from gunshot wounds in both legs.

Soon five French emigrant miners, unaware of the outbreak, arrived from downriver. When they heard Benedict's story, they left one man to assist the family while the remaining four hastened back across the river to get their weapons. Isabella gave the miner the family breechloader in case the warriors came back. Only a few minutes passed before she saw Indians approaching, and she hurried to tell her husband. Benedict told her to flee. She and her two children ran out of the house toward the back gate but quickly returned when they spied warriors on the hillside across the creek. Entering the room where her husband had been, she could not find him. As she turned toward the Frenchman standing in the front doorway, shots suddenly rang out. The man pitched back into the room and collapsed on the floor, blood-spattered and dead. The warriors rushed into the house and, finding only Isabella and her children, ordered them to leave. Once outside, the three hid in some nearby willows.

Meanwhile, Benedict had abandoned the house and was struggling across a small bridge over White Bird Creek when the warriors discovered him. They shot and he fell dead into the creek. Then the raiders returned to the house, pillaging the adjacent store of ammunition and a keg of whiskey.

At two o'clock that afternoon, a warning reached Harry Mason and William Osborn, whose homesteads were above White Bird Creek on the Salmon River. When the news came, Mason had just finished lunch and was lying on a cot in a corner of his store. With no illusions about his unpopularity with the Nez Perce, Mason led a party downriver late that evening consisting of his sister, Helen Walsh, and her two children; Osborn, his wife, Elizabeth, and their four children; and an employee, William George. Arriving at Baker's, they stumbled on the raiders and a fight began. Neither side advanced, and as darkness settled over the valley, the whites decided to escape back upriver.

William George—who had the tip of his little finger blown off in the scuffle—volunteered to go for help at Mount Idaho. The others made their way back to Mason's ranch, arriving at daybreak to find François Chodoze and another employee known only as Shoemaker eating breakfast. This was either a brave or foolish feat, considering that the Nez Perce had raided the homestead just hours before while the two men lay hidden in the brush. Fearing the Indians' return, Mason suggested they travel on to Osborn's ranch. Shoemaker lingered behind to let the calves out of the corral.

But the party no sooner arrived at Osborn's homestead when the Nez Perce discovered them. "We all ran in," said Helen Walsh, "and the Indians rode up and called on the men to come out; Mr. Osborn told them to *Clatawa!* They called out again, and Mr. Osborn told them to leave." Harry Mason sprang onto one of the beds to fire through an opening between the logs. He had a clear shot at several Indians and was about to pull the trigger when Osborn called out, "Don't shoot yet!" Then Elizabeth Osborn repeated, "Don't shoot, Harry!" Osborn knew several of the warriors and still hoped to avoid bloodshed. Harry "turned and looked at them, lowering his gun without a word," said Walsh. "I shall never forget that look. There was a prophecy in it. He knew he was giving up his last chance."[10]

From outside the Indians began firing at the only window in the cabin. The three men positioned themselves around the broken glass and had just raised up to shoot when the warriors fired another volley. Osborn and Chodoze were killed almost instantly. A bullet shattered Mason's right arm and he fell to the floor, bleeding heavily. As more bullets came crashing through the window, the women and children scrambled under a bed and Mason recovered enough to roll under another. When no returning fire came from the house, the warriors battered down the front door. As they charged in, Helen Walsh pushed a revolver across the floor toward Mason, but he was too weak to hold it. "If I could only shoot," she remembered him saying.

The warriors jumped up and down on the beds until the women and children crawled out. One man grabbed Mason by his injured arm, pulling him toward the door. "Oh, shoot me!" Helen Walsh heard him beg, and holding a revolver against Mason's head, the Indian obliged. Then the raiders turned to the two women. In all published accounts she gave later, Helen Walsh claimed that she and Elizabeth Osborn were treated kindly by the war party. "They told us that they did not want to kill us; that we could go to Slate Creek or Lewiston without fear." But a man who saw them a week later claimed the women would not show themselves because of their shame. Another settler suggested that they had "received treatment that was but little better than death," leaving no doubt what either one really meant.[11] Rape was not an unknown allegation during the first few days of the outbreak, but if the women were so abused they took the secret to their graves; they were never pressed for a public admission.

But they did survive. Finally the raiders rode away, leaving the women and children staring at the dead bodies. Stunned and in shock, Elizabeth Osborn insisted on changing into a black dress; her husband was dead and it was only proper. A dazed Helen Walsh led the survivors to a nearby ranch, where they found some milk and fed their children. "As for ourselves," recalled Walsh, "we did not seem to realize that we should ever want anything." While they rested, Shoemaker overtook them, wet and shaking from cold. After letting out Mason's calves, he went to the cabin, arriving just as the attack began. With no cover about, he ran to the river, jumped into the frigid water up to his neck, and stayed there until it became unbearable. All eventually made it to safety at Slate Creek, where about forty women and children and thirty men had taken shelter behind a stockade built of heavy timbers. One week later a group of volunteers ventured out and buried the dead men, saying of the corpses that little remained but their feet encased in boots.

That same afternoon some twenty miles north, Benjamin Norton stood on his front porch and greeted a wagon driven by Lew Wilmot and Pete Ready. The teamsters were hauling freight from Lewiston to Mount Idaho, and Norton's home, known as Cottonwood House —a combination store, saloon, hotel, and stage station about eighteen miles west of Grangeville—was a popular stop between Lewiston and the settlements. Norton managed the outpost with his wife, Jennie; their nine-year-old son, Hill; and his wife's teenage sister, Lynn Bowers. Norton was well liked, had a special love of horses, and was known as one of the best horse breeders in the country.

As the teamsters prepared to leave, Lew Day, a messenger from Mount Idaho, arrived bearing bad news. Day carried dispatches for the army post at Fort Lapwai announcing the killings that morning along the Salmon River. He told Norton and the teamsters that settlers were coming to Mount Idaho for protection. Moments after Day rode away, John Chamberlin appeared with his wife and two children, traveling to Lewiston with a wagon load of flour. Norton told Chamberlin the news, and the two men then tried to convince the teamsters—particularly Wilmot, who was known as a crack shot with a rifle—to spend the night at Norton's and travel with them to Mount Idaho in the morning. The men were in a hurry, however, and soon departed, camping later that night along Cottonwood Creek.

If those remaining at Norton's were uneasy, their fear must have been palpable when Lew Day suddenly returned less than twenty minutes after he had left, shot in the right shoulder. Three or four Indians had jumped him in a running fight, and he had barely managed to escape. While Jennie Norton dressed Day's wound, Norton and Chamberlin lost no time preparing to leave immediately for Mount Idaho. Departing Cottonwood House about nine o'clock under a starry sky with good visibility, Chamberlin drove his wagon containing the women and children while Day, Norton, and a hired man, Joe Moore, rode horseback.

They had not gone far before they overtook Wilmot and Ready. Norton tried to convince the teamsters to come with them, but already camped for the night, the two men declined. "This is the last time we will see you boys alive," Norton called out as their wagon bumped down the road.[12] It would turn out to be true, but not as Norton imagined. An hour later, the teamsters heard what sounded like faint shots far off in the night. After a restless sleep, they rose just before daybreak and had traveled only three miles when they heard a piercing war cry. Unhitching their team and with only a quarter-mile lead, the two men fled, riding bareback toward Grangeville. Two miles from town, the Indians gave up the chase and returned to the abandoned wagon. There they found a dozen baskets of champagne, twelve bottles of brandy, and a barrel of whiskey.

It had been gunfire that the teamsters had heard the night before. Several miles from Cottonwood House, Norton's party ran into the raiders. For a brief time they managed to gain slightly on their pursuers until a bullet dropped Lew Day from his horse. Chamberlin stopped the wagon long enough for the twice-wounded man to climb on, then suddenly Norton was hit in the leg and another bullet felled his horse. As Norton climbed aboard, a warrior shot one of the harness horses, and the wagon plowed to a halt.

Day jumped out and hid behind one of the dead horses. With his own horse down and two of his fingers shot away, Moore took cover next to Day only to be hit in the hip. The two men managed to hold the warriors at bay while Norton and Chamberlin hurried the women and children under the wagon. The Nez Perce kept up their desultory but accurate fire throughout the night. Day received four additional bullet wounds and, in the manner of victims who have lost much blood, his thirst became uncontrollable. When Norton stood up to fetch him a container of water, a warrior shot him in the thigh, severing his femoral artery. Jennie Norton—described by a journalist as "a very pretty brunette, with soft, large eyes, like an antelope" —was desperate.[13] She pleaded with her husband to let her go to the Indians and beg for their lives. Norton reluctantly agreed; there was no alternative. As she stood up, a bullet ripped through the calves of both her legs and she fell, dislocating an ankle.

Meanwhile, John Chamberlin decided to run for it. Gathering his wife and two daughters, he moved off into the night. But soon they became disoriented. A short while later, young Hill Norton heard screaming in the distance, several shots, then silence. With the Chamberlins gone, both Day and his father mortally wounded, and Moore and his mother crippled, only he and Lynn Bowers remained capable of going for help. Hill recalled that his tearful father "choked out that I should try to get away, but mother did not want me to go. Father said, 'He'll be killed here anyway.' "[14] Nothing seemed closer to the truth. Along with Lynn Bowers, who removed her heavy skirt to run faster, the two slipped away into the darkness.

The night dragged on for Jennie Norton as she watched first Lew Day then her husband drop into unconsciousness, slowly bleeding to death. The only hope she had was Moore, who refused to give up. Painfully crawling out from under the wagon and returning with ammunition he found scattered about, Moore kept up a constant fire until it was exhausted. When he located rounds he was unable to use in his gun, he dug out the powder and loaded Norton's shotgun. The retort carried no lead, but the bright flashes held off the warriors until daybreak.

By first light, the Indians had disappeared. When Day regained consciousness and began moaning again for water, Jennie crawled to some nearby grass and with a tin cup "tried to dip up enough dew to wet Lew Day's lips." She had gone only a short distance when she heard a horse approaching. Knowing the warriors had returned, she lay deathly still, covering her head, afraid to move. The rider dismounted and as he walked up behind her, she heard a pistol cock. "Don't shoot, for God's sake! It's us!" shouted Moore from under the wagon. Jennie looked up into the barrel of the revolver. Holding the gun was Frank Fenn, a settler from Mount Idaho.[15]

Just after dawn, Fenn and five others had found Hill Norton on the outskirts of Grangeville and immediately rode to where the party was under siege. The first to arrive and convinced that Jennie Norton—covered in blood—was an Indian, Fenn was about to shoot her when Moore cried out. The men quickly loaded all but the dead Norton into the wagon, cutting the fallen horses from their traces. Hitching their own horses to the wagon, they looked up to see a large war party bearing down on them. With Indians in hot pursuit, the men ran the horses at top speed, arriving at Grangeville just as more volunteers rode out to meet them, forcing the warriors to abandon the chase.

Later that morning, a search party of about forty men found the body of John Chamberlin "cold in death," a few hundred yards from where he had wandered from the wagon. Cradled in his arms was his three-year-old daughter, "beyond all earthly harm." Huddled underneath Chamberlin's legs, the men discovered his younger daughter, terrified and wounded, but alive. By most accounts, the child had a severe wound on one side of her neck, as if a knife had been stuck diagonally through it, barely missing her jugular vein. The tip of her tongue was also gone. An imaginative journalist thought the Indians had grown tired of her crying and "had tried to cut off the end of her tongue," but others believed she probably had fallen and bitten it off accidently.[16]

About a mile away, rescuers led by John Rowton found Chamberlin's pregnant wife wandering about hysterically after having been repeatedly raped, an ugly arrow wound in her breast. The men had to "run her down and surround her before we could make her believe we were friends," said one of the volunteers. Idaho district attorney J. W. Poe later alleged the older daughter had been killed as the mother watched "by having its head placed between the knees of a powerful Indian and crushed to death."[17] History records that Mrs. Chamberlin and her daughter survived, but how and in what state we can only surmise.

The following morning, June 16, twenty volunteers under George Shearer discovered three warriors at an abandoned homestead near Grangeville. On seeing the horsemen, two of the Indians quickly mounted and galloped away. But an older man named Jyeloo had a game leg, a bad back, and only a single bullet for his old rechambered 50-70. He had trouble catching his horse, who turned out to be a poor runner, and the volunteers, eager for revenge, soon overtook him. After shooting Jyeloo several times in the back, Shearer emptied both barrels of his shotgun into the man's body. Dismounting, he then broke the stock of his gun over the head of the old warrior, crushing his skull.

. . .

Two weeks before the outbreak, the Lewiston *Teller* described Mount Idaho as a "lovely burg nestled at the fringe of the precious metal bearing hills of Northern Idaho, about sixty-five miles east of Lewiston, with a fertile valley spreading out before it, where grain is raised in abundance and superb quality. Fruit such as apples and their kindred flourishes majestically. There is no church and no minister in that infant town, yet its citizens are good, true and moral. . . ."[18]

Nearby Grangeville was also young and growing and eventually would become the larger of the two towns. Farms and ranches were springing up along the edge of Camas Prairie, and what had once grown only wild camas before the whites began to till the soil now promised a wealth of agricultural riches. Just beyond the prairie, in the mountains, lay untold fortunes awaiting the miner. The only impediment to progress were the "savages" who occupied the land, claimed the newspaper, but deep down everyone knew they hungered for the tempering hand of civilization.

Town spokesperson and hotel owner L. P. Brown became alarmed when some Nez Perce entered Mount Idaho on June 14 and offered a storekeeper $2.50 for a can of black powder, a price so beyond its worth that some observed correctly that hostilities had already commenced. Brown quickly sent a messenger to Fort Lapwai warning of tribal unrest. Later that day, as word of the murders spread, Brown dispatched Lew Day to Fort Lapwai, and the town began turning into a stockade. Volunteers blocked the street with wagons and logs and lost no time constructing a small fort just above town. The residents took refuge inside the stockade that night, singing "Onward Christian Soldiers" and "Nearer My God to Thee." The war fever was so high-pitched that hardly anyone could sleep. To soothe the children, who were particularly fearful, John Rowton, the volunteer who would find the deranged Mrs. Chamberlin on the prairie and who possessed an unusually melodious voice, climbed to the top of a large pine tree growing inside the stockade and quieted them all with a lullaby.[19]

Early on the morning of June 15, Arthur "Ad" Chapman, a rancher who raised horses near Grangeville, spoke fluent Nez Perce, and had an Indian wife, met with Looking Glass and several other

FLIGHT OF THE NEZ PERCE 1877

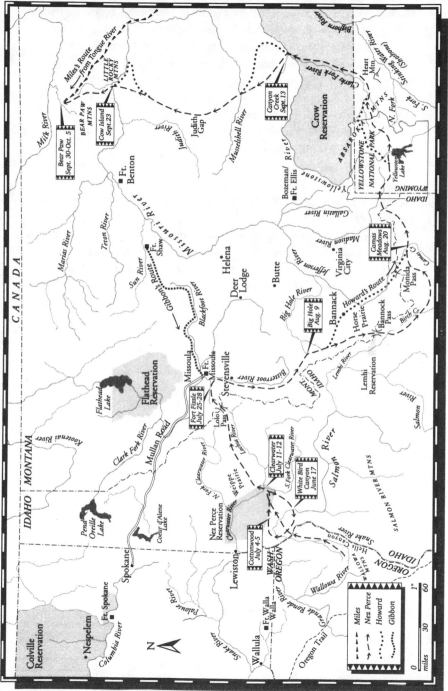

Indians who claimed to be noncombatants. Chapman had had a stormy relationship with the Nez Perce; however, his relations with Looking Glass were apparently good. The men told Chapman the names of whites who had died so far. When he learned that Lew Day had failed to reach Lapwai, Chapman talked Looking Glass's brother into carrying another dispatch to the fort. To maximize the chances of their message getting through, L. P. Brown also separately sent another courier. About this time the volunteers discovered Hill Norton and were on their way to rescue survivors.

Women in Mount Idaho were terrified when Mrs. Chamberlin was brought into town, convinced of the fate awaiting them if the Indians overran the stockade. Outraged District Attorney Poe charged that during these few days no fewer than five women had "suffered from the brutal fiends' outrages" after being "stripped of their clothing and dragged about naked by the heels." Although all had defended themselves "to the last extremity," they had become "the victims of the lust of the hell hounds."[20] Poe never acknowledged that there were Nez Perce women who had received similar treatment in the past at the hands of whites, treatment they would experience again before this conflict ended.

Jennie Norton and Mrs. Chamberlin were cared for in Brown's hotel, although friends held scant hope for either one. With the town doctor away, one of the treatments used was the running of a silk handkerchief through the wounds in Jennie's legs. But both recovered, and Jennie Norton was reunited with her son. Lew Day and Joe Moore were placed on litters in the hotel dining room. Day lived for six days; Joe Moore died of his wounds two months later. Lynn Bowers was found alive and unharmed, hiding in brush close to town, incoherent with fear. Although the exact number is disputed, at least eighteen whites eventually died as a result of the outbreak. Convinced that alcohol would fuel the war flames, Lew Wilmot led an expedition of volunteers to Cottonwood Creek to recover the liquor left behind in his wagon, hoping at the same time to "get us some Indians."[21] But when the men reached the location where the Norton party had been attacked, they saw sixty warriors approaching and quickly retreated. By June 16, Mount Idaho swelled to 250 people and anyone not there was given up for dead.

Fifteen miles away, the Nez Perce were just as restless, feeling nervous and vulnerable, squeezed between Fort Lapwai and the settlements with no clear route of retreat if it should become necessary. A council was held and the bands made their way to Lahmotta, known to whites as White Bird Canyon. Here, where many of the murders had taken place, their camp was protected by ridges and hills at the bottom of the steep but open valley, with ample escape routes. By Saturday, June 17, both settlers and Indians spent their hours strengthening defenses, waiting anxiously for the soldiers they knew would soon come. Each side began to comprehend the shock and horror of the past three days. It was enough for John Rowton to conclude, "May such trials be forever gone."[22]

But indeed, they had only just begun.

2

In 1492, perhaps five million aborigines inhabited the conterminous United States. By 1865, there were fewer than half a million, some the victims of war but most having succumbed to disease introduced by Europeans, particularly smallpox, measles, and influenza. Few of the newcomers expressed concern. Native people had become an obstacle to that holiest of grails: Manifest Destiny. As America looked westward after the Civil War, the mood toward Indians was decidedly ugly and getting more so every day.[1]

The nineteenth century had not begun that way. Some sixty years before, the official spirit was one of tolerance and brotherhood toward Native Americans living beyond the frontier. "Made by the same Great Spirit, and living in the same land with our brothers, the red men," Thomas Jefferson had declared, "we consider ourselves as the same family; we wish to live with them as one people, and to cherish their interests as our own."[2] Lewis and Clark carried Jefferson's peace message on their journey to the Pacific, and returning, they told a wondrous tale about a Columbia River tribe they called the Chopunnish or Pierced-Nosed Indians.

The explorers had just separated into two groups after crossing the Bitterroot Mountains between what were to become Idaho and Montana, a range one of their men termed "the most terrible mountains I ever beheld."[3] In late September 1805, the journey became increasingly difficult as their food supply dwindled. The entire expedition was on the verge of collapse. With six hunters, Clark set out ahead to obtain game. As the men made their way out of the mountains, they stumbled on a small village of Chopunnish, who welcomed them and provided food and shelter.

In their haste to winter on the western coast, the explorers soon departed, retracing their route back to the Rocky Mountains the following spring. There, late-melting mountain snows kept them guests of the Chopunnish for several weeks. Now they took time to study their hosts. The rugged, hilly land of the plateau country had molded this largest tribe in the Northwest, whom Lewis estimated numbered nearly six thousand, into a virile people. They practiced no agriculture but were good hunters and fishers. In spring and summer, the tribe traveled to root-gathering grounds where they dug kouse and camas.

In their own language, they called themselves *Nee-Me-Poo,* roughly translated as "the people." There seems little doubt that when Lewis and Clark first met them, some of the tribe pierced their noses and wore the colorful dentalium shells or wampum obtained from coastal tribes. The practice soon faded away, although the French-Canadian sobriquet *Nez Percé* (now anglicized and pronounced "nez purse") would stick. Some authorities believe the Nez Perce never had pierced noses to any great extent, that their name was a mistake in sign language translation. One of the Plains Indians' signs for the Nez Perce was made by passing the index finger from one side of the nose to the other, suggesting a brave person who refused to flinch even at an arrow shooting right past his or her nose. The Kiowa name for the Nez Perce, *Adalkatoigo,* meaning "the people with hair cut across the forehead," may have been more apropos since early paintings reveal that this was a common practice. Red and ochre were favorite colors, and often the forehead was painted brilliantly, with strips of ermine fur woven into the sidebraids of the men.[4]

Lewis and Clark noted that males were affable and gentle, rarely moved to passion, but were not lacking courage when attacked. Women were short and had bright, intelligent, and "handsom" faces. The Nez Perce did not practice the sun dance of the Plains Indians, and much to the explorers' surprise, they did not eat dog and were repulsed that the white men did. The travois was used to carry items when traveling in open country, with packs on horses the preferred method in the mountains. Buffalo disappeared from the plateau country sometime before the whites first made contact with the Nez Perce, but by then the tribe had begun making hunting forays across the Bitterroot Mountains to the eastern plains. In their trips to buffalo country, they would set out in the spring and return as much as a year or two later; often there would be two parties, one going and one returning, meeting on the way. Men, women, and children might go on these excursions, although often males traveled without their families. Highly valued buffalo hides were the main item brought back, since the meat was heavy and spoiled unless thoroughly dried.

The Nez Perce used three main trails to the buffalo country: one to the north near present-day Coeur d'Alene, the Lolo Trail in existence long before Lewis and Clark, and the longer and infrequently used Salmon-Bitterroot trail to the south, known as the Old Nez Perce Trail. As the Nez Perce learned to train and raise horses, they traveled these high country routes to the plains until they had as much in common with that culture as their traditional neighbors in the fishing villages along the Columbia River.

The origin of Nez Perce horsemanship is unknown, but it probably developed at least a century before contact with whites. According to oral tradition, they learned to ride by having one man lead the horse slowly while the rider attempted to balance himself with the aid of two long sticks, one in each hand, reaching to the ground like crutches. It was not long before they were breeding horses. The animals thrived and multiplied, and the Nez Perce soon became the major supplier of horses to neighboring tribes, one man owning as many as fifteen hundred head. Fifty years after Lewis and Clark, Henry Miller, editor of the Portland *Oregonian*, noted that "the Nez Perce horses are much finer than any Indian horses I have yet seen. A great many are large, fine-bred American stock, with fine limbs, rising withers, sloping well back, and are uncommonly sinewy and sure-footed." Another observer declared Nez Perce horses "infinitely superior to any in the United States."[5]

By the time of contact with whites, they were practicing selective breeding, perhaps the only Indians to do so on the continent. Lewis thought their gelding method "preferable to that practiced by ourselves," and he remarked that their "active and durable" horses were often pied "with large spots of white irregularly scattered and intermixed" with darker colors.[6] From this early description, the Nez Perce and the closely related Palouse have been credited with developing the Appaloosa, a popular breed marked with such distinctive spots. Doubtless the Nez Perce maintained a number of these horses, but there is no direct evidence that they actually favored one pattern over another, endurance and speed being the sought-after qualities.

For weapons, early Nez Perce crafted a powerful bow made from wild sheep horn that was widely admired by other tribes. An arrow from such a bow was said to drive clear through a deer. A bone whistle eight inches long, made from the leg or wing of a sandhill crane or eagle and carried about the neck, was used in battle or times of great need when the bearer wanted to call upon his *wyakin* —a kind of guardian or tutelary spirit—for assistance.

Of all the plateau tribes, the Nez Perce were the least warlike, but they were quick to fight when threatened. The Bannock Indians to the south, called *te-wel-ka*—loosely translated as "an enemy to be fought"—were the most feared traditional foe, one that was always formidable and demanded respect. Indians living at nearby Celilo Falls on the Columbia River called them the Rattlesnake People because they believed them always watching, ready to strike, like the rattler. In Nez Perce legend, Bannocks are incredibly tough. Once when nearby Cayuse Indians were searching for killers who had raided a village, they captured a Bannock chieftain. Binding his hands, they demanded to know about the murders. Every time he was asked a question, he spitefully told how the Cayuses had been cruelly killed, even though his interrogators cut off one of his fingers after each answer. When ten questions had been asked and none of his fingers remained, the Cayuses hacked off his hands and left him to bleed to death.

The longer Lewis and Clark remained with the Nez Perce, the more their respect grew. What impressed them most was that they were energetic and able, happy "but not gay" people, somewhat introverted and reserved, with a dignified, proud bearing and high moral standards. The expedition's Patrick Gass called the Nez Perce "the most friendly, honest, and ingenuous" of all Indians. Clark, who is said to have fathered one or more children of a Nez Perce woman, said they were "much more clenly in their persons and habitations than any nation we have seen," and praised them for "greater acts of hospitality" than the explorers had witnessed from any nation or tribe since passing the Rocky Mountains.[7]

Theft from either a tribal member or a guest was seriously frowned upon and punishment was often public disgrace. Rape was punishable by death or enforced marriage. Lying was regarded as among the worst infringements of morality, and the epithet *liar* an insult. Their language had no profanity; the worst they said of an individual was that they were *kap-seese*, a no-good or bad person, or the somewhat stronger *yi-hell-lis*, scum of the earth.[8] A small portion of their population consisted of slaves who were not usually purchased but acquired as prisoners of war. Treated well, many eventually became members of the tribe, and the children of slaves were always free. Although far from a strict rule, marriage was generally matrilineal with the husband taking up residence with his wife's family. There was little private ownership, but any personal property belonging to prominent males was frequently given away at their funerals to family members and close friends. The large communal house was owned in common, as were salmon fishing grounds and camas and kouse meadows. As in most Indian cultures, while men hunted and provided security, women handled all domestic chores: gathering berries and making clothing, baskets, mats, and dress skins, as well as cooking and infant child care.

Nez Perce society was remarkably egalitarian and decentralized, a loosely grouped federation of bands based on kinship, ranging in size anywhere from thirty to two hundred people. Although bands frequently intermarried and shared a basic language and cultural heritage, each resided separately with extended forays to temporary hunting, fishing, berry-picking, and root-digging camps. Loose tribal associations for common defense and trade were formed from time to time, but bands remained mostly autonomous. A leader was accepted by several villages in day-to-day affairs, but he spoke only for his own followers in time of crisis. Even then authority was limited, headmen giving counsel and advice rather than orders. Major decisions were most often settled by men in tribal councils. While they had no voice in these meetings, women, through their husbands, nevertheless were influential in tribal decisions.

Lewis and Clark noted that the Nez Perce possessed a long tradition of oratory. There was considerable use of gesticulation and a great display of dignity. Any conclusion of collective business was reached only after extensive and eloquent debate, often lasting for days, the end of which was less majority rule than simple consensus. Accord by persuasion was usually successful, but if an individual or a band disagreed it could go its own way.

Undoubtedly, the Nez Perce valued the useful items of trade that they knew whites would soon bring, and this influenced their friendliness toward the explorers. When the expedition finally left the Nez Perce, Lewis recorded that "these affectionate people [demonstrated] every emotion of unfeigned regret at separating from us."[9] Good relations fostered reciprocity. In the thirty years that followed Lewis and Clark, trade prospered between the Nez Perce and "Americans," the Nez Perce calling them "Big Hearts of the East" due to their liberal trading policies, as compared with the stingy and taciturn British.

To Americans or "Bostons" trapping the beaver country, there came to be no Indians equal in popularity to the Nez Perce. Praised as an unusual species of red men, the tribe was consistently described in unprecedented terms. With unabashed ethnocentrism, the Americans said they were like the best of white people: honorable, sincere, and trustworthy. In their letters and journals they commented on Nez Perce generosity, self-esteem, and dignified bearing; on their cleanliness, well-crafted garments, weapons, and wealth in horses; and on their courage and valor in battle. Most frequently, however, they mentioned what Lewis and Clark had already discovered: that the Nez Perce possessed a high quality of character and were proudly independent. In 1833, an American visiting the upper Snake River wrote, "The people who are most used to this country are so little afraid of the Indians that they either travel without guns or with them unloaded."[10]

This was as close as whites and the Nez Perce would ever come· to Jefferson's vision.

In March 1833, a letter appeared in the New York *Christian Advocate and Journal,* written by G. P. Disosway, a prominent Methodist interested in missionary work. In a passionate appeal, Disosway described four Nez Perce Indians who had traveled "on foot 3,000 miles through thick forests and extensive prairies" seeking God. He called for a mission to "penetrate into these wilds where the Sabbath bell has never yet tolled since the world began" and save "these wandering sons of our native forests."[11] The four visitors were part of a delegation of Nez Perce and Flatheads who had traveled east with trappers after the 1831 fur rendezvous. With no immunity against Euro-American diseases, three of the Nez Perce grew sick and died either while in St. Louis or en route back to the Northwest. One survived the return journey but was killed by Blackfeet before he reached Nez Perce country. The exact purpose of their visit is still debated, but at the time a hue and cry arose that they had come seeking teachers of the "Heavenly Book."

Although isolated, the Nez Perce and nearby Flatheads had certainly heard of Christianity and its Bible from other tribes and fur trappers. At least a decade before Lewis and Clark, a Spokan shaman had prophesied that "soon there will come from the rising sun a different kind of man from any you have yet seen, who will bring with them a book and will teach you everything."[12] Many Indians thus welcomed whites and were anxious to learn of their power since better "medicine" would increase their prestige, although it is doubtful whether they initially discerned any distinction between reading, writing, and white people's religion. It is also highly likely that the Indians had come to encourage increased trade with the "Bostons." Quick to seize such an opportunity, churches rallied around Disosway's letter, and in 1834 a tall, powerfully built man, Reverend Jason Lee, along with three companions, arrived in the Northwest to begin the first Christian mission to the Nez Perce and Flatheads.

Like fur trappers at the rendezvous that year, tourist William Marshall Anderson questioned Lee's intentions, writing in his journal that the Nez Perce were "remarkable for their more than Christian practice of honesty, veracity and very moral virtue which every philosopher and professor so much laud, and practice so little." If the four missionaries en route to save these souls "only succeed in making them such as the whitemen are, not such as they should be," Anderson opined, "it would be charity for these messengers of civilization to desist."[13]

However impressed he was with the eagerness of the Nez Perce for Christian instruction, Lee soon discovered he was not cut out to minister to "heathens," admitting it was easier "converting a tribe of Indians at a missionary meeting than in the wilderness." He soon departed for western Oregon's Willamette Valley, but not before writing in his diary the fervent wish that would come to epitomize white attitudes of supremacy toward the Nez Perce: "O that these sons of nature may soon be the children of grace."[14]

Other Protestants heeded the call, and by 1836 Henry Spalding and his wife, Eliza, settled among the Nez Perce near Lapwai, or Valley of Butterflies, named because the valley periodically attracted large numbers of these insects. Stern and fierce, jealous, with a bitter and furious temper, Spalding had been born a bastard to an "unfeeling mother," who abandoned him when he was fourteen months old. These scars must have flamed inside of him his entire life, for his puritanical methods of converting the Nez Perce to Christianity included beatings and whippings, an action the proud Nez Perce found particularly repugnant. But Lee encouraged Spalding, writing, "Let not the Indians trifle with you, let them know that you must be respected, and whenever they intentionally transgress bounds, make them feel the weight of your displeasure." Spalding could expect to have trouble with them, said Lee, for "the truth is they are *Indians*."[15]

Other missionaries soon joined Spalding, and the history of their relationship is fraught with petty jealousies, false accusations, and behavior so antithetical to Christian precepts that Marshall Anderson's fears proved grossly understated.

By 1842, his influence waning, Spalding welcomed Dr. Elijah White, the new government subagent to Oregon Indians, who had decided to back up the missionaries' authority by imposing a set of laws on the region's tribes. With Spalding's assistance, White inveigled the Nez Perce to agree to regulations that required severe punishment, even death, if violated. White also directed the bands to choose for the first time in their history a single "high chief" of the tribe, an action that was to lead to bitter and lasting tribal conflict.

Instead of strengthening the missionaries' position, White's laws further reduced Spalding's prestige. By 1847, the number of Nez Perce attending his mission school dwindled to almost nothing. Still Spalding's influence and that of his wife, who was well respected among the women of the tribe, was great among certain Indians. Spalding introduced farming, and while he never mastered the Nez Perce tongue, he oversaw efforts to transform their language into writing, eventually printing part of the Bible in Nez Perce. Under the Spaldings, hundreds of Nez Perce learned to read and write in their own language, and a few learned English. Among Spalding's converts was the Wallowa headman variously known as Tu-ke-kas or Old Joseph, as he was called by whites, born sometime between 1785 and 1790, the son of a Nez Perce woman and a Cayuse chief. Tu-ke-kas eventually settled with his mother's people and had a number of wives and children, among which were Young Joseph and his younger brother Ollokot, who would figure prominently in the coming war. There is some indication that both brothers briefly attended Spalding's mission school, although their exposure was minimal and neither ever spoke English.

Not all Nez Perce accepted Spalding's teachings. Those that did became known as "progressives," or Upper Nez Perce, because of their close location to Spalding's mission along the Clearwater River. The bands that resented the missionaries' demands that they give up their traditional ways lived mostly along the lower Salmon and Snake, spoke a slightly different dialect, and were known variously as "heathens," "nonprogressives," or Lower Nez Perce.

By 1853, Congress had created Washington Territory, and settlers were rapidly moving into the Northwest. The new territorial governor, Issac Ingalls Stevens, saw Indian land ownership as an impediment to progress and persuaded tribes to conclude a treaty in 1855. Nez Perce oral history records that Stevens warned that settlers would soon arrive and simply take their land if the tribes refused to come to terms. The council included thousands of Indians and was the largest ever held in the Northwest. The Nez Perce alone purportedly sent twenty-five hundred people.

At the council's conclusion, fifty-four Nez Perce headmen had signed away over a third of their ancestral territory, managing to retain a twelve thousand square mile reservation that, had it survived, would be one of the largest Indian reservations in the United States today, encompassing most of central Idaho and including portions of northeast Oregon and southeast Washington. The treaty boundaries included an irregularly shaped area as much as 100 miles wide, spreading from the Bitterroot Mountains in the east to the western Wallowa Valley, and some 120 miles in length.[16] The use of "ardent spirits" was outlawed, and no whites were allowed within reservation boundaries without the tribe's permission.

It was at this gathering that Hallalhotsoot, whom whites called Lawyer, a subchief from a Clearwater band, gained ascendancy over all other Nez Perce headmen. Disdaining the tribe's customary rule by council, Stevens insisted on dealing with a single chief. Lawyer probably received his name because of his abilities to argue and to write in the Nez Perce language, and because he was one of only a few Nez Perce who spoke some English. Records of early fur trapper rendezvous indicate Lawyer attended many of them and was friendly with whites. In earlier years, he was known as a "tobacco cutter chief," the Indian to whom traders gave lengths of gift cloth or tobacco, which were then cut up and distributed among the tribe. It soon became an unflattering term, connoting an Indian Uncle Tom. However, Lawyer eventually managed to consolidate major political power, representing probably half of the approximately three to four thousand members of the Nez Perce tribe.

Shortly after it was signed, Issac Stevens immediately violated the agreement by announcing that Indian lands ceded in the treaty were open to white settlement, even though no land was to be occupied until after congressional ratification. There is no doubt that Stevens's action was responsible for the uprising that immediately followed the onrush of settlers into Indian land in Oregon and Washington; many Indians believed that they had been tricked into giving up ownership. Although a few Nez Perce voiced support for neighboring tribes, most seemed satisfied that they had retained the majority of their lands in the treaty. Then there was Lawyer's longtime friendship with whites. When nearly every other Columbia Basin tribe revolted, some Nez Perce, led by Lawyer, aided the Americans in their campaign against the Yakimas, Spokans, Coeur d'Alenes, and Palouses. By 1860, nearly all major tribes were subdued, and the Nez Perce were left internally divided and without Indian allies.

Much to the distress of the Nez Perce, Congress refused to approve the treaty for several more years, not ratifying it until 1859. One year later, their greatest fear came true. Violating both the treaty boundaries and the exclusion of whites from the reservation, prospector Elias Pierce discovered gold in the northeast foothills of the reservation. When Pierce spread the tale that he and his companion had "found gold in every place we tried," the government agent to the Indians rapidly capitulated to miners' demands that the reservation boundaries be redrawn.[17] In 1861, the agent, along with the Superintendent of Indian Affairs for Oregon and Washington, induced the Nez Perce to cede all of the land lying north of the Snake and Clearwater rivers. That same year, six years after the 1855 treaty, promised goods and annuities finally began to arrive from the government.

In early summer, before Congress approved the new agreement, five thousand miners swarmed into the area. "Scarcely anything short of a Chinese Wall or a line of Troops will restrain Land Jobbers and the Incroachment of Settlers upon the Indian Territory," a frustrated George Washington had once remarked about America.[18] Sixty years and as many gold rushes later, it was still true.

Unable to navigate the upper Clearwater, ferries unloaded miners and supplies downriver at the junction of the Snake and Clearwater rivers, and the settlement of two thousand people dubbed Lewiston sprang up almost overnight on reservation land. Settler

P. W. Gillett wrote in his diary that the town was crudely constructed of "canvas, poles, logs and split boards," and that "drunkenness, gambling, crime and murder were in full blast." Real estate thrived with town lots all the rage, selling for $50 to $100. "Yet Lewiston is situated upon an Indian reservation," observed Gillett uncomfortably, "and no one has any title to the lots, save squatter's rights—squatter's sovereignty."[19]

The Indian agent posted signs warning the whites, but the miners were in no mood to comply, stating they had given Lawyer "some compensation" for the parcel. A local newspaper, *The Golden Age*, advised whites to settle, occupy, plow, and cultivate the reservation without regard to Indian treaty rights. In Boise, an editor suggested blankets infected with smallpox be distributed to the Nez Perce. By early 1862, $3 million in gold had already been mined from Indian land. When troops finally arrived later that year, the commanding officer of the District of Oregon, General Benjamin Alvord, estimated fifteen thousand people, of whom most were gold miners, were settled illegally on the Nez Perce reservation.

The results of such rapid acculturation were devastating to the tribe, particularly those who lived close to major mining areas. Indian protestations were buried under the sheer number of invading miners, many whom the Indian agent bluntly termed "robbers and cutthroats." Alcohol flowed freely and inevitably reached Indians, prompting one miner to mockingly observe: "What Christianity and civilization could not accomplish in decades, liquor has accomplished in a few short months."[20]

With the government deeply enmeshed in the Civil War and eviction of the miners politically unpopular if not impossible, Senator J. W. Nesmith of Oregon made an impassioned plea to Congress that "for the purpose of preserving peace" the Nez Perce should be removed from danger.[21] This was dubious reasoning at best, but in no mood to quibble, Congress authorized a new treaty, and a year later, in May 1863, Indian Affairs Superintendent Calvin H. Hale called a council with the Nez Perce at Lapwai. Within several days, fifty-three headmen arrived, including Old Joseph, White Bird, Big Thunder, Eagle-from-the-Light, and Lawyer and his subchiefs.

Hale told them he wanted to reduce the reservation's size and would compensate them for their ceded land. The new reservation, entirely within Idaho, included territory belonging to nearly all of Lawyer's following, while those bands outside the boundary would be forced to give up their land and move within the new reservation. With Spalding and another white man interpreting, Hale insisted that the government could not guarantee the existing boundaries from the miners' invasion, thus it was necessary that the Nez Perce all live close together.

After listening in silence the headmen withdrew, but on returning they rejected Hale's offer. They would give up the land where gold had been found, but they could not reach an agreement concerning a reduction in the remaining reservation. The council broke apart, but later that night, the chiefs reconvened. Oregon cavalryman Captain George Currey, who observed the meeting, recalled that "the debate ran with dignified firmness and warmth until next morning," when Big Thunder, speaking for the nontreaty headmen, those whose land fell outside the new boundaries, announced they would take no further part in the negotiations and, in a warm but "emotional manner, declared the Nez Perce nation dissolved; whereupon the Big Thunder men shook hands with the Lawyer men, telling them with a kind but firm demeanor that they would be friends, but a distinct people."[22]

The next day Lawyer quickly came to an agreement with Hale, meeting almost all of his terms. A few weeks later, he and fifty-one members of his faction signed the treaty. Nearly all signatories resided on land inside the new boundary, while none of the nontreaty headmen who lived outside the boundary signed the document. Indian oral history records that not only were the final terms of the signed treaty never presented to all the nontreaty headmen, but indeed, many of them had not even been invited to attend the original meeting. When the legality of Lawyer's action was later challenged, the government argued that the minority was bound by majority rule, refusing to acknowledge just how that majority had been determined. Several years later, the Indian agent, in one of his annual reports—mostly tedious documents but whose ingenuousness can sometimes inadvertently spotlight past deceit—admitted that the tribe was about equally divided between treaty and nontreaty Nez Perce. Captain George Currey believed the proportions less than equal. "Although the treaty goes out to the world as the concurrent agreement of the tribe, it is in reality nothing more than the agreement of Lawyer and his band, numbering in the aggregate not a third part of the Nez Perces tribe."[23]

Hale was ecstatic and wrote to the Commissioner of Indian Affairs that he had managed to secure "very nearly six millions of acres" obtained "at a cost not exceeding eight cents per acre."[24] The actual figure was closer to seven million acres, with the new reservation of 784,996 acres about one-tenth the size of the former one. By announcing the signing of the treaty, Hale officially endorsed Lawyer as head chief, driving a bitter schism between the Nez Perce people that had begun with Issac Stevens and has remained well into the present century. The treaty also required that all Nez Perce move inside the new reservation within one year. The government would pay $265,000 to the tribe, but part would go toward removal, plotting, and fencing—payment out of their own sale price for "benefits" proposed in the treaty.

Not long afterward, an angry Old Joseph tore up both his copy of the 1855 treaty and the Gospel of Matthew, a gift he had carried ever since the missionary Spalding had baptized him years before. He would never trust whites again.

In the following years, the nontreaty bands continued to reject the treaty (today's Nez Perce refer to it as the "steal treaty"), refusing any part of the payments or assistance offered in either it or the 1855 treaty. When congressional ratification finally came in 1867, the Indian agent complained of spades and axes made of iron rather than steel, blankets glued together that dissolved when wet, and forty dozen elastic garters sent to a tribe who owned not a single pair of stockings. In 1868, Lawyer and several others agreed to some minor revisions, among which allowed for a military reservation at Lapwai. As for enforcing the requirement that all Nez Perce move to the new reservation, the government hesitated, indicating lingering doubts about the treaty's rejection by the nontreaty bands.[25]

During this period, inaction, theft, and dishonesty of officials continued to plague the government and the Nez Perce alike, both becoming a target of unscrupulous Indian agents in particular. After the 1863 treaty, a pattern emerged. No sooner did a new agent take over at Lapwai than he issued a complaint about the dishonesty of his predecessor and then promptly absconded with funds meant for the tribe.

A government weary of scandal and ineffective Indian agents responded in 1870 by transferring the administration of all Indian reservations to selected religious denominations. Churches, it was believed, would end corruption and the hostility it had caused, hastening the assimilation of Indians into white society. "Peace is better than War," reasoned Indian Inspector E. C. Kemble in describing the plan, "so the Peace Policy which makes Christian men and women of Indians must be better than the old policy of whiskey alternated with whippings to keep them quiet."[26] None of the reformers, however, advocated allowing Indians to choose their own religion, and most were interested more in Sunday school head counts than in carrying out the government's treaty obligations. The upshot, remarked one early critic whose voice was buried under the avalanche of self-congratulatory rhetoric, was agents so busy preparing the Indians for heaven that they made hell for them on earth.

For the Nez Perce, who had a long history of Christian domination, it was the same wine in the same cup. When it appeared Catholics might receive jurisdiction over the reservation, Presbyterians cried foul, protesting that they had been first and most active. The government conceded, and in 1871 John B. Monteith, a stubborn, strong-willed son of a Presbyterian minister with both a face and determination not unlike Henry Spalding's, became the new Indian agent. By most accounts Monteith was fiscally honest, unlike most agents before him, but any hope that the Nez Perce had of maintaining their traditional identity rapidly vanished with his administration.

The same year Monteith took over, Old Joseph of the Wallowas died. He was buried near Wallowa Lake, at the foot of a prominent hill. One of the old headman's favorite horses was killed and its skin hung on a pole over his grave, as befit a Nez Perce funeral for a leader. Before he died, Old Joseph charged his son, who would assume both his leadership and his name, with a dire warning. Recalled by Young Joseph years later, the old chief said: "Always remember that your father never sold his country. You must stop your ears whenever you are asked to sign a treaty selling your home. A few years more, and the white men will be all around you. They have their eyes on this land. My son, never forget my dying words. This country holds your father's body. Never sell the bones of your father and your mother."[27] In 1886, long after his people had been forced from the Wallowa Valley, someone opened the grave and took the old chief's skull. Years later, it could be seen in a dentist's office in Baker, Oregon.

By August 1872, conflict between settlers and the Nez Perce had grown so tense that Monteith traveled to the valley to meet with Old Joseph's band. Here, for the first time, Monteith met the new chief of the Wallowas, Heinmot Tooyalakekt (Thunder Traveling to Loftier Mountain Heights), although whites would come to call him Young Joseph, or simply Joseph. Of all Nez Perce, he would be the most remembered by whites, his character first vilified then venerated in that paradoxical manner that nineteenth-century America had of destroying Indian people while revering their memory. Soon myth would grow around Joseph until he became "marblized," embedded like a fossil in American frontier history, the legend inseparable from the fact. But we know that before Monteith that day stood a thirty-two-year-old man, six feet, two inches tall with handsome, well-defined features. Large black eyes gave his face a calm, impassive, some said an almost sedate, expression. Like his younger brother Ollokot, to whom he was very close, he wore his hair long, braided in two strands below his shoulders and combed above the forehead in the upswept curl of their traditional religion. Unlike Ollokot, described as "gay, fun-loving and daring, an able hunter," Joseph had his father's mild and gentle disposition, his quiet strength and dignity, qualities that made him more of a civil chief than a warrior.[28]

Perhaps more than any other characteristic, Joseph possessed the gift of oratory. Although his precise words were often lost in the rough-and-tumble translations and embellished print of those frontier days, there is a graceful, often eloquent quality that repeatedly shines through. In 1877, F. J. Haynes photographed then thirty-seven-year-old Joseph in Bismarck, North Dakota. His head was held high, chin firm, with dark eyes looking far beyond, still proud, still confident even after his capture at the Bear Paw Mountains. A quarter of a century later, in 1903, the inveterate photographer E. S. Curtis, after years spent ennobling Native Americans on film, would decline to use a photograph of Joseph in an exhibition, claiming that his aged face was not representative of the Nez Perce Curtis knew. But the eyes that stare out from Curtis's photograph are hardly those of the man of earlier years—eyes full of pain, the proud, faraway look gone, the terse mouth drawn low at the edges of the lips, the shoulders stooped. Curtis had photographed a defeated man.

At his first meeting with Monteith, Joseph demanded that the settlers leave, reminding the agent that none of his band had signed away the Wallowa Valley in the 1863 treaty. Nonetheless, Monteith argued, they were bound by majority rule, and "it was useless for them to talk about sending the whites away," that he could not remove them. Monteith left with no agreement other than Joseph's assurance that "he would not let any of his men do anything that would cause trouble, but would have the trouble settled peaceably." Back in Lapwai, however, Monteith relented, writing to the Commissioner of Indian Affairs that "it is a great pity that the valley was ever opened for settlement." So high and cold, he said, settlers "can raise nothing but the hardiest of vegetables." Concluding that "raising stock is all that can be done to any advantage," Monteith advised that "if there is any way in which the Wallowa Valley could be kept for the Indians I would recommend that it be done."[29]

In March 1873, another council was held at Lapwai, attended by Oregon Indian Affairs Superintendent T. B. Odeneal, Monteith, and Joseph. With reasoned sincerity, Joseph convinced the two men that his band had been wronged at the treaty talks ten years earlier. Odeneal and Monteith concluded that if the government determined that the treaty did not extinguish Indian title to the valley, then Joseph and his band should be permitted to remain there. In his report, Monteith noted that the band does not "desire a separate reservation made of the Wallowa Valley. They claim the whole valley belongs to them, and are opposed to the whites settling there."[30] As a compromise, Odeneal and Monteith proposed the area be divided between the white livestock owners and the Nez Perce, the whites given the lower part of the Wallowa Valley and Joseph's band a reservation encompassing the upper valley.

Acting on this report, President Grant signed an executive order in 1873 establishing a "reservation for the roaming Nez Perce Indians in the Wallowa Valley, in the State of Oregon." Something went awry, however, for when the boundaries of the new reservation were announced, they proved to be contrary to those recommended by Odeneal and Monteith. Through what appears to be simple bureaucratic ineptitude, the Nez Perce were given the western Wallowa Valley where most whites had settled, while whites received the eastern portion, an area too cold for farming and inaccessible to nearby settlements.

Once this had been decreed, Grant refused to budge; the boundaries would stand. While some settlers welcomed a government buyout, others were furious and enlisted Oregon's governor, Lafayette Grover, to protest their plight. Grover, who had senatorial ambitions, insisted that Grant rescind his order, claiming that removing "enterprising white families" to make way for "nomadic savages" is against "the spirit of our frontier people in their efforts to redeem the wilderness and make it fruitful of civilized life." Grover demanded Joseph's band be removed to Lapwai.[31]

Monteith was deeply chagrined. Not only had his superiors altered his boundary recommendations, but he had raised the ire of settlers throughout the area by what many considered his "Indian-coddling" methods. Monteith was also having trouble at Lapwai with Catholic priests who had secured a small mission on the reservation. Stung by Catholic allegations that Protestant missionaries were "self-styled ministers" and "selfish professors of false doctrines," Monteith feared the Catholics' increasing influence, although only a small number of Nez Perce ever converted to Catholicism. The conflict was not lost upon Joseph, who earlier had refused missionaries access to the Wallowa Valley, claiming, "they will teach us to quarrel about God, as the Catholics and Protestants do on the Nez Perce reservation and at other places. We do not want to learn that. We may quarrel with men sometimes about things on this earth, but we never quarrel about God."[32]

Since their first meeting, Monteith had relentlessly pressured Joseph to give up his band's nomadism as stockbreeders, hunters, and fishers and to become farmers, even though he knew the Wallowa Valley was unsuitable for agriculture. Finally, at a meeting in Lapwai that year, an angry Monteith accused Joseph of creating the trouble in the valley and declared that, regardless of the president's order, the only solution was for the band to move to the existing Idaho reservation. Unable to convince Monteith otherwise, Joseph told the agent that he wanted to go to Washington to appeal to the Indian Bureau himself. Monteith promptly refused, and an irreconcilable Joseph returned to the Wallowa for the winter.

In the spring of 1875, Joseph chanced on a meeting with the new commanding officer of the Department of the Columbia, General Oliver Otis Howard. The general recalled that their exchange was brief. Joseph was perhaps aware that Grant was vacillating about the Wallowa, and through an interpreter, he asked if the president had a message for him. "There is no word from Washington," answered Howard.

The men, who were to figure so prominently in the coming war, then shook hands and parted. "Joseph put his large black eyes on my face," remembered Howard, "and maintained a fixed look for some time." It was not an audacious stare but one "endeavoring to read my disposition and character." In the first of many such misjudgments for which he was soon to pay dearly, Howard said, "I think Joseph and I became then quite good friends."[33]

3

O liver Otis Howard was forty-five years old when he first met Joseph. From his Civil War photograph ten years earlier shines a youthful face in full beard. Howard's empty right sleeve is pinned to his dress uniform; his arm was amputated midway between shoulder and elbow after the battle of Fair Oaks in 1862, when thirty yards from Confederate lines two lead minié balls shattered his arm. Because of his wound, the Nez Perce called him Cut Arm. In the photo, Howard holds a Bible in his left hand.

Born in Maine, Howard graduated from Bowdoin College and then the U.S. Military Academy, standing fourth in his class.[1] Within the year, he married his childhood sweetheart, Lizzie. When the Civil War broke out, Howard was a lieutenant but had been contemplating entering the ministry. He fought as a colonel in the Maine volunteers, having gained a political appointment, and emerged before the year was out as a full-fledged brigadier general. Two years later he was promoted to major general, one of only a few in his West Point class to rise to such a rank.

Early on Howard resolved any personal conflict between fighting and Christianity. Nonresistance was all right for individuals, he declared, but not for those serving government. Fearless in battle, he was a favorite of General George McClellan before McClellan's star fell with President Lincoln. Then Howard served under "Fighting" Joe Hooker. Although he liked Hooker at first, their relationship soon soured.

At Chancellorsville—despite orders from Hooker that he claimed he never received—Howard failed to fortify his position and was overrun in what many consider the worst rout of the war. Charges were never brought against him, but Hooker held him responsible. By war's end, an unforgiving Hooker charged that Howard could command "a prayer meeting with a good deal more ability than he would an army."[2]

Howard survived Chancellorsville only to be swept into Gettysburg. With most of the Union army not yet there, he suddenly found himself in charge. Overwhelmed by Lee's forces, he retreated, losing thousands of soldiers to the Confederates. The secure position he chose, Cemetery Hill, cost Lee Gettysburg and perhaps the war, but Howard's critics saw it only as another retreat. Frustrated, he transferred to the command of William Tecumseh Sherman.

Sherman was impressed with Howard's abilities. On the march through Georgia, he commanded half of Sherman's army and did much to redeem his reputation. But the public's first impression was hard to shake; many still referred to him as the man who ran at Chancellorsville and Gettysburg.

When the war ended, President Lincoln appointed Howard commissioner of the Bureau of Refugees, Freedmen, and Abandoned Lands (Freedmen's Bureau). For seven years, he was in charge of protecting the rights of four million freed slaves throughout the difficult period of Reconstruction. During this time he helped found Howard University for blacks.

In many ways Howard seemed the best choice for the bureau: he was patient and understanding, and he epitomized Christian virtues of kindness and sympathy, even courageously resisting a church-led movement in Washington to outlaw mixed-race marriages. Sherman, however, advised him that soldiers should leave "education, charity and religion" to civilian philanthropists. He wrote Howard that "I feel you have Hercules' task."[3] It was true. With over a thousand employees, during a time when corruption flourished in public office, Howard lost control over the bureau amid accusations of fraud and mismanagement.

Although Howard was later exonerated, Grant temporarily relieved him of his duties and sent him to the Southwest to settle the decade-long war between whites and the Chiricahua Apache leader, Cochise. The commanding officer in Arizona, General George Crook, was preparing for an Indian war and resented his involvement. Howard, said Crook, "told me that he thought the Creator had placed him on earth to be a Moses to the Negro. Having accomplished that mission, he felt satisfied his next mission was with the Indian." Nevertheless, riding into Cochise's camp almost alone and unarmed, Howard convinced Cochise to surrender. Thirteen years of war in southern Arizona suddenly ceased.[4]

Crook later derided Howard's assertion that the treaty had been concluded "by God's help," accusing him of making an oral agreement with Cochise and establishing a reservation without a written treaty. There seems little doubt that Howard's actions contributed greatly to the ease with which the Chiricahuas were removed from their reservation by the government two years after Cochise's death.[5]

In 1872, weary of political turmoil, Howard returned to active duty as a brigadier general, eventually becoming the commanding officer of the Department of the Columbia in the Northwest. His accomplishment in Arizona gave him confidence that he could do the same with the Nez Perce, but within two months of Howard's meeting with Joseph, his hopes for a quick settlement were dashed. In June 1875, capitulating to political pressure, Grant rescinded his executive order and reopened the Wallowa Valley to settlers. Fearing an outbreak was imminent, Agent Monteith petitioned Howard to send troops to the valley. In August Captain Stephen Whipple, who was in charge of the cavalry detachment, wrote a long letter to Howard, telling him that most settlers there were disappointed that the government had rejected the reservation buy-out. Whipple declared that "this band of Indians are by no means a vagabond set," calling them "proud-spirited, self-supporting and intelligent."[6]

To understand the situation in the Wallowa more fully, Howard directed his adjutant, Major H. Clay Wood, to investigate. After reviewing records and interviewing Joseph and Monteith, Wood prepared a lengthy report that reads like a scholarly legal treatise. Wood reasoned that because Joseph's band had never signed the 1863 agreement, extinguishment of title was "imperfect and incomplete." Therefore the band could not be forced to move. The further he looked into the dilemma, the more discomforted the major became. Because their land had been excluded from the treaty, it was "this God-given sentiment—the love of home" that was the true cause of the difficulty. Wood regarded Grant's rescindment of the Wallowa reserve a mistake, saying, "if not a crime, it was a blunder." He was shocked at how settlers had treated the Nez Perce. "I could fill page after page in portraying the number and nature of outrages the Indians and their families were subject to." If the government could not keep faith with the Nez Perce, if it had "no sense of honor left," said Wood, then "there is reason to fear a chapter in our history remains to be written which mankind shall tremble to read."[7]

Howard was so impressed with Whipple's letter and Wood's report that he wrote to the War Department. "I think it a great mistake to take from Joseph and his band of Nez Perces Indians that valley. The white people really do not want it. . . . Possibly Congress can be induced to let these really peaceable Indians have this poor valley for their own."[8]

Howard must have held scant hope for congressional action, but for the time being he was content not to press a solution to the Wallowa problem. Sometime in early 1876, however, his attitude began to change, due largely to a Portland Presbyterian minister, Reverend A. L. Lindsley. Major Wood was correct, maintained Lindsley, that Joseph's band had never agreed to give up the Wallowa Valley. But unlike Wood, Lindsley sided with Monteith in calling for Joseph to settle on the Presbyterian controlled reservation, and he suggested that the government appoint a new commission and purchase the valley from the Indians. If they did not come willingly, he concluded, "harsher methods" would be appropriate.[9]

Lindsley's idea seemed ill-advised in the face of Wood's admonition about the importance of the valley to the Nez Perce. The idea appealed to Howard, however, particularly when he learned of the latest conflict between settlers and Indians. That June one of Joseph's young men, Wilhautyah (Wind Blowing), was accused by two settlers of stealing horses that had been missing. Exactly what happened is unknown, but during an ensuing scuffle one of the whites shot and killed Wilhautyah. Days later the wandering horses showed up, and worried valley settlers feared retaliation. Howard seized this opportunity to send Major Wood to convince both Monteith and Joseph that a peace commission was necessary.

Wood soon met with Monteith, Joseph, and about forty Nez Perce, promising justice for the murderers. Joseph declared that "since his brother's life had been taken in the Wallowa Valley, his body buried there, and the earth there had drunk up his blood, the valley was more sacred to him than ever before." As recompense for that life, his people wanted the Wallowa "from this time forward forever, and that all the whites must be removed from the valley." When Wood broached the idea of a commission to review the entire problem, Joseph agreed to attend "if good honest men were sent."[10]

Two months later the murderers still had not been brought to trial, and Joseph demanded the two men be turned over to his band for justice. The whites refused and, as words threatened to turn into bullets, Howard was again forced to send troops to the valley. When the two accused men were finally apprehended, only one was tried and he was acquitted, the judge ruling he had acted in self-defense. With soldiers preventing further conflict, Joseph placed his hopes with the upcoming commissioners, little realizing that their only purpose was purchasing the Wallowa Valley and removing his band to the reservation.

In early November 1876, the commission convened at Lapwai. General Howard and Major Wood constituted two of the five members, with the other three coming from the East. While they waited for Joseph to arrive, Monteith described the background of the Wallowa problem, dwelling at length on how the Dreamer or Washani faith of the plateau Indians was causing the bulk of the conflict. His explanation was hardly news to Howard or Wood, both of whom were aware of the growing regard of northwest Indians for the prophet Smohalla.

"He is a large-headed, hump-shouldered, odd little wizard of an Indian," said Howard later, after meeting Smohalla, "and exhibits a strange mixture of timidity and daring, of superstition and intelligence." Smohalla lived at Priest Rapids on the Columbia River, an ancient gathering place for Indians during the salmon season before whites flooded it behind a dam, an event he is said to have foretold. If Indians returned to their traditional ways, Smohalla promised that the white invaders would simply disappear.[11]

He had reason to wish for this to happen. From a population of about two thousand in 1800, his Wallula tribe numbered less than three hundred by 1875. Having lost all of his children and grandchildren to disease, Smohalla held whites in vile contempt. What particularly irked him was what they were doing to the land. Native people, he said, "no more harm the earth than would an infant's fingers harm its mother's breast. But the white man tears up large tracts of land, runs deep ditches, cuts down forests, and changes the whole face of the earth. You know very well this is not right. Every honest man knows in his heart that this is all wrong. But the white men are so greedy they do not consider these things."[12]

Dreams became the method of holding communication with the Earth Mother and the great unknown. Smohalla is said to have fallen into cataleptic trances, then been cut with knives or stuck with needles without showing any pain. Witnesses claimed blood did not flow from his wounds.

Although Smohalla refused to take up arms or advocate violence, whites suspected treachery. The Tacoma *Herald* called him the most dangerous "savage" in the country, ready at a moment's notice to "murder, rapine and pillage." It is a "peculiar religion," admitted Oregon Indian Affairs Superintendent Odeneal, one that held that a "new god is coming to their rescue; that all the Indians who have died heretofore, and who shall die hereafter, are to be resurrected; that as they will then be very numerous and powerful, they will be able to conquer the whites, recover their lands, and live as free and unrestrained as their fathers lived in olden times." It is incredulous, declared Odeneal in calling for suppression of the Dreamers, but "their model of a man is an *Indian.*"[13]

Some nontreaty Nez Perce were readily drawn to this prophet

and his call for a return to traditional values; although few of them believed in the resurrection of dead warriors, and many maintained vegetable plots in their villages, a practice that Smohalla believed was too much like agriculture. In fact, far from being allies, Smohalla actually expressed disdain for Joseph's band, who he later claimed were driven from their land because they had no business planting fields like whites. Such subtleties were lost on Monteith, however, who only saw the similarities between Smohalla and the nontreaty Nez Perce, concluding their beliefs were identical. To Monteith, any Indian religious independence threatened his control of the reservation. Now he had a convenient scapegoat. By the start of the council, all except Major Wood seemed convinced that the nontreaty Nez Perce were bent on nothing less than the extermination of the white race.

When Joseph and some sixty followers reached Lapwai on November 13, they were obviously in no haste. Joseph's delay demonstrated to the commissioners that he considered himself on equal footing with them. "Never was the policy of orderly inactivity more fully inaugurated," their report dryly stated. Joseph answered "every salutation, compliment, and expression of good-will, in kind, and duplicated in quantity. An alertness and dexterity in intellectual fencing was exhibited by him that was quite remarkable." When the commissioners demanded he give up his claim to over a million acres in return for sixty twenty-acre parcels at Lapwai, Joseph lectured them that when the creator made the earth, "[He] made no marks, no lines of division or separation upon it, and that it should be allowed to remain as then made. The earth was his mother. He was made of the earth and grew up on its bosom. The earth, as his mother and nurse, was sacred to his affections" and therefore "to part with the earth would be to part with himself."[14]

Joseph reiterated that he did not desire Wallowa Valley as a reservation, for "that would subject him and his band to the will of and dependence on another, and to laws not of their own making." He wanted to live peaceably, he said, but above all, freely. He and his band had suffered wrong rather than done wrong. The serious and feeling manner in which he uttered these sentiments, the commissioners conceded, was "impressive."[15]

On the final day of the council, Howard described what had happened to the Modocs, the Sioux, the Seminoles—all Indians who had refused to move to reservations. "Everything that they might want was offered and extended to them if they would submit to governmental authority," said Howard. But they answered, "sometimes very roughly: 'We want nothing from you. We have not given you our land. You have no right to take it from us.' "[16]

Listening to this exchange was Emily FitzGerald, twenty-six-year-old wife of Lapwai's Post Surgeon John FitzGerald. Contrary to the commission's official report written by Howard, Emily wrote in a letter to her mother that the general threatened Joseph, saying that "if the trouble in the Wallowa is brought up again, he will send out two men to Joseph's one . . . and whip him into submission." When some Nez Perce rose to their feet in anger at Howard's words, the chairman abruptly adjourned the meeting, later declaring, "I thought that a report would be better than a massacre."[17]

Later that evening, Major Wood confided to FitzGerald that he was sure Joseph would acquiesce, "knowing that this is our last chance and that we leave in the morning." Joseph failed to appear, however, and the commissioners left for Portland early the next day. About nine o'clock, four "most gorgeously gotten up" Indians rode up to FitzGerald's backgate and asked for General Howard. As far as she could understand, "they had come to make terms of some sort with General Howard. They all were very smiling and pleasant and seemed very sorry about not finding him. We don't know whether this is the beginning of a settlement, but we hope it is."[18]

No one knows if the Nez Perce had actually decided "to make terms," but Major Wood's confidence is strong evidence since he had come to know Joseph better than any other white man. Regardless, the opportunity was lost by three hours. The commission's final report appeared a month later, stating that Joseph and his band were under the spell of Dreamer "fanaticism." The report called for removal to Indian Territory (Oklahoma) of the leaders of the Dreamer religion, and unless Joseph's band came on the reservation within a reasonable time, they should be placed there by force.

Major Wood declined to sign the document. Later he submitted a dissenting opinion, which the other commissioners refused to include in their report. It was Wood's last public statement in defense of the Nez Perce before the war, his words calling for patience, reason, and justice blown away like so much chaff before a storm. Less than a year later, with the U.S. Army focused more on how to stop Joseph and his people in their bid to escape to Canada than on how the threat of force may have precipitated the violence, Wood's voice surfaced in a final indignant cry, this time in an open letter to the *Army and Navy Journal.* "Did the necessity exist for *forcibly* placing him upon a reservation? What wrong had he committed? Cite the act of hostility!"[19]

In light of Howard's early support for Joseph, his long history of championing black emancipation, and his compassion in a profession known more for warriors than humanitarians, his sudden reversal seems harsh and imperious. He was simply in no mood to bargain. What changed the man's mind? It appears that Wood's argument— no matter how principled—was less interesting to Howard than finding an immediate solution to this vexing Indian "problem." Howard had begun to believe, like Spalding, Monteith, and most other Christians of their generation, that while racial extermination was unacceptable, cultural extirpation was imperative. (Throughout his life, Howard continued to heap praise on Spalding, calling him an "honest teacher" and a "grand pioneer of our civilization.") Indians must cease their nomadic ways, settle down, farm, and give up their traditional life that so obviously obstructed their adoption by civilization. What these utopists failed to realize was that most whites had no intention of accepting Indians—reformed or not—as equals, and that once shorn of past traditional values, Indians would be abandoned to a twilight zone between cultures. The Indian needs "patient and constant perseverance, instructing, correcting, and reproving," the commissioners concluded in their report. "They are grown-up children, and must be personally educated to work."[20]

But Howard had deeper and more personal reasons for his handling of the conflict, for, after all, this was a man who harbored both religiosity and an equally intense desire for public approbation. Howard's inability to quickly and cleanly resolve the Nez Perce dilemma as he had the Apache conflict undoubtedly rankled him. He had encouraged the idea of the commission, gaining the support of his superior in San Francisco, General Irvin McDowell, commander of the Division of the Pacific. But McDowell was wavering, openly questioning Howard's participation and warning him not to be responsible for "any step which may lead to hostilities."[21]

Adding to Howard's problems was the fact that he had recently been accused again of mismanagement during his years as head of the Freedmen's Bureau, and it had cost him a great deal in personal legal expenses. A frustrated Howard wrote his friend General Sherman that "more than half my pay" was going for legal fees as the government held him personally responsible for hundreds of thousands of dollars. His annual salary of $5,500, considered well above most other high government officials' earnings, was simply not enough. "You laugh at this," he told Sherman, "everybody does; & says 'Wait it will come right.' Yes, but my hair is whitening, and my heart is very heavy." Later Howard would finally be cleared of all charges, but now this prideful man, who had never weathered criticism well throughout his career, was under fire from all directions.[22]

Howard's reaction was entrenchment. In the months to come, the dogged determination of the Nez Perce to keep their homeland would come up against Howard's increasingly intractable defense of his own reputation, until he believed that only a judgment from heaven could explain the reasons behind Indian resistance. "The rule is as fixed as the stars," Howard maintained in a burst of then fashionable Lamarckism, "that the sins of the fathers shall be visited upon the children unto the third and fourth generations of the men who hate God. Smart as these youths were, their tendency to evil . . . was undoubtedly inherited."[23]

In early January 1877, the Bureau of Indian Affairs approved the commission's report and ordered that its recommendations be implemented but cautioned Monteith to give Joseph's band "reasonable time" for compliance. Ignoring these directions, Monteith immediately requested that Howard send two troops of cavalry to the Wallowa Valley. At the same time, the agent dispatched a delegation of Nez Perce who had signed the 1863 treaty to demand that Joseph move to the reservation by April 1.

By setting such an early date, Monteith completely ignored the difficulties the Nez Perce would face in transporting their families, possessions, and newborn livestock across the Snake and Salmon Rivers, then beginning to rise with early spring run-off. Curiously, he also neglected to notify Howard of the deadline.

The men soon returned with Joseph's answer: "I have been talking to the whites many years about the land in question, and it is strange they cannot understand me; the country they claim belonged to my father, and when he died, it was given to me and my people, and I will not leave it until I am compelled to."[24]

By now newspapers in Walla Walla and Lewiston, aware of Joseph's opposition to removal, were openly forecasting war. In March, Joseph sent his brother, Ollokot, to meet with Monteith at Lapwai. Interpreter James Reuben, a treaty Nez Perce who was also Joseph's nephew, was present and later wrote a letter to the Lewiston *Teller* denying rumors that the Wallowa band would fight the whites. "Why should I undertake anything to lose all my property for nothing?" Ollokot had asked Monteith. He likened Indians to deer, white men to grizzly bears. "If I should fight the whites, I would lose it all."[25] Convinced that Joseph's words had been misinterpreted at the meeting in November, Ollokot proposed another council with Howard.

Monteith was encouraged. Although troops might have to enforce the order to remove Joseph's band, it seemed likely that their defiance was a face-saving move, that they would not take up arms. Soon after the meeting with Ollokot, the *Teller* reported Joseph had told a settler that while he refused to go to the reservation willingly, "nor would he fight." Then, with a knowing look, Joseph purportedly told the man, "But you know they won't kill us for General Howard and Monteith are Christians."[26]

During the following month, Joseph's emissary, Ollokot, attended two meetings with army personnel, the final one at Walla Walla on April 20 with General Howard. Described by Howard as over six feet tall and "perfectly formed," Ollokot had "small hands and feet, was very intelligent, and had, an unusual feat for an Indian, made quite good maps of the country about Wallowa." Howard thought him "frank, open-hearted, and generous" and "very quick and graceful in his motions," and when he spoke in council, he always agreed with his brother. Howard was sure that in private, however, Ollokot "took the side of the reckless young men, who would rather than not have a fight with the white men." The council, Howard said, was really a ruse "to observe how many troops there were at Walla Walla and the character of our armament." At this meeting, Ollokot requested another council between the general and all nontreaty Nez Perce bands. Howard agreed to meet in Lapwai in twelve days. "Really," concluded the general, "matters did not look much like war."[27]

On the morning of May 3, Howard watched as Joseph's band rode into Lapwai, "a long rank of men, followed by women and children, with faces painted, the red paint extending back into the partings of the hair—the men's hair braided and tied up with showy strings—ornamented in dress, in hats, in blankets, with variegated colors, in leggings of buckskin, and moccasins, beaded and plain; women with bright shawls or blankets, and skirts to the ankle, and 'top moccasins.' All were mounted on Indian ponies as various in color as the dress of the riders." Suddenly the Nez Perce broke into song, one that Howard described as "wild and shrill and fierce, yet so plaintive at times it was almost like weeping, and made us sorry for them, although we could not but be glad that there were not five hundred instead of fifty." They then "turned off to the right and swept around outside our fence, keeping up the strange song all the way around the fort, where it broke up into irregular bubblings like mountain streams tumbling over stones." Dismounting and stacking their arms, the men entered the large tent that had been pitched on the parade ground while women and children waited outside.[28]

Inside the tent, General Howard, Monteith, and several officers greeted Joseph and his men. The other nontreaty bands had not yet arrived. There seems little doubt that Howard and Monteith considered the council meaningless, since just two days before Howard had ordered two companies of cavalry to the Wallowa Valley in preparation for the removal of Joseph's band. Strangely, what was to be Howard and Monteith's final meeting with the Nez Perce was the first to include all nontreaty bands, who together numbered nearly four times Joseph's band of two hundred people. The Wallowa conflict had completely absorbed the attention of Howard and Monteith, and only now were they to discover that nontreaty discontent was far greater than they had realized.[29]

The following morning, May 4, dawned "a glorious day," wrote Howard. "The sun shone without a cloud and a gentle breeze coursed through the valley and over the smooth hills, causing the flowers to ripple and sparkle in long noiseless waves." White Bird, Looking Glass, and Toohoolhoolzote, another nontreaty band leader, had arrived and now the council began in earnest. White Bird's band included some fifty warriors living along the Salmon River, and at the time of the council the chief was about fifty years old. According to trader Duncan McDonald, who became the first Nez Perce to chronicle the coming war, White Bird was "a handsome man, of about five-feet-nine in his moccasins, square shouldered, long-waisted and of clear sinewy limbs." His hair had been dark chestnut, rather than black, although it was now quite gray with a face "longer than rounder." White Bird's name, Peopeo Hihhih, has been variously translated as White Goose, White Brant, or White Pelican, the last having particular numinous power. Throughout the council, he sat impassively, a large ceremonial eagle wing hanging in front of his eyes and nose to show he was a medicine man or *tewat*.[30]

Looking Glass lived near the confluence of the South and Middle forks of the Clearwater River, an area within the eastern edge of the reservation boundary. While his land was not in immediate jeopardy, he had never signed the 1863 treaty and was largely sympathetic with the others. About forty-five years old, well built, hair streaked with gray and nearly six feet tall, he was a respected warrior, having made numerous trips to the buffalo country and fought in battles with the Sioux and Blackfeet. The other bands revered him as well, and his influence and personal confidence made him a likely leader, although his band only numbered about forty warriors. Like Joseph, he counseled against armed conflict with whites.

Representing some 180 Nez Perce, including about 30 warriors residing near the confluence of the Salmon and Snake rivers, was Toohoolhoolzote. Howard described him as "broad-shouldered, deep-chested, thick-necked, five feet ten in height, had a heavy guttural voice, and betrayed in every word a strong and settled hatred of all Caucasians."[31] By most accounts, he was exceptionally homely and extraordinarily strong. Stories attested to his ability to carry a dead deer on each shoulder for long distances. An eloquent and persuasive orator who could passionately invoke the beliefs of his people, he was mistakenly identified by the general as a *tewat*.

At the beginning, Joseph announced that Toohoolhoolzote would speak for the nontreaty bands, and the "ugly, obstinate savage of the worst type," as Howard termed him, spoke "with a flourish of words and illustrations, but with no attempt at conciliation even in manner." At one point during the chief's lengthy discourse, Howard interrupted him, reminding him that "we are all subjects, children of a common government, and must obey its requirements." Toohoolhoolzote quickly took offense at such metaphor, telling the general, "You have no right to compare us grown men to children. Children do not think for themselves, grown men do think for themselves. The government at Washington cannot think for us." When it looked as if the two men were about to come to blows, Joseph quickly asked for adjournment. Howard readily agreed, having decided from the inauspicious beginning that "it would be wise to have the troops that were already on the march in position." The meeting would begin again on Monday.[32]

Over the weekend, Howard ordered Whipple and his cavalry to move closer to Lapwai in case of trouble. He also ordered a company of troops from Walla Walla to Lewiston, and another from Portland's Fort Vancouver to Fort Walla Walla.

Monday, May 7, proved to be the final day of the council. More Nez Perce arrived over the weekend, including two small bands totaling sixteen warriors headed by Hahtalekin and Huishuis Kute (Little Baldhead), Palouse Indians who had close familial ties with the Nez Perce and lived on the north side of the Snake River, below Lewiston. Also known as the Preacher, Huishuis Kute purportedly lost his hair years before when a cannonball came very close to removing his entire head as he assisted the Americans in their campaign against the Spokans. Huishuis Kute was an "oily, wily, bright-eyed young chief who could be smooth-tongued or saucy, as the mood seized him," said Howard. Holding forth like an Old Testament Pharisee, the general believed that "in the words of Scripture, his heart was deceitful above all things and desperately wicked."[33]

As the meeting opened, Toohoolhoolzote began speaking about "the earth being his mother, that she should not be disturbed by hoe or plough, that man should subsist on what grows of itself, &c., &c. He railed against the violence that would separate Indians from lands that were theirs by inheritance."[34]

Howard interrupted. "We do not wish to interfere with your religion," he declared, "but you must talk about practicable things. Twenty times over you repeat that the earth is your mother, and about chieftainship from the earth. Let us hear no more, but come to business at once."

"You white people get together, measure the earth, and then divide it," Toohoolhoolzote replied. "Part of the Indians gave up their land. I never did. The earth is part of my body, and I never gave up the earth."

"You know very well that the government has set apart a reservation, and that the Indians must go upon it," said Howard.

"What person pretends to divide the land, and put me on it?" said Toohoolhoolzote.

"I am that man," Howard shot back. "I stand here for the President, and there is no spirit good or bad that will hinder me. My orders are plain, and will be executed. I hoped that the Indians had good sense enough to make me their friend, and not their enemy." Stepping toward Toohoolhoolzote, Howard said, "Then you do not propose to comply with the orders of the government?"

"So long as the earth keeps me," replied the chief, "I want to be left alone. You are trifling with the law of the earth!"

Howard was furious. Turning to the others, Howard asked, "Will Joseph and White Bird and Looking Glass go with me to look after their land? The old man shall not go. He must stay with Colonel Perry."

"Do you want to scare me with reference to my body?" demanded Toohoolhoolzote.

"I will leave your body with Colonel Perry!" exclaimed Howard. With that, Howard grabbed his arm and along with Perry, commander of Fort Lapwai, escorted Toohoolhoolzote across the post grounds to the guardhouse where a soldier took him inside the building.

Returning to the tent, Howard again asked the chiefs, who had watched this exchange in silence, if they would go with him to look for reservation land.

Stunned, they all nodded agreement.

In defending his actions later, Howard maintained that the government's previously "kindly manner and patient tones" had been interpreted as weakness and had enlarged the Indians' "ideas of their own importance." He had no doubt that "the time for loving persuasion had now gone by" and was confident that "fearless sternness always produced the most wholesome and immediate consequences." A far different spirit now prevailed among them, he declared. "Their tones changed. They spoke pleasantly, and readily agreed to go with me to examine the [reservation]. With this satisfactory conclusion," Howard recalled in almost the identical words Issac Stevens had used in 1855, "the council again adjourned."[35]

Some Nez Perce who attended the meeting took issue with Howard's account of the dialogue published in both his official War Department report and his book *Nez Perce Joseph,* which appeared shortly after the war. Thirty-four years later Yellow Bull, leader of the initial Salmon River war party, said that Toohoolhoolzote's language was less severe, that he told Howard that Indians and whites were like two trees standing close together, that eventually their limbs would intertwine and unite while still maintaining their unique identity. "The great law has planted us separately on the earth, and when these two trees grow together, your race and mine, the branches unite between earth and sky." But, he concluded, "I shall not move to any reservation at all. I will live where I am." Other Nez Perce claimed Howard used rude and inconsiderate language, occasionally telling Toohoolhoolzote to "shut up" and even pushing him angrily at one point.[36]

There is no way of knowing exactly what transpired; no impartial record of the meeting exists. The only thing that seems certain was Toohoolhoolzote's total humiliation. As one Nez Perce who was present ruefully recalled, "All that hurt us. In peace councils, force must not be talked. It was the same as showing us the rifle."[37]

On May 14, at the request of the chiefs, Howard released Toohoolhoolzote from the guardhouse and announced that the bands would have thirty days in which to move to the reservation. Like Monteith, Howard ignored the fact that the Snake and Salmon rivers were in spring flood. Doubtless, both Howard and Monteith believed the longer the Nez Perce were given, the less likely they were to comply. Although the general denied that anyone objected to the deadline, Joseph later maintained that he had tried unsuccessfully to get Howard to change his mind. This harsh ultimatum would only exacerbate feelings of unfairness and injustice.

As far as Howard was concerned the matter was concluded, and he wired the good news, albeit somewhat prematurely, to McDowell: "We have put all nontreaty Indians on reservation by using force and persuasion without bloodshed. Have not exceeded my instructions." Howard prepared to return to Portland "feeling that a difficult task had been done."[38]

Just before departing, Howard warned the headmen that any delay on their part risked a confrontation with whites anxious to see them on the reservation. To drive home his point, he read a petition he had recently received from settlers along the Salmon River that accused the Nez Perce of stealing horses and destroying property, and demanded their prompt removal. The chiefs listened in stony silence as Howard concluded by reading the names of fifty-seven settlers who had signed the document.

One month later, many of these same settlers were dead.

4

*A*bout the time that Isabella Benedict looked out her window at White Bird Creek on the morning of June 14 and saw her wounded husband, Sam, fall from his horse, General Howard was arriving by steamboat at Lewiston some ninety miles away. Howard had left his headquarters in Portland two weeks earlier on an inspection tour accompanied by Indian Inspector Erwin Watkins. With the deadline for the Nez Perce's removal to the reservation the following day, the general thought it wise to be near Lapwai in case of trouble.

Waiting to greet Howard and Watkins at the landing were several officers and townsfolk, including Captain David Perry, commanding officer of Fort Lapwai. Like many officers of the period, Perry had been awarded a brevet title for past meritorious and gallant service and was commonly addressed by his higher honorary rank. Howard asked anxiously, "How is Joseph, Colonel?"

Perry reassured him, "All right, at last accounts. The Indians are, I think, coming on the reservation without trouble."

Young Charles Monteith, the agent's brother and reservation clerk, told the same story. "Indians seem to be acting in good faith;

guess they will make no trouble." The citizens of Lewiston agreed, Howard said. "All united in the same testimony, 'The Indians are all right.' "[1]

Howard seemed satisfied but decided to remain in Lewiston until the bands arrived on the reservation, then continue his travels with the inspector. He both liked and respected Watkins, a former Civil War officer whom he described as "a large, wholesome man possessing genuine courage that never failed." Charged with carrying out policies formulated by each of the fourteen Indian agents in his department, Howard had been frequently frustrated, protesting that "it is not scriptural to obey so many masters." Since Watkins had seniority, Howard had "transferred my allegiance to him at once, and placed him over all agents."[2]

While Watkins attended to business in Lewiston, Perry suggested that the general would be more comfortable at Fort Lapwai. Howard agreed, and that afternoon they traveled on to the fort some twelve miles upriver. No sooner had Howard gotten comfortably settled in, however, than a messenger arrived from Mount Idaho, sent by innkeeper and town spokesperson L. P. Brown. Addressed to Perry, the message expressed Brown's concern over the congregation of nontreaty Nez Perce at Tolo Lake (near Tepahlewam), complaining that "they are insolent, and have but little to say to the whites, and that all their actions indicate trouble from them." Brown did not "feel any alarm, but thought it well to inform you of what was going on among them." He ended the letter by requesting Perry send troops "as soon as you can, a sufficient force to handle them without gloves, should they be disposed to resist."[3]

Neither Perry nor Howard was particularly concerned, but Perry suggested they order a small detachment to Mount Idaho to investigate the charges and placate the settlers. Howard agreed and the following morning at dawn, two enlisted men and an interpreter named Rabusco set out for Mount Idaho, some sixty-two miles away. Only a few hours passed before the three came riding breathlessly back, accompanied by two friendly Nez Perce they had met on the trail coming from Tolo Lake. As Rabusco tried to interpret their rushed words, a tale began to unfold that no one at Fort Lapwai wanted to believe. To be sure of what they were saying, Howard and

ROUTE FROM NEZ PERCE HOMELAND TO BIG HOLE

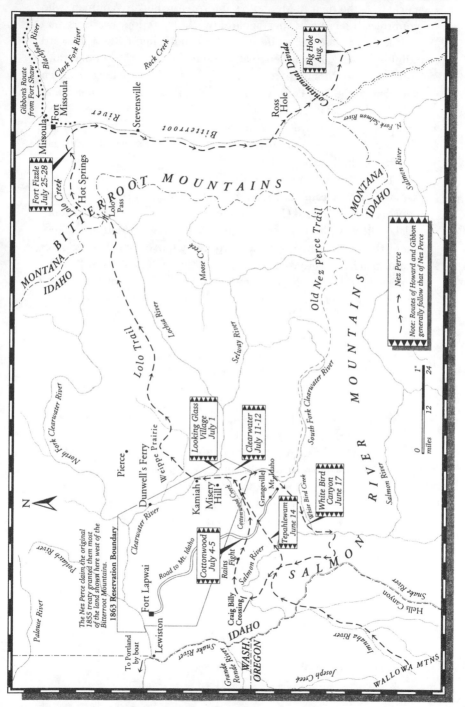

Perry took the men to Monteith's interpreter, Perrin Whitman, who confirmed their news that apparently three or four warriors had murdered at least one white man along the Salmon River. Howard admitted that "all believed that matters were getting into serious trouble," and Monteith recommended they immediately dispatch someone to the Nez Perce camp to quell any additional violence that might erupt. Jonah Hayes, the acting chief of the treaty Nez Perce, and James Reuben, Joseph's nephew, volunteered to go, convinced that any killings had to be the work of rebellious warriors beyond control of the bands' headmen.[4]

The two men started down the trail to Tolo Lake, but within the same hour they came galloping back accompanied by the two messengers Brown and Ad Chapman had sent that morning from Mount Idaho. "It was a time to be remembered," Howard said of the moment the men reigned up their worn-out horses and handed over the dispatches. A crowd of officers and their wives along with some agency Nez Perce had gathered on Perry's front porch. Howard instantly opened the messages and, making every effort to remain "perfectly cool and self possessed," he read the startling news:

Mount Idaho, 7 A.M., Friday, June 15, '77
COMMANDING OFFICER, FT. LAPWAI:

Last night we started a messenger to you, who reached Cottonwood House, where he was wounded and driven back by the Indians. The people of Cottonwood undertook to come here during the night; were interrupted; all wounded or killed. Parties this morning found some of them on the prairie. . . . One thing is certain, we are in the midst of an Indian war. Every family is here, and we will have taken all the precautions we can, but are poorly armed. We want arms and ammunition and help at once. Don't delay a moment. . . . You cannot imagine people in a worse condition than they are here. . . .

Yours truly,
L. P. Brown[5]

Then Howard read the second message Brown had written an hour later, describing the dead and wounded. "Give us relief and arms and ammunition," wrote the frantic man. "Hurry up! Hurry!"[6]

From one of the messengers, who spoke English, the crowd heard a graphic if somewhat overdrawn account of the murders.

Howard turned to Perry. "Well, Colonel, this means business!"

"Yes, sir."

"Are your men in readiness?"

"Everything but some transportation that must come from Lewiston," answered Perry.[7]

Now the irrevocable wheels of war began to turn. As an editorial in the New York *Tribune* observed, "When frontier towns are ravaged and settlers are murdered, all question as to which side violates treaties is out of order."[8] Howard penned a quick note to Brown, telling him that help was coming. Then he sent his aide-de-camp to Walla Walla to telegraph orders for additional troops. Finally, he dispatched his quartermaster to Lewiston to return with pack mules to carry supplies for Perry's command. With only two companies of cavalry numbering about a hundred men at Fort Lapwai, Howard summoned two additional companies on duty in the Wallowa Valley and a detachment of infantry headquartered at Walla Walla.

As Howard and Perry planned their strategy, neither man was comfortable sending so few troops against the Nez Perce. With the benefit of hindsight, it is difficult to know exactly what they hoped to accomplish with such a small force. Since none of the nontreaty bands had arrived within the reservation on the appointed date, it was possible that as many as two hundred or more warriors might be involved in the outbreak. But Brown's message about the settlements had been urgent. Perry's force would have to stop further depredations until reinforcements arrived. It is also unclear why Howard failed to encourage Perry to attempt to negotiate with the bands for the surrender of the murderers. According to several accounts, the general brushed aside repeated admonishments by treaty Indians that the murders had been the work of a small number of warriors who had betrayed the wishes of the bands. Added to all of this was the uncertainty over what kind of combatants the Nez Perce might be. Undoubtedly, bravado was no small factor in their decision to forcefully crush the rebellion, since rarely did the army consider any Indian an equal match for a soldier.

Standing on Perry's front porch as the final messengers arrived was Emily FitzGerald. Her husband, Surgeon John FitzGerald, was temporarily away from Lapwai, but she had no doubt that had he been present he would now be preparing to leave with Perry in pursuit of the Nez Perce. In a long, colorful letter to her mother that day, she remarked that "the parade ground is full of horses, the porches are full of trunks and blankets, everybody is rushing about, and everything is in confusion. . . . The two companies of cavalry will leave in a few hours. They don't dare wait even for more troops, though dispatches have already been sent everywhere to gather up the scattered troops in the Department. My dear old husband will have to follow Colonel Perry's command as soon as he gets back here. These poor people from Mt. Idaho say, 'One thing is certain. An Indian war is upon us.' You know these devils always begin on helpless outlying settlements. Poor Mrs. Theller is busy getting up a mess kit for her husband. Major Boyle remains in charge of the post. The talk among the officers is that there will be a great deal of trouble."[9]

Late that evening, Perry believed he could wait no longer for the mule train from Lewiston. With orders to catch up as best it could, some one hundred cavalrymen of Companies F and H, along with twelve treaty Nez Perce scouts, prepared to depart for Mount Idaho. Emily FitzGerald remarked that it was well that Captain Perry's wife was absent, for although she was a gracious hostess who "adored" her husband, she was also "a very foolish and hysterical woman" who would have made Perry's departure even more difficult.[10]

The man riding at the head of the column, Captain David Perry, senior officer of the First Cavalry's Company F, was no greenhorn. Like so many frontier army officers, thirty-six-year-old Perry had learned his soldiering in the Civil War. A year later, he found himself on the Owyhee River in Idaho Territory at battle with a large band of Bannock Indians. In a resounding victory, Company F killed thirty warriors while losing only one soldier. For his leadership,

Perry won a brevet, that of lieutenant colonel. In 1873, he fought against the Modocs in the Lava Beds of Oregon and was wounded in a battle near Tule Lake. Crook, that ever eccentric but highly respected general (except perhaps in Howard's view), called Perry "an excellent officer," one who was conversant with his duty and "willing to do it and do it thoroughly." Crook was particularly complimentary of Perry's abilities as an Indian fighter.[11]

In describing him, Howard said Perry was "a little over six feet in height and standing straight, he is so gracefully formed and young looking, that he does not seem tall. He has a clear Saxon eye and usually wears a pleasant smile—pleasant, but with a reserve in it." After all, the general noted, "one can hardly command men and go into battle often and still keep altogether sunshiny."[12]

The junior officer of Company F was Lieutenant Edward R. Theller, a native of Vermont. Theller served with a volunteer regiment during the Civil War but somehow missed the entire conflict while stationed in California. In 1866, however, he saw duty in Arizona, fighting in several skirmishes with Apaches, and later in the Modoc War. Howard thought he was "a generous, brave man, with a warm heart," who was particularly interested in the "speed of his stallion." Forty-four years old in 1877, Theller apparently was fond of horse racing and had come under criticism for his "associations" with a gambling element in Lewiston. He and his well-liked, energetic wife, Delia, frequently entertained at their quarters in Lapwai. Of the four major officers, Theller had the least combat experience.[13]

Commanding Company H was Captain Joel G. Trimble, "another good officer" in the general's opinion. A year older than Theller, Trimble had fought Indians as a private in Oregon before joining the Army of the Potomac in 1861. By the end of the war he had secured a commission, earning two brevets as well as two wounds in numerous engagements. Like Theller and Perry, Trimble fought in the Modoc War and actually was the officer to whom the Modoc chief, Captain Jack, surrendered in 1873. "Spare" was how a fellow soldier described him, and while Trimble was almost as tall as Perry, he probably weighed no more than 140 pounds. Howard thought that

Trimble had a slight cast in one eye from one of his Civil War wounds, but he was in fact partially blind in both eyes and would soon muster out of the service on a disability pension.[14]

Trimble's junior officer was William R. Parnell, one of the most experienced men ever to fight on the Indian frontier. Parnell was Irish, yet he served with the British in the Crimean War and was one of the few survivors of the famous Charge of the Light Brigade at Balaklava. As soon as Parnell immigrated to the United States in 1860 he enlisted in the Union army and went on to serve in no less than eighteen major Civil War battles. After the war, Parnell fought Indians in California under Crook and again in Oregon against the Modocs. Described by another soldier as "a large fleshy man" who "taxed the powers of his horse quite heavily," Parnell lacked Trimble's stamina. Little more is known about him in 1877 except that he was suffering from numerous past wounds. Shot in the hip during the Civil War, he still carried the bullet embedded in his pelvis. Parnell also had wounds from several deep saber cuts, one of which had severed his nose. Infection had caused part of the nasal bone to rot away, leaving a gaping hole in the roof of his mouth, making speech difficult. He wore a metal plate over the hole that allowed better articulation, but because it was fragile he lived in constant fear of breaking it.[15]

As was typical of the post–Civil War U.S. Army, many of the enlisted men were foreign-born. Twenty-three men were from Ireland, thirteen from Germany, five from Canada, three from England, and one each from Denmark, Scotland, France, and Austria. Before joining the army, twenty-two men had worked as laborers, seven as farmers, four as teamsters, three as blacksmiths, two as tailors, and two as bricklayers. Others had been painters, bookkeepers, barbers, gardeners, bakers, miners, jewelers, and musicians. Twenty of the men had previous military experience, and Company H had ten men who had fought Indians—on the whole, however, hardly seasoned troops. Their average age was twenty-eight and most were single.[16]

Why had these men joined the army? Some were down on their luck, trying to escape poverty or the drudgery of farm life, or simply felt they had no other skills after four long years of fighting in the

Civil War. Others had just immigrated and did not speak passable English. A few probably enjoyed the frontier fighting life, although it is difficult to understand why. All that most could look forward to was fear of brutal death by Indians, miserable rations and wages, and ungratefulness from a nation that couldn't decide if Native Americans should be reconciled or exterminated. Frontier soldiering, remarked one disgruntled officer, consisted of being shot and killed by savages, then having one's name spelled wrong in the newspapers. Tired of war, Congress reduced the army by one million men after 1865, setting a ceiling of twenty-five thousand enlistees in 1874 and not allowing any increase for the next twenty-five years. Some officers called this period the army's Dark Ages due to the skeleton forces they commanded as well as the quality of the average soldier, who was widely considered to lack the mental, physical, and moral competence of Civil War volunteers.

In 1876, 24,742 men were enlisted in the army, nearly two-thirds of whom were involved in the Indian wars. Of these, 16,665 were privates. Once a soldier was enlisted, his term usually lasted five years. At the conclusion of the Civil War, a private made sixteen dollars a month, but in a cost-cutting mood, a parsimonious Congress slashed salaries to thirteen dollars in 1871. Because of such low wages many privates were continually in debt to their sergeants and post sutlers. During 1877, Congress delayed passing an appropriations bill, and those wearing army blue were not paid for five long months.

Private William Hurlburt of Company F was typical of those who fell on hard times: after losing all his "property" and with nowhere to turn, he enlisted. What made Hurlburt unusual was that he had a wife and two children who could not bear the separation and longed to join him in distant Idaho Territory. In 1876, Hurlburt secured a loan from the army to pay his family's $400 travel expenses, but the army deducted $10 every month from his pay, leaving them only $3 to live on for each of the next forty months. When Alice Hurlburt and her children arrived in St. Louis on their way to Lapwai, an army clerk took interest in her plight, describing her as a woman with "a pretty, lady-like little body" who evidently had passed "a good portion of her life under happy auspices. There was a shadow of trouble on her smooth brow," remarked the smitten clerk, "that made her really charming ways irresistible." Before she had been in the office fifteen minutes, "she could have counted a friend in every one of the good-looking young men about the establishment" (among whom the clerk no doubt included himself). Not to be distracted, Alice Hurlburt finally joined her husband in Lapwai and took employment as a laundress to make ends meet.[17]

Frontier life was hard by any measure and campaign life the most difficult. Food supplied by the government became a prime cause of discontent among troops in the field. Hardtack, salt pork, and coffee were the staples, but bureaucratic corruption often resulted in shipments of maggot-infested bread and flat stones cleverly placed between slabs of salt pork. With nothing else to eat soldiers would dunk their hardtack in hot coffee, spoon off the maggots as they rose to the surface, and devour the softened biscuit. In 1890, a trooper with the Eighth Cavalry observed that the label on his field rations indicated they were twenty-seven years old. "The hardtack had a green mould on it, but we just wiped it off. . . ."[18]

Coffee came in the form of green beans, which a trooper usually roasted in his mess kit and pounded into grounds with a stone or the butt of his revolver. Salt pork—termed bacon, sowbelly, or Cincinnati Chicken—was often eaten raw after being dipped in vinegar, particularly when nighttime campfires might attract Indians. Seventh Cavalry Trumpeter Frank Mulford commented on the monotonous fare in 1877: "We now have a change of diet: hardtack, bacon and coffee for breakfast; raw bacon and tack for dinner; fried bacon and hard bread for supper." Scurvy was not uncommon, and cholera was a constant threat on long field maneuvers. For every soldier who died of wounds or accidents on the frontier, nearly two died of disease. Between 1866 and 1868, the Seventh Cavalry alone reported thirty-six men lost to Indians, six drowned, and two missing in action. During this period, fifty-one men died of cholera. "For all these evils," remarked General George A. Custer in 1867, "desertion became the most popular antidote." In that year alone, 14,068 men decided they could endure no more. Oddly, only 1,844 men discharged themselves in 1877, whereas during the twenty-four years of frontier warfare over 88,000 men—fully one-third of the U.S. Army—deserted.[19]

Many made it through only one winter, then slipped away in early spring when civilian jobs returned with warm weather. "Snowbirds," as they were called, often succeeded in escaping military authorities only to fall prey to civilians anxious to collect the thirty-five-dollar reward for capturing a deserter. In 1870, one deserting soldier chose suicide when confronted by suspecting citizens near Fort Dodge, Kansas (punishment was frequently severe). Before the Civil War, a deserter who was caught was flogged unmercifully, but for some years after 1861, branding was the preferred method. Sergeant John Ryan recalled that "deserters were laid on their left side with the right hip exposed, and the letter 'D' was branded on them with a heated iron an inch or more in diameter." Then there was the ball and chain. A blacksmith forged an iron ring around the deserter's ankle attached to a short length of chain and a twenty-five-pound iron ball. It was an experience to be avoided, recalled Private Harvey Ciscel in his account of one unpleasant campaign against the Sioux that resulted in a high number of desertions. "You could hear the screams of the men being shackled a mile out on the prairie." Finally, the army resorted to tatooing. Besides being a lasting humiliation, a tattoo also served another purpose. It was not uncommon for men to desert and then sign up at a distant post, collecting a reward for each enlistment. One soldier successfully reenlisted thirty times before he was finally caught. Tattooing put an end to his lucrative career once and for all.[20]

If they survived maggots, disease, poor wages, and the constant threat of brutal death at the hands of Indians, soldiers barely survived the boredom between campaigns. History records that nearly one thousand hostile engagements occurred between 1866 and 1891, but accounts fail to mention the long periods of ennui and inactivity of frontier military life. In 1877, Secretary of War George W. McCrary believed he had the answer to desertions, readily admitting that for the most part the life of the soldier is one of "dull and monotonous routine of which it is natural, if not inevitable, that men of spirit and ambition should weary." What could be done to render the daily life of the common soldier more agreeable? The good bureaucrat suggested "taking measures for the supply of more and better reading-matter for the Army."[21]

When not campaigning, soldiers were often employed as carpenters, painters, or common laborers around a post, work hardly conducive to keeping in fighting trim. First Cavalry Sergeant Michael McCarthy of Company H, who kept a most revealing journal, recalled that at Fort Lapwai "most of the enlisted men were employed on extra duty—clerks, carpenters, blacksmiths, officers' servants, etc. The men so employed rarely attended a drill and target practice was not . . . encouraged." Only twenty rounds or less per month were issued for practice, and as a result, soldiers were often ridiculed by Indians and settlers alike for poor marksmanship. All in all, "we were poorly supplied with ammunition," stated McCarthy, and the men's guns were "rusty and foul."[22]

In 1873, the government finally provided decent standardized weapons. The infantry's Springfield rifle and the shorter-barrel carbine used by the cavalry were both breech-loading guns that fired single-shot .45 caliber cartridge ammunition. The cavalry also carried a side arm: the .45 caliber Colt revolver. Seven-or-more-shot repeaters such as Winchester, Spencer, and Henry rifles were well liked by settlers and Indians but were unpopular with army officers who claimed their nervous men often shot away all their ammunition at the first alarm. Early-model repeaters also frequently misfired or jammed and had only half the range of Springfields. By modern standards, bullets fired from these weapons were slow, about 1,500 feet per second as compared to present-day cartridges that are often double that speed. Such slow velocity necessitated a high trajectory when shooting beyond short distances, so accuracy was a learned skill, one which soldiers with inadequate practice rarely acquired. But Indians who frequently hunted as well as warred with their weapons were often excellent shots.

The soft lead bullets these weapons fired were heavy. When they struck, they did so with much force, often exploding on impact. The bullets shattered any bone they hit, taking out huge chunks that left a surgeon little choice but amputation, often without antiseptic or anesthesia. In an age when the wounded were seldom treated until after a battle, amputation was the preferred "cure" for myriad ailments including "frostbite, gunshot wounds, fractures and dislocations," according to one army surgeon. Abdominal wounds were nearly always fatal. Officers knew this and instructed their men to "fire low," for while bullets might glance off bones of the head or upper torso, stomach wounds almost always developed into deadly peritonitis. This knowledge was shared by Indians and used effectively on their enemies as well. There were worse ways to die. An 1885 publication from the U.S. Government Printing Office entitled *The Soldier's Handbook* makes peritonitis out to be the gentlest of departures, for "the person lives a day or two, with perfect clearness of intellect, and often not suffering greatly."[23]

When guns were unavailable, Indians readily took up their time-honored skill with bow and arrow. Before the advent of repeating weapons, a good archer could launch a dozen arrows while the opponent awkwardly reloaded a muzzle loader. Flaked-stone arrowheads were difficult enough for surgeons to remove, but arrowheads made of strap iron tended to bend like a fishhook when striking bone. Army surgeons devised a removal technique using a wire loop pushed in alongside the shaft of the arrow in an attempt to snag the arrowhead, backing it out as carefully as possible to avoid ripping open an even greater wound. This operation had to be performed soon after the victim was wounded, however, for the animal sinew securing the arrowhead to the shaft would soften and loosen if long immersed in the victim's blood. Then the shaft came out and the arrowhead remained buried inside, sometimes working its way to the surface years later in what must have been unforgettable agony.

Pain and death were probably not far from the minds of Perry's men when they arrived at Cottonwood House, exhausted after having ridden forty miles in darkness and through thick timber from Lapwai. Traveling on, they soon reached the overturned wagon of Wilmot and Ready, cigars strewn across the road and an empty whiskey keg nearby.

Outside Grangeville, a group of volunteers led by Ad Chapman rode out to meet the tired troops. A tall, lanky man with black hair, a walrus moustache, and darkly sunken eyes, Chapman urged Perry to hurry to the Salmon River since he believed the bands were moving their stock and belongings to the opposite shore where the terrain made concealment easier. Howard recorded later that Chapman beseeched Perry: "Oh, Colonel, you can easily whip the scoundrels!

They are cowardly wretches. We could destroy them if we only had the arms! You will have to hurry up, or you will not be able to overtake them! We will go and help you, as many as have arms and horses!"[24] Chapman promised at least twenty-five or thirty men.

The soldiers arrived in Grangeville just before nightfall and prepared to finally rest after twenty-four hours and sixty miles in the saddle. But townsfolk badgered Perry, some people spuriously claiming that the bands' stock was actually theirs. Perry vacillated, saying later, "I saw at once that if I allowed these Indians to get away with all their plunder without making any effort to overtake and capture them, it would reflect discredit upon the Army and all concerned." Perry summoned Trimble, Parnell, and Theller, and they all agreed that "the only thing to do" was to stop the Indians from crossing the Salmon River.[25] "The call for boots and saddles" came at nine o'clock, and men who had lain down to sleep were awakened, some attempting to wolf down half-cooked beans before saddling their horses. A half hour later, accompanied by Chapman and only ten of the volunteers he had promised, the command moved out toward White Bird Canyon and the Salmon River.

Soon after midnight, the column arrived at the edge of trees near the head of the canyon some ten miles from Mount Idaho. From here, the mostly treeless valley descended some 2,600 feet in a distance of nearly three miles down to White Bird Creek, then a few miles farther to the Salmon River where Perry believed the Nez Perce were camped. When the troops were hidden among the trees at the summit, Perry ordered them to dismount and await first light before advancing down the canyon. No one was to sleep, and there would be no fires or smoking. Well into their second night without rest and with over seventy miles behind them, Sergeant McCarthy recalled that he had to continually wake the dozing men. Even their mounts were so tired that "in many instances the horses lay down beside their riders."

Near dawn, disregarding Perry's orders, one of the soldiers struck a match to light his pipe. A coyote instantly howled. Lieutenant Parnell thought the last note was different than any he had ever heard before, indicating an Indian sentry. Private John Schorr of Company H declared the howl "a shivering one" that was enough "to make one's hair stand on end."[26] At four o'clock, the eastern sky started to lighten, and the mounted troops began their descent into White Bird Canyon.

Whether any Nez Perce heard the warning, if indeed it was one, is doubtful. Accounts vary on exactly how, from their camp a few miles away at the bottom of the canyon, they were alerted to the approaching soldiers. What seems certain is that the night before many warriors had gotten drunk on stolen whiskey, and much of the camp was still suffering the effects. According to the Nez Perce's Camille Williams, four sentinels had been posted partway up the canyon some distance from Perry's bivouac. At first light, Payyenapta (Hand in Hand) discerned soldiers moving about high up the canyon and succeeded in rousing his drunken companions "by the severest usage of his riding quirt, swinging it without mercy."[27] Soon Sees-koomkee (No Feet), an ex-slave and not a Nez Perce, mounted a horse and rushed down the mountain. That the man could ride at all is a wonder since years before, as a slave of another tribe, he had been caught stealing and had iron bindings put on his wrists and ankles as punishment. He was banished outside on a winter night and his limbs froze, resulting in the loss of both feet and a hand. By the time he came to the Nez Perce he had become a free man, although his position was somewhat less than a full-fledged tribal member. Now this cripple, who had become a splendid horseman, galloped into camp sounding the alarm.

As Toohoolhoolzote, Joseph, and White Bird hurriedly consulted, the soldiers made their way down the valley in the gathering light. Suddenly a woman, scantily clothed, appeared in the trail, holding a small child in her arms while another stood at her side hanging on to her skirt. All three, recalled Sergeant McCarthy, had hair so blond it was almost white. After Isabella Benedict and her daughters had escaped from their house, they had first hidden and then, having despaired of rescue, finally started for the settlements. When they met up with Perry and his men, they had not eaten for three days. She asked Perry for an escort back to Mount Idaho and begged him to give up the chase, declaring that only a massacre awaited the soldiers a few miles away. Ignoring her warning and with no soldiers to spare, Perry offered to send her back to Mount Idaho with one of his Nez Perce guides, but Isabella Benedict declined, mistrusting any Indians by now. Instead she said she would wait for the soldiers on their return trip—if there were any survivors. One man gave her a blanket and Trumpeter John Jones gave her a loaf of bread. The column moved on, more determined than ever. Such suffering, concluded Lieutenant Parnell, called for "sympathy, compassion, and action."[28]

As dawn began to break, the men could make out the ever-widening valley as they descended. To their west was a massive ridge that separated them from the Salmon River. Looking east, White Bird Creek dropped down through forested foothills. The trail to the canyon bottom led through grassy slopes intersected by numerous ridges and ravines thick with brush. Perry believed the Nez Perce camp was near the confluence of the creek and the river, several miles downstream and out of sight. As a precaution, however, he decided to detail an advance party consisting of Lieutenant Theller and eight men, including Ad Chapman and several Nez Perce scouts. Theller's party rode about a hundred yards ahead, then came Perry's Company F with Trimble's Company H about forty yards behind. A few moments later, Perry gave the order to remove overcoats and load carbines.

Just beyond Perry's view and hidden by trees along the creek, the Nez Perce were rousing every man who was not hopelessly drunk. Although the camp contained some 140 warriors, probably no more than 70 took up their weapons; these were bows and arrows and about forty-five guns, many of which were old muzzle loaders.[29] The chiefs had decided on a plan. They would send out a peace party and offer to surrender the murderers. If that failed, they would position warriors to flank the soldiers as they approached a rock outcrop just above the creek. Beyond that, their plan ended in typical Indian fashion. "Unlike the trained white soldier, who is guided by the bugle call," said a warrior named Weyahwahtsitskan, "the Indian goes into battle on his mind's own guidance. . . . All the warriors, whoever gets ready, mount their horses and go."[30]

Reaching the rock outcrop, two of Theller's Nez Perce scouts suddenly halted, indicating by signs that the Indian camp was near. Ad Chapman, wearing a large white sombrero, quickly rode forward to see for himself. There only a hundred yards away were six mounted warriors riding slowly toward him. The Nez Perce said later they were displaying a white flag. On seeing Chapman and the soldiers, one of them shouted, "What do you people want?" Chapman immediately raised his gun and fired, and the warriors turned and ran for cover.[31]

As Sergeant McCarthy came over the ridge moments later, all he saw were "a few Indians riding back toward the creek." Theller ordered his men to spread out along the ridge and commence firing. Then he told Trumpeter Jones to sound the call to battle. Known as "Jonesy," the thirty-year-old trumpeter was a well-liked young man whose passion for strong drink had at least on one occasion landed him in the guardhouse. When Toohoolhoolzote was imprisoned by Howard at the May council, his cellmate had been Jones. The two struck up such an amiable friendship that the private bragged that Toohoolhoolzote had promised that if the soldiers ever fought the Nez Perce he would not be harmed. Now, as Jones raised the trumpet to his lips, Fire Body, an elderly warrior, shot him dead out of his saddle.

On hearing the shots and seeing Theller's men dismount, Perry quickly moved his company up to the ridge and prepared to charge the warriors below. When he turned to Trumpeter Daly to give the order, Daly informed him he had earlier dropped his trumpet along the trail. Only a few moments into the battle, Perry had lost his most important means of communication. Turning back to the fight commencing before him, he decided a charge would be foolish since the warriors would only fall back to the line of trees along the creek, leaving his men exposed and vulnerable. Whoever possessed the high ground held the most defensible position, and here Perry decided to remain. Sending his horses to the rear, protected by a swale, Perry ordered Trimble up on his right. The men deployed along the crescent-shaped ridge, Trimble's Company H to the right of Perry while the volunteers took up a position on a small knoll to his left along the ridge.

Trimble had barely positioned his men, who were still mounted, when warriors led by Wahlitits, Sarpsis Ilppilp, and Strong Eagle began to ride around his right flank. The men were wearing red blankets to show their contempt for the soldiers. Since the warriors were riding in traditional Plains Indian style, hanging over the side of the horse, away from the troops, the inexperienced soldiers thought the horses riderless at first and were surprised when Indians popped up and began shooting at them. Shot in the groin, Corporal Roman Lee fell to the ground in shock. The last anyone saw the dazed corporal alive, he was wandering toward the Indian camp, his waist and legs awash in blood. About this time, the remaining men began to dismount in order to fire more accurately.

Acutely feeling the loss of his ability to convey battle orders, particularly with his men so separated, Perry started toward Trimble's line to retrieve Company H's trumpet. Looking back, he saw the volunteers retreating from their position on the knoll. One of the men had been wounded in the hip and another in the thigh. When Perry chanced to look again, the volunteers had mounted their horses and were in a headlong scramble back up the canyon, one rider even leaping over an Indian in his rush to escape. Later a soldier wryly recalled that Ad Chapman, always wanting to be the head of everything, was far in the lead.

The small knoll the volunteers had held was now too far away to defend, and believing his men too scattered, Perry ordered them to tighten up the line toward Company H. Arriving at Trimble's position, he learned Trimble's trumpeter had been killed. All was confusion, with horses bucking and rearing and many of Trimble's men fearfully huddled together in the center of the line, scared witless. Looking back, Perry saw that several warriors had gained the knoll, and their deadly accurate fire quickly felled six soldiers. Theller, whom Perry had left in charge of Company F, "seemed much excited and did not seem to know what he was doing."[32] What was to have been a slow consolidating movement of Company F toward Trimble's line now suddenly turned into a rout, men stumbling over one another, some discarding their weapons in panic as they madly dashed for their horses.

Seeing his company in unceremonious retreat and with Company H ready to do the same, Perry ordered Trimble to retreat in an orderly fashion. Falling back two men at a time while others covered them, Trimble had gone only about four hundred yards before he encountered Lieutenant Theller on foot, a carbine in his hand, wandering around in shock. Trimble quickly ordered a horse brought up for him. No sooner had the men placed the lieutenant in the saddle than he recovered enough to gallop off up the canyon after his fleeing command.

Trimble saw that a handful of men led by Sergeant Michael McCarthy had not heard the retreat order and were still fighting on the rock outcrop. Believing McCarthy's position the most defensible, Trimble shouted to his men to turn back, but they ignored the order. Meanwhile, McCarthy had started toward the rear, then returned with his men to the rocks when he heard Trimble's second order. They fired about ten rounds each before realizing no other soldiers were joining them. In a few seconds they would be completely cut off.

Ordering a retreat, McCarthy was bringing up the rear when his horse took a bullet and collapsed. On foot and with Indians beginning to close, he ran to catch up with a group of ten men led by Lieutenant Parnell who had separated from Trimble, moving "over the ground quite freely, for I am now thoroughly scared." One-half mile later he was still running, but beginning to fall behind. Just then, two men saw his plight and returned. McCarthy was so exhausted that he had to have help mounting behind one of them, riding double until they managed to catch a riderless horse. The detachment slowly worked its way up the hill, stopping to fire on pursuing warriors until they were flanked, then gaining higher ground to repeat the same. In one of the ravines about halfway up the canyon, McCarthy's horse went down, crippled by a bullet, and he soon fell behind again, unable to keep up with the others. Desperately fatigued, he slipped on the steep hillside, rolled down, and lay still as warriors rushed by him.

Everywhere men like McCarthy who were wounded or unhorsed and who had failed to keep up with their retreating companions were quickly overrun. Husis Owyeen (Wounded Head), armed with an ancient pistol containing a single cartridge, recalled overtaking an unidentified soldier. "As he raised his gun I drew the old pistol with its last bullet. I shot first and he fell backwards and did not move. The bullet struck between his eyebrows. I jumped to the ground and took his gun and belt of cartridges. I left the dead soldier the old pistol as a present. Laid it on his breast."[33]

Not far away, Wounded Head was astonished to discover a white woman on foot, stumbling up the slope trying to escape. Isabella Benedict, whose struggles never seemed to end, had been given a horse a few moments before by retreating soldiers. At first, none of the fleeing men would stop. As each horse bounded past, she could hear their hard-drawn breaths and feel the flecks of foam thrown from their nostrils. Finally, two men halted long enough to catch a horse for her and take up her children on their own mounts before galloping up the hill. Told to cling tight and let the animal run at top speed, Isabella hung on until the saddle slipped and then turned, and she found herself flung into the brush.

Now Wounded Head overtook the woman and, making a sign that he would not harm her, motioned for her to get on the horse behind him. Carrying her down the trail, the warrior stopped at the bottom of the canyon. There, according to Benedict, some Nez Perce women persuaded him to let her go. "I think she was scared when I told her to get off to the ground," said Wounded Head. "I instructed her to escape with her life, and I shook hands with her." The next day, not far from Grangeville, Isabella Benedict was finally rescued by a settler named Edward Robie who had gone out alone in search of the woman he had long admired. Three years later they were married. After the war, Wounded Head declared Isabella Benedict "a very great friend to me, and the first time I met her after my return she gave me six dollars as a present."[34]

While Parnell's detachment struggled up the canyon, Perry and Trimble were attempting an orderly retreat up the steep west ridge with the bulk of the warriors in close pursuit. Perry repeatedly ordered the men to form a line, but it was hopeless. Pleading and begging, even threatening to shoot them, would not stop the soldiers in their haste to get up the hillside. One of the men, Private John Schorr, called it "a race of 'God for us all and the devil take the hindmost.' "[35] His horse having been shot out from under him, Perry rode double behind another man until he managed to catch Trumpeter Jones's riderless horse.

As the men gained higher ground, the warriors became more

wary. Perry managed to split his command, one squad firing while the other retreated a short distance, then those men covering for the squad in front. Repeating this method over and over, the men—their sweat-soaked horses heaving with exhaustion—finally made the summit of the canyon. Looking around, Perry saw Trimble and a number of men farther along the ridge. He called and motioned for Trimble to come to his aid, but the men waved once and then disappeared into the trees in the direction of Mount Idaho. Since he had not seen Theller for some time, Perry assumed he was also on his way to the settlements.

Today, looking down the steep, brush-choked hillside, it is difficult to imagine how the men and horses made it to the summit. Some did not. Lieutenant Theller and seven men had gotten trapped in a rocky ravine thick with thorn bushes that proved too steep for their weary horses to climb. Joseph's nephew, Hemene Moxmox (Yellow Wolf)—twenty-one years old, strong, quick, and who would survive the war to provide one of the most remarkable accounts ever made by an Indian during frontier years—was one of the warriors who witnessed their end. When the bodies were found later, the ground was littered with spent cartridges, a fact some said proved the men had sold their lives dearly. "Those soldiers put up a fight," remembered Yellow Wolf, before being "wiped out." The Nez Perce later reported, however, that only three warriors were wounded in the battle and none of those mortally, hardly a testimonial to the accuracy of the soldiers' fire.[36]

About a mile from the main battleground, five soldiers dismounted and sought shelter among some rocks. Riding up unaware, Yellow Wolf was shouted a warning by a fellow warrior. Jumping from his horse, he struck a soldier with his bow as the man was putting a cartridge in his gun. The soldier fell backward and a warrior shot him before he could get up. As Yellow Wolf leapt down the bank toward another soldier, he slipped on the grass, sprawling in front of the man. The soldier fired pointblank, but the bullet passed over the warrior's shoulder. Yellow Wolf grabbed the barrel of the gun, and as they wrestled, an Indian shot the man from above, killing him instantly. Looking around, Yellow Wolf saw that "a soldier was pointing his rifle at me. In that I saw danger. I jumped and ran, springing from side to side. I did not look back. Before the soldier got sights on me, a warrior threw a rock. It struck the soldier above the ear and killed him." Farther on, Yellow Wolf and his companions came upon two other soldiers. "They hardly slowed us," declared the warrior.[37]

Near the top of the canyon where the command had waited in the dark only hours before, Perry encountered Parnell, whose small squad had retreated up a more direct route. Together the two dozen men continued their retreat several miles to an abandoned ranch. The shock of battle was so great that during a brief lull in the fighting, Perry looked at his watch and told Parnell that since it was seven o'clock, he thought they could hold their position until dark. A disbelieving Parnell turned to Perry and informed him that it was seven o'clock in the morning, not evening, and that each man had left only a few rounds of ammunition.

At one point warriors almost flanked them, and Parnell provided protection while Perry and the others quickly mounted and rode away. When he looked around for his horse, Parnell found it gone. As bullets began to zip dangerously close and with no immediate cover, the lieutenant did what anyone would have done—he started running after the column. A few hundred yards away, some of his command realized he was missing and returned just before the Nez Perce closed in.

With Parnell safely in tow, alternately fighting and retreating, the men made their way back to Grangeville. Along the way, one soldier fell or was thrown from his horse, breaking his neck. As they neared the settlements at the end of the thirteen-mile chase, the warriors withdrew. There the survivors found Chapman's volunteers, Trimble, and a number of men from both companies. A quick headcount revealed the bad news. Out of the one hundred or so soldiers who had left Lapwai less than two days before, thirty-eight were missing. Perry thought a few men might yet straggle in, but he held little hope for the rest.

Back in the canyon, the scattered wounded and dismounted cavalrymen had all been killed with the exception of one man: Michael McCarthy. The sergeant lay quietly were he had slipped and fallen at the bottom of a ravine until no warriors were in sight. Then, "wiggling like a snake so as not to disturb the top brush," he crawled about one hundred yards down the creek into more dense cover. As McCarthy lay hidden underneath some rose bushes, two warriors rode "so close that I could almost touch the blankets trailing by their pony's side, which they had flung across their saddles." He scarcely believed they could miss seeing him, but the two men rode by.

Moments after they passed, two women came riding up, and, calling the men back, one of them told the warriors in Chinook (a pidgin widely used on the northwest frontier) that there was a soldier in the bushes. "She described me quite accurately," recalled the sergeant, "not even forgetting my stripes and chevrons."[38] Evidently, the women had seen where McCarthy had first sought cover but were unaware he had moved downstream. Now the warriors went back to where the women indicated he was hiding and fired several shots into the brush. McCarthy lay as still as possible, "my right hand resting on a rock with pistol cocked, determined to have a shot if discovered." He even considered shooting himself to avoid being captured alive, "but I found life too sweet to commit suicide." After a few minutes, the warriors lost interest and departed.

The two women, however, continued to search the brush, accompanied by an elderly man. "I could look into their faces as they leant down toward the bush in which I was concealed, and I could, if I so wished, grasp the muzzle of the old smoothbore musket that the old reprobate carried." Lying absolutely motionless, McCarthy held his breath, "trying to stifle even the beating of my heart." It seemed impossible, "but these three vicious pairs of eyes with all their Indian acuteness again pass me unobserved, and they disappear down the road."

In the creek for over an hour and with the battle sounding ever more distant and sporadic, McCarthy reasoned that the warriors would soon return and make a thorough search of the battlefield for survivors and weapons. Stripping off his heavy boots, he determined to make a run for it. At the edge of the brush and with no one in sight, he "commenced creeping up the hill." Partway, he discovered a small piece of the bread Trumpeter Jones had given Isabella Benedict earlier that morning. Finally reaching the summit, he looked back down on the creek far below, "expecting to see some other unfortunate trying to escape," but he saw no one. All who had fallen behind had been "dispatched, and it was barely two hours since the first shot was fired. How many there were I could only guess."

Two days later, tired, hungry, and footsore, Sergeant Michael McCarthy—who would receive the Medal of Honor for his participation in the battle—walked up to some startled settlers near Grangeville and asked directions to town.

5

*T*he night of June 16, while Perry's command was awaiting
daybreak at the head of White Bird Canyon, General Howard
was awakened by loud voices coming from the porch of his quarters
at Lapwai. Going outside, he recognized the wife of Jonah Hayes
(acting chief of the treaty Nez Perce), "a large-sized Indian woman"
sitting on her horse. "She was accompanied by another woman, the
one, as I understood, that had just come from the hostiles. One of
the half-breeds interpreted. She spoke so emphatically and so excitedly that she wakened everybody." The woman related a harrowing
tale. The Nez Perce had fixed a trap. The troops had run straight
into it and all been killed.[1]

Of course, this is nearly what happened the following morning.
Whether the messenger had a premonition about the ensuing battle
or only had been told that the bands intended to entrap the soldiers
if they chose to fight is uncertain. The translation may also have
been jumbled. Howard was not alarmed. He had just received a
message from Perry a few hours before stating the command had
reached Grangeville that afternoon, and there had been no word of
an impending fight. Howard went back to bed.

Late the next day, two of Perry's cavalrymen rode into Lapwai with news that made Howard think twice about his hasty dismissal of the woman the night before. The men had been among the first to bolt at White Bird, bypassing Grangeville and pushing their horses all night back to the fort. They were unsure what had happened to the rest of the command, feared they all might be dead, and declared that the Nez Perce were on their way to attack Fort Lapwai.

Howard was dumbfounded but wasted no time in barricading the post. Cordwood was stacked around one building where women and children were sheltered, and rumors of the defeat spread rapidly as far away as Lewiston. With almost all troops in the area with Perry, there was little to do but wait for more accurate news. The next afternoon, June 18, the long-awaited messenger arrived. "The fight resulted most disastrously to us, in fact scarcely exceeded by the magnitude of the Custer Massacre in proportion to the numbers engaged," wrote Perry in describing his casualties to Howard. "We saw about 125 Indians today and they are well armed, a great many of our guns and much ammunition must have fallen into their hands. I think it will require at least 500 men to whip them." The message concluded, "Please send word to Mrs. Perry that I am safe. Am too tired to write. . . . Please break the news of her husband's death to Mrs. Theller."[2]

Howard immediately sought out Delia Theller, endeavoring to "break the tidings gently. But Mrs. Theller read them in my face before I could speak, and words had no place. 'Oh, my husband!' " During the coming days before his body was found, the shock hardly diminished as Delia Theller refused to acknowledge her husband's death, believing he was only captured or would be found asleep. For weeks she kept his uniform neatly pressed, ready for his return.[3]

Also among the casualties was Private William Hurlburt who, having joined the army after losing all of his "property," had now lost his life as well. His distraught and pregnant wife, Alice, and her two children—whose transportation expenses the year before had sunk the family deep in debt—were taken in by Emily FitzGerald. "She is a very nice little woman, and her children are as nice as I know," wrote FitzGerald. "She is left destitute. After her sickness, we will all help her. A purse will be raised to take her back to her friends.

She is a helpless sort of a little woman, and I never saw such a look of distress in my life as has taken possession of her face." An article in the *New York Times* a month later was hardly as sympathetic, pragmatically noting "that in losing Private Hurlburt the Government will probably lose also its claim for transportation advanced."[4]

Soon after he received Perry's message, Howard wired General McDowell the "gloomy news," placing the number of dead at 34. Although Perry had said he had encountered some 125 warriors, Howard stated the enemy was "about two hundred strong." Thirty years later, calling the rout "a kind of Bull Run on a small scale," he would claim more than 500 Indians had faced Perry's beleaguered force, while most Nez Perce sources maintain that no more than 70 warriors took part in the battle. Several days after the fight, Emily FitzGerald heard Agent Monteith state that the Nez Perce force "does not number much over a hundred." But she warned, "that hundred is prepared to fight to the death."[5]

In requesting additional troops from McDowell, Howard proclaimed that the Nez Perce are "gradually increasing in strength, drawing from other tribes. The movement indicates a combination uniting nearly all disaffected Indians, [and] probably will reach a thousand or fifteen hundred when united."[6] McDowell later ridiculed this estimate, but Howard believed what everyone (including himself) was saying about the Dreamers throughout the Northwest. Weeks would pass before the perceived threat of a general uprising dissipated, and the delay in assembling such a large force of soldiers to combat this chimera would cost Howard the chase of his life.

Meanwhile, the entire citizenry between Lewiston and Montana became unnerved as news of the defeat spread, and missionaries, settlers, and treaty Nez Perce flocked to Lapwai for protection. The military post, made up of scattered homes, a clinic, and a horse stable, was hardly built for a siege, making everyone feel particularly vulnerable. Four days after the battle, vigilantes gave chase to two friendly reservation Nez Perce who came galloping at top speed back to the fort for safety. Before anyone could identify them, the cry arose that Indians were attacking. The handful of remaining troops quickly took up defensive positions, and officers' wives and children came running, "wild with fear," to the barricade. Emily

FitzGerald was sure that "for a few moments, I think, we women with our helpless little children suffered as much as if the Indians had really come."[7]

By June 21, eight companies had arrived from nearby forts and garrisons, and more were on their way from as far away as Georgia, Arizona, and Alaska. The next day, Howard prepared to move against the Nez Perce with 20 civilian volunteers from Walla Walla, a large number of guides and packers, and 227 regulars consisting of five companies of infantry, two of cavalry, and one of artillery. Besides the soldiers' personal weapons, the command was armed with two Gatling guns and a mountain howitzer. As the noisy procession assembled on the parade ground with officers barking out orders and men falling into ranks, Howard recalled, "a little of the old thrill of war comes back to me."[8]

Emily FitzGerald thought it hardly thrilling. "You can't imagine how sad it all is here," she wrote her mother. "Here are these nice fellows gathered around our table, all discussing the situation and all knowing they will never all come back. One leaves his watch and little fixings and says, 'If one of those bullets gets me, send this to my wife.' Another gave me his boy's photograph to keep for him, as he could not take it. He kept his wife's with him, and twice he came back to look at the boy's before he started off. One officer left a sick child, very ill; another left a wife to be confined next month. What thanks do they all get for it? No pay, and abuse from the country that they risk their lives to protect." It was enough to "wish all the Indians in the country were at the bottom of the Red Sea," she declared. "I suppose the country will have trouble until they are exterminated."[9]

The following afternoon, June 23, Howard's command reached Cottonwood House where he allowed the men to rest while he gathered intelligence concerning the whereabouts of the Nez Perce. The next day Perry arrived from Mount Idaho and delivered a verbal report of the battle, expressing his disappointment in his men's performance, particularly Trimble's apparent abandonment of Perry's squad at the summit of White Bird Canyon during the retreat. Howard decided he needed men too badly to take disciplinary action against the officer. Instead he ordered Trimble's company to assist the settlers stockaded at Slate Creek along the Salmon River. Howard reasoned that if the Nez Perce were still at the battlefield and he managed to push them up the river, Trimble would provide a flanking offense. Their losses now made up with reinforcements, Company H began the long, tedious ride around the headwaters of White Bird Creek, arriving at Slate Creek early the morning of August 26 after some twenty hours in the saddle.

Among the column was Sergeant Michael McCarthy, sporting a new pair of boots, a hat, and a pair of gloves that had been donated by a patriotic Mount Idaho merchant (the man changed his mind later and presented McCarthy with a bill). While the men and horses rested for a day at Slate Creek, McCarthy talked to some of the settlers. In his journal that day he noted there had been many causes that had precipitated the initial murders, but "in nearly every case the whites were to blame."

On the morning of June 25, Howard left orders for the infantry to proceed to White Bird Canyon, while he and Perry, accompanied by the cavalry, made a side trip to the settlements. "The soldiers who were left alive of Perry's command here met us," said Howard. "How different they were in numbers and appearance from the brisk and hearty troopers that had left Fort Lapwai the week previous!" At Mount Idaho, Howard visited the wounded. "Poor Mrs. Norton was there, very sadly wounded through her limbs. A lady [Mrs. Chamberlin] lay in another room, pale as death and suffering from a gunshot wound, and from other savage and repeated violence. Her little child was playing, to all appearance quite happy, on the outside of the bed, but a part of its tongue had been cut off." Howard concluded with a short speech to the settlers, promising that "no stone will be left unturned to give you redress and protection in the future."[10] Then the column traveled on to rendezvous with the infantry.

Since the battle over a week before, the Nez Perce had not moved far. Combing the battlefield for weapons, the Indians found as many as sixty-three guns, enough to arm those warriors who had fought with bows and arrows or smoothbore muskets. Several treaty Nez Perce who had guided Perry's command had been captured, and after much debate, they were freed with the warning they would be beaten or killed if caught again aiding soldiers. One elected to remain with the bands while the others immediately departed for Fort Lapwai, one scout running his horse to death in his eagerness to escape. Undoubtedly, the use of their own people against them must have been unsettling, but this successful army practice had a long history in the wars with Indians. General George Crook, who more than any other frontier commander refined this technique, was convinced that nothing more destroyed the will to fight than turning tribesman against tribesman. "To polish a diamond," observed Crook, "there is nothing like its own dust."[11]

The morning after the battle, Rainbow, Five Wounds, and a small party of warriors rode into camp, having just returned from hunting buffalo in Montana. These men were some of the tribe's most experienced and renowned warriors, with a reputation for bravery and fierceness that would now prove invaluable to the Nez Perce.

Soon after their arrival, the bands—surmising correctly that they had not seen the last of soldiers—decided to escape west across the Salmon River. The country was rugged and forested, offering numerous defense positions if they were pursued. Such a plan also allowed them to escape farther westward to the Wallowa and Snake River country, or double back eastward across the Salmon in the direction of the Clearwater River. They knew that soldiers would have difficulty crossing any of the large rivers in the area, and each delay of Cut Arm's army allowed them more time to determine their next move. Later that day, the bands moved six miles upstream from White Bird Creek to camp along the Salmon River at a traditional crossing called Horseshoe Bend. Just before dark, some Nez Perce approached the nearby stockade at Slate Creek under a flag of truce. Fearful settlers knew most of the Indians, who seemed friendly and told them about the battle. In one of the remarkable incongruities of this war, a few Nez Perce—despite their uncertain future—paid a startled merchant their outstanding debts on past accounts, lest whites think them dishonest.

The next morning the bands crossed the river, leaving a small force behind to watch for soldiers. Using waterproof buffalo hides that doubled as tipi coverings, they stretched the hides over bent willows into the shape of a large cup. These "bullboats" were pulled by horses and steadied by two swimmers, one on each side. Everything they owned—extra tipi covers, food, clothing, blankets, cooking pots—was piled inside, with children and the elderly on top of the load. The rest swam and herded their 2,500 to 3,500 horses to the west side of the river. The crossing was made without loss, and now they camped and awaited Cut Arm.

Early on the morning of June 26, the general's command broke camp and cautiously moved down White Bird Canyon. Howard had two purposes: locate the Nez Perce and bury the dead soldiers, by now nine days exposed. Shortly after the fight, Mount Idaho citizens had encouraged Perry to return with them to the battlefield and bury the dead, but after first agreeing, Perry had refused to go, citing the danger to his diminished force. Ad Chapman, along with several other volunteers, now scouted the steep western ridge Perry's retreating men had struggled up and soon reported seeing Indians across the Salmon River in the distant hills.

Meanwhile, soldiers in burial details combed the ravines of the canyon for bodies. They had only gone a short distance, recalled volunteer E. J. Bunker, when they began discovering "corpses in an advanced state of decomposition, the flesh falling from their faces, glaring with glazed eyeballs upon us, their comrades." Ripening in the hot sun, the bodies had turned black, "swollen and changed into awful shapes," said Lieutenant Harry Bailey. The smell was so overpowering that "we had to run a distance every little while," before returning to dig the shallow graves in the rocky soil with the only tools the soldiers had—entrenching bayonets. The bodies could not be pulled into the graves, as one man discovered when he gave a tug on an arm and was left holding the detached limb in his hands. They soon learned to dig a grave as close to a corpse as possible, said Bailey, then roll the body into it. Others resorted to dragging a corpse on a blanket, then pitching it off into the grave.[12]

A few of the bodies had had their blue cavalry jackets removed, but most were still clothed. No one found any weapons. Animals had fed on some of the corpses, and a few eyewitnesses claimed more than one body had been scalped and mutilated. Corpse disfigurement by Indians was not uncommon in frontier warfare. Some believed flaying the back and legs of a brave enemy and cutting out the sinew or tendons to use in bowstrings and weapons would bring good luck in future battles. Teeth, fingers, and even infant hands were particularly valued as necklaces by several Plains tribes; at least one Sioux medicine bag consisted of numerous human scrota, used as containers for body paint. Others thought a mutilated corpse prevented entry into the spirit world. The official report of the Fetterman massacre eleven years before had been particularly gruesome: eyes torn out and laid on rocks, noses and ears cut off, teeth chopped out, brains removed, hands and feet hacked off, genitals severed and stuffed in their victims' mouths.[13]

The Nez Perce, however, had no tradition of such practices and they emphatically denied the charges of mutilation. According to Penahwenonmi (Helping Another), wife of Wounded Head: "I rode out over the field with other women and saw dead soldiers lying about. None of the dead showed disfiguring knife cuts. No one knifed those dead soldiers."[14]

As for scalping, Lieutenant Albert Forse thought such reports in error, explaining that due to the effects of heat, sun, and rain, when "a body was lifted up or rolled over into his grave, his hair and whiskers would adhere to the ground, tearing off the scalp and skin." Several Nez Perce declared that their chiefs had forbidden such behavior. Joseph agreed, saying, "We do not believe in scalping."[15]

Such denials aside, it remains unclear why no scalps were lifted since at least some Nez Perce regularly took enemy scalps in traditional Plains Indian fashion on their forays to buffalo country. Yellow Bull, interviewed years later by E. S. Curtis, perhaps came closest to the mark, claiming that short-hair scalps of whites were not only worthless, but taking them disparaged previous exploits of Indians fighting other Indians. Of the battle, Yellow Bull said, "Their guns were taken, but no scalps; their hair was short." Regardless of the reason, during the battles to follow, allegations of scalping and mutilation by the Nez Perce soon ceased. By the end of the war, the Nez Perce were routinely praised for their "civilized" conduct in battle, an "extraordinary" accomplishment, claimed General Sherman, for savages.[16]

On the lookout for Indians waiting in ambush as he moved down the canyon, Lieutenant Bailey was startled to see a figure hiding in a small thorn-studded hawthorn tree. Cocking his pistol and approaching slowly, he discovered the swollen corpse of a soldier thrust hard into the tree in the full and lifelike position of firing. "He must have worried his foes very greatly for his body was torn and torn with bullets," remarked Bailey. "It was very difficult to remove that body."[17]

The search halted when a thunderstorm rolled in over the mountains and it began raining. Only eighteen of the dead had been buried; the rest were covered with blankets and left for interment the following day. Meanwhile, some of the command rode to the smoldering remains of the Manuel homestead. There, in a nearby outhouse, thirteen days after the outbreak, they found Jack Manuel alive. Shot through both hips, the homesteader had dragged himself into the brush, then finally to the nearby shed. Using his hunting knife, Manuel had dug out the four-inch metal barb from his neck and covered the wound with a poultice of horseradish leaves. Living on whatever wild berries he could find, he was near death when rescuers found him. The following day, the soldiers rigged an Indian-style travois and sent him back to Mount Idaho. There Manuel would recover enough to eventually walk and reunite with his six-year-old daughter, Maggie, who not surprisingly maintained long afterward that her father was never the same man again.

That evening in camp, Howard wrote a letter explaining his views on the battle to Indian Inspector Watkins at Lapwai, saying that "had all behaved as well as the few who remained together, the Indians might I think have been beaten, though we cannot despise the fighting of savages."[18]

In this backhanded compliment to the Nez Perce, Howard overlooked Captain Perry's mistakes, charges that would continue to haunt both men. Perry had made an inadequate reconnaissance ahead of his ride down the canyon, held no reinforcements in his rear, placed volunteers in charge of a vital position, and unduly wore his men and horses down ahead of battle. But above all, he had been completely unprepared for a surrender initiative by the bands, a blunder at least equally shared by Howard. Had not most of the Nez Perce warriors been inebriated, probably few, if any, of Perry's command would have escaped alive. With the notable exception of the 1866 Fetterman and 1876 Little Bighorn battles—both instances in which soldiers were overwhelmed by vastly superior numbers—the White Bird defeat proved to be the worst ever suffered by the U.S. Army on the Indian frontier.

The following morning, a detail of soldiers led by Lieutenant Sevier Rains discovered the body of Lieutenant Theller and the seven enlisted men who fell with him. The corpses were located in a steep ravine. Theller had a single bullet hole in his skull. Like the others, the men were buried in shallow graves. This must have been a relief to Delia Theller, who had often told Emily FitzGerald, "If he was only buried. Oh, my poor Ned, lying there with his face blackening in the sun."[19]

That night the command camped near the mouth of White Bird Creek. Realizing the campaign might take longer than he had first thought, Howard sent Perry back to Lapwai for more rations and ammunition. Additional reinforcements arrived, bringing the total number of troops to about 530 men, 65 of whom were citizen volunteers. Among the new soldiers was Lieutenant Charles Erskine Scott (C. E. S.) Wood, Howard's aide-de-camp for the remainder of the war. Wood recorded in his diary that night: "Rain—eternal rain—veal & no veal—supper in camp. Visiting the different messes, youngsters with neither bedding nor shelter, rough it jokingly—night duty, posting the pickets—rough times all night standing in the rain—no fire—no talking, no bedding—no sleeping. Up at 2 o'clock for fear of Indian habits of attack—roll call at 6—the alarm [sounded] at midnight—one of our own pickets shot by one of our men."[20]

Lieutenant Bailey remembered that his troops were particularly nervous that night as coyotes howled nearby. Aware that such a signal may have preceded Perry's fight, Bailey expected an attack at any moment, with "a sudden rush upon the tired soldiers and every throat cut." About midnight, a guard returning from duty on the picket line startled a sleeping lieutenant and was shot. According to Bailey, "the poor fellow had lingered in painful but brave resignation until morning, when he died, forgiving the wretched lieutenant, saying that it was an unavoidable accident." Burdened with guilt, claimed Bailey, the unidentified officer suffered immensely in the days that followed.[21]

On June 28, the command moved upriver to Horseshoe Bend and prepared to cross the Salmon. Terming the river "swift, deep and difficult," Howard praised the Nez Perce, convinced that "no general could have chosen a safer position," the river being a "wonderful natural barrier" to his pursuing force. As his men constructed a cable ferry, fifty warriors suddenly appeared on the hillside and rushed toward the troops from across the river. But after some brief long-distance shooting, they disappeared downriver. Howard was sure it was a diversion and ordered the crossing to proceed. The next day the men started over, but the going was slow after the cable failed and each boat had to be rowed across the raging river. It would be three days before the entire command managed to cross.[22]

That evening Howard summoned Captain Stephen Whipple, who had recently arrived with two cavalry companies from the Wallowa Valley. Forty years old, "dark-browed, strongly built," and "reliable," Whipple was ordered to proceed with one of his companies to the Clearwater River and arrest Looking Glass and his band. Afterward, Whipple was to turn them over "for safe-keeping" to the volunteers at Mount Idaho, a desperate order that clearly demonstrates either Howard's naivete about settlers' intentions toward the Nez Perce or how little he believed he could spare any of his command to guard the would-be prisoners. Precisely what prompted Howard to take this action that was to become one of his gravest mistakes of the war is unclear. He seems to have known that Looking Glass had played no part in the settlers' murders. But since the chief had never signed the 1863 treaty and he had participated in the May council at Lapwai (even though his bands' land was not in jeopardy), Howard mistrusted him. His official report states that Looking Glass had provided the nontreaty bands at White Bird Canyon with "at least twenty warriors, and that he proposed to join them in person with all his people on the first favorable opportunity."[23]

Howard fails to cite his source, but rumors were rampant. A few days earlier, Lewiston *Teller* editor Alonzo Leland reported that Inspector Watkins met with about one hundred treaty Nez Perce at Lapwai. One of the chiefs had declared that while some of Looking

Glass's band "were anxious to join the hostiles," calmer heads had "talked much with them and had allayed their anxiety to fight." In the same issue, however, in a report that later proved false, an unconvinced Leland alleged: "Indian runners and Chinamen say the Looking Glass band has been increased in numbers, that they have plundered Jerome's place at the Clearwater bridge, that their whole movements indicate hostile intention though they pretend to yet be friendly to the whites."[24] Another article accused Looking Glass of stealing stock, an act for which white men were later apprehended.

Whether any of Looking Glass's warriors actually joined the bands prior to Howard's arrest order is uncertain. Josiah Red Wolf, a child in the band and the last survivor of the Nez Perce war (he died in 1971), said, eighty-six years after the fact, that "a few of our men had been in White Bird's fight." Yet Duncan McDonald, a relation of Looking Glass, claimed that the chief sent word to the other bands after the White Bird Canyon battle that "my hands are clean of white men's blood, and I want you to know they will so remain. You have acted like fools in murdering white men. I will have no part in these things, and have nothing to do with such men. If you are determined to go and fight, go and fight yourselves and do not attempt to embroil me or my people. Go back with your warriors; I do not want any of your band in my camp. I wish to live in peace."[25]

Evidently, Looking Glass was having difficulty controlling some of his warriors—particularly the younger ones—but there is no indication that the chief or a majority of his followers planned to join the other nontreaty bands. Poised to pursue Joseph and White Bird across the Salmon River, Howard thought otherwise. Looking Glass was "only waiting his favorable chance," declared the general, and since he was "near the line of my supplies, I must take care of him."[26]

Whipple, after picking up an additional twenty volunteers at Mount Idaho, arrived just after sunrise on July 1 at Looking Glass's camp on Clear Creek, not far from present-day Kamiah. The band of 40 warriors and 120 women and children was prosperous with horses and cattle, vegetable gardens, and even several milk cows.

Peopeo Tholekt (Bird Alighting) was in Looking Glass's tipi eating breakfast when the soldiers appeared. The headman told him to

92

go and "say to them, 'Leave us alone. We are living here peacefully and want no trouble.'" Peopeo Tholekt then rode across the creek to where Whipple and his detachment waited. An interpreter greeted him "friendly" in Nez Perce, and he began telling the soldiers what his chief had said. Before he could finish, a volunteer jabbed a gun into his chest and demanded, "You Looking Glass?" The interpreter pulled the man away, explaining that the Indian was only a messenger. Then he instructed Peopeo Tholekt to "go back and tell Looking Glass to come."[27]

Those in camp had seen Peopeo Tholekt threatened with a gun and were mistrustful. Someone raised a white cloth on a pole near Looking Glass's tipi, and, returning to the soldiers, Peopeo Tholekt told them, "Looking Glass is my Chief. I bring you his words. He does not want war! He came here to escape war. Do not cross to our side of the little river. We do not want trouble with you whatever!"

The same volunteer again threatened to kill him, saying, "I know this Injun is Looking Glass!" But the interpreter interceded, and finally Whipple and two or three soldiers started back across the creek with Peopeo Tholekt. Before they reached Looking Glass's tipi, a volunteer behind them raised his rifle and shot an Indian, wounding him in the thigh. "At this," recalled Peopeo Tholekt, "the white men whirled their horses and hurried to their own side of the stream," and the shooting began.

As soldiers "poured a fire" across the creek into the camp, men, women, and children scattered over the hillside, seeking shelter in nearby brush. Tahkoopen (Shot Leg), named for a wound he had received years before, was unlucky enough to be struck once again by a bullet in his leg. Two mounted men rode up alongside of him and, each grabbing an arm, dragged him out of danger.

Jumping on a horse, Peopeo Tholekt urged the animal forward, but he "proved a bad one. He was at a standstill. Finally, when I did get him to move, he began hard bucking, and I got nowhere." As soldiers moved closer, the horse suddenly quieted, stood perfectly still, and Peopeo Tholekt received a bullet in his leg. He then began beating the animal about the head until it started up the hill after the fleeing band. Along the way, he encountered a warrior running alongside, and, seeing "death for that Indian if left to be overtaken by the enemy," the two men rode double up the hill. "Soon I found something wrong," said Peopeo Tholekt. "Then all color, all light went from me," and he blacked out, his companion keeping him from falling as they ran from the soldiers.

A quarter of a mile away he regained consciousness, and the two men were overtaken by Etemiere (Arrowhead), riding a horse and wearing a wolf cape around her shoulders. The three stopped briefly and the woman, "who was ready to fight the soldiers," dressed the wound tightly to stop the bleeding; then they hurried on after the others. By the time the shooting ceased, a youth had been killed and several men wounded. One woman carrying her baby mounted a horse and tried to cross the Clearwater River, but she was drawn under and drowned, her body later recovered downstream. The child was never found.

Deciding pursuit was impractical, Whipple ordered the village ransacked, and they captured over seven hundred horses. When the band returned later that day, they found their possessions looted. "Many objects [were] destroyed or badly damaged. Brass buckets [kettles] always carefully kept by the women, lay battered, smashed and pierced by bayonet thrusts. Growing gardens trampled and destroyed. Nearly all our horses were taken and every hoof of cattle driven away," remembered an embittered Peopeo Tholekt. "Of course that settled it. We had to have a war."

White reports of the raid are sketchy and woefully incomplete. Howard simply recorded that "an opportunity was given Looking Glass to surrender, which he at first promised to accept, but afterwards defiantly refused." Failure to apprehend Looking Glass and his "treacherous companions" had now "stirred up a new hornet's nest," one that was to prove particularly painful in Howard's efforts to defeat the Nez Perce. Instead of 140 warriors, he would soon face 200 or more since not only Looking Glass and a smaller band led by Red Owl eventually joined the rebellion but also the sympathetic Palouse. More important to the conflict, however, Looking Glass's forced defection gave the bands the war leader who most strongly advocated retreat to the buffalo country.[28]

Howard had only himself to blame for Looking Glass's—and the additional bands'—involvement, yet he was unwilling to admit it.

Due to Joseph's prominence before war erupted, coupled with a misunderstanding of the Indian tradition of band autonomy and rule by tribal council, Howard continued to believe that Joseph was the one in command. Soon the legend of Joseph became unassailable, subsequently deceiving a public (along with not a few historians) reluctant to concede that more than one Indian leader could bring repeated defeat to the U.S. Army. By heaping praise on Joseph as a "shrewd savage," a veritable "Indian Napoleon," Howard managed to partly offset public criticism of his own inability to resolve the conflict. But the truth is that although Joseph participated in tribal councils, he was never a military strategist, and Nez Perce sources agree that he was involved in "some fighting" but did "no leading" on the battlefield. Indeed, Joseph's pacifism before the outbreak caused many of his fellow tribesmen to distrust his intentions. During the coming retreat to Montana, Joseph was more the indifferent player, at times even depressed and morose over what he saw as a hopeless endeavor. In the months to follow, experienced warriors such as Ollokot, Rainbow, Five Wounds, Toohoolhoolzote, and, in particular, Looking Glass were the primary leaders.[29]

Returning to Mount Idaho, Whipple received orders from Howard to proceed to Cottonwood to protect the command's supply line and to notify Howard immediately if the bands should recross the Salmon River and head east. Meanwhile, back at Horseshoe Bend, Howard had finally completed his crossing. After ordering Trimble to catch up from Slate Creek, the command began the grueling ascent of the Salmon River Mountains. Continuous rain had turned the trail into a quagmire, and the mountains were "so steep and lofty," reported journalist Thomas Sutherland in an embellished account, that "it was absolutely necessary to cling to the rocks with fingers and nails."[30]

Twenty-seven-year-old Sutherland had just arrived from Portland. A Harvard graduate and the only professional journalist to follow the war to its conclusion, he soon struck up such a genial relationship with Howard that the general included him within his command retinue. Unlike Howard's mentor General Sherman, who loathed journalists, calling them "gossip mongers" and "hounds and whores"—convinced that even if he could kill them all, there would still be news from hell before breakfast—Howard was yet untouched by critical press. His friendship with Sutherland would prove beneficial since the journalist's colorful pieces for the San Francisco *Chronicle,* Portland *Standard,* and the New York *Herald* were often biased in Howard's favor.[31]

The going was frustratingly slow. Major Edwin C. Mason, Howard's Chief of Staff, wrote to his wife that the country of the Salmon River "is broken beyond my power of description—a perfect sea of mountains, gullies, ravines, canyons." A drenching rain made the 3,500-foot ascent exceedingly treacherous. Lieutenant Parnell wrote that several pack mules were lost during the steep climb, the animals slipping and floundering in the mud, "and in the struggle to get foothold in some particularly steep places several lost their balance and went rolling down the mountainside, nearly two thousand feet, with frightful velocity. Of course," observed the lieutenant, "there was not much pack and very little serviceable mule left when the bottom was reached."[32]

Halfway up, the men discovered a cache of supplies the bands had stolen from settlers along the Salmon River, including one hundred bags of flour, cigars, meerschaum pipes, and store clothing, along with some five hundred horses that had separated from the Indian remuda. The cache was destroyed and Howard ordered the horses driven to the other side of the river, although Sutherland records that cooks tried to turn some of the horses into *fricandeau de cheval,* a dish that came out tasting more like "elastic beef." Food was short that night for soldiers camped on the summit as the packers were still struggling to get supplies up the mountain. Wrapped in blankets, hugging immense fires, the men shared their coffee, hard bread, and salt pork as far as it would go. The pack train camped along the steep trail in the mud, dubbing it "Camp Misery," not reaching the fog-shrouded summit until the following day. No one was happy about the situation, but Sergeant McCarthy observed that the worst complainers were young soldiers. "Many of them were very helpless and appeared unused to campaigning, and growled terribly and so loud that the general must have heard them."[33]

Unknown to the soldiers as they labored up the mountain, the Nez Perce were twenty miles away at a traditional fording place on the Salmon River known as Craig Billy Crossing. The tactic had worked. As Joseph said later, "we crossed over the Salmon River, hoping General Howard would follow." Now Howard was days behind, and the bands were deciding their next move. There was disagreement, some wishing to move to the Wallowa Valley while others suggested the buffalo country to the east, perhaps even Canada. "Some wanted to surrender to Howard," declared Duncan McDonald, "but they feared they would be shot or hung." More than one account portrays Joseph as among those who argued against leaving their homeland.[34]

Yellow Bull claimed later that a message reached the bands at the crossing informing them of the raid on Looking Glass's camp and requesting help. When the council broke up, the decision had been made: they would recross the Salmon River, climb up to Camas Prairie, and head east to the Clearwater River. Later Sutherland wrote that Howard "drove the Indians from their mountain fastnesses and kept them from reaching the naturally fortified country of the Wallowa," but the truth appears otherwise.[35] The Nez Perce were in full control of the direction and pace of their retreat and now with Howard far behind, the only obstacle that blocked their path was Whipple's small force at Cottonwood House.

Early the next morning, civilian scouts William Foster and Charles Blewett rode west from Whipple's camp. After several miles, they were startled to see a large herd of horses driven by several Nez Perce. The Indians gave chase and as the two men fled, Blewett's horse reared and he fell. By the time Foster realized his companion's predicament, it was too late to help. Yelling to Blewett to take to the brush, Foster headed for Cottonwood to sound the alarm. Upon arriving, he hurriedly told Whipple what had happened, saying he felt sure Blewett was now dead. No doubt Foster was correct. Volunteers later found Blewett's remains, one dubious report claiming he had been decapitated.

Whipple immediately prepared to ride to Blewett's aid. He asked for a small detachment of volunteers to scout ahead, and Lieutenant Sevier Rains, ten enlisted men, Foster, and another civilian started toward where Blewett had last been seen. "I particularly cautioned Rains," recalled Whipple, "not to precede the command too far, to keep on high ground, and to report the first sign of the Indians." Following minutes later with about seventy-five men, Whipple had ridden several miles when he heard shooting and suddenly came upon a "large force" of Indians. Ordering his men to dismount, they formed a firing line, every fourth man holding the others' horses in typical cavalry fashion. Although the warriors outnumbered them, after some desultory shooting they withdrew, and Whipple began looking for Rains.[36]

In a nearby ravine, he found the thirteen men, all dead. The corpses were stripped to their underwear but none were mutilated. Rains, an extremely well-liked officer, was found wearing his riding gloves, his West Point gold ring still on his finger.

Signs of the struggle told the tale. Rains had stumbled into an ambush, the soldiers tried to flee, but six men fell in a deluge of crossfire. After running a short distance, the rest dismounted and attempted to cluster around some small boulders. Yellow Wolf was in the attacking party and said that while one of the warriors acted as a decoy, the others led by Five Wounds circled around in the tall grass until they were close enough to shoot. After the fight, Yellow Wolf recalled:

> One soldier was sitting up, leaning against a rock. He was shot in the forehead, almost level with the eyes. He had two other shots, through the breast, and he still lived. He washed his face with his own blood, and looked around. He made a clucking noise, a sound like that of a chicken. The Indians, hearing, wondered! They asked one another, "What about him? He must be more like us!"
>
> From that day the warriors who are left remember what they saw and heard. All stood around that soldier, many of them saying, "He can not live. His body is too bad hurt."
>
> But one man thought differently and he said, "He can live if he wants to!"
>
> "He is too many times shot," answered one. "Head too bad shot!"
>
> Then one oldlike man name Dookiyoon [Smoker], who had

a gun with flint to set the powder afire, spoke, "We shall not leave him like that. He will be too long dying."

With those words, Smoker raised his gun and shot the soldier in the breast. The bullet knocked him over, but he raised up again. He sat there, still calling to his Power. Calling with that same clucking. He washed his face again with his running blood, and still looked around.

The warriors, all silent, said nothing. Then some of them taunted Smoker about his gun, that it was not strong. Smoker reloaded and shot once more, but it did no good! The soldier still sat against the rock, still making the clucking of the hen.

While the warriors stood silent and wondering, one man stepped forward and knocked the soldier over with his kopluts [war club]. Others spoke to save him, but our leader said to us, "We have no doctor. Poor fellow! He is suffering. We better put him out of trouble."

When our leader made this talk, we all became one-minded. I then helped with my kopluts.[37]

Before dark, Whipple retreated to Cottonwood and set up a defensive camp on top of a nearby hill. Then he dispatched two messengers to notify Howard about Lieutenant Rains. That evening, couriers rode in from Fort Lapwai announcing Perry's arrival the next day with supplies and badly needed ammunition. After a sleepless night anticipating attack and fearing that Perry and his twenty men might meet the same fate as Rains, Whipple set out the following morning. About eight miles away, both columns met and promptly returned to Cottonwood, Perry assuming command as senior officer of the three companies composed of 113 men. The soldiers spent the remainder of the morning digging rifle pits, building a barricade of fence rails, and generally strengthening their position. At noon the warriors attacked. "For hours they made the most frantic efforts to dislodge us," claimed Whipple. "Every man of the command was kept on the lines until about sundown when the enemy withdrew for the night."[38]

While the soldiers at Cottonwood were engaged with the Nez

Perce during the afternoon of July 4, Howard's command was making camp some twenty miles across the river. Learning of Rains's fight, Howard dispatched two citizen volunteer companies of about sixty-five men, directing their leader, Ed McConville, to cross the river and proceed as quickly as possible to aid Whipple.

Howard was criticized later for not immediately crossing his entire force. But the Indian trail continued west, and he disbelieved they would all turn east or could be so far ahead of him, despite Whipple's message and a warning he had received earlier from area settlers. Frank Fenn, who helped rescue the survivors of the Norton party, claimed he told the general the Nez Perce would probably cross the river at Craig Billy Crossing, and that the narrow ford could easily be defended by a handful of men. Howard, said Fenn, "politely listened to our suggestions" and then remarked "that he believed himself fully competent to manage his own campaign."[39]

At ten o'clock the following morning at Cottonwood, Whipple's two couriers returning from Howard were seen riding hard pursued by Indians. The men arrived safely, but soon other figures were observed in the distance on the road from Mount Idaho. "Captain" D. B. Randall, who had only days before assisted Whipple in his failure to arrest Looking Glass and who the Nez Perce claimed was illegally squatting on reservation land, had organized a volunteer force of seventeen men from Mount Idaho after hearing of the Rains massacre. Now just a few miles away from Cottonwood, the volunteers halted and "Lieutenant" Lew Wilmot, who had narrowly escaped death only weeks before with the Norton party, put down his binoculars and informed his companions that the large body of horsemen on the road ahead were not soldiers but Indians.

Moving around the Cottonwood defenses was the entire Nez Perce camp—men, women, and children with all of their possessions and thousands of horses. The halfhearted attack on Cottonwood the day before had been only a feint. Confident that the soldiers would not leave their stronghold to attack, the Nez Perce were now traveling east across Camas Prairie toward the South Fork of the Clearwater River. It was the poor luck of the volunteers that directly below them, spread out in a line nearly a half mile long between the soldiers at Cottonwood and the Indian caravan, were at least a hundred Nez Perce warriors. Wilmot, who had a wife, a two-day-old baby, three other children, and an aged father, "tried with all of my persuasive powers to get the Company to retreat." But Randall, also married and the father of five children, refused.

> *Randall:* Lew, if you want to go back, you can go. I and the rest of the boys have started to Cottonwood and we are going.
> *Wilmot:* Randall, you know I am not going back unless the rest go. You know we have nearly all the arms of the settlers and you can see we have the Indians between us and Cottonwood to fight, and they outnumber us ten to one.
> *Randall:* Well, if you are afraid, you can get behind me.
> *Wilmot:* Randall, this is too serious a situation to be made a joke of and I can stand it if the rest can. But the best thing we can do is to go back before it is too late.[40]

Wilmot then asked Randall what he proposed to do. Randall replied, "We are going to charge the Indians."

With that, the men who would forever after be known as the Brave Seventeen galloped straight toward the warriors, firing their guns. Astounded by their audacity, the Indian line opened up then quickly recovered, closing on their flanks as the men rode through. In the intense crossfire, one volunteer was wounded and several had their horses shot out from under them. Less than a mile and a half from the soldier's defenses, they were forced to dismount and make a stand on a small rise but not before sending two men on to request assistance.

The soldiers could hear popping in the distance and, with all eyes on the volunteers, were awaiting Perry's order to go to their aid. By some accounts, they were still waiting hours later. Whipple heard the shots and asked Perry what was happening.

> *Perry:* Some citizens, a couple of miles away on the Mount Idaho road, are surrounded by Indians and are being all cut to pieces, and nothing can be done to help them!
> *Whipple:* Why not?
> *Perry:* It is too late![41]

Exactly what happened is unclear, lost in the bitter accusations between volunteers and officers after the fight. One volunteer said that Perry remarked, "They cannot last a minute, they are gone, men ought to know better than to travel that road as dangerous as it is." What seems certain is that Perry hesitated to aid the volunteers, doubtlessly wary of the number of warriors and unwilling to risk another defeat. While Perry waffled, the two volunteers rode up, requested and received ammunition, then rode back to their besieged companions. One account claims that at this point, soldiers fed up with Perry's inaction briefly rallied behind a Sergeant Simpson when he cried, "If your officers won't lead you, I will." The effort fizzled, however, when Simpson was threatened with insubordination, a charge later withdrawn after he was seriously wounded in a subsequent battle. Finally, George Shearer—the volunteer who had brutally killed the old warrior Jyeloo three weeks before, fought in the White Bird battle, and reputedly had served on General Robert E. Lee's staff during the Civil War—mounted his horse, exclaiming that "it is a shame and an outrage to allow those men to remain there and perish without making an effort to save them," and galloped off alone. Soon after he departed, Perry gave permission for Whipple to rescue the men.[42]

By the time Shearer arrived, with Whipple's troops right behind, the warriors had broken off the attack and were almost out of rifle range. Addressing the volunteers, Shearer told them the danger was past and to follow him to Cottonwood. "Just then," said Lew Wilmot, "I saw smoke from an Indian rifle and soon a bullet passed through the withers of [Shearer's] horse." Collecting his men, Wilmot learned three were wounded (one mortally), and one was dead. A short distance away, Wilmot found Randall lying by his fallen horse, shot through the spine. Randall asked for some water and a soldier offered his canteen. "I lifted Randall's head and he said, 'Tell my wife—' I gave him a drink. This he threw up, and died without finishing what he wanted to say."[43]

Volunteers claimed between nine and thirty warriors were killed in the fight. Sergeant McCarthy was dubious, admitting later that "this statement must be taken with a grain of salt." The Nez Perce said one man had been wounded, and an older warrior named Weesculat killed when his horse spooked and ran too close to the volunteers. They also professed that they had little interest in fighting that day, their purpose being to engage the whites only long enough to allow safe passage for their families. If Nez Perce accounts of casualties can be believed (they are more often in agreement than those of whites), during the three weeks since the outbreak, only five Indians had been killed compared to some seventy whites, forty-six of whom were soldiers. The army had suffered two humiliating defeats and Howard was still days behind, living up to the sobriquet the Nez Perce now bestowed on him: General Day After Tomorrow. Arriving that evening after the fight, Ed McConville and his volunteers were discouraged with Perry's failure and soon departed for Mount Idaho with a daring plan to try to halt the bands long enough for Howard to catch up.

As for Captain Perry, his troubles were just beginning. Lew Wilmot complained to Howard several days later about "the cowardice of Col. Perry," and Mount Idaho spokesperson L. P. Brown wrote a letter to the *Teller*, accusing Perry of abandoning the men "until the Indians had drawn away out of range."[44]

In order to clear his name, Perry requested two separate military courts of inquiry, the first convening in September to consider the Cottonwood allegations. Two months later, the court announced that although Perry had delayed "about ten minutes" in ordering troops to the relief of the volunteers, it did not consider his delay "excessive under the circumstances."[45] Perry had been both surrounded and outnumbered and had acted correctly by not unduly risking the lives of his men. Outraged editor Alonzo Leland cried "Whitewash!" declaring some witnesses had not been allowed to testify. Although Leland's blistering invective bordered on the irrational, it seems clear that the battle actually lasted within Perry's full view for an uncomfortably long time, not "ten minutes."

Reaction was mixed within the military. One officer labeled the charges "a wicked falsification." Howard's support was subdued, the general perhaps unwilling to appear too favorable, realizing that Perry's name would not be cleared unless he survived the second inquiry. Exactly how his fellow troops felt surfaced in November when Perry was transferred to another post. Emily FitzGerald wrote that "Col. Perry . . . has gotten into trouble with Gen. Howard, and we feel sorry for him, tho he has scarcely behaved exactly as he ought to." The new commanding officer of Fort Lapwai, Colonel Frank Wheaton, bluntly wrote Howard after the inquiry that "the two, David P. & his wife together are a severe load for any regiment to carry." Wheaton was anxious "to be rid of them" for their continued presence made him feel "persecuted for life with such a field officer with such a family."[46]

Allegations resulting in the second court of inquiry came from a fellow officer. In December 1877 Captain Joel Trimble, still smarting from Perry's insinuations concerning his lack of bravery, prepared a stinging report. His criticism was twofold: Perry's failure to start immediately against the Nez Perce after the first message describing Indian unrest arrived at Lapwai (he started toward White Bird Canyon twenty-six hours after the first message and nine hours after the killings had been reported) and his apparent eagerness to withdraw soon after the warriors had attacked. When the court convened a year later, most testimony of fellow soldiers supported Perry. Perry himself blamed the defeat on the volunteers, declaring, "a panic was caused by the Indians getting on my left flank, by the citizens abandoning the knoll, thus exposing my whole line and lead horses."[47] In February 1879, the court found Perry had done all that had been expected of him and that his conduct had been prudent and proper.

Exonerated and with his military reputation secure, Perry soon drifted into the background of frontier history. At the close of his career he was promoted to brigadier general; he died in 1908 at the age of sixty-seven.

Some remained unconvinced, however. In a letter to a friend nearly thirty years after the war, an unforgiving Sergeant Michael McCarthy could bring himself to refer to Perry only as "that coward."[48]

6

At the same time George Shearer was riding to the aid of the Brave Seventeen on the afternoon of July 5, sixteen miles away at Craig Billy Crossing, Howard's command was descending the Nez Perce trail down the steep canyon to where it crossed the Salmon River. Here a disappointed Howard reluctantly admitted his prediction had been wrong—instead of continuing on to the Wallowa Valley, the bands had taken the trail toward Cottonwood. The problem now was how to cross the torrent "foaming and tumbling like a boiling caldron" that stretched some 250 feet wide and was racing at over seven miles per hour.[1]

Undaunted, a young artillery lieutenant named Harrison Otis dismantled a nearby cabin constructed of twelve-inch hewn logs, thirty or forty feet long, and began fashioning a crude raft. As Lieutenant Parnell recalled, Otis's idea was "to take all the cavalry lariats (light three-fifth inch rope), tie them together, make one end fast to a tree and the other to the raft, and then let the current carry the raft near enough to the other side to be able to throw a line from it to the shore." Parnell was doubtful. The slender rope "was not strong enough to hold even a single log . . . but the young and inexperienced 'sub,' who was on his first campaign, knew better." The next morning, while Parnell and fifteen others stripped naked, mounted bareback and prepared to swim the command's horses across the river, Otis and a half dozen men cast off in the raft from shore. The thin rope immediately parted and to the howls of fellow soldiers, the men drifted three or four miles down the river, Lieutenant Otis forevermore burdened with the nickname "Crusoe."[2]

The morning's humor was short-lived, for Howard was anxious to make the crossing. Nez Perce messengers James Reuben and John Levi had arrived the night before with news that the bands had left Cottonwood and were headed in the direction of the Clearwater River. Demonstrating for the soldiers how Indians crossed rivers, James Reuben swam his horse to the other side and back. When one of the white scouts tried the technique, Howard wryly noted, the man failed to get but a few yards from shore. With no safe way to cross the river and realizing the Nez Perce were now days ahead, Howard concluded that "my shortest line was to turn back via White Bird Canyon."[3]

Leaving orders for the infantry to follow as quickly as possible, Howard and his cavalry began the long and arduous retrograde back over the same route they had just traversed, crossing the river by boat at White Bird Creek the next evening. The following night, July 8, a weary Howard camped outside of Grangeville, having arrived exactly where he had begun thirteen days earlier. Here he learned the Nez Perce were encamped along the South Fork of the Clearwater northeast of Grangeville. Fearing the bands would escape across the river as soon as he appeared, Howard eschewed a direct route to their camp and instead devised a plan "with the hope of taking the enemy in reverse." The next morning the command crossed the upper reaches of the Clearwater at Jackson's Bridge, which the Nez Perce had damaged but not destroyed. By the evening of July 10, Howard had amassed all of his troops, including Perry's command, at a camp above the bluffs along the east side of the Clearwater. Fully assembled with four companies of cavalry, six of infantry, and five of artillery, plus volunteers and about fifty packers, the command numbered well over five hundred armed men.[4]

That night a weary Sergeant Michael McCarthy lay down to

sleep, only to be awakened by the "psalm-singing" of one of Howard's staff officers, Lieutenant Melville Wilkinson. "He was a great annoyance to everybody within the sound of his voice," recalled the sergeant, himself a devout Catholic but exhausted by the march from the Salmon River.[5]

After the Cottonwood skirmish, the Nez Perce had camped along the South Fork of the Clearwater, about seven miles downstream from the eventual location of Howard's camp. Here Looking Glass and his band joined the others, raising their force to nearly 200 warriors and some 500 women and children, who with both older and younger men not bearing arms, probably totaled about 750 people. Accusations arose later from both Howard and the regional press that tribes sympathetic to their plight joined the encampment, swelling the number of warriors to over 300, but there is no surviving evidence other than newspaper gossip. Those present denied that any disaffected Indians other than Nez Perce joined the bands here or at any other time during the war. During the following days, the Nez Perce kept watch for approaching troops coming across Camas Prairie from the direction of Cottonwood and the settlements. They did not have long to wait, but to their surprise, the attackers were not dressed in army blue.

On the evening of July 8, while Howard was struggling toward Grangeville, "Colonel" Ed McConville and some seventy-five citizen volunteers, mounted on fresh horses confiscated during the raid on Looking Glass's band—men, according to Howard, "disgusted with the slowness of the regulars"—discovered the Nez Perce camp on the Clearwater. Wisely determining that his force was outnumbered, McConville sent a courier requesting assistance, telling Howard that "I would keep as quiet as I could" until the troops arrived.[6]

The following day, however, one of his scouts accidently discharged his rifle. Alerted, the warriors immediately attacked, forcing the volunteers to the top of a hill several miles away. Here the volunteers hastily built rifle pits, barely repulsing repeated charges throughout the day and night. Incurring no casualties but suffering from lack of water and losing most of their horses in a successful midnight raid, the disheartened volunteers named their fortification Misery Hill. Sometime that evening McConville dispatched Lew

Wilmot and Benjamin Penny to find Howard, inform him of their dire predicament, and request reinforcements. Early the next morning, Wilmot and Penny rode into Howard's camp. With his infantry and artillery not due until later that day, the general sent Penny back to McConville with the message that while he was not yet ready to attack, he would be shortly, and that the volunteers should hold out until he could bring his forces into position.

Lew Wilmot, feeling ill and unable to return with Penny, was looking for a place to rest when Howard called him over. Standing next to Howard was Captain Perry. "Lieutenant Wilmot," the volunteer recalled the general saying, "this is Colonel Perry whom you have charged with cowardice." Wilmot replied that he had not seen anything in Perry's actions that had made him change his opinion. Perry then accused Wilmot of telling falsehoods. "I asked him wherein, said he, 'You told Gen. Howard that I never sent you any aid.'" Infuriated, Perry ordered Wilmot to leave, for his presence filled him with contempt. "God damn you!" replied Wilmot. "You have not got one-half the contempt for me that I have for you so I will leave your camp!"[7]

As Wilmot stalked away, Howard ordered him arrested, telling the volunteer it made his blood boil to hear a man blaspheme an officer, "to which I replied that it did not make his blood boil half as much as it did mine for a man to tell me I had told a falsehood." Howard soon cooled down, asking Wilmot to guide the command to where the Nez Perce were camped, but the scout refused, saying he preferred Indians to Howard's officers. Gushing bitterness, Wilmot later wrote a vitriolic letter to the *Teller* proclaiming that when Perry died he would be turned away from the gates of both heaven and hell, that "the coyote would tuck down his tail and sneak off, the buzzard would soar aloft from his vile remains, and the little worm that would delight to worry in the carcass of a dog would crawl away from him in disgust."[8]

The morning of July 11, with his command together again, Howard started down the east side of the South Fork, his men spread out in a long line following an old mining road that stayed well behind the bluffs some eight hundred feet above the river. Deeply incised ravines covered with scattered pines made travel along the edge of the canyon practically impossible. Although Howard had some idea of the approximate location of the bands, his untimely brouhaha with Wilmot had deprived him of the one man who might have shown him their exact location. Without accurate maps, and forced to make wide detours at each ravine, the command's scouts ventured only periodic glimpses of the river. Despite their slow progress, summer was finally underway, with the rain and cold that earlier had plagued the troops gone, the days now uncomfortably warm.

Across the river the Nez Perce had finally withdrawn, and McConville's weary and thirsty volunteers were ready to give up the fight. Neither Penny nor other messengers Howard had sent the day before had managed to get through. Unaware the troops were only a few miles across the river, the men began walking back to Mount Idaho. There they learned Howard's whereabouts, but it would be days before they would catch up.

About midday across from the mouth of Cottonwood Creek, Ad Chapman and Lieutenant Robert Fletcher decided to detour toward the river. As they rode out on a steep bluff and looked back upstream, they discovered the Nez Perce camp across the river. Howard wasted no time in ordering his artillery pieces to the bluff, directing Lieutenant Otis to fire one of the command's two howitzers. The shots Otis fired, however, proved no more successful than his ability to cross rivers, most falling short and only serving to alert the Nez Perce. But it was hardly Otis's fault. Of Civil War vintage and capable of lobbing a single twelve-pound spherical shell only about 1,300 yards with any hope of accuracy, the howitzer was simply not enough weapon to reach the camp over a mile away.

Realizing he had to move closer to wage an attack, Howard ordered his men back around the head of the ravine they had just passed to a bluff directly across from the Nez Perce. While soldiers scrambled back, the Indian camp was utter bedlam. Lulled into complacency by their victories of recent weeks and caught completely by surprise, they had failed to keep track of the soldiers' movements, never expecting an attack from the east side of the river. As cannon shot exploded in the distance, warriors were seen "scampering over the hills in every direction," wrote Thomas Sutherland.[9]

Although the exact movements of the troops could not be viewed from their camp, Toohoolhoolzote anticipated Howard's intentions and with about twenty-four men rushed across the river and ascended the steep bluff to meet the soldiers. Taking up positions along the plateau near the head of the ravine, they poured a withering fire into the oncoming troops, killing several and forcing them to dig in, thus establishing the battlefield. Sutherland reported later that "General Howard displayed true military genius in the way in which he opened the battle," but the truth appears quite the opposite.[10] In the precious hour spent firing the howitzer from out of range, Howard lost his advantage and now was unable to assault the camp. His troops numbering in the hundreds were pinned down with only tall grass for protection as Toohoolhoolzote's handful of men fired from the brow of a small rise, some with trees for protection. Soon two other warrior groups led by Ollokot and Rainbow moved up the nearby ravine, and as the soldiers formed a rough semicircle about seven hundred yards wide, the battle was on.

Howard's pack train, carrying food and ammunition, was attacked first, and warriors killed two packers. Captain Trimble's company rode up as they were wrestling with one of the mules laden with howitzer ammunition, chased them off, and led the animals to safety behind the battle line. There they unloaded the mules, stacking the aparejos and supplies in the grass and forming a temporary structure that would be used by Howard and his staff as headquarters. From behind this scant fortification, one lieutenant dryly observed, the general had no trouble observing and directing the battle.

On the firing line, Sergeant Michael McCarthy found himself in the thick of battle with warriors "fronting us or galloping by us firing from horseback," the shooting sounding "like firecrackers on fourth of July" with howitzers and Gatling guns booming, "Indians yelling, soldiers cheering, and the mules of our immense pack train braying loud enough to drown all other sounds. The sun pouring down on burnt necks, with thermometer somewhere around the 100 mark, and no water."[11]

In the murderous hail of bullets, Lieutenant Harry Bailey had difficulty getting his men to stay on the firing line. As soon as he got some placed at proper intervals and moved on down the line, "as many men would run back to the holes or trenches" in the rear. Not far into the battle, he came upon two officers "lying flat behind small head shelters with dusty sweat streaks down their faces, dodging bullets. They yelled at me to get down as I was drawing fire." When two bullets "tipped the earth between their heads and my ankles," Bailey dove for cover. Soon he realized that a nearby company of soldiers and his own had mistaken each other for Indians in the tall grass, "bobbing up and down firing at each other at a lively rate." Bailey ran out between the two lines, yelling, "Cease firing, you're firing into your own men!" At least one of his men, Private Frances Winters, "always believed his dreadful hip wound was by a friendly bullet."[12]

The Nez Perce marksmen were terrifyingly accurate. Private John Lynch saw "one man shot through the heel as his foot became exposed for an instant above the trench rim. A sergeant lost an eye, destroyed without a skin break. He continued with the command, wearing a green patch over the wound. One soldier displayed a freakish bullet mark. The ball had struck just above the right ear, traversed the contour of the skull to his left ear, leaving a seared, blackened and hairless trail along its entire course. That soldier was rendered hors de combat for a long time, knocked entirely senseless." Lieutenant C. E. S. Wood recalled that "one man, raising his head too high, was shot through the brain; another soldier, lying on his back and trying to get the last few drops of warm water from his canteen, was robbed of the water by a bullet taking off the canteen's neck while it was at his lips."[13]

Thomas Sutherland, "wishing to enjoy all the experiences of a soldier," took a rifle and crept out to the front line, "prepared to take notes and scalps. My solicitude in the former direction was nearly nipped in the bud, for the moment I inquisitively popped up my head, a whine and thud of bullets in my proximity and a very peremptory order to 'lie down, you damned fool,' taught me that hugging mother earth with my teeth in the dirt was the only attitude to assume while in that vicinity."[14]

Lieutenant Bailey was appalled at the marksmanship of his command. Writing years later to historian Lucullus Virgil McWhorter, Bailey said that "a number of us saw a poor old horse, probably wounded, standing for some hours out in my front, and I suppose several hundreds of bullets were fired at him without apparent effect." Bullets coming the other way were relentlessly on target. One man near Bailey had his hat shot off three times, "when he concluded to leave it off. His clothing was grazed two or three times, and his cartridge box cut entirely off by a bullet, the leather belt cut as by a knife, as I saw it at the moment it occurred. Rather a hot place, wasn't it?"[15]

At least one warrior was grateful for the soldiers' poor marksmanship. Far out in front, Yellow Wolf had joined the initial charge led by Toohoolhoolzote. Now looking around, his face cut and bleeding from rock chips flying off bullet-riddled boulders, he saw that his companions had retreated under the heavy fire. Running back to a clump of pines where his horse was tied, he quickly mounted and with soldiers rushing toward him, their bullets "singing like bees," successfully reached the Indian line. "I thought it my last day. I was not much excited [for] if we die in battle, it is good. It is good, dying for your rights, for your country."[16]

As the hot afternoon wore on, the warriors continually pressed the soldiers, "their brown naked bodies," said Lieutenant Wood, "flying from shelter to shelter. Their yells were incessant as they cheered each other on or signaled a successful shot." Some even wore bundles of grass attached to their heads as they crawled close enough to shoot, then quickly moved to another position. Wood was convinced he saw Chief Joseph "everywhere along the line; running from point to point, he directed the flanking movements and the charges. It was his long fierce calls which sometimes we heard loudly in front of us, and sometimes faintly resounding from the distant rocks." Nevertheless, most Nez Perce accounts credit Ollokot as the principal leader of the fight that day, Yellow Bull declaring later that Joseph was present but "fought like anybody else."[17]

The soldiers attempted several charges, but none got far. At one point, word spread that some companies along the firing line were low on ammunition. Who would volunteer to carry it out? "Ad Chapman jumped on his spirited horse," said Sutherland, "and with a heavy box of cartridges on his back hip, started at full run amid a shower of balls for the front, where he safely landed his precious burden." Apparently unaware of Chapman's reputation during the

White Bird Canyon fight, Sutherland was so impressed that he acclaimed him "one of the most intelligent and bravest men in the command."[18]

In one case, bravery assumed a dark twist. Earlier, Sutherland had struck up a friendship with Sergeant James Workman of the Fourth Artillery. "He was a very intelligent young man," he recalled, "being one of the best Shakespearian scholars and readiest quoters from standard English poets" he had ever met. But Sutherland thought the sergeant depressed, "weighed down with troubles and bitter recollections" from his past. During the battle, Sutherland was startled when Workman suddenly stood up and charged alone toward the Indians. Almost instantly he fell "flat on his face, pierced by Nez Perce bullets on every side." It was tragic, concluded the correspondent, but the man seemed "determined to die."[19]

To make for himself a "brave name," one warrior mounted a horse and galloped the entire length of the battlefield in front of the soldiers, then turning, rode back. Before he was out of range, a bullet pierced his back just above the shoulder, coming out his breast. Still mounted and joined by a companion, the injured man rode down to the river where he dismounted and began washing his wound in the water. Calling on his guardian *wyakin,* described by Yellow Wolf as a buffalo bull, the warrior crawled out of the stream on all fours with hands closed, imitating a buffalo's hooves. There he walked about emitting the deep, rumbling bellow of a challenging bull. Clotted blood gushed from the wound, and after his fellow warrior applied bandages, he remounted his horse and returned to the fight. Henceforth known as Kipkip Owyeen (Wounded Breast), he survived the entire war. Such courage was uncommon, declared Roaring Eagle, and bordered on the reckless. "The Indian way of fighting is not to get killed," he maintained in what today might be termed the first rule of guerrilla warfare. "Killed today, there can be no fighting tomorrow."[20]

Late in the day, both soldiers and warriors were astonished when a trusted Nez Perce army scout named Elaskolatat, known to whites as Joe Albert and wearing a blue soldier's jacket, suddenly bolted across the battlefield toward Indian lines. Only moments before he had learned that his father, Weesculatat, had been killed at the Cottonwood skirmish. Shot at by both sides, Elaskolatat managed to join the warriors where he immediately turned and led a charge against the soldiers.

Toward nightfall the fighting lessened, and by dark it had almost ceased. His work not done, Surgeon George M. Sternberg, who would go on to become the Surgeon General of the U.S. Army, was still tending the wounded. In the field hospital just to the rear of the packsaddle headquarters, a packer was brought in "badly wounded and bleeding profusely" from a severed artery. Deciding it was unsafe to move the man, Sternberg instructed his assistant "to light a candle and screen it with a blanket." No sooner had the candle been lit, however, "than the bullets came thick and fast at this faint little mark, and it had to be quickly extinguished." Later that night, Sternberg managed to shield his operating tent from snipers long enough to operate on another man who had been shot through both hips. This time Indians were not the problem, for Sternberg's patient suddenly "died under the operation and was buried on the spot."[21]

Throughout the night, soldiers remained on the firing line, fearing attack. Captain Joel Trimble recalled "Indians could be distinctly heard in various forms of expression, sometimes in earnest talk, sometimes in harangue; the chief exhorting the hardy to greater bravery on the morrow and on reproving the delinquent. Now and then the female voice could be detected in a plaintive wail of mourning, sometimes in low and tremulous unison, then breaking into a piercing cry. . . . The clear sky, the stillness of the night, added to a feeling of weariness on our part, made the distant sounds strike the ear with an intensely mournful cadence." As Trimble reflected on the fighting that day, he concluded that the Nez Perce were no despicable foe, "and in this opinion the troops coincided to a man." In light of their pacifism before the war and subsequent bravery in defense of their homeland, there was never a tribe more worthy of respect. "But," he observed afterward, "no recollection of former service or common ties of humanity could stand before the white man's greed."[22]

During the long, hot day, the soldiers had no food, but their greatest deprivation was water. Suffering even more were the three hundred horses and mules picketed behind the firing line, confined for some thirty hours before the battle finally ended. When a small spring was located at the head of a ravine at midday, sharpshooters quickly discouraged soldiers from filling their canteens. It was not until the following morning that a force managed to rout the Nez Perce and secure the spring.

At dawn the sporadic firing increased and the battle resumed, with every available soldier on the firing line. When Howard ordered food and coffee be carried to the front, the men ate for the first time in nearly twenty-four hours. Sutherland observed that the warriors seemed "disinclined to expose themselves, so the forenoon passed off without any particular incident." By midafternoon, Howard devised a plan to charge the Indian left flank, using Captain Marcus Miller's battalion. But with Miller nearly in position, someone reported a dust cloud approaching along the road from Jackson's Bridge. Soon a pack train of 120 mules rode into view, escorted by a cavalry company accompanied by twenty treaty Nez Perce scouts. Bringing up the rear was Captain Birney Keeler, General McDowell's aide-de-camp, sent by the general to evaluate the progress of Howard's campaign.[23]

Howard quickly realized the new arrivals were at risk and redirected Miller and his men forward to protect the train. Soon the men and animals were safely inside the command's firing line. As his troops brought up the rear, Miller suddenly shouted an order, and, surprising onlookers on both sides, his men charged the Indian line. At first the warriors held, then tried to turn Miller's flank, but another soldier charge turned the would-be flankers. Trimble, watching from Howard's command post, termed it "a very pretty movement" as Miller quickly began "rolling up the enemy's line." Thomas Sutherland recalled there was a moment of hesitation, then suddenly a cheer went up and down the line. The remaining soldiers, who had been watching Miller's maneuver, sprang to their feet and rushed toward the Indians, shouting, "To the river! To the river!" To the journalist's amazement, the Nez Perce turned and fled.[24]

The reason for the rout seems evident in retrospect: prolonged warfare was simply not the Indian way of fighting. According to E. S. Curtis, "their hearts are not of the mettle which endures long punishment, and they are so strongly fatalistic that if a battle cannot be won in the first grand rush, they begin to question the medicine power of the leader and think it better to fight at another time and place, where the spirits may be with them." That the Nez Perce had fought the entrenched battle as long as they had, said Curtis, was extremely unusual. Also dissension was widespread in the warrior ranks long before the charge that afternoon. Some wanted this fight to be their last, either crushing the soldiers or perishing in defeat. Others advocated continuing flight. Wottolen, who along with Yellow Wolf was one of the last warriors to leave the battlefield, could not hide his contempt. "There was a quarrel among the Nez Perces, some kept riding back and forth from the fighting to the camp. That was not good. The leaders then decided to leave the fighting, the cowards following after."[25]

With soldiers in pursuit, fleeing warriors rushed down the bluff to their waiting horses. There they forded the river and, quickly gathering women and children and whatever personal belongings they could manage, began escaping up the timbered slope. When soldiers suddenly appeared across the river and began pouring heavy fire into the camp, panic seized those remaining and they quickly followed, passing close by the fortification held the day before by McConville's volunteers.

Yellow Wolf had been shot in the forearm that morning and was one of the last warriors to mount his horse and descend the steep, rock-strewn bluff to the river. As he reached the nearly deserted camp, with soldiers beginning to fire howitzers and Gatling guns from the bluff, he saw a woman mounted on a horse she could not control. Her husband, thinking all the women and children had gone ahead, had become separated in the confusion. "The animal was leaping, pawing, wanting to go. Everybody else had gone. I hurried toward her, and she called, 'Heinmot! I am troubled about my baby!' " Lying on the ground was an infant wrapped in its *tekash* (cradleboard). "It was the cannon shots bursting near that scared her horse. She could not mount with the little one. She could not leave it there." Yellow Wolf picked up the baby, handed it to the woman, and together they hurried up the slope after the fleeing bands. The woman's name was Toma Alwawinmi (Springtime), wife of Chief

Joseph, and their baby had been born at Tepahlewam the day the war began.[26]

After descending the bluff, the foot soldiers stopped at the stream's edge, the water being too deep and rapid for the men to ford. Directly behind them was Captain Perry leading a company of cavalry, who crossed the river and began pursuing the retreating Indians. In his official report, Howard claimed that upon seeing warriors attempting a rear guard action, he ordered Perry back to help transport foot soldiers across the river. "While doing this," said Howard, "time was consumed, and the Indians . . . got well in advance of us, so that I concluded to postpone further pursuit until next morning." Lieutenant Parnell tells a different story, claiming that Perry's charge "was so dilatory and irritating that General Howard became annoyed" and ordered him back. The lost opportunity, declared Parnell, was "inexcusable." Two weeks later, General McDowell agreed, calling the failure to pursue a fleeing enemy "a capital mistake."[27]

As soldiers rushed into the Indian camp, Sutherland could hardly believe what they had left behind: "Knives and forks, groceries, plates, clothing, in fact, the miscellaneous stocks of plundered country stores, mixed with articles of Indian dress, handsome furs, adorned with stained feathers, moccasins, immense feather headdresses, quantities of Camas-root bread, kouse, dried berries and jerked beef." Searching for souvenirs, Sutherland found a child's pair of moccasins and "an absurd little rag doll under a tree." The correspondent was sure they had gotten away "with nothing more than their guns and horses. Hundreds of buffalo robes, skins of all kinds in abundance, camas and kouse roots dried and in flour, quantities of dried beef, with their different utensils—in fact their entire camp equipage was captured." Later Joseph maintained that "eighty lodges" fell into Howard's hands, representing at least half of the bands' possessions.[28]

Lieutenant Bailey was impressed at how quickly the packers and volunteers discovered caches buried earlier and containing "tons and tons of flour and other foods," along with "gold dust, jewelry, and fine silver tableware, some of which I judged dated from an early Hudson's Bay period." Bailey watched as the packers and citizens "helped themselves" before complying with Howard's order to "burn everything."[29] That evening, the men ate their first decent meal in days: potatoes, fried bacon, boiled beef, tea, and coffee.

Soldiers discovered an aged woman left behind during the hasty retreat, described by Sutherland as "an old hag of at least 90 years," who told him "that Joseph is not 'big chief' of the non-treaty Indians, as he is too young." But Howard, by now convinced that Joseph was the leader of the Nez Perce, was not listening. Although Joseph had fought with "skill and the utmost obstinacy," wrote the general in a report several days after the battle, his defeat had ended in total victory for the army. Not everyone agreed. Sergeant Michael McCarthy's matter-of-fact entry in his diary termed Howard's leadership "slow and timid." A skeptical Lieutenant Parnell believed that despite an advantage in numbers as well as position for the army, "strictly speaking, the Indians were not defeated." They had been forced to give up many of their possessions, but their loss was "insignificant" and their retreat "masterly, deliberate and unmolested, leaving us with victory barren of results."[30]

Howard listed his battle casualties as thirteen killed and twenty-seven wounded, two of whom soon died. At least twenty-three warriors had been killed, he claimed, with "about forty wounded, many of whom subsequently died." Not so, said the Nez Perce. Most agree with Yellow Wolf, who maintained only four warriors were killed outright, with four or five wounded. It is difficult to resolve the disparity between accounts. Sutherland believed the exact number would never be known as Indians, if given the opportunity, always "carry off their dead and bury them almost immediately." Regardless of the reason, Sergeant McCarthy recalled seeing only one dead warrior after the battle. "He was nearly naked, and lay as if asleep on his back, one arm drawn over his head and knee bent. He was a magnificently-shaped man and very large, a fierce figure, in fact almost gigantic." That the Nez Perce cared for their dead was evident three days after the battle when Wayakat (Going Across), the bereaved mother of the warrior whom McCarthy had likely seen, secretly returned alone to the battlefield and buried her son.[31]

On the day following the battle, the dead soldiers were buried in temporary graves and the wounded began the tortuous journey back to Fort Lapwai. One of the most seriously injured, Captain Eugene Bancroft, had been shot through the chest and was not expected to live. Wagons were procured, but since they had no springs, most men preferred the relative comfort of a travois. By the time the wounded reached Grangeville the next day, two men riding in the wagons had died. On July 20, the Portland *Weekly Standard* reported Captain Bancroft "has since died from the effects of his wounds." But three days later, propped up in a hospital bed and very much alive, Bancroft wrote to his father that "it is twelve days since I was wounded, and the doctor thinks I am out of danger." Since he had left Wrangel, Alaska, one month before, he had seen more of battle than "I ever experienced during the whole War of the Rebellion."[32]

Early on the morning of July 13, Howard set off north on the trail along the Clearwater River. Hours before, James Lawyer, son of the deceased chief and a prominent headman of the treaty Nez Perce, had sent a message saying that the bands had arrived at Kamiah, a small, prosperous village about twelve miles downstream from the battlefield. By midafternoon, Howard topped a rise and through binoculars saw the last of the bands fording the river several miles away. The villagers, led by James Lawyer and refusing to directly oppose the nontreaty bands, had removed the ferry boats normally used to cross the Clearwater, forcing them to resort to traditional bull boats. Since most of their buffalo hides had been lost during the rout, the crossing had taken much of the day.

Charging down the trail, the soldiers soon reached the river and, setting up a Gatling gun, "peppered" the defensive positions taken by warriors on the opposite shore. Slightly downstream, across from a rocky point, a detachment of cavalry led by Captain Perry reigned up short when warriors suddenly appeared from behind rocks and fired "about forty times in quick succession." One man was wounded when a bullet creased his scalp, but Howard declared that "little damage resulted, except the shame to us and a fierce delight to the foe."[33]

From across the river, warriors hooted and laughed as the troops ungracefully scrambled back from shore and out of range. A disgusted Major Mason was not surprised, admitting that Indians held "the cavalry in profound contempt—as well they may, for the truth is they are almost worthless. They cannot fight on horseback and *will* not fight on foot."[34] Unwilling or unable to mount an attack across the river, Howard ordered the weary command into camp for the night.

The next day, scouts reported the bands encamped only four miles away and showing no obvious signs of preparing to travel. Anticipating that as soon as he crossed the Clearwater, the Nez Perce again would quickly retreat, Howard devised a plan. The following morning, July 15, with infantry and artillery troops remaining at Kamiah, the general led his cavalry up the road toward Fort Lapwai. Hoping to convince the Nez Perce that he was returning to Lapwai, Howard planned to abandon the main road after several miles, then move north "twenty miles down the Clearwater to Dunwell's Ferry, and crossing there, to attempt to gain the trail to the rear" of the bands. The command had traveled only six miles, however, when word came that the bands had broken camp and were headed toward Weippe Prairie and the start of the Lolo Trail leading to Montana. Soon afterward, another courier arrived bearing a startling message from Joseph, "asking on what terms he could surrender."[35]

Howard hurriedly returned to Kamiah, sending the cavalry on to Dunwell's Ferry. That evening a messenger named Ta-min Tsi-ya (No Heart) crossed the river under a white flag, and began talking to Howard and Mason. A precise account of what transpired at this meeting (indeed, even the identity of the messenger) is disputed. Sutherland, who was not present, claimed that the man said Joseph desired to surrender. Howard answered that Joseph and his people could give themselves up the following morning, but they would be tried by a court of officers whom Howard would appoint. Suddenly, a single shot was fired from the Indian side of the river which "struck near the consulting parties." The messenger quickly explained that while Joseph wanted to quit fighting, White Bird, Looking Glass, and Toohoolhoolzote "are desirous of immediately making for the buffalo country in Montana" and did not "want to talk peace or anything else." The meeting broke up with Howard apparently believing that Joseph would surrender. The following morning, however, Joseph failed to appear, and scouts reported the Nez Perce had moved some fifteen miles away.[36]

Howard recorded little about the meeting, confident the offer had been "doubtless a ruse, intended to delay our movements," but there is ample evidence to the contrary. Years later, Lieutenant C. E. S. Wood claimed that he had been told by an unidentified Indian that "Joseph wished to surrender rather than leave the country or bring further misery on his people, but that, in council, he was overruled by the older chiefs . . . and would not desert the common cause."[37]

Also Josiah Red Wolf maintained in 1963 that "not only was Joseph hard to persuade to stay in the fight, but he tried to drop out after the [Clearwater battle]." Rumors drifted into Fort Lapwai from treaty Nez Perce, said Emily FitzGerald, claiming Joseph "says he is tired of fighting. He was drawn into it by White Bird and other chiefs, and he wants to stop." Even General McDowell's aide, Captain Keeler, wired Division Headquarters in San Francisco that while Joseph wanted to surrender, he "was forced by White Bird and other chiefs to accompany them."[38]

If Joseph's offer was sincere, there seems little doubt that Howard's strict terms of unconditional surrender were less than appealing. Sutherland was convinced that "Joseph and White Bird and other chiefs were determined upon not surrendering, as they would all be hanged." The chiefs had every reason to believe this true. Only four years before, five Modocs had swung at the gallows after waging unsuccessful war. Still fresh in the minds of tribes of the upper Columbia Plateau were the summary hangings of numerous Indian leaders following the tribal uprisings resulting from the 1855 treaty, leaders whom the Nez Perce had helped apprehend. Although probably few Indians were aware of what appeared in newspapers, one had only to turn to a Portland *Daily Standard* editorial that appeared shortly after the outbreak to understand where most whites stood. Joseph was descended from "inhuman butchers of the most merciless type," the paper opined. The only punishment for such a "cunning, treacherous, brutal, blood-thirsty savage" is hanging "by the neck until dead."[39]

That some Nez Perce were fearful of being drawn into the deepening conflict became evident later that day when thirty-five men, women, and children walked into Kamiah and surrendered. Howard immediately had them arrested. Sutherland reported that "they consist of fourteen warriors, and the remainder are squaws and their children." The journalist was optimistic, saying "this surrender is looked upon by the officers of our command as the beginning of a general disintegration." Captain Keeler reported to McDowell that "the war is practically ended," because the captives indicated "want and demoralization among the late hostiles is very great."[40]

While the surrender may have appeared encouraging, most of those who gave themselves up were women and children, and of the men, several were elderly, possessing in total only two guns and no ammunition. Sutherland claimed six were Joseph's warriors and three belong to Looking Glass, but the Nez Perce maintained the entire group consisted of a small band led by Red Heart. This band had recently arrived from Montana, having been unlucky enough to return to their home along the Clearwater River just as Whipple raided Looking Glass's camp. Losing their possessions in the foray and attempting to escape the entire conflict, they had moved to Weippe Prairie where they found themselves directly in the path of the retreating bands. Although Red Heart steadfastly claimed to have taken no part in any of the hostilities, Howard confiscated all of the band's remaining horses and ordered them taken to Fort Lapwai.

In a forced march on foot of sixty miles with little food and water, the ragged group arrived on July 20. The *Teller* triumphantly reported that the Indians had "their hair cut short (it should have been under the scalp) and then they were placed in irons." In early August, thirty-three of the prisoners were taken via steamboat to Fort Vancouver near Portland, where they remained incarcerated without trial until their release nine months later. Emily FitzGerald witnessed their departure from Lapwai, moved by the unforgettable despair of the captives, who had been persuaded they would be hung. "One poor woman moaned and cried and really looked distressed. Just before she left, she took some ornaments of beads and gave them to the interpreter to give to her little girl who is up somewhere near Kamiah. One old man cut the bead ornaments off his moccasins and left them for his wife."[41]

As the Nez Perce went into camp at Weippe Prairie on July 15, a tribal council was held that went on long into the night. Sixteen Palouse warriors and their families under Hahtalekin and Huishuis Kute had finally joined them, and it was time to determine their next move. They had lost many of their possessions at the Clearwater fight, but in one regard this proved an advantage for now they had less to carry. Although there is no precise record of the discussion, it appears Looking Glass argued persuasively for fleeing to the buffalo country, saying there was every reason to believe the soldiers would not follow. On the open plains of Montana they would receive aid from their allies the Crows. If the soldiers pressed them, there was always the possibility of retreating to the Old Woman's Country (Queen Victoria's Canada) and joining forces with Sitting Bull, recently self-exiled there after his row with Custer. Another inducement to move on to Montana was that many returning buffalo hunters recently had left horses with the Flatheads in the Bitterroot Valley. The whites would not remain angry forever, Looking Glass reasoned, and in a few years—perhaps as early as the following spring—they would be allowed to return.

According to one account, Joseph spoke in opposition:

What are we fighting for? Is it for our lives? No. It is for this land where the bones of our fathers lie buried. I do not want to take my women among strangers. I do not want to die in a strange land. Some of you tried to say once that I was afraid of the whites. Stay here with me now and you will have plenty of fighting. We will put our women behind us in these mountains and die on our own fighting for them. I would rather do that than run I know not where.[42]

Other sources claim he had little to say, refusing to abandon his people but unwilling to play a leadership role for a cause he deemed hopeless. After interviewing Yellow Bull, E. S. Curtis remarked that "depression seemed to have taken possession of Joseph from the start, and he drifted as the tribe desired."[43] By the council's conclusion, although most participants voiced more indifference than enthusiasm for the plan to escape to the plains, Looking Glass prevailed, thereby assuming influence if not outright dominance over the other chiefs. Although he continued to have a voice in councils and would occasionally take up arms, Joseph assumed the responsibility of protecting the camp and its women and children.

The next morning, leaving a small group of warriors behind to watch for soldiers, the bands broke camp to begin their hegira over the Lolo Trail to Montana. During the days at Weippe Prairie and with many of their provisions lost on the Clearwater, they had killed cattle belonging to a white rancher, jerking the meat for the long trek over mountains they knew held little game. In an irony that could hardly have been lost on the bands, the site of their Weippe Prairie camp was where the starving Lewis and Clark Expedition had wandered out of the mountains seventy-two years earlier to be welcomed, fed, and sheltered by the Nez Perce.

When Joseph failed to surrender at Kamiah on July 16, Howard ordered the infantry across the Clearwater using makeshift ferryboats. By evening all were camped on the eastern shore. Word soon arrived from the cavalry at Dunwell's Ferry that the ferryboat there had been cut loose, drifted miles downstream, and surrounding buildings had been destroyed. Howard concluded that the Nez Perce had discovered his scheme and sent a raiding party ahead (although they later denied knowledge of Howard's plan), and with the bands now at Weippe Prairie and showing every indication of full retreat, he abandoned hope of encircling them. Unsure if they were planning to head east over the Lolo Trail into Montana or north into Washington and northern Idaho, Howard ordered his chief of staff, Major Mason, and five companies of cavalry to scout ahead and determine their direction.

Before daybreak the next morning, Mason's cavalry, led by six Nez Perce scouts, along with Ad Chapman and some of McConville's volunteers, departed Kamiah for Weippe Prairie. Here Mason found the trail entered a "narrow defile, densely wooded and almost impassable with undergrowth." On the lookout for a trap and aware that the trail was "almost impossible to handle a mounted force on," Mason sent the scouts ahead, led by James Reuben and John Levi, followed by the volunteers and cavalry. The command had gone only a short distance when shots rang out, and several of the scouts came running back. Mason dismounted and deployed his men behind trees, sending a small party forward to learn what had happened.[44]

There the men discovered James Reuben wounded in the wrist and Abraham Brooks shot in the shoulder. A little farther on they found John Levi "lying in the grass," said volunteer Eugene Wilson, "with forty-five bullets through his lungs." There were probably more holes than truth in Wilson's statement, but it did appear that the bands were making good on their pledge to treat Indian army scouts as the enemy. Yellow Wolf, one of the avenging warriors waiting in ambush, claimed that Levi was still alive when a fellow warrior calmly walked up to him and, without speaking, "shot him through the heart."[45]

Having fulfilled Howard's orders and determined the direction of the retreating bands, Mason ordered the entire command back to Kamiah, arriving the following morning after twenty-eight hours in the saddle. McConville brought up the rear, claiming the men had to stop frequently to let the wounded rest. But surviving scouts were adamant that both the cavalry and the volunteers abandoned the wounded. Seekumses Kunnin (Horse Blanket) said that he carried Abraham Brooks, who eventually died from his wound years later, alone on his horse, getting "blood-soaked" during the long ride. Only once did they stop long enough to bury John Levi in a shallow, hastily dug grave, the scout claimed, while anxiously watching back over the trail. Twenty-three years later, Congress passed a bill compensating the heirs of John Levi for "services rendered" in the form of $79.50.[46]

When Mason reported that the Indians had started on the Lolo Trail, Howard faced a dilemma. As soon as the Nez Perce crossed the Continental Divide between Idaho and Montana, they would pass from his jurisdiction into that of Brigadier General Alfred H. Terry's Department of Dakota, a wholly separate military department of the Division of the Missouri, commanded by Lieutenant General Philip Sheridan. Howard was correct when he observed that "this really ended the campaign within the limits of my department."[47]

Only a few days before, on July 15, confident he had soundly defeated the Nez Perce at the Clearwater and pushed them beyond any immediate danger to white settlements, Howard had wired McDowell. The bands have "made a pretty clean retreat," he said, adding that he planned to move the command north and "settle with the malcontents who have furnished aid to Joseph, and secure a permanent peace." Howard seemed certain that the Nez Perce would reappear somewhere near Spokane, and he planned to be present to meet them. Now that he had information they were retreating to Montana, he hesitated to follow, although it seems certain that he possessed orders to do precisely that.[48]

Soon after hostilities had broken out in June, General Sherman had left Washington, D.C., on an inspection trip of western army divisions. Anticipating just such a predicament, he had told McDowell before departing on June 25 to order Howard "to pay no attention to boundary lines of the Division; only in case the Indians retreat toward Montana, to send word as much in advance as possible."[49] McDowell had telegraphed Sherman's order to Howard's Portland headquarters the next day and again on July 16 when it appeared Howard had halted pursuit. Official records indicate that the original order was passed on to Howard in the field. Although he never directly acknowledged its receipt, based on concurrent communication he did receive and statements by his staff, it seems likely that he was well aware of its content as he pondered his next move.

By all accounts, Mason's grim description of the Lolo Trail was supported by settlers who warned that the route was even worse than the terrain the soldiers had encountered along the Salmon River. The command was exhausted after nearly a month of forced marches over more than two hundred miles of rugged country. The idea of as many or more miles under harsher conditions would hardly be welcome. Also, Howard was increasingly concerned about removing most of the department's available soldiers from the region, particularly since he feared the recent successes of the Nez Perce were creating unrest among neighboring Columbia River Basin tribes. Emily FitzGerald, with her ear close to Fort Lapwai's scuttlebutt, gave support to this anxiety, writing that "another victory for Joseph would bring to his standard all the disaffected Indians in the Department, and the whole Nez Perce tribe is wavering. . . ."[50] Even if these estranged Indians never joined forces with the Nez Perce, Howard reasoned, they might take up arms if the department had no deterrent force present. A large detachment of Second Infantry troops under Colonel Frank Wheaton was en route from Atlanta, Georgia, and Major John Green was leading a force of cavalry and infantry that was due to arrive within the week from Boise, Idaho. Until additional troops reached the area, Howard decided he dare not follow the escaping bands.

Within a day he had devised a plan. He would return to Fort Lapwai with most of his command, move on to Lewiston and resupply, then depart for Montana via the Mullan Road as soon as reinforcements arrived. Although twice as long as the 150-mile Lolo Trail and scarcely more than a cleared path wide enough to pass a small wagon, this northerly route across the Idaho mountains provided the easiest access to the settlements of western Montana. Leasing wagons to carry his infantry, Howard somewhat naively hoped to arrive in the Bitterroot Valley a few miles below Missoula just as the Nez Perce were exiting the mountains. There was always the possibility the Nez Perce might turn north from Missoula and attempt a direct route to Canada through the Flathead Valley, in which case he would be positioned to meet them. At the same time, he believed his show of force along the northern route would do much to quell the region's Columbia River "renegades."

Based on the limited intelligence he had gathered about the bands' movements and the nature of the Lolo Trail, Howard's plan seems prudent, if not exactly ambitious. The Nez Perce had already killed nearly ninety people and had done well over $200,000 worth of damage in a time when a common laborer made no more than seventy-five cents a day. Like Perry at Cottonwood, Howard was reluctant to jeopardize his department's strategic safety for a bold, possibly dangerous tactical move. He was playing by the book. But no sooner had he concluded his plan than it began to unravel.

On July 19, the command started on the road to Fort Lapwai and had almost reached the halfway point at Cold Springs when messengers brought news that bands were threatening the handful of troops left at Kamiah. Soon other messages arrived saying warriors were "stealing some of the Kamiah Indians' horses," and that "parties of Indians were burning houses along the North Fork of the Clearwater." Only the horse theft proved true, as a small raiding party lingered behind the fleeing bands and stole four hundred horses, but Howard determined that "the excitement was too real to admit of my leaving the vicinity" until reinforcements arrived. Sending the cavalry back to Kamiah but leaving the infantry and artillery temporarily at Cold Springs, Howard and a small escort under Captain Perry rode on to Fort Lapwai to make arrangements for departure via the Mullan Road as soon as Wheaton or Green appeared.[51]

The ride of thirty miles was exhausting, but Howard had received word days before that his wife was arriving by steamboat that very night in Lewiston. When the boat docked at ten o'clock, however, Lizzie Howard was not aboard. "The story proved false," Howard wrote later, "and the disappointment real." One of the passengers, however, was Mrs. David Perry, who upon seeing her husband had an attack of hysterics—sentiment that "rather disgusted" Howard.[52]

The trip to Lewiston proved even more disappointing when Howard picked up the first newspapers he had read since taking to the field and saw he was under unmerciful, personal attack from San Francisco to New York. Lewiston *Teller* editor Alonzo Leland, with an ear close to the grumblings of returning volunteers (his son was wounded at Cottonwood), was livid with sarcasm. Howard may be "a very pleasant and amiable gentleman," declared the editor, but he was no Indian fighter. "The sheep is a very pleasant and amiable animal and has none but sterling qualities, but we do not expect him to chase wolves and coyotes; we assign the task to the dog—also an amiable brute, but better adapted to the purpose." General Crook was much better suited for the job. "He sticks his breeches in his boots, keeps his powder dry, eats hard tack and goes for 'em." Unlike Howard, who "regards the army as a kind of missionary society" for the Indians and "himself as the head of a kind of red freedman's bureau," Crook was a first-class Indian fighter who brooked "no foolishness about him." If Howard continued to command the chase, Leland prophetically forecasted, it would be a "six month's campaign, hunting the enemy in the mountains."[53]

Even more alarming was an item reprinted in the San Francisco

Chronicle that only days before had appeared in Chicago and New York newspapers, claiming Howard's removal was virtually imminent. "The Cabinet yesterday secretly but seriously considered the propriety of displacing Howard and putting Crook in his place." Howard had "made such a sad mess of the campaign," the article concluded, that it was "quite possible that he will be removed today."[54]

Word of his success at the Clearwater had not yet reached national newspapers, and Howard must have been relieved when he opened a telegram from General McDowell that in part read:

Your dispatch and that of Captain Keeler of your engagement of the eleventh and twelfth gave us all great pleasure. I immediately reported them to Washington to be laid before the Secretary of War and the President. These dispatches came most opportunely, for your enemies had raised a great clamor against you, which the press reported had not been without effect in Washington.

They have not been silenced, but I think like Joseph's band, have been scotched not killed, and will rise again if they have the chance.[55]

Long afterward, Howard was the very example of equanimity toward the press, coolly observing "how wonderfully news can spread. It is like the cloud no bigger than a man's hand, when it leaves us; it is magnified several times before the journals at Lewiston and Walla-Walla have put it into type, and by the time it has reached Portland and San Francisco it has become a heavy cloud, overspreading the whole heaven." Newspaper editors, said Howard, would be more patient with Indian chases "if they could be made to realize how deceptive the small-scale atlases are."[56] But these circumspect comments came much later, and at the time neither he nor his men were so generous.

Confident that the accusations had originated with citizen volunteers, Major Mason bitterly complained to his wife that he had never seen "a more worthless set of trifling rascals," calling them "utterly worthless, a cowardly pack of whelps." Major Keeler reported to

McDowell that the rumors volunteers had circulated about Howard's campaign were "wanton, systematic lies," and to employ any
more men of such character would be "worse than useless." On July
21, Howard joined in the indignation, wiring McDowell that he
would like to put a few of his "lying rear enemies on these mountain
trails, under a broiling July sun."[57]

Sutherland echoed this sentiment, revealing that newspaper aspersions had stung Howard, who was enraged at what he considered
scurrilous and unfair attacks upon his integrity. As a result, declared
the journalist, Howard resolved to scrap his previous plans and "start
with the rest of his command through the impenetrable Lolo Pass,
and follow Joseph to the very death."[58]

Returning to Cold Springs on July 22, Howard left orders for
Colonel Wheaton, upon his arrival, to send a detachment of cavalry
led by Captains Perry and Trimble to Missoula via the Mullan Road.
As soon as Major Green arrived from Boise to protect the settlements against other potential uprisings, Howard would directly pursue the Nez Perce over Lolo Pass, linking up with Perry and Trimble
in the Bitterroot Valley. While waiting for Green, the command
began preparing for the long march.

It was not all work and no play, however. Sutherland said that
while camped near Cold Springs, he and the general discovered a
trout stream "that would have made Issac Walton brave all the Indians in Christendom for one day's 'whipping' at it." After catching
enough fish to "drive amateur fly-flingers" into hospitals with sheer
envy, Sutherland could not help but reflect "how nice it would be if
Joseph and his warriors could only be caught as easily."[59]

Four additional companies soon arrived via Lewiston, and Howard immediately added them to his force. Among the officers was
Second Lieutenant Guy Howard, the general's eldest son, who was
made an aide-de-camp. By July 27, when the forward column of
Major Green's detachment finally arrived at Kamiah, Howard had a
command consisting of over 735 men, along with about 50 packers
and 350 mules. A few days before they were due to leave, the packers—mostly whites but with a smattering of those of Mexican descent—went on strike for higher wages, which they promptly
received. Sutherland was impressed with the packers, terming them

"a splendid class of men physically," with just enough of an accent "to give proper pronunciation to aparejos, and swear in a musical tone." They were always first to build their campfires at night, cook their meals, and never faltered in battle or on long marches, he declared.[60]

Howard also dispatched three citizen volunteers—apparently ones still in good graces—led by James Cearley over the Old Nez Perce Trail, a lengthy and difficult passage through the southern Salmon River Mountains to the head of the Bitterroot Valley. Cearley carried a message for Captain Charles Rawn, commanding officer of the small army post at Missoula. Howard was convinced the Nez Perce were demoralized, writing Rawn that "if you simply bother them, and keep them back until I can close in, their destruction or surrender will be sure." Still smarting from criticism, he closed with the admonition that "we must not let these hostile Indians escape."[61]

Howard's messages to McDowell continued their characteristic upbeat tone, reassuring him that "in another month I shall surely be able to make clean work of the whole field." A few days later, he sounded only slightly less optimistic: "Cannot troops at Missoula or vicinity detain Joseph till I can strike his rear? The two companies there with a little help from volunteers ample, considering present condition of hostile Indians. My troops will push through rapidly."[62]

But by now eleven days had passed since the Nez Perce had departed for Montana, and McDowell began to openly question Howard's unhurried pursuit. In the margins of one of Howard's telegrams that McDowell forwarded on to General Sherman, he penned a curt note, expressing belief that the pursuit would prove to be nothing but a "military promenade." As commander of the division, McDowell was feeling pressure to produce results. He had already received three frantic telegrams from Benjamin Potts, Governor of Montana, describing the bands' progress toward the Bitterroot Valley. Although it would be days before Howard would receive them, McDowell passed these messages on, each with a nearly identical postscript strongly encouraging Howard's "rapid movement up the Lolo trail."[63]

By Sunday, July 29, the command was fully assembled and en-

131

camped on the east side of the Clearwater, ready to move out toward Weippe Prairie and the Lolo Trail the following morning. Howard and a few officers crossed the river and attended church services at Kamiah, where a nontreaty Nez Perce delivered the sermon. Never one to neglect an opportunity to continue his vilification of Howard, *Teller* editor Leland condemned the general for refusing to campaign on the Sabbath, although it appears this was one of the few exceptions during the many months of war.

Emily FitzGerald's husband, Surgeon John FitzGerald, having finally caught up with the command, spent the day completing last-minute details. Late that night, he wrote a letter to Emily saying that the men doubted if they could catch the Nez Perce and describing a conversation he had just had with Colonel Marcus Miller. "I said to Colonel Miller, 'Colonel, what are we going to do over there?' He replied, 'Oh, we will have a big mountain picnic with no Indians to trouble us.' "[64]

7

The unusually hot and dry summer of 1877 had barely gotten underway in Montana's capital of Helena when Governor Benjamin Franklin Potts began to experience acute discomfort. He was a large man, well over two hundred pounds, with fierce blue eyes, a closely trimmed beard, and receding hairline, and his popularity was rapidly waning after seven years as territorial governor. In May, Montana Republicans had accused his administration of malfeasance and openly demanded his impeachment. No less a personage than President Rutherford Hayes exonerated him of any wrongdoing, but Potts's detractors were far from satisfied. A scathing editorial in the *Bozeman Times* lambasted him as "the two hundred and fifty pounds *avoirdupois* of bone and muscle and the thimble full of brains that runs our government."[1]

Then in June, word arrived from Idaho that the Nez Perce were on the warpath. Bitterroot Valley residents were convinced the bands would soon turn eastward, join their allies the Flatheads, and together seek vengeance on every white settler in western Montana. To say that Potts welcomed the diversion of an Indian conflict to save his faltering political career may be somewhat disingenuous, but there is ample proof that he threw himself into the fray with consummate energy.

On June 29, only a week into Howard's campaign, Potts nervously wired General McDowell: "Have Indians retreated toward Montana? Great excitement prevails in western Montana. Flathead and other Indians seriously disaffected. Serious trouble anticipated." Two days later Potts again wired McDowell: "Charlos [Charlot], Flathead chief, controlling two hundred fighting Indians, has disappeared from Bitter Root Valley, probably to join Joseph's band." A third telegram from the governor, however, reported that Charlot and his followers had been discovered some seventy miles away, "seeking safety" and claiming they were fearful of being drawn into the conflict.[2]

If McDowell was confused as to the intentions of Montana's Flathead Indians after receiving these messages, it appears most whites in the territory were similarly bewildered. The only thing that seems certain is that nearly everyone agreed the Flatheads harbored multiple grievances against whites, and scarcely anyone doubted that they would pass up this opportunity for retribution.

Such belief in the inevitability of violence reflects just how desperate Indian-white relations in Montana had become by 1877; only a short time before, whites had considered the Flatheads or Salish unusually peaceable. They are a "meticulously clean, amiable, truthful, upright" people, declared trapper David Thompson. The Hudson's Bay Company's Ross Cox found them "honest, brave, quiet and amenable to their chiefs, cleanly . . . [and] decided enemies of falsehood of every description." In the 1840s, the young Belgian Jesuit Pierre Jean De Smet voiced only praise for their warmth and conviviality. These early descriptions sound remarkably similar to those of the Nez Perce, and indeed, long before white contact, the two tribes had struck up a friendship based on intermarriage, trade, and mutual defense. The Nez Perce frequently left horses and other possessions with the Flatheads while traveling back and forth to the plains, and both were firm allies in their ongoing war with the Blackfeet.[3]

For all their kindred attributes, the Flatheads fared little better than their neighbors in dealing with whites. Soon after concluding the Treaty of 1855 with the Nez Perce, Issac Stevens attempted an identical agreement with Montana's Kootenais, Pend d'Oreilles, and Flathead Indians. A reservation was established north of present-day Missoula, but Victor, chief of the Flatheads, opposed giving up his Bitterroot home. Stevens convinced him to leave the decision up to the president. Until the valley was surveyed and the decision made, the Bitterroot would remain closed to white settlement.

For the next sixteen years, the government failed to act. Victor died and was succeeded by his son Charlot, who interpreted the government's neglect as consent to remain in the valley. By 1870, Bitterroot settlers, having ignored the treaty and numbering a thousand strong, pressed Congress to evict the Flatheads. The next year, President Grant authorized their removal. When Charlot balked, the government sent envoy James A. Garfield to persuade Charlot to vacate the valley. Upon Garfield's arrival, however, Charlot promptly informed the man who would become president that he considered the original treaty invalid.

Unlike Howard with the Nez Perce, Garfield stopped short of threat of force, but he did manage to convince two lesser chiefs to sign a new treaty agreeing to move to the reservation. Charlot, variously reported to have between 360 and 550 followers, refused. Garfield went ahead with the treaty anyway, saying that he believed Charlot "would ultimately come into the agreement." The following year, either by deception or a printer's error, Charlot's mark appeared on the published document (although not on the original). When word spread that he had signed the treaty, the chief was furious, accusing whites of forging his name. The government ignored his protestations, and Congress went on to ratify the treaty.[4]

During ensuing years, Charlot stubbornly refused to leave the Bitterroot, even though his people fell into wretched poverty. In their attempt to abnegate the treaty, the Flatheads, like the nontreaty Nez Perce, pointedly avoided accepting any governmental assistance lest such behavior be interpreted as de facto acceptance of the agreement.

In an attempt to force their capitulation, the territorial government in 1876 tried to impose a property tax on the indigent Flatheads. Charlot bitterly denounced the proposal, incredulous that the white man wanted money "for things he never owned and never gave us." Whites had become "a foul thing," he declared, spoiling "what the Spirit who gave us this country made beautiful and clean. But that is not enough: he wants us to pay him, besides his enslaving our country. . . . His laws never gave us a blade of grass nor a tree, nor a duck, nor a grouse, nor a trout. No; like the wolverine that steals your cache, how often does he come? You know he comes as long as he lives, and takes more and more, and dirties what he leaves."[5]

Now a year later, with an Indian war only a mountain range away and potential violence already brewing, Governor Potts was increasingly apprehensive that the Flatheads might join the Nez Perce. As recently as April, a large contingent of Looking Glass's and Charlot's bands had camped together near Missoula. Then, just after war had broken out, some thirty lodges of Nez Perce had stopped briefly in the Bitterroot before heading back to Idaho. Settlers, who generally welcomed trading with Nez Perce traveling to and from buffalo country, began pressuring the governor to provide defense. Potts wired Washington for permission to form a militia, but his request was denied. In mid-June, an army detachment led by Captain Charles Rawn had left Fort Shaw to construct a post at Missoula, but the fort was unfinished and Rawn's skeleton force inadequate for protection. Rawn, along with Indian Agent Peter Ronan, had recently sought out Charlot and elicited his promise that if the bands arrived in Montana, the Flatheads would "not fight with them against the whites," but neither would they "fight against the Nez Perces." Despite this assurance of neutrality, both Rawn and Potts remained mistrustful.[6]

Meanwhile, settlers began constructing three strongholds throughout the valley and arming themselves. Panic was great when news of the Idaho uprising first spread to Montana, then cooled somewhat as Howard took to the field. When it became apparent by mid-July that the Nez Perce were unsubdued, unrest began to flame again. *Weekly Missoulian* editor Chauncey Barbour wrote to Potts warning that the region's combined tribes of some two thousand Indians could easily crush the area's few hundred white defenders. Barbour claimed he had information that "restless young men from all tribes, lured by the prospect of plunder," had already joined the Nez Perce in Idaho. The Flatheads, he said, were only waiting for an opportunity "to come down and clean out Missoula."[7]

At least one band of Nez Perce, consisting of eleven lodges led by Eagle-from-the-Light, had joined the Flatheads more or less permanently, resisting Howard and Monteith's efforts to place them within the Nez Perce reservation. But they also feared war. As rumblings of hostilities grew louder in July, Eagle-from-the-Light approached Agent Ronan, requesting permission to camp on the reservation north of Missoula in an attempt "to keep out of trouble" should the Nez Perce invade Montana. In what soon would prove a costly mistake, Ronan refused, declaring "it was a bad policy to throw the Reservation open as a shelter as suspicion could not be avoided." Thus the band remained camped just south of where the Lolo Trail exited into the Bitterroot Valley.[8]

Reacting to settlers' fears, Potts telegraphed Washington a second time on July 13 requesting permission to form a militia. "The Idaho Indians appear to be heading for western Montana. I respectfully ask authority to raise five hundred volunteers to meet the Indians soon as they reach our borders." The Secretary of War sent back a hazy reply, saying that General Phil Sheridan's staff in Chicago was carefully watching the situation. Neither they nor General Terry, commander of the Department of Dakota, deemed such a move necessary.[9]

Five days later, Captain Rawn responded to settlers' demands that he position scouts up the Lolo Trail by dispatching Lieutenant Francis Woodbridge and four enlisted men. The eastern side of the trail began several miles south of Missoula where Lolo Creek emptied into the Bitterroot Valley. From there it ascended the creek some thirty miles to a pass separating Idaho and Montana, then bounded up and down steep forested mountains for over another hundred miles before debouching near Weippe Prairie. During their trip west in 1805, Clark had reported the trail "most intolerable," with the party "much fatigued" after encountering immense quantities of fallen timber. Some seventy years later—as Howard was soon to learn—the trail had changed little, General Sherman calling it "one of the worst *trails* for man and beast on this continent."[10]

When Woodbridge failed to appear back in Missoula by July 21, Rawn sent Lieutenant Charles Coolidge up the trail. The next day, near Lolo Pass, the two parties met. Woodbridge had crossed some thirty miles into Idaho but had seen nothing. In possession of fresher mounts, Coolidge returned to Missoula that evening while Woodbridge camped along lower Lolo Creek. During the night, two white youths claiming to have escaped after briefly being held prisoners of the Nez Perce rode into Woodbridge's camp with the unsettling news that the bands were camped at Lolo Hot Springs several miles up the valley. How Woodbridge had missed seeing the bands on the narrow trail remains a mystery, but he lost no time notifying Rawn the following day.

Upon hearing this news, Governor Potts responded with alacrity, and a flurry of telegrams shot back and forth between Helena and San Francisco. "Nez Perces arriving in Montana by Lolo trail in large numbers; profess to want to pass peaceably through settlements; have wounded with them," Potts told General McDowell. "If possible," the general wired back, "they should not be allowed to pass, but be arrested or detained, and treated as hostiles. What, if anything, can you do?" Potts tersely replied that the Secretary of War had granted him no authority to form a militia, consequently he was "powerless to arrest and detain Joseph's band."[11]

Meanwhile, others across the country were listening to this exchange on what Indians so poignantly called the "talking wire." When McDowell telegraphed the adjutant general requesting assistance, General Sheridan sent a message to Fort Shaw's commanding officer, Colonel John Gibbon, directing him to proceed at once to intercept the Nez Perce. Gibbon quickly ordered a company at Bozeman's Fort Ellis to Missoula. Then he began collecting his troops, who were scattered across northern Montana on temporary duty that summer. It would be almost a week before he could assemble his men and begin the 150-mile trek to Missoula. Because his troops were infantry—called "walk-a-heaps" by Indians—Gibbon wired Sheridan saying he feared their movements would be "very slow."[12]

With reinforcements a week away, fewer than 35 troops in his command, and some 750 threatening Indians at his doorstep, Captain Rawn suddenly found himself in a most uncomfortable predicament. He nevertheless began making plans to halt the Nez Perce before they reached the Bitterroot Valley. On July 25, Rawn moved his command and fifty volunteers up Lolo Creek about sixteen miles from Missoula. Here the canyon narrows to some two hundred yards, with precipitous mountains on the south side "densely covered with standing and fallen timber," wrote *Missoulian* editor and volunteer Chauncey Barbour, "so that escape on that side was impossible." The steep, grassy slopes on the north side of the canyon appeared more negotiable, maintained another observer, but he was confident "a goat could not pass, much less an entire tribe of Indians with all their impedimenta."[13]

As his men dug rifle pits and felled trees for a barricade, Rawn learned from scout E. A. Kenney that the Indian camp was located only two or three miles up the canyon. Arriving the night before, Kenney had been met by Nez Perce messenger John Hill. Kenney reported that Hill had been sent by Joseph "to find out whether he can leave the pass and go through Missoula and so on to the buffalo country. Says he will go peaceably." Kenney sent Hill back with the message "to come to our camp and have a talk." Another account disputes Hill was allowed to return to the bands, maintaining he was made a prisoner. Regardless, a meeting was arranged for the following day.[14]

While Rawn continued to fortify his position late into the night, Governor Potts traveled by stagecoach from Helena to Missoula. By noon the next day he had joined Rawn at the Lolo barricade, expressing the opinion that it was "madness" to attack the bands with an inadequate number of men, that the only thing that could be done was "to hold the Indians in check until such a force arrived as to compel a surrender." To this end, Potts returned to Missoula and issued an emergency proclamation calling for a volunteer militia. Although he lacked federal authority to provide citizens with arms and ammunition or pay them for their services, Potts promised to "use every effort in his power" to reimburse those who volunteered.[15]

The order went out July 26 but failed to reach outlying communities when it was mysteriously lost at Deer Lodge by the stagecoach driver. Banner headlines in a special edition of the *Missoulian* read, "Help! Help! White Bird Defiant. Come Running!" Upon hearing the call, nearby Montana settlements hastily formed volunteer companies who began moving as fast as horses could go toward the barricade on the Lolo Trail.[16]

That same afternoon, waving a white hankerchief tied to a gun barrel, Rawn met with the Nez Perce. There was wariness on both sides. Looking Glass expressed his intention to travel through the Bitterroot without violence. The bands' argument was with Idaho settlers, he said, not those in Montana. Rawn responded by demanding the bands "surrender arms and ammunition or fight." When several warriors took offense at Rawn's brusqueness, the two sides withdrew, agreeing to meet the following day when Governor Potts would be present.[17]

The next morning, Potts again visited the barricade, and he and Rawn discussed the wisdom of another parlay with the Nez Perce. Although the governor's militia call had come belatedly, volunteers had begun arriving. By that evening there would be over two hundred men at the barricade, including fifteen or twenty Flatheads sent by Charlot, who had had a change of heart and now openly supported the whites. Rawn invited Potts to accompany him to the meeting, to which the governor—perhaps recalling the recent Modoc War when negotiator General Edward Canby was assassinated during such talks—declined.

Finally, Rawn headed up the valley with one hundred mounted volunteers. About a half mile below the bands' camp, Looking Glass came out, offering to meet Rawn "alone and unarmed" midway between the two forces. In his somewhat confused and bare-bones account of the meeting, Rawn claims he reasserted his demands, and Looking Glass again refused but said "he would talk to his people" and give his final answer the next morning. Rawn quibbled about the exact time, and the council broke up without reaching an agreement to meet again. When he returned to the barricade, Rawn told his command what had happened, saying that he fully expected "to be attacked." To his amazement, when the volunteers learned that the Nez Perce promised to pass peaceably through the settlements, the men began leaving "in squads of from one to a dozen," determined that "no act of hostility on their part should provoke the Indians."[18]

In the days that followed, no single event of the war in Montana would be more hotly debated than how this failure of will to battle the Nez Perce came about. Accounts vary dramatically as to the exact number of meetings that took place between Rawn and the bands and even more about what was actually said. During coming weeks, as allegations raged back and forth across the territory, nothing less than the sacred manhood of every white man present at Lolo Canyon came into question. As the rhetoric became more virulent, explanations, excuses, and outright lies would obscure the truth forever.

Nearly everyone had an opinion about what happened. After interviewing Looking Glass's Nez Perce interpreter, Duncan McDonald maintained that in the final meeting Looking Glass agreed to give up ammunition but not weapons, saying, "It is foolish to think of a whole camp going to the buffalo country and not carrying a single gun." Most Nez Perce also remembered only one meeting between the two sides. More than one white account accuses Rawn of promising the bands he would not fight, some going so far as to include Governor Potts at the final meeting and implicating him as well. But if the governor was privy to any of the discussions, it seems his influence was at best indirect. Joseph later endorsed the view that Rawn capitulated, saying, "We then made a treaty with these soldiers. We agreed not to molest any one and they agreed that we might pass through the Bitter Root country in peace." John Humble, captain of the Corvallis volunteers, told Rawn, "If you are going to fight those Indians, I will take my men and go home." Captain Rawn, said Humble, "promised me he would not fight."[19]

Regardless of who made this decision or when, the following morning fewer than one hundred men remained at the barricade, most having departed during the night. At ten o'clock, someone noticed Indians filing by on the steep, grassy ridge north of camp, just beyond rifle range. Some eyewitnesses say sporadic shots were fired, either by whites or warriors, but apparently these soon ceased. A mile below Rawn's fortification—forever after dubbed "Fort Fizzle"—the Nez Perce descended the ridge and continued their journey down Lolo Creek toward the Bitterroot.

Volunteer W. R. Logan, whose father, William Logan, was an officer in Rawn's command, followed them down the trail, noting that the warriors "were good-natured, cracked jokes, and seemed very much amused at the way they had fooled" the whites. Several other men sent downstream by Rawn to observe their movement ran into the Nez Perce rear guard. As soon as Looking Glass saw them, wrote Chauncey Barbour, the chief "waved his hat, and came up and exchanged friendly greetings." The maneuver, declared the disbelieving editor, was "one of the most brilliant strategically of modern warfare." To guide their women and children through country that was literally swarming with armed men was a move whose "audacity was stunning."[20]

The Nez Perce continued at a relaxed pace to the mouth of Lolo Creek, then they turned south up the Bitterroot Valley before encamping. With his small group of soldiers, a weary Rawn followed at a distance, returning to Missoula when he determined the bands were headed in the opposite direction. The remaining volunteer force of about fifty men had started toward their homes in the valley when they inadvertently stumbled into the Indian camp. Looking Glass ordered the men released, repeating his promise to harm no one. To show good faith, the chief then shook hands all around. With over two hundred women and children at nearby Stevensville, said Volunteer W. B. Harlan, "we were not silly enough to uselessly incite the Indians to devastate our valley, and I do not think our critics would have done otherwise had they and their families and homes been situated as were ours." Harlan unabashedly declared, "If they want Indians for breakfast, they are still within reach."[21]

Fourteen-year-old William Cave of Missoula recalled that earlier that afternoon Rawn had sent a string of pack mules back to town. An older settler with poor eyesight immediately "jumped at the conclusion that they were Indians coming, did not tarry to ascertain to the contrary, but mounted a saddle horse, rode across the flat as fast as the horse could travel, coming into town and excitedly announcing that the Indians were right upon us." Cave remembered that there was "sure enough hurrying in hot haste about the burg" before the panic subsided.[22]

Duncan McDonald may have witnessed this ride. Arriving at the hotel in Missoula that afternoon, the trader noticed Governor Potts with some of his staff and several ladies lounging on the hotel veranda. Suddenly a cloud of dust signaling a fast rider appeared on the horizon from the direction of Lolo Creek. "I was standing in the doorway," recalled McDonald, "and at the cry, 'Nez Perce Outriders!' the Governor nearly upset me in his hurry to get inside."[23]

No sooner had the crisis passed than Governor Potts and others began receiving arrows from a source from which there was no protection: newspaper editors still chafing over the failure to fight the Nez Perce. Robert Fisk of the Helena *Daily Herald*, a longtime foe, called the volunteers "useless as boys with popguns" and, accusing Potts of "negligence," demanded his prompt dismissal. "Dreadful," bemoaned editor James Mills of Deer Lodge's *New North-West*, "the worst thing I have ever known." On July 31, the *Missoulian*'s Chauncey Barbour begged Potts to "wipe out the disgrace that has been put upon us," and to "take command yourself, and don't let good men be humiliated by imbeciles or cowards." Perceiving his political fortunes in rapid decline, a desperate Potts responded by issuing yet another proclamation requesting three hundred volunteers and naming himself commander-in-chief. Calling the Nez Perce "public enemies," Potts declared, "compromise with them is cowardice, and the honor of Montana demands that they shall be fought down."[24]

Two days later, however, when the order was forwarded to General Phil Sheridan, the army again refused permission, and Potts's effort ground to a halt. In disgust, the Helena *Daily Herald* cynically quipped that the federal government "fears volunteers more than Indians." A week later, General William Sherman wired Potts and offered a tentative apology, admitting he had underestimated the situation and endorsing repayment of the volunteers' expenses.[25]

But by then, attacking the Nez Perce was the farthest thing from the governor's mind.

Governor Potts's apostasy came three days after receiving Barbour's letter, when the editor suddenly reversed himself, writing Potts that "if you had taken command of the militia and precipitated hostilities, you would have merited our unmixed condemnation. It is best as it was, and our people now with one accord congratulate themselves that our welfare was in the hands of discreet men. There were some restless spirits among us . . . who have nothing to lose, who would have precipitated a fight even at the expense of seeing this country ravaged."[26]

That Barbour had been one of those very spirits a few days before bothered him not a whit. In truth, the editor was now echoing sentiment first heard from volunteers and increasingly expressed by a majority of settlers throughout Montana. The price of admission to Valhalla was simply too great. A potentially devastating conflict had been avoided, and instead of feeling shame, citizens were applauding, conveniently forgetting that early on they had hotly clamored for war, and probably would have had it if Potts had not hesitated in the face of repeated federal disapproval over raising a militia. By not acting until too late, the governor now found himself back in favor, his actions (or inactions) hailed more for their wisdom than any dishonor they might have brought the territory. His political future secure, Potts went on to serve six more years as governor and become one of the most popular territorial administrators in Montana's history.

The newspaper war, however, was far from over. Unable to sink their verbal talons in Indians or politicians, Montana's editors took on one another. The *New North-West*'s James Mills, incensed at the government's inane Indian policy, "which has drenched the American settlements in blood," uncovered an earlier *Missoulian* editorial written by Barbour advocating the outright pocketing of Indian "money and property" by white Indian agents. Claiming that such "infernal scoundrelism" supported the Nez Perce contention that they had been "outrageously swindled and mistreated in Idaho," Mills labeled Barbour's actions "dishonest, disreputable and atrocious." Barbour retaliated, asserting that Mills "stands before the world a falsifier and perverter of holy truth," a bleeding heart who has taken "the noble red man to his perturbed bosom."[27]

The latter was hardly true, for in early July Mills had written

Governor Potts demanding that if the Nez Perce retreated to Montana, whites should "whip hell out of the red-skins." Still, in the weeks to come, as the Nez Perce distanced themselves from Montana settlements and the war fever subsided, Mills—more than most other Montana editors—softened his view. Attributing the Nez Perce with behavior of the highest character, the editor admitted that "wrong in the outset may not have been wholly theirs."[28]

When the editors tired of one another, their target became the absent U.S. Army, in particular, General Howard. More than a few column inches raked the general for having driven the Nez Perce into Montana. Captain Rawn received his share of brickbats also. Volunteer W. B. Harlan later maintained that a Missoula saloonkeeper had provided a demijohn of whiskey to Rawn, and by the time the bands had evaded his force, "the commanding officer could hardly sit in his saddle and the second in command (Captain Logan) could not, but was hauled out, stretched out upon an army wagon load of tents and bedding." Harlan faulted Rawn's "contemptuous manner that too often characterizes regular army officers in their intercourse with mere citizens" and accused the captain of trying to initiate "another Custer massacre."[29]

Although Harlan appears to have been inordinately venomous toward Rawn, there may have been more than a little truth to some of his allegations. Liquor had reportedly flowed freely in the Seventh Infantry's ranks during the march from Fort Shaw to the Little Bighorn the summer before, markedly increasing as the men approached the Sioux and Cheyenne camp. Rawn had been absent from most of the march, however, suffering from snowblindness. By late August, after the battle of the Big Hole, an exasperated Rawn could take no more and would ask the army for a court of inquiry to clear his name. Colonel Gibbon denied the request, stating his belief that if Rawn's participation in the battle did not vindicate him "from previous aspersions of irresponsible newspapers, it is not thought a Court can do it."[30]

If the Nez Perce were aware of the battle of words being waged over their unwelcome arrival in the Bitterroot Valley, they showed little concern as they camped several miles upstream from the mouth of Lolo Creek and discussed their next move. The day after exiting the Lolo Trail, they encountered six lodges of some ten warriors from Eagle-from-the-Light's band. Among them was a half-breed named Tom Hill, brother of John Hill, recently returned from hunting buffalo on the plains and earlier refused permission by Indian Agent Peter Ronan to camp out of harm's way on the reservation north of Missoula. Some accounts claim these disaffected Nez Perce were physically coerced into joining the bands, but considering their willing participation in subsequent events, this seems unlikely.

Among these Nez Perce was a subchief of mixed blood called Wa-wook-ke-ya Was Sauw, known to whites as Lean Elk, Joe Hale, or more commonly Poker Joe, who had traveled over the Lolo Trail to Idaho a month before, only to learn of the outbreak upon arriving at Kamiah. Not wishing to become involved in hostilities, he and his family quickly returned to the Bitterroot. Along the way, Poker Joe —described by William Cave as speaking passable English, frequently making "a general cleanup" at any gambling, and whose pinto pony often won local horse races—accidently cut his leg with a knife, and he returned to the valley with a limp. Settlers were suspicious and accused him of having been wounded in battle. Now Poker Joe joined up with the buffalo hunters, who decided to accompany the bands since it appeared the fighting had ended.[31]

Also joining the bands at this camp were three young warriors led by Grizzly Bear Youth, who had just returned from scouting for Colonel Nelson Miles in his campaign against the Sioux in eastern Montana. These men advised the chiefs that the most direct route to Canada and away from the U.S. Army was north through Missoula and the Flathead Reservation. According to Duncan McDonald, six chiefs took part in the discussion. White Bird and Red Owl argued for the northern route, while Looking Glass, Rainbow, and Five Wounds favored Montana's Crow country. Joseph refused to endorse either option.

Undoubtedly, Charlot's decision to aid the whites at Lolo Canyon nettled the Nez Perce, and they may have feared additional resistance should they travel north through the reservation. By the end of the council, Looking Glass again prevailed. The bands would go south some seventy-five miles to the head of the Bitterroot Valley, cross over the mountains to the Big Hole Valley, and continue east to the plains.[32]

On July 30, Henry Buck, who with two brothers owned the Buck Brothers' General Store in Stevensville, sat on the fifteen-foot-high sod wall of old Fort Owen just outside of town and watched from across the Bitterroot River as the Nez Perce moved up the valley. Built twenty years earlier as protection against periodic attacks by Blackfeet Indians, the fort had been patched up by volunteers, who renamed it "Fort Brave" due to the secure feeling the structure imparted. The storekeeper took out his pocket watch as the first Indians approached, recording that it took one hour and fifteen minutes for the entire column to pass by. There were no gaps in the line, "no unusual confusion or disorder and none came over on our side of the river."[33]

About three miles farther, the bands stopped and camped. The next morning, Buck and his brothers began moving the goods and supplies they had been storing at the fort back to their store in Stevensville. No sooner had they restocked the shelves than several Nez Perce women accompanied by warriors appeared. "They soon made known their wants to us," said Buck, "saying that they needed supplies and had money to pay for them, but if we refused to sell, would take them anyway." The brothers decided they had little choice and began trading with the bands.

The following morning, Buck was surprised when 115 well-armed warriors rode into town under the leadership of White Bird. "Never shall I forget their formidable appearance, their stern looks, their aggressiveness and their actions, which in themselves placed us immediately on the defensive." All were well dressed with new "showy" blankets, rode the finest of horses, and "seemed to have plenty of money, all in gold coin." Many who came into the store Buck recognized from past visits. Speaking "good English," they told the merchant "that they held no animosity against the white people of the Bitter Root, as they had always treated them kindly. They also told me of their troubles at home, causes leading up to the outbreak, depredations they had committed, and . . . their determination to seek a new home rather than submit to the will of their oppressors."

Waiting outside the store across the street, Chief White Bird "sat on his horse all the time the Indians were in town and talked to them constantly in the Nez Perce tongue." Nearby, Buck observed "a goodly number" of armed but friendly Flatheads, who, fearing trouble, had arrived to defend the whites. When Buck learned another merchant, "in his eagerness for the almighty dollar," was selling whiskey to the bands, he and several citizens marched down the street to the man's store and demanded the barrel. When the merchant resisted, asking by whose authority, the local Methodist minister stepped forward with pistol in hand, leveled it at his head, and exclaimed, "By this authority!" The man knuckled under and the whiskey was loaded on a wagon and taken to the fort for safe keeping.

Soon afterward, Buck observed several drunk warriors outside his store growing ever more belligerent. Suddenly one pointed a rifle at Buck through the window. But before he could fire, a nearby Flathead Indian wrenched the weapon away. Almost simultaneously, White Bird slipped off his horse and, springing on the youth, "gave him a whipping with his quirt and then sent him and his little band up the road to camp." The others soon disbanded, and when all were gone, a shaken Buck locked the door and hurried to Fort Owen. "Upon arriving, my nerves gave way to the awful strain and I collapsed, trembling like a leaf . . . realizing how near we came to the close of our earthly careers."

Henry Buck had no doubt that the settlers owed their lives that day to Chief Charlot and his warriors, calling him a "true friend." Later Howard scoffed at the idea that the Flatheads were anything but "good spies" for the Nez Perce, keeping them informed about the army's movements. But this seems only another instance of Howard's eagerness to spread blame, for the Nez Perce were soon to clearly demonstrate their total ignorance of the army's whereabouts.

After the war, in reward for casting their lot with whites, Charlot and his followers were continually hounded to move to the Flathead Reservation. In 1889, after successfully resisting removal for thirty-four years, desperately poor, hungry, and with many ill, Charlot and his band were assembled and a last attempt was made to convince them to voluntarily leave the valley. "Chief Charlot hung his head in silent meditation for a time," remembered Buck, "then, lifting up his voice, he said, 'I will go.' " Congress delayed authorizing the necessary funds until 1891, forcing the Flatheads, destitute of any means of support, "to live mainly on roots," according to the treaty commissioner who had delivered the ultimatum. Finally the day arrived. As the Indians folded tents, packed belongings, and saddled their horses, citizens of Stevensville lined the main street. One by one the Flatheads filed by, many of them openly weeping, bidding good-bye to whites they had befriended over the years. "It was a sad sight indeed to see those people so ruthlessly driven from our midst," said Henry Buck, "as they went slowly winding their course down the valley, while we stood silently watching them moving away until lost in the distance."

As the Nez Perce moved up the valley, they encountered other whites. John Deschamps, a volunteer who spoke Nez Perce, counted 250 guns among them. Of the two thousand or so head of horses, many "are fine American horses and very valuable." The horses appeared much jaded, however, and Deschamps believed that the bands were making such slow progress in order to fatten their mounts. When they encountered whites, they disarmed them, often taking ammunition and returning the guns. They paid "for everything they got, but if they could not buy, proposed to take it anyhow." Deschamps was amazed at the "many relics of their outlawry in Idaho," including weapons obviously taken from dead settlers and soldiers. One man even tried to sell Deschamps a gold watch "with the former owner's name in it for $30."[34]

Some whites reported they were offered as much as a dollar a cartridge in payment. Prominent Missoula attorney Washington McCormick claimed that "the Indians have plenty of Gold dust, Coin and greenbacks, and have been paying exorbitant prices for flour, Coffee, sugar and tobacco."[35] By one account, the bands spent $1,200 while in the Bitterroot Valley.

Despite Looking Glass's tight reign on young warriors, depredations took place, particularly by Toohoolhoolzote's band, described by Duncan McDonald as "the worst band in the whole camp and a very unruly lot." While passing Myron Lockwood's ranch in the upper valley, some of the band looted the abandoned cabin. Looking

Glass was incensed and demanded as payment from the warriors seven of their own horses, insisting that they be branded with Lockwood's brand before being returned to the settler's corral. Lockwood later made a claim against the government for $1,600, complaining of the horses' poor quality. There is no record that he ever received compensation, and in coming days, Lockwood, like several other valley residents who were reluctant to let the Nez Perce pass by without resistance, would be lucky to get away with his life.[36]

As the bands reached the upper valley, they encountered fewer homesteads. A short distance above the West Fork of the Bitterroot they passed a ponderosa pine, a tree considered sacred by both the Nez Perce and Flatheads. It was known to them as the Medicine Tree, and fur trader Alexander Ross in 1823 was astonished to discover embedded in the tree about five feet from the ground the skull and horns of a wild sheep. "All Indians reverence the celebrated tree," declared Ross, unable to explain the phenomenon, "which they say . . . conferred on them the power of mastering and killing" animals. In time the tree became a "wishing tree," and whenever Indians passed, tokens of colorful ribbon or small gifts were draped over its lower limbs.[37]

It is unknown if offerings were made by the Nez Perce this day, but near here a man named Peopeo Ipsewahk (Lone Bird) claimed he had a premonition. A tragedy would soon befall the bands if they lingered in retreat, and he purportedly warned Looking Glass that "death may now be following our trail." The chief was unalarmed, however, as were most others, convinced that Howard's forces were far behind. "We traveled through the Bitter Root Valley slowly," said Yellow Wolf. "The white people were friendly. We did much buying and trading with them. No more fighting! We had left General Howard and his war in Idaho."[38]

Several miles above Medicine Tree, the bands camped in the high spur valley called Ross Hole. The next day they ascended the seven-thousand-foot Continental Divide separating the Bitterroot from the Big Hole Valley. On the evening of August 7, they reached a traditional camp located along the willow-studded banks of the Big Hole River called Iskumtselalik Pah, named for a small ground squirrel that frequents the high, flat, grassy basin, then considered too harsh an environment for permanent settlement by most whites.[39] After journeying nearly a hundred miles since exiting the Lolo Trail, the bands—now numbering almost eight hundred people after gaining additional family bands both at Weippe Prairie and the Bitterroot—rested and cut fresh pine lodge poles in preparation for the journey east.

On the same day the Nez Perce passed Stevensville, Thomas Sutherland and over seven hundred men of Howard's command were struggling from Kamiah toward Weippe Prairie. Rising at three o'clock—"a most unreasonable hour for those indifferent to worm gathering"—the correspondent was greeted by a drenching rain that had turned the trail into a stream of mud. Those mounted soon became "pedestrians," the trail so "greased" that on one particularly steep downhill section Sutherland found himself embracing a nearby tree "like an island in the tropic sea." As he watched, his miserable horse slipped past, turning crude pirouettes in the mud before finally sliding to a halt. Uphill was hardly better, claimed the bombastic journalist, convinced that none but "a mucilaginous-footed fly could climb over fallen timber and through sloughs of despond." By the time the command completed the fifteen miles to Weippe Prairie and the start of the Lolo Trail, the men were plastered with mud, their boots gushing water like "miniature wells." The next day the sun came out, clouds lifted, and with them everyone's spirits.[40]

Then the men ascended a rise and beheld the sobering and stupendous sea of mountains stretching before them. "A rougher country one could hardly imagine," said Howard. Sutherland agreed, declaring New York's Adirondack Mountains "holes in the ground" by comparison.[41]

The next peak did not appear far away, and a "hog-back" ridge could be seen in the distance leading east beyond the earth's curvature some one hundred miles toward Montana. But such a straight route, admitted Howard, was impossible. The constant up and down between heights "made the distance three times greater than by straight lines," and the ground was "too stony, too steep, the canyon too deep, to attempt the shorter course" along the Lochsa River. As the command struggled up the trail, Howard saw traces of blood left by Nez Perce horses that had been forced over and around rocks and logs. At one point, Ad Chapman turned to the general and remarked that "no man living can get so much out of a horse like an Indian can."[42]

Although the Nez Perce were miles ahead, Indians were constantly in sight. Besides several treaty Nez Perce scouts, twenty Bannocks led by Buffalo Horn recently had joined the command from eastern Idaho. "Buffalo Horn is a small, gracefully-built Indian, with beautiful eyes, not unlike a cross between an eagle's and an antelope's," said Duncan McDonald. "One side of his long hair is bound round with threads of brown bark, which, resembling a buffalo horn, is probably the occasion of his name. He is a very daring rider, a good shot, brave, intelligent and proud as Lucifer. He speaks very little English, but seems to enjoy the society of whites." Wearing soldier's jackets, colorfully decorated with a blue sash of stars and stripes, Sutherland thought the Bannocks all "fiendish and cruel looking as any Apache."[43]

Before long the command settled into a routine: reveille at four, breakfast at five, and march by six. Twelve hours later, they would halt wherever they found themselves, at times, said Sutherland, "on the summit of bald rock mountains, at others on the sides of steep declivities, and at others in rank swamps," having made a daily average of sixteen miles. With tents pitched at steep angles, the men often "slept almost erect or standing on our heads." Rations were monotonous—hardtack, salt pork, occasional potatoes, and coffee. Grass for their stock was practically nonexistent, and it was with the greatest difficulty that they kept their horses moving every day. At first Sutherland had only admiration for his general, saying that for "an old gentleman," Howard had the most "vigorous body in the service." But a few days later, the journalist was beginning to suspect that Howard planned "to kill us all by hard marches before we can perform a similar service for Joseph."[44]

Four days into the march, the command was joined by Captain William Spurgin and fifty "skilled laborers" hired to help clear the trail with axes and crosscut saws. The valued men soon were nicknamed "Spurgin's skillets." As the command gained elevation toward Lolo Pass, Major Mason wrote his wife that the column had entered "the thickest of forests," so that every few feet "there is a log to climb over or crawl around." The men often spread out for miles, but there was hardly any danger of flank attack, maintained the major, for one could "hardly travel a foot off the trail." At one point, Howard suddenly heard gunfire ahead. Believing his scouts had located Indians, the general spurred his horse for miles until he came upon his men standing knee deep in the headwaters of a creek, shooting "the nicest of salmon" with their carbines.[45]

Just before reaching Lolo Pass on August 4, Howard received his first word about the location of the Nez Perce since leaving Kamiah. Into camp rode James Cearley and two companions who had been sent five days earlier with Howard's message for Captain Rawn. "Mr. Cearley's face was cheery," recalled Howard, "but he brought us bad news."[46]

On learning of the Montana volunteers' failure to halt the bands at Lolo Creek, Sutherland was dismayed, terming it "the most disgraceful feature in the entire Nez Perce war." To let them pass unchallenged, said the unsympathetic journalist, was the same as "breathing new life into a corpse." Still seething from criticism heaped on the command by Idaho citizens, Major Mason declared, "It is for such cattle that we risk our lives."[47]

Writing two years after the war, Howard was surprisingly uncritical, saying one could hardly blame "these citizen-volunteers for letting 'General Howard's Indians' go on, provided they promised to do no damage." Had the volunteers stopped the Nez Perce long enough for his command to arrive, he concluded, "it might have saved us a long march, much public abuse, and perhaps have secured to us the enviable reputation of being good Indian fighters."[48]

News of the Lolo Creek debacle was disheartening, but Howard learned from the scouts that Colonel Gibbon was expected soon in Missoula. By splitting his command, allowing the slower infantry to proceed at their own rate while he pressed ahead with the cavalry, Howard rekindled hope of combining forces with Gibbon and bringing the fleeing bands to bay. Two days later, Howard's advance force traveled over the pass and went into camp at Lolo Hot Springs, having taken eight days to travel the same distance the Nez Perce had accomplished in seven. Here the troops rested, bathing and washing their clothes in the steaming water, fishing in Lolo Creek, and allowing their horses to freely pasture for the first time in a week. The break came none too soon, believed Major Mason, particularly for their horses who were in "wretched condition." Surgeon John FitzGerald agreed, writing to Emily that his horse Old Bill "is but the shadow of what he was when I left Lapwai."[49]

The men had hardly begun to relax when a messenger rode in from Gibbon. The colonel had arrived in the Bitterroot Valley and needed a hundred more soldiers to close on the Nez Perce. Howard dashed off a note saying that he was "coming on, as fast as possible, by forced marches, with two hundred cavalrymen" and called for a courier. As darkness fell, Sergeant Oliver Sutherland (no relation to the journalist), along with an Indian scout, rode out of camp and traveled all night, finally reaching the Bitterroot Valley at daybreak. Here the Indian "deserted," claimed Howard, while Sutherland continued south up the valley in pursuit of Gibbon's command.

The sergeant stopped at a homestead near Stevensville to trade his worn mount for a "wild" but fresh one; as soon as he leapt into the saddle the new horse began bucking. As horse and rider careened around the corral, the girth cinch gave way and Sutherland crashed against a post, severely injuring his back. After calming the horse, Sutherland—now in "considerable pain and quite lame"— managed to remount and ride on, finally locating Gibbon on the morning of August 10, three and a half days after leaving Lolo Hot Springs.[50]

But the dispatch that the sergeant carried had come too late to help the men in Colonel Gibbon's command.

8

A little more than a week before the Nez Perce arrived at the Big Hole in early August, Colonel (Brevet General) John Gibbon could be seen tirelessly preparing his Seventh Infantry troops to depart their headquarters at Fort Shaw in northern Montana and commence the long march to Missoula. Although he still occasionally suffered from a severe left shoulder wound that he received fourteen years before at Gettysburg, the fifty-year-old Gibbon appeared to his soldiers as eager as always on the eve of a campaign. But they also thought there was little chance they would actually fight—their commander, many of the men believed, was simply too cautious.

The previous summer, as his column hesitantly approached the Little Bighorn to join Terry, Custer, and Crook in what the army hoped would be the final crushing blow against the Sioux and Cheyenne, a young, newly commissioned army surgeon mistook Gibbon's reluctance for cowardice. "He is trembling & frightened so it is pitiable to see him—If I am to be under the command of such imbecile damned fools I think I'll get out of it as soon as possible."[1] But what the surgeon and others did not realize was that Gibbon had reason to believe the number of Sioux and Cheyenne the army faced was much greater than previously thought, numbering possibly in the thousands. Far from a coward, once in battle John Gibbon was the coolest of warriors, as men who had served under him during the Civil War could attest; he was given the affectionate nickname Old War Horse.

After graduating from West Point and fighting in the Mexican War, Gibbon attained the rank of captain and briefly taught artillery at the U.S. Military Academy. Not unlike other regular officers seeking rapid advancement at the outbreak of the Civil War, he accepted a higher rank as a brigadier general of volunteers. Early in the conflict, General George McClellan lauded Gibbon's "Iron Brigade" as "equal to the best soldiers of any army in the world." Promoted to brevet major general and in command of a full division, Gibbon suffered a grueling defeat at Fredericksburg, taking some forty percent casualties. At the end of the battle, after being severely wounded in the hand, he purportedly shook his bloody fist at his failed command and shouted, "I'd rather have one regiment of my old brigade than to have this whole damned division."[2]

In 1866, the recipient of no less than five brevet promotions, not to mention numerous wounds, he accepted a colonelcy in the regular army. By 1877 he found himself commander of the District of Montana under General Terry's Department of Dakota. One early historian described Gibbon as an example of the army's old school: dependable, straightforward, not full of "fuss and feathers" as were some contemporaries. Like many frontier officers of reduced rank who had once risen high and commanded much responsibility during the Civil War, Gibbon—sporting a graying Vandyke and at an age considered over the hill for a field officer—was also bright, articulate, and anxious to silence critics who deemed him faint-hearted after last summer's disaster. Now, learning of the Nez Perce Indians' "inroad into my district," he lost no time preparing "to move up the Bitterroot after the Nez Perces & fight them if they will stand."[3]

On July 28—the same day the bands skirted Fort Fizzle—Gibbon departed Fort Shaw via the Blackfoot River. Seven days later he arrived in Missoula, many of his men having walked the entire 150 miles. The next day, after enlisting Rawn's command, Gibbon loaded his infantry in commandeered wagons, and the column of 15 officers and 146 men struck off after the Nez Perce.

Near Stevensville, the colonel met briefly with Charlot and tried to induce him to supply scouts. But if the chief was willing to help protect valley whites, he was not eager to do the same for the army, and he "declined very positively to take sides in the contest." Gibbon heard from Father Rivalli, who had spent forty years as a Catholic missionary among the Flatheads, that the Nez Perce are "a very dangerous lot" and quickly dispatched a messenger up the Lolo Trail requesting a hundred more cavalry from Howard. He also learned that the bands were armed with as many as 260 guns and were well supplied with ammunition they had bartered from Bitterroot settlers. Dismissing the claim that the Nez Perce had threatened to take whatever they needed had citizens refused, the colonel condemned the settlers' actions as a "pitiful spectacle." By furnishing fresh supplies, they had enabled the Nez Perce "to continue their flight and their murderous work."

There was no evidence of depredations until the command approached Ross Hole, where the men found Myron Lockwood's ranch "thoroughly gutted." Now with "sad and revengeful eyes," Lockwood joined the column. Here Gibbon also received word that the bands had only hours before left Ross Hole and begun the climb toward the Big Hole; but his advance slowed as it encountered difficulties ascending the spur valley, taking "four hours in pulling up the worst hill I ever saw." Even so, at his present rate of travel, Gibbon knew it was only a matter of time before he eventually caught up. He hoped that the Nez Perce would not discover his presence, claiming that "to *surprise* them" was absolutely vital. Otherwise he feared they would "either hasten their march, or, what was more probable, turn upon us, and with their superior numbers so cripple us to render any further pursuit out of the question."

Before they reached Ross Hole, the column was overtaken by several late-arriving cavalrymen along with two companies of thirty-five volunteers, led by "Captains" John Humble and John Catlin. Both men later claimed that although they were personally opposed to pursuing the fleeing bands, their men had insisted. Humble recalled that Gibbon "appeared rather surly," doubting their worth as soldiers. By Ross Hole, however, the colonel asked Humble to take his men, scout ahead, and engage and halt the Indians until his command could catch up. Humble refused; it was too risky. Then Gibbon tried to embarrass the volunteer by exposing his reluctance in front of his men, prompting Myron Lockwood to step forward, demanding to " 'see the color of the feller's hair' that refused to go. I said, 'Mr. Lockwood, you better look at mine! I am the man! If you get into a scrap with those Indians you will know that you have been somewhere!' " With those prophetic words, Humble mounted his horse and, announcing that he "was not out fighting women and children," rode off toward home alone.[4]

As the command went into camp at the foot of the pass leading to the Big Hole on the evening of August 7, Gibbon sent Lieutenant James H. Bradley and some sixty mounted men, including John Catlin's volunteers, to scout ahead and locate the Indian camp. Ascending the ridge in the dark, the men encountered so much fallen timber that it was daylight before they managed to work their way down to the open basin of the Big Hole River. Bradley suspected he had found the camp when scouts reported that a few miles ahead they had heard sounds of voices and the chopping of wood. Taking two men along, the lieutenant cautiously advanced, climbing a tree to get a better view when he reached the last of the timber. Spread before him in the meadow at the foot of the mountain was the Nez Perce camp.

The men immediately returned to the others, dispatched a messenger to Gibbon, and prepared to remain hidden until the remainder of the command arrived. In the note he sent Gibbon, Bradley admitted that the Indians "have seen my camp, but I do not expect them to attack me."[5] Some Nez Perce later acknowledged they observed white men on the hillside that day, but thought little of it. Since traveling through the Bitterroot, whites had been watching their movements, and they had grown accustomed to the followers. They were confident Bitterroot settlers had been mollified by their pledge of nonviolence in return for safe passage. As for the army, they believed General Howard was still in Idaho.

By one o'clock that afternoon, using draglines to assist the wagons up the rough road to the pass, Gibbon's column crested the ridge and began the descent down Trail Creek, following the route Bradley had taken only hours before. Arriving at the scouts' camp about sundown, and no doubt with the army's favorite method of assault in mind, Gibbon ordered a surprise dawn attack. Each man was given two days' rations, ninety rounds of ammunition, and a cold supper of hardtack and raw salt pork since fires were forbidden. Then they lay down to sleep. But "to sleep, one's mind must be at rest, and mine was very far from it," Gibbon said, unable to shake the belief that the Nez Perce were aware of his movements and were preparing a trap.[6]

At 11 P.M., the command was awakened. Some twenty men stayed behind to guard the wagons, and another squad was ordered to follow with the howitzer and two thousand rounds of rifle ammunition at daybreak. Then Gibbon set off with 149 soldiers and 35 volunteers toward the Indian camp four or five miles away. With no moon and only starlight to guide them, the column noisily stumbled over rocks and fallen timber. About 1 A.M., the men rounded the shoulder of a slope and saw campfires and the outline of tipis at the edge of the meadow below, just beyond where a bench of small lodgepole pines jutted away from the hillside. As the command worked their way down to the trees, Gibbon was suddenly startled when he saw "moving bodies directly in our path on the sidehill"; he realized they had come upon the Indian horse herd. There were several anxious moments when the horses began to neigh and whinny, and dogs in the camp began barking. Soon the remuda moved away up the hillside and the dogs quieted. In the dim starlight, Gibbon could make out the Big Hole River, only a waist-deep creek this high in the valley, meandering between the bottom of the slope and the camp, with the marshy ground between covered with scattered willows.

The men awaited daybreak, shivering in the cold morning air, only a couple hundred yards away from the village. Lieutenant Charles A. Woodruff, the colonel's adjutant, recalled distinctly hearing the occasional bark of a dog, the "cry of a wakeful child, and the gentle crooning of its mother as she hushed it to sleep."[7] Suddenly a soldier struck a match to light his pipe, echoing a similarly thoughtless action at White Bird Canyon two months earlier. Although Gibbon said later that the man deserved to be either "shot on the spot or knocked over with the butt of a musket," an officer quickly extinguished the light and the incident passed undetected. Reflecting on his good fortune to be precisely in the position he desired, Gibbon began worrying about the horse herd, believing it was critical to run off the horses and set the camp afoot. When he told his scout, H. S. Bostwick, to take some men and quietly drive the herd back along the trail, Bostwick—"who had spent all his life among the Indians" —assured Gibbon that the Nez Perce "would never allow the herd to remain unguarded" and that to try to drive them away would certainly "create alarm and render a surprise impossible." Later, when it became obvious the horses had actually not been guarded, Gibbon would regret his decision, saying if he had gone after the herd Bostwick's life would have been saved.

Just before first light, the scout turned to Gibbon and whispered, "If we are not discovered, you will see the fires in the tipis start up just before daylight, as the squaws pile on the wood." Not long after, "the sky in the east began to brighten, the fires began to blaze all through the camp," and Gibbon deployed his men along the bottom of the hill. Soon came whispered orders to begin moving quietly through the brush across the creek bottom toward the camp. When the men heard the first shot, they were to fire three volleys and "charge the camp with the whole line."

Dawn came early that morning for a Nez Perce man nearly blind with old age. Mounting his horse and riding through the camp on his way across the creek in search of the horse herd, he passed women beginning to kindle cooking fires. Some were uncovering small pits where they had buried camas roots the night before in the traditional manner of baking with hot rocks or coals. Nearby lay green lodge poles, freshly cut, peeled, and drying; others supported the eighty-nine tipis that stretched up and down the open ground along the creek.

As the herder rode through camp, there were few people awake. The day before there had been an argument when the *tewat* Pile of Clouds had purportedly warned Looking Glass, saying, "Death is behind us; we must hurry; there is no time to cut lodge poles or hunt!"[8] So much were this man's premonitions valued that some wanted to move immediately. But the bands had been living in brush shelters since their rout at the Clearwater, and the Big Hole was one of the last locations to cut prime poles before heading east. The chief apparently was determined they not arrive in Crow country as paupers. Others suggested sending scouts to watch over the back trail. Several theories have been advanced on why Looking Glass did not encourage this endeavor, which in retrospect appears only prudent. He may have feared more depredations if he allowed warriors to return to the settlements, or he may have felt confident that since whites had offered no resistance, they tacitly approved of the Indians' intentions. Some of his people later accused him of simple stubbornness and arrogance in flaunting his ascendancy over the other headmen. At any rate, the warriors needed fresh horses for scouting and they had been unable to convince an older, wealthy warrior to provide the required mounts. Instead the camp had spent the night running footraces, dancing, and celebrating their successful journey through the Bitterroot.

The horse herder crossed the creek near the north end of camp and began riding through the willows. About halfway to the hillside, he stopped, leaned forward on his horse, and attempted to make out in the dim light what was before him. Three or four volunteers suddenly stood up and fired, killing the man instantly. Up and down the line, the men fired three salvos and, yelling at the top of their lungs, charged through the remaining willows toward the camp.

The surprise was sudden and complete.

The closest troops rushed the center of camp, spreading out as men, women, and children stumbled half-asleep from their tipis, most having difficulty comprehending what was happening. As "squaws yelled, children screamed, dogs barked, horses neighed, snorted, and many of them broke their fetters and fled," recalled an early chronicler of the attack, warriors "usually so stoical [ran] wild and panic-stricken like the rest," too badly frightened to use their weapons.[9] Almost at once, the fighting became hand-to-hand. One soldier reported bewildered warriors running away a short distance, then rushing back to their tipis for weapons; many shot at such close range that their flesh was burned by the powder from the blast.

Entering the camp, Lieutenant Woodruff saw tipis "suddenly light up," shadowy figures momentarily silhouetted as soldiers stepped inside and fired at the occupants, many still under buffalo robes. Before long "the ground [was] covered with the dead and dying, the morning air laden with smoke and riven by cheers, savage yells, shrieks, curses, groans. No one asks or expects mercy—our only commands are: 'Give it to 'em, push 'em, push 'em!' " Later Woodruff stated that Gibbon's plan was to force the Nez Perce out into the open grassland and separate them from their weapons and horses. Beyond that there was no plan. More than one account claims that Gibbon unofficially told his men that "we don't want any prisoners."[10]

When the shooting began, six-year-old Josiah Red Wolf's father covered his son with blankets and told him not to move. "I had no intention of leaving," he said, "but my mother started out of the tipi with my sister on her back. She was shot and my little sister shot right there in the tent and both were killed. . . . I was very frightened as sound of guns and screams of wounded increased . . . but I never moved."[11]

Chief Joseph's ten-year-old nephew Suhm-Keen was asleep under a buffalo robe next to his grandmother Chee-Nah in a tipi at the southern end of the camp. "Suddenly a rifle shot, then neighing of startled horses roused us. Chee-Nah rose to peer out and a bullet pierced her left shoulder . . . blood streamed from the wound as she pushed me from the tipi crying, 'Suhm-Keen run to the trees and hide!' I raced up the slope as fast as I could . . . bullets kept whizzing past clipping off leaves and branches all around me. I was very afraid. . . . Soon some other boys joined me there and we watched trembling at the awful sight below."[12]

Emerging from his lodge unarmed, Wounded Head—who had spared Isabella Benedict during the White Bird battle—was shot point blank in the head, the bullet deflecting off his skull after piercing hair rolled into a tight ball on his forehead. He fell, momentarily stunned, unable to move. As he watched, his two-year-old child crawled from the tipi and began toddling toward some soldiers. His wife ran after the child but before she reached it, a soldier raised his rifle and shot it through the hip. Picking up the child, she turned to flee and was shot in the lower back, the bullet coming out near her breast. Like several other warriors who managed to escape being killed or wounded in those first minutes, when he recovered, Wounded Head stopped fighting long enough to remove his injured family to safety. Although his wife survived, the child died four days later.

Chief White Bird's nephew, who subsequently took the chief's name and was then about ten years old, woke up when the shooting started. His mother grasped his hand, and once outside their lodge, they began running toward the only available protection: the scattered willows the troops had just charged through. As they ran, a bullet cleanly took off her middle finger and end of her thumb, also severing her child's thumb. Reaching the shallow creek, the woman and boy jumped in, squatting down in the cold water with only their heads above the surface. Soon several other women and children joined them and huddled in the creek, young White Bird recalling that "one little girl was shot through the under part of her upper arm. She held the arm up from the cold water, it hurt so. It was a big bullet hole. I could see through it."[13]

Nearby on shore, a woman shot through the left breast "pitched into the water and I saw her struggling. She floated by us and mother caught and drew the body to her. She placed the dying woman's head on a sandbar just out of the water. She was soon dead. A fine-looking woman, and I remember the blood coloring the water." Suddenly soldiers appeared on the bank. One pointed and they all began aiming at the women and children in the creek. "Mother ducked my head under water. When I raised out, I saw her hand up. She called out, 'Women! Only women!' When mother called those words, the order must have been given those soldiers to quit. They brought their guns back, and turned the other way."[14]

Young White Bird and his companions were fortunate. From most accounts, it appears soldiers made little distinction between men and the camp's women and children. There were exceptions, such as when a small girl saw a soldier pick up a baby lying beside its dead mother and hand it to another woman who was wounded, and again when an officer stopped his men from killing two women. But by and large, the greatest number of victims in those first minutes were women and children. Nez Perce claimed a soldier entered one lodge and killed five children attempting to hide under a buffalo robe. Corporal Charles Loynes of Company I recalled seeing a young woman with a baby "lying dead with the baby on her breast, crying as it swung its little arm back and forth—the lifeless hand flapping at the wrist broken by a bullet." Not far away a woman who had given birth the night before was killed in a tipi along with another woman serving as her nurse, still holding the baby in her arms. "Its head was smashed," said Yellow Wolf, "as by a gun breech or boot heel."[15]

Gibbon would say later that in the poor morning light, identification was difficult and thus the killing of women and children was "unavoidable." When tipis were broken into, "squaws and boys from within fired on the men, and were of course fired on in turn." Doubtless this was sometimes true, considering the nature of the attack, particularly for those who refused to accept a passive death.

Wounded Head recalled seeing one woman charged by a soldier with a bayonet on his rifle, seize the gun, wrest it from him, and throw him to the ground. The man jumped up but was shot and killed by a nearby warrior.

At least one soldier, Private Charles Alberts, entered a tipi only to find himself surrounded by women and children coming at him with knives and hatchets. Grasping the barrel of his rifle, the private "dealt blows fast and vigorous, right and left," until he managed to fight his way back outside. Private George Lehr was struck in the head by a glancing bullet and knocked unconscious. Recovering, he realized a woman was dragging him by the heel, an action that ceased when he "secured a rifle and dispatched her."[16]

Gibbon's further claim that "the poor terrified and inoffensive women and children crouching in the brush were in no way disturbed" appears less accurate. Later he would say that when women begged for mercy and held their babies out to him, "it touched his heart" enough to spare them. With few exceptions, such protection has been emphatically denied by Indian as well as some white survivors.

Eelahweemah (About Asleep), a child of fourteen, hid in the creek with his younger brother and five women and watched as all the women, including his mother, were killed by soldiers shooting at them from the shore. As the women fell one by one, the two boys scrambled out of the water and escaped. That the creek offered scant protection was echoed by Corporal Loynes, who witnessed several women throw a buffalo robe into the water, then submerge themselves beneath it. But they had to have air, so where the buffalo hide was slightly raised, said Loynes, "a bullet at that spot would be sufficient for the body to float down the stream."[17]

Others tried hiding in willows along the bank. One woman lay down with her arm around a young girl. "Bullets cut twigs down on us like rain. The little girl was killed. Killed under my arm," recalled the woman in disbelief many years afterward, as if the horror of what had happened was still unthinkable. Decades later when historian Lucullus Virgil McWhorter began collecting Nez Perce accounts of the battle, those who were children at the time were often the only witnesses willing to relate their stories, many of the older people finding it still too painful to speak. Returning to the Big Hole with McWhorter some fifty years after the war, Yellow Wolf was frequently overcome with both anger and grief, able to account for the deaths of women and children only by saying that "some soldiers acted with crazy minds."[18]

During those first few minutes of attack, a brief defense started when twenty warriors took cover behind some willows and began shooting into the charging troops near the center of the camp. Corporal Loynes was wading the creek when a fellow soldier a few feet away suddenly "leaped into the air giving the most awful yell and dropped dead."[19]

Leading the initial attack on the right or southern flank, the soldiers of Company A had a somewhat longer distance to travel than others, arriving just in time to catch the Nez Perce defenders from behind. The company captain, William Logan—described as an Irishman with "much of the rollicking humor and warm geniality of his race" and who had played a role in the Fort Fizzle affair—was three years away from retirement and still "suffering the recent death" of both his daughter and granddaughter (the wife and child of another officer in the battle). Now, as Logan led the charge into the camp, warriors turned and fired, killing him instantly.[20]

Rainbow, considered by many in the bands as their greatest warrior, was one of the first to die, shot through the heart. At least one warrior—Wounded Head—was so shocked by his death that he lost the will to fight, making his way to the yet unattacked northern part of the camp. Two Moons recalled that Rainbow had told him, "I have the promise given that in any battle I engage in after the sunrise, I shall not be killed. I can therefore walk among my enemies. I can face the point of the gun. My body no thicker than a hair, the enemies can never hit me, but if I have any battle or fighting before the sunrise, I shall be killed."[21]

Such belief—along with a taboo that served as an explanation should it fail—was not unusual among warriors, although it was often met with derision from whites eager to demonstrate its fallibility. No doubt, an unshakable belief in their own invincibility gave warriors a fearlessness their enemies found intimidating, thus enhancing their chances of survival—and perpetuation of the belief—in battle, where fear itself is often the greatest killer. Beyond that, such stories are difficult for non-Indian minds to cogently explain. Yellow Wolf, whose entire account of the war resonates with such forthright and uninhibited candor, is not easily dismissed when he relates the story of a "very old man" who sat outside of his tipi throughout the battle smoking a pipe.

> He was shot many times! As he sat on his buffalo robe, one soldier shot him. He did not get up. Others shot him. Still he sat there. Others shot him. He did not move. Just sat there smoking as if only raindrops struck him! Must have been twenty bullets entered his body. He did not feel the shots! After the battle, he rode horseback out from there. He grew well, but died of sickness in the Eeikish Pah [Indian Territory] where he was sent after the surrender. The wounds did not seem to grow. It was just as you see mist, see fog coming out from rain. We saw it like smoke [steam] from boiling water, coming out of his wounded body.[22]

Another warrior who died early into the battle was Wahlitits, one of the original young trio whose violence precipitated the war. He and his pregnant wife took refuge in a small depression near the creek. According to a relative, when the soldiers drew close Wahlitits told his wife to flee. As she rose to go, a bullet slammed into her shoulder, knocking her down. Wahlitits killed one of the soldiers just before another shot the warrior through the chin, killing him instantly. Struggling to aim her husband's rifle, the woman managed to shoot the soldier but others quickly returned the fire, a bullet entering her throat, passing down her spine, and exiting near her lower back. Found after the battle, Yellow Wolf said she was "lying across her husband's body as if protecting him."[23]

Twenty minutes into the battle, soldiers had gained control of the southern end of the village, consisting mostly of the bands of Joseph, White Bird, and Poker Joe. Those who escaped made their way toward the camp's northern end. One was Seeskoomkee, the limbless ex-slave who had warned of the soldiers' approach at the White Bird battle, observed alternately rolling and hobbling on his one hand and knees until he gained a shallow depression at the edge of camp. Also seen was Joseph, carrying his two-month-old daughter, who once again had managed to escape from soldiers at the seemingly last possible moment.

Confident the Nez Perce were demoralized and near defeat, Gibbon now made a blunder, ordering his men to stop pursuing them, sweep the nearby willows for survivors, and torch the camp. Soldiers began setting fire to several tipis, but the morning dew had dampened the skins and with the lodge poles still green, the men succeeded in burning only eight tipis. One woman, Owyeen (Wounded), later recalled that children who had avoided detection earlier by hiding under buffalo robes in one of the tipis began screaming when it went up in flames.

Soon Gibbon learned that the attack on the northern part of the village (his left line) had failed when Lieutenant James Bradley had fallen early in the charge, shot through the heart. Without a leader, the men had simply drifted back toward the center of the line, leaving that part of the camp unchallenged.[24]

When Gibbon failed to press his advantage, White Bird and Looking Glass began exhorting the survivors, their loud voices heard even by soldiers at the far end of the camp. One warrior recalled that White Bird was enraged, shouting, "Why are we retreating? Since the world was made brave men fight for their women and children. Are we going to run to the mountains and let the whites kill our women and children before our eyes? It is better we should be killed fighting. Now is our time. Fight!"[25]

For warriors who had the desire, the difficulty was finding weapons. When the battle started, Yellow Wolf had been sleeping unarmed in a tipi in the northern part of the camp. At the first shots he ran toward the fighting, unsuccessfully imploring several returning wounded warriors to give him their weapons. Finally he saw an injured soldier "crawling like a drunken man." He clubbed the man with his *kopluts* and took his gun. "I saw teeth loose in his mouth, and easily took them out. I had never seen such teeth," recalled the startled warrior.[26] Following Yellow Wolf's example, or using their own or borrowed weapons, some thirty or forty warriors began attacking the soldiers with telling accuracy. "At almost every crack of a rifle," said Gibbon, "some member of the command was sure to fall."

Spurring his horse across the creek toward the camp, Gibbon dismounted, realizing that in the withering fire of the counterattack, "horseback was not the healthiest position to be maintained." As the colonel watched the fight, a fellow officer remarked that Gibbon's horse's leg had been broken by a bullet. Only then did Gibbon realize that "the same bullet which broke my horse's leg passed through mine" as well. The colonel promptly sat down on the bank and began washing his wounded thigh. As the Nez Perce approached, Gibbon saw several warriors moving to cut off his line of escape back toward the hillside. With bullets coming "from all directions" and finding his position "untenable" and sure to result in "increased losses," Gibbon called a retreat.

Encouraged by the soldiers' withdrawal, the warriors quickly charged. Grizzly Bear Youth remembered one particularly "tall, ugly looking man" who, suddenly turning around and cursing, "made for me," swinging his gun by the barrel and attempting "to strike me over the head with the butt end. I did the same thing. We both struck and each received a blow on the head. The volunteer's gun put a brand on my forehead that will be seen as long as I live. My blow on his head made him fall on his back. I jumped on him and tried to hold him down. The volunteer was a powerful man. He turned me over and got on top. He got his hand on my throat and commenced choking me. I was almost gone and had just strength left to make signs to a warrior, who was coming up, to shoot him. This was Red Owl's son, who ran up, put his needle gun to the volunteer's side and fired. The ball passed through him and killed him. But I had my arm around the waist of the man when the shot was fired, and the ball after going through the volunteer broke my arm."[27]

The retreat became a rout when the soldiers crossed open ground and, in the intense crossfire, left their wounded to make their way as best they could. When volunteer Tom Sherrill jumped into the creek and began wading across, he was startled to see a white girl about sixteen years old cowering in the waist-deep water. No one else remembered her during the battle, although an unknown young woman of light complexion had been reported traveling with the bands as they passed through the Bitterroot Valley.[28]

Approaching the hillside, a young corporal cried out, "To the top of the hill—to the top of the hill, or we're lost!" A limping Gibbon, who wrote later that "the top of the hill was the last place I wanted to go or *could* go," reminded the man amid a few nervous chuckles from soldiers within earshot "that the commanding officer was still alive" and ordered the men to the nearby timbered bench.

Here on about an acre of ground, the command dug in behind pine trees some three or four inches in diameter—trees, Gibbon remarked, that now appeared unusually "large" considering the circumstances. With Nez Perce snipers in trees on the hillside above them, the men frantically dug rifle pits with their trowel-shaped bayonets—large, unwieldy instruments soon to be discarded by the army (although Gibbon credited them with saving his force from annihilation). Others used tin cups, knives, and even an empty canteen split in half to scoop and dig. Corporal Loynes recalled that one man would scrape up the dirt while every second man continued to fire. Those lucky enough to drop behind logs and stumps, said Gibbon, were "millionaires (for the time being) in safety." For volunteer Luther Johnson, this particular wooded spot was intimately familiar.

In the 1860s, he had prospected the area for gold but had found nothing. Now Johnson and another volunteer fought for their lives from the very prospect hole he had dug years earlier.

As the men prepared for the attack they knew was coming, Gibbon's attention was suddenly drawn to the "wail of mingled grief, rage, and horror which came from the camp four or five hundred yards from us when the Indians returned to it and recognized their slaughtered warriors, women and children." Reentering the destroyed camp and seeing their dead, men and women alike were overwhelmed with grief, many falling to the ground and openly weeping for those lost. Owyeen was shocked by dead children she earlier had heard screaming in a burning tipi. "We found the bodies all burned and naked," the woman said, "lying where they had slept or fallen before reaching the doorway."[29]

In a shallow ravine, Duncan McDonald reported that several women were found killed, one with the bodies of three dead children cradled in her arms. Pahit Palikt, a young boy about ten years old, wandered through the camp and, discovering dead women and children lying about, wondered why so many were asleep. Walking among the smoldering tipis, Yellow Wolf saw the bodies of soldiers and warriors, some in deathly embrace. "Wounded children screaming with pain. Women and men crying, wailing for their scattered dead! The air was heavy with sorrow. I would not want to hear, I would not want to see, again."[30]

Warriors lost no time stripping dead soldiers of their weapons to use on those yet alive. Yellow Wolf stopped by one man sprawled face down with a knife still gripped in his hand. "When I stooped to get the gun, the soldier almost stabbed me. His knife grazed my nose. I jumped five, maybe seven, feet getting away from that knife. Approaching, I struck him with my *kopluts*. He did not raise up." The Nez Perce discovered other whites across the battlefield who were still alive. One young soldier, Francis Gallagher, listed as a musician on Gibbon's roster, was shot through both lower legs. Unable to retreat with the others, he was found later with his throat "stabbed in three places."[31]

When volunteer Campbell Mitchell was discovered, some Nez Perce suggested questioning him; others wanted to kill him immediately. One account has Mitchell telling his interrogators that "Howard would be there in a few hours and that volunteers were coming from Virginia City to head the Indians off." (It is unclear how the volunteer would have known this since the command had received no messages from Howard.) While the man was talking, a sobbing woman who had lost both her children and a brother in the fight walked up and slapped Mitchell in the face. When the volunteer kicked the woman in return, a nearby warrior promptly shot him. Another account claims that Mitchell "died a more fearful death," implying he was tortured, and years later Corporal Loynes maintained that he could plainly hear "the cries of our wounded when the Indians finished them." But Yellow Wolf denies this happened, saying that all prisoners were quickly killed by warriors furious at what the "cowardly coyotes" had done. Whatever the truth, it appears that of the whites who fell in the initial battle, as many as seven may have been found wounded but still alive by the Nez Perce. None survived.[32]

Unsure of the Indians' intent, Gibbon and several officers ventured to the edge of the trees to reconnoiter in the direction of the village. Here the bench fell away sharply fifteen or twenty feet down a steep embankment to the creek and willows below. As the men watched, they could see warriors "creeping forward through the brush," and several stood up and commenced firing. Standing next to Gibbon, Lieutenant William English suddenly "fell backward with a cry," wounded by a sniper from behind, the bullet entering his back and lodging in his lower abdomen. The soldiers "now began to fire rapidly," said Gibbon, "and were excitedly throwing away their ammunition."

As the men hunkered down, some sixty warriors led by Ollokot took up positions around them. There they kept up a fierce barrage of both yelling and gunfire, forcing the soldiers to remove their hats to avoid drawing fire. Particularly vexing were several sharpshooters who positioned themselves both in and behind large trees about 150 yards away. One of these snipers wounded no less than seven men before being felled; Lieutenant Woodruff recalled his dread at hearing the "dull thud" the bullets made hitting flesh. In addition to the sniper attacks, the soldiers' line was constantly being tested. Sergeant Edward Page was shot and killed by a mounted warrior who brazenly rode out of the willows. When he reappeared a moment later in an attempt to repeat his success, the soldier next to Page shot the warrior dead.

South of the siege area, a shallow draw led up from the creek. Whites were startled when a lone warrior on foot suddenly made a suicidal charge up the draw, nearly penetrating their line before enough guns managed to kill him. The man's name was Pahkatos Owyeen (Five Wounds), and he had only recently learned of the death of his closest friend, Rainbow. "A man of strong feeling, strong in battle," Ollokot's wife Wetatonmi described him. "Never was known to cry and show tears. Rainbow lay dead where the fighting had been hard. He and Pahkatos had grown up together. Always went together when hunting buffaloes or on warpath. Had never been separated for long. He cried over his friend. Cried long. He said, 'This sun, this time, I am going to die. My brother is killed, and I shall go with him.' "[33]

Also killed early during the siege was Sarpsis Ilppilp, who with Wahlitits had murdered the first whites in Idaho. According to Nez Perce accounts, the warrior had taken up a position behind a boulder only a few yards from the defended line, drawing much fire after wounding or killing several soldiers. A single bullet struck him in the neck, cutting one strand of a tight-fitting wampum necklace he was wearing, his talisman against death. He was also wearing a white wolfskin cape which had special spiritual powers. At least eight warriors tried to recover the body and cape, and several were wounded before one, himself shot in the attempt, finally succeeded. Because he was injured in the back of the neck, the man's hands reportedly shook uncontrollably for the remainder of his life.

Of the four horses taken into battle, only Lieutenant Woodruff's reached the siege area alive, but the animal thrashed about so much from its wounds that when it began to draw fire, the men shot it. As the morning wore on, several Nez Perce positions became preferred targets for soldiers. One large boulder in particular sheltered a warrior calling on his *wyakin* for success, attracting considerable fire from those unnerved by his constant chanting (the rock's bullet pockmarks are still quite visible). Between brief lulls in the fighting, men treated their wounds. Without a surgeon or medical supplies, most made bandages out of shirttails after resorting to that dubious but time-honored frontier practice of spitting tobacco juice into their wounds. Others more desperate may have resorted to another technique: splitting a rifle cartridge, pouring black powder into the wound and striking a match, cauterizing the blood vessels to stop the bleeding.[34]

At one point in the fight, Private Charles Alberts crawled up to Lieutenant Woodruff, exposed the wound in his left breast, and asked the lieutenant if he would live. "Knowing from the bubbles of air in the flowing blood that the shot had entered the lungs," said Woodruff, "I told him to let me see his back, where I found the ball had come out. I described the nature of the wound and said: 'Alberts, you have a severe wound, but there is no need of your dying if you have got the nerve to keep up your courage.' Two years later Alberts, a hotel runner, was the first man I met in getting off a train at St. Paul [Minnesota]. He rushed up to me, grasped my hand and luggage and said, 'You see, I had the nerve, Lieutenant.' "[35]

Not long into the siege, the soldiers were momentarily heartened to hear the distinct sound of two shots from the howitzer. Gibbon, however, quickly realized the danger when no more rounds followed. The distant sound of gunfire and yelling soon confirmed his fears that warriors had captured both the gunnery piece and the commands' reserve rifle ammunition. Following Gibbon's orders to start after the command at daybreak, six soldiers and two civilians had led mules hauling the wheeled howitzer and a horse laden with ammunition to a nearby hillside position. When they saw Indians approaching, the men managed to get off two shots before the warriors closed in. Two privates immediately fled, Gibbon saying later that "they never stopped until they had put a hundred miles between themselves and the battlefield." One man was killed and two were wounded. Private John Bennett, riding one of the team mules, became entangled in the harness when the animal was wounded, landing underneath as it fell. Cutting himself loose and frantically prodding the dying animal with his knife, he managed to roll free and escape back down the trail along with the other survivors and eventually reached the wagon train camp.

For the warriors' trouble, they managed to capture two thousand rounds of .45/70 caliber ammunition, usable in Springfield rifles taken from dead soldiers. Exactly what happened to the howitzer is disputed, Gibbon claiming his men hid the friction primers necessary to fire the piece before abandoning it, the Nez Perce saying they found the cannon in working order, then dismantled and hid it lest it fall back into the soldiers' hands. The howitzer was found later at the bottom of the slope and resides today in the battlefield's visitor center.

As Gibbon was fretting about the howitzer and ammunition, his men suddenly smelled smoke. Soon "a line of burning grass made its appearance on a hill close by, sending its stifling smoke ahead of it." As the men prepared for a charge by the warriors, those with revolvers placed them close at hand "as a final guard against torture" should their defense be overrun. Gibbon recalled that only a year before, Looking Glass's band had visited Fort Shaw on their return from hunting buffalo and, at the behest of "ladies at the post," had given a "sham-fight" exhibition. Lighting a grass fire, "one side charged under the supposed cover of smoke and drove the other party from the field." Now, with yells of these same warriors growing ever louder just behind the smoke screen, the identical technique "meant possibly defeat and death, perhaps worse." But it was not to be. Soon the wind shifted and gradually died down, the grass fire "vanished," and with it the threat of a charge.

By late afternoon, the shooting fell off. A quick count of remaining ammunition showed at least nine thousand rounds had been expended by Gibbon's men since that morning. Peering through the trees, soldiers could see the Nez Perce packing up their camp and moving away from the battlefield. The injured were placed on travois or tied to horses. One volunteer judged the camp had been "badly crippled" by the number of animals he saw burdened with wounded. Still, the men feared to move. Lingering behind, their number unknown to the soldiers, some thirty Nez Perce continued to exact a toll. By nightfall an occasional shot was just enough to keep the men awake, most having slept no more than a few hours during the last two days or eaten since the previous night. One exhausted volunteer, who shared a rifle pit with twenty-year-old Tom Sherrill, managed to fall asleep lying on his back, snoring, his mouth open. Sherrill was astonished that anyone could sleep when a bullet struck nearby, filling the man's mouth with dirt and gravel. After coughing and gasping for a few moments, he rolled over and promptly fell back asleep. Moments later, a bullet passed through Sherrill's hat, "cutting a trail through my hair and just missing the piece of ivory in which I had been trying to carry my brains around with me for the past twenty years. . . ."[36]

Hunger kept some awake. Hardtack carried in their packs had dissolved when they waded the creek, and men began to eye Lieutenant Woodruff's dead and bloated horse. Unwilling to risk a fire, some crawled to the animal and sliced strips of muscle from its haunches, eating the meat raw. Others preferred to remain hungry.

Of the 183 soldiers and volunteers who attacked the camp that morning, 7 out of 17 officers had been killed or wounded, with a total of 29 men dead and 40 wounded (two mortally), many severely, with more than one wound. Lieutenant English was in constant pain, wounded in the wrist, the scalp, the ear, and through the bowels. To quiet the pleading of the wounded for water, three men slipped down the gulch to fill canteens, volunteer Homer Coon saying that "as thirsty as I was, I actually forgot in my excitement to get a drink myself." Throughout the night, Corporal Loynes recalled the agonizing cries of the wounded man next to him in his rifle pit, drummer Thomas Stinebaker, "moaning from pain and crying for water until he died near dawn."[37]

Sometime during the night, between five and seven volunteers slipped away and headed back to the Bitterroot Valley. Becoming disoriented in the dark, they eventually stumbled into Howard's command the following day. After leaving Howard, the men apparently lost their way in the mountains and didn't arrive back in the settlements until almost two weeks later.

Believing the attack would be renewed in the morning, Gibbon—that day marking his thirtieth year in the army—sent several messengers for help. One man carried a message for Howard that Gibbon had scribbled on a small scrap of paper, briefly describing the battle, the command's location, and the need for both "medical assistance and assistance of all kinds." A fervent postscript read: "Hope you will hurry to our relief." The man failed to discover Howard's forward detachment along the back trail but did find Major Mason and the remainder of the cavalry the following evening. Without delay, the major dispatched two of the command's surgeons to aid Gibbon.[38]

Two other men were sent separately to Deer Lodge that night, volunteer Billy Edwards slipping through the Indian line and arriving first in what must have been an incredible journey. Alternately running and walking some forty miles, he came to a homestead and obtained a horse, then rode the remaining forty miles, arriving in Deer Lodge thirty-four hours after leaving the command. One of the messages Edwards carried was addressed to Governor Potts and implied certain defeat, describing the besieged troops and saying, "We need a doctor and everything (food, clothing, medicines and medical attendance). Send us such relief as you can." With a telegraph office at Deer Lodge, this brief first news of the fight was wired to Helena and that same afternoon appeared in a special edition of the Helena *Daily Herald*.[39]

Gibbon's message to General Terry telegraphed that same day was just as terse, if not entirely the whole truth:

Big Hole Pass, August ninth

Surprised the Nez Perces camp here this morning, got possession of it after a hard fight in which both myself, Captain Williams and Lieuts Coolidge, Woodruff and English wounded, the last severely.[40]

Terry passed on this message, along with the first newspaper reports, to General Sheridan, who in turn telegraphed the adjutant general in Washington, D.C. All of the generals, upon hearing two seemingly disparate accounts, chose to disbelieve the published version in favor of Gibbon's telegram, so much did they doubt the possibility of what had happened to his command. Not until the second messenger straggled into Deer Lodge with additional details were they forced to admit the newspaper had been correct.

Just after dawn on the second morning of the siege, both Indians and soldiers alike were startled when a white man suddenly appeared on horseback and charged past the warriors into safety behind the soldiers' defenses. A moment later the Nez Perce heard loud cheering, which they understood to mean that reinforcements were coming. By now, probably fewer than a dozen warriors remained, most having slipped away during the night to join the fleeing camp some dozen miles to the south. Asked later why they declined to press the attack, Yellow Wolf responded that their obligation lay with their families. "If we killed one soldier, a thousand could take his place. If we lost one warrior, there was none to take his place." In his official report, Gibbon claims the Indians continued to fire upon his men until late into the night of the second day, but Yellow Wolf later derided this, saying with probably some truth, "Afraid of armed warriors, they lay too close in dirtholes to know when we left!" Other testimony and events occurring after the arrival of the messenger lend support to Yellow Wolf's statement that after a cursory look down the back trail that morning, these last warriors fired a "goodbye" salvo at the troops and soon left to join the bands.[41]

The courier, a civilian sent by Howard, delivered the welcome news that the general and a relief detachment were only a day away. Gibbon became concerned, however, when the man reported he had not seen the command's wagon train camped some five miles up the trail. Tensions eased somewhat when Sergeant Sutherland finally appeared a short time later. Stumbling on Gibbon's wagons the day before and warned of the ongoing fight ahead, the sergeant had elected not to carry his message, now nearly four days old, to Gibbon until the following morning. The camp had been moved off the trail after the return of the howitzer fight survivors, accounting for the first messenger's inability to find it. Not long after Sutherland arrived (unchallenged by warriors if they were present), Gibbon sent a detail to escort the wagons to the siege area. Why the Nez Perce had not found the men and wagons when they searched the back trail that morning is puzzling, although it appears they may have come close, missing them by only several hundred yards.

That the men refused to abandon the wagons in light of the Indian force they knew was only several miles away does not deny the fact that they feared attack. Lieutenant Joshua Jacobs's servant, William Woodcock (some blacks continued to serve former white masters long after the Civil War ended, an accommodation the U.S. Army conveniently overlooked for officers), was put on guard duty one night with the lieutenant's shotgun loaded with birdshot. Described as "a vigilant sentry, but a poor shot," Woodcock is said to have mistaken the wagon master for an Indian and challenged the man and, without waiting for a reply, emptied both barrels at him. When the smoke cleared, the charge of buckshot had torn up "the ground and cut down the brush," but the wagon master was unhurt.[42]

When the wagons rolled in late that afternoon, the men cheered, built fires to cook salt pork, and tried to make the wounded more comfortable. Many had suffered throughout the heat of the day, the air thick with flies on the dead and wounded. One man later claimed he lost several inches of bone in his wounded arm to maggots. For the first time in nearly sixty hours, the exhausted men slept.

Since sending Sergeant Sutherland with his message for Gibbon, General Howard had moved quickly to close the gap between the two commands. When he arrived at the terminus of the Lolo Trail in the Bitterroot Valley on August 8, he learned that Colonel Wheaton's force, commanded by Captains Perry and Whipple and due to arrive in Missoula via the Mullan Road, was so hopelessly behind that they would never effect a timely rendezvous. Thus he sent Lieutenant Harry Bailey back with a message ordering them to return to Idaho.[43]

On the day Gibbon attacked the village, Howard's command traveled thirty-four miles up the Bitterroot. The next morning, the general left orders for Mason to follow with the remainder of the cavalry. Taking his staff, twenty cavalrymen and seventeen Bannock scouts, Howard pushed over the pass into the Big Hole Valley, remembered by saddle-sore Thomas Sutherland as a "tremendous ride" of fifty-three miles. That night the volunteers who had abandoned Gibbon walked into camp. Gibbon "has lost half his men," they told Howard. "It was going hard with him when we left." Howard recorded that "no offer of favor or money . . . could induce one of those brave men to go back, and guide us to the battlefield." The general ordered additional campfires struck to give the appearance of more men in case Indian scouts were nearby. Then he dispatched a runner back down the trail to tell Mason to bring up the troops.[44]

The next day, Howard and his party of about forty men rode into Gibbon's camp. The camp appeared more like a hospital than a fortification, said Howard. Near one corner "reclined the wounded commander. His face was very bright, and his voice had a cheery ring as he called out, 'Hallo, Howard! Glad to see you!' "[45]

There was little anyone could do until morning when Surgeon John FitzGerald and another doctor arrived and began ministering to the wounded. A few hours later, Major Mason and the remainder of the cavalry finally caught up. Although Gibbon would soon report that there was but one man "who could have been benefited by the presence of a surgeon with our command," FitzGerald wrote to Emily that upon reaching the camp, "we found a horrible state of affairs. There were 39 [actually 40] wounded men without Surgeons or dressings, and many of them suffering intensely." FitzGerald also observed that had not the messenger arrived alerting the remaining warriors that help was rapidly approaching, "I think it probable they [the warriors] would have finally annihilated them. As it was, he [Gibbon] 'stood them off' for two days, when all but a few warriors left." Such was hardly the case if Nez Perce sources are to be believed, but this conviction undoubtedly gave FitzGerald and others of Howard's command satisfaction that their arduous journey had not been in vain.[46]

That day the survivors set about burying their twenty-nine dead —two officers, twenty-one enlisted men, five civilian volunteers, and one army scout. At the same time, the Bannock scouts began to disinter the Nez Perce dead (apparently without objection from Howard), scalping and mutilating the bodies. Tom Sherrill watched as they first scalped one dead warrior, then "kicked him in the face, and jumped on his body and stamped him. In fact they did everything mean to him that they could."[47]

When it comes to an accurate count of the exposed bodies, virtually no two white reports agree. With the exception of warriors who fell too close to the soldiers' defenses, all corpses had been buried by the bands before leaving the battlefield, for the Nez Perce believed that burial was highly desirable for passage to a spiritual hereafter.

Although some graves were concealed, most had been hastily dug and were shallow. Many of the bodies were wrapped in buffalo robes. Several had been laid in a row under an eroded creek bank, and then the bank had been collapsed, the earth barely covering the corpses. When the Bannocks were done, Amos Buck, brother of Henry and a participant in the fight, counted sixty-seven bodies, although he noted that additional corpses he had not seen were reported downstream of the battlefield. Howard claimed his men reburied the exhumed dead, but ill-equipped for digging, the effort was at best superficial.

Gibbon officially reported eighty-three dead Nez Perce were found, with six additional bodies located later in a nearby ravine. Some said more had died, one white source claiming 116 corpses and another as many as 208. A few days after the battle, Surgeon FitzGerald wrote to Emily that he had seen "30 dead bodies (mostly women and children)." FitzGerald went on to disparage Gibbon's official denial of harming women and children who had taken shelter in the creek and willows after the initial charge. "I was told by one of General Gibbon's officers that the squaws were not shot at until two officers were wounded by them, and a soldier or two killed. Then the men shot every Indian they caught sight of—men, women, and children."[48]

Almost as conflicting are Nez Perce accounts of the number dead. Wounded Head claimed sixty-three died (ten women, twenty-one children, and thirty-two men). After interviewing survivors in Canada the following year, Duncan McDonald reported seventy-eight dead, of whom thirty were warriors. Closer to this estimate, Chief Joseph put the number at eighty to thirty warriors and some fifty women and children.[49]

Some of these inconsistencies may be attributed to the confusion immediately following the fight, as the bands quickly buried their dead and fled the battlefield. Several youths seeking shelter from the fight became separated from the bands and made their way back to Idaho and eventual imprisonment, thus avoiding an after-battle head count.[50] Also, the wounded who subsequently expired along the trail may not have been tallied among those who died on the battlefield. Whatever the actual number, most authorities believe between seventy and ninety Nez Perce died as a result of the battle, of whom probably no more than thirty-three were warriors.

Perhaps more revealing than body counts is how whites viewed the attack. It was "the most gallant Indian fight of modern times," acclaimed the *Missoulian,* one that will forever "cause a thrill of pride to every Montanian." From his headquarters in Minnesota and anxious to regain lost ground after his deplumation the summer before, General Terry proclaimed Gibbon's effort a "brilliant success." Expressing "feelings of great admiration" for those soldiers and volunteers who waged the battle, Terry sidestepped any discussion of Gibbon's methods, seizing the opportunity to blame congressionally mandated troop reductions resulting in an army so emasculated that its "distinguished" commander had to fight "rifle in hand" like a common private. Certainly Gibbon's actions did not hurt his chance for promotion; he went on to serve as commander of the Department of Columbia and the Division of the California.[51]

In a statement released three days after the fight, Terry's superior, Phil Sheridan, sounded only moderately less upbeat, terming the battle a "substantial success." Interviewed later by a gadfly New York *Herald* reporter who questioned the army's optimism about a battle that seemed more like a defeat, the general became apoplectic. If Gibbon appeared overeager, it was only because his command under Rawn had been roundly accused of "cowardice" a week earlier for not attacking with even fewer men. Now newspapers were calling Gibbon "a fool for venturing to put 150 men against four times that number of Indians," huffed Little Phil.[52]

Any rationalization about a battle that had left so many women and children dead is conspicuously absent from official reports. Every surviving officer received a brevet recommendation, and six enlisted men eventually received the Medal of Honor, including one who was purportedly responsible for the deaths of nine women and children. There seems little doubt that no officer felt compelled to address this issue since Sherman himself had defended war against noncombatants time and again, claiming that in the end it is more humane because it speedily ends resistance. Only eleven years before, after Wyoming's Fetterman Massacre, it was Sherman who had written Grant a widely circulated letter declaring that "we must act with vindictive earnestness against the Sioux, even to their extermination, men, women and children."[53]

Writing in one of his many published accounts after the war, Howard defended Gibbon's actions. Of course he was "horror-stricken" upon seeing the bodies of women and children, but outrages committed by Indians against whites "are a thousand times worse." When it came to accounting for the deaths of children, volunteer John Catlin wavered not at all. In words that might have fallen from the lips of men in past centuries as well as those to come, Catlin steadfastly maintained, "They were there with their fathers and mothers . . . violating the laws of our land and we as soldiers were ordered to fire, and we did."[54]

Others were less certain. Eighteen years after the battle, Gibbon —then near the end of his life—harbored that disturbingly paradoxical attitude maintained by more than a few soldiers who served on the frontier long after the last official shot had been fired at an Indian: that soldiers had been nothing more than reluctant instruments in carrying out government policies. Defending their personal actions, they lamented what those actions ultimately accomplished. Killing women and children at the Big Hole had been "unavoidable," said Gibbon. In almost the same breath, he admitted that the war against the Nez Perce was a "cruel fate" marking "the culminating point of the maltreatment of the Indians in this country."

Some of those lower in the chain of command were even more uneasy. After viewing the exhumed bodies, Major Mason wrote to his wife that "it was a dreadful sight—dead men, women and children. More squaws were killed than men. I have never been in a fight where women were killed, and I hope never to be." And Corporal Loynes, writing Lucullus Virgil McWhorter over half a century after the battle, revealed that "in the few living members of my regiment whom I receive letters from, they have mentioned with regret that it was their duty to attack those people." One can only imagine how Stevensville merchant Henry Buck, temporarily conscripted as a teamster for Howard's command, must have felt when after the battle he stumbled on the partially exposed body of a woman, recognizing "the calico dress that she wore as being made from cloth that I had sold her only a few days before."[55]

In coming weeks, curious citizens would travel to the high, wind-swept valley to view the battlefield, one journalist remarking that the odious sight of "festering, half putrid corpses" of the scalped and mutilated Indians was the most "horrible and sickening I ever beheld." Anticipating exactly what had happened, several Nez Perce managed to return in the first few days and, under cover of darkness, rebury some of their dead. Soon, however, white grave robbers exhumed the bodies yet again, searching for Indian souvenirs and artifacts. One party from Deer Lodge reported finding fresh dirt and a tuft of buffalo robe protruding from the ground. They attached a lariat to the robe and took a turn around a saddle horn, and up came several bodies.[56]

In late September, Captain Rawn sent a burial detail to the battlefield after receiving reports that bears had come down out of the mountains and dragged several corpses to the surface. The men reinterred the whites, counted more than eighty exposed Indian bodies, but made no attempt to rebury them.

One year after the battle, fur trader Andrew Garcia and his Nez Perce wife, In-who-lise, who had been shot in the shoulder, had her mouth smashed with the butt of a soldier's rifle, and lost her sister and father during the battle, returned to the Big Hole to locate and bury their remains. Garcia found "human bones and leering skulls" of Indians scattered throughout the tall bunchgrass and among willows near the creek, while nearby white graves appeared undisturbed.[57] Late that evening, as dusk fell across the western sky, In-who-lise began wailing for the dead, a sound so eerie and mournful that Garcia would never forget it.

"You can hear it a long way," said the frontiersman, "and it haunts you for days. As her piercing wails came and went, far and near through this beautiful still valley of death, they would come echoing back in a way that made me shiver, as though in answer to her sad appeals."[58]

Photographed by Orlando S. Goff in November 1877 in Bismarck,
Dakota Territory, after one of the longest and most arduous military
pursuits in history, thirty-seven-year-old Joseph was about to begin
eight years of exile in Indian Territory.   *Montana Historical Society*

Ollokot, Joseph's younger brother, photographed a few days before war erupted in 1877. A mapmaker and daring battlefield leader whom Joseph consulted before each battle, Ollokot was considered the abler man in the field.

Washington State University

The only surviving photograph of Looking Glass was taken in 1871 when the chief was about forty years old; the capable but vain warrior was the advocate of the flight to the plains.

Smithsonian Institution

Freed by the Nez Perce, ex-slave Seeskoomkee had both feet and a hand frozen when he was shackled and left outside on a winter's night as punishment for stealing. A superb horseman and scout, Seeskoomkee escaped the final battle to live out his days among the Sioux in Canada.

Smithsonian Institution

Yellow Bull, the father of one of the three youths responsible for the murders that ignited the white reaction at Salmon River, survived the war and eight years of exile to deliver a stirring eulogy at Joseph's funeral.

Smithsonian Institution

Only sixteen in 1877, Black Eagle, the son of Wottolen, escaped to Canada during the final battle. He returned to Idaho with twenty-nine fugitives the following summer; threatened with arrest, he and his father escaped again to Canada. They were allowed to settle on the Nez Perce Reservation three years later.

Smithsonian Institution

Tom Hill joined the fleeing bands in Montana's Bitterroot Valley after being denied sanctuary on the Flathead Reservation. Sending his wife toward Canada on horseback, he fought in the final battle and later served as a Nez Perce interpreter during surrender negotiations.

Smithsonian Institution

A member of Looking Glass's band, Peopeo Tholekt served as interpreter between the chief and Captain Stephen Whipple's command sent to arrest them. When Whipple's men began shooting, killing several Indians, Peopeo Tholekt remarked: "That settles it. We have to have a war."

Smithsonian Institution

LEFT: General Oliver Otis Howard's Bible-thumping humanitarianism failed to embrace Native Americans; his threatening actions played a significant role in precipitating the Nez Perce outbreak.

Idaho State Historical Society

RIGHT: Surgeon (Captain) John FitzGerald wrote his wife before the final battle, "Poor Nez Perces!...I am actually beginning to admire their bravery and endurance in the face of so many well-equipped enemies."

Fitzgerald Hiestand Family

OPPOSITE PAGE:

TOP: Flathead Chief Charlot was convinced that armed rebellion by the Nez Perce was hopeless; Montana settlers rewarded him by forcing his removal to the Flathead Reservation in 1891. *Montana Historical Society*

BOTTOM LEFT: In-who-lise was shot in the shoulder and smashed in the mouth with the butt of a soldier's rifle at the Big Hole. The wife of frontiersman Andrew Garcia, she was bludgeoned to death by Blackfeet raiders on the Montana Plains in 1879, not long after this picture was taken. *Montana Historical Society*

BOTTOM RIGHT:Yellow Wolf, nephew of Joseph, provided one of the most remarkable accounts of the war and frontier life now available. *Montana Historical Society*

Accused of cowardice at the Little Bighorn in 1876, Colonel John Gibbon was repulsed in a predawn attack at the Big Hole, where women and children were slain along with many of the bands' most accomplished warriors.

Montana Historical Society

General Philip H. Sheridan oversaw the army's efforts to block the Nez Perce once they crossed into Montana on their way to Canada.

United States Military Academy Library

Colonel Nelson "Bear Coat" Miles was already a veteran of many Civil War and Indian battles when he defeated the Nez Perce at the Bear Paw Mountains in what he called the hardest fight of his life. Miles alone called repeatedly for the Nez Perce's repatriation to the Northwest.

Montana Historical Society

Lieutenant C. E. S. Wood, General Howard's aide-de-camp, recorded Joseph's words of surrender from a messenger after the Bear Paw battle. Wood later claimed that Joseph spoke the dramatic words himself upon surrendering his rifle to General Miles. *The Huntington Library*

General William Tecumseh Sherman, whose order caused jealousy among commands by giving General Howard carte blanche to follow the Nez Perce regardless of military divisional boundaries. *National Archives*

Colonel Samuel D. Sturgis, who commanded Custer's mangled regiment after the Little Bighorn, made the error of abandoning the sure trap he had laid for the Nez Perce at the mouth of Clarks Fork Canyon, allowing them to slip by him and continue toward Canada.

National Archives

Henry Spalding, head of the first Presbyterian mission to the Nez Perce, was described by fellow missionary William Gray as "a sincere, though not always humble Christian."

Smithsonian Institutio

BELOW:

Joseph Roberts (LEFT) and Frederic Pfister (RIGHT) escaped into the woods with several other tourists from Helena, Montana, after being surprised by warriors at their Otter Creek campsite in Yellowstone Park. Shortly afterward, Andrew Weikert (CENTER) was wounded in an encounter with the raiders. *Montana Historical Society*

TOP LEFT: As the Nez Perce fled Idaho, Montana's Governor Benjamin F. Potts responded to settlers' call to arms by proclaiming, "The honor of Montana demands that they shall be fought down." Denied the army's permission to raise a militia, Potts allowed the Nez Perce to pass through peaceably.

Montana Historical Society

TOP RIGHT: Stanton (S. G.) Fisher proved the best of Howard's scouts. Along with several Bannock Indians, he trailed the Nez Perce through Yellowstone Park and the Absaroka Mountains.   *Idaho State Historical Society*

Emily FitzGerald's letters illuminate the quiet desperation of frontier women whose husbands were setting out for war "knowing they will never all come back."   *Fitzgerald Hiestand Family*

Richard Dietrich, a German music teacher who had immigrated to Helena, Montana, narrowly escaped the Nez Perce near Yellowstone Falls, only to be killed by warriors near Mammoth Hot Springs.

Montana Historical Society

When Emma Cowan was released along with her brother and sister by the Nez Perce near Yellowstone Lake, she was convinced that her husband, George (OPPOSITE), had died in her arms during their captivity; two weeks later, she learned that he had managed to crawl ten miles to safety.

Montana Historical Society

Former enemies met for the last time at Pennsylvania's Carlisle Indian School in 1904. Joseph remarked that though he had once desired to kill General Howard in battle, "today I am glad to meet him...and be friends. We are both old men, still we live and I am glad." *Bowdoin College Library*

9

White Bird Canyon . . . the Clearwater River . . . and now the Big Hole. One can almost feel the U.S. Army shrinking with embarrassment at its third major failure to bring the rebellious Nez Perce to heel. To add to its misery, not a few eastern newspapers began to portray its most senior officers as bumbling dimwits and the flight of the Nez Perce as a cause célèbre, a nineteenth-century David and Goliath. The man who would normally attend to such matters, General William Sherman, was touring military installations in the West and at this moment was deep in the heart of the nation's new Yellowstone National Park. Second in command and within whose jurisdiction the Nez Perce now resided was General Philip H. Sheridan.

If Sheridan at his headquarters in Chicago had not shown much interest up to now in the trials and travails of Howard's pursuit of the Nez Perce, it was not because of a disinterest in Indians. Indians —or primarily their wars—were Sheridan's business. His Division of the Missouri had its hands full with renegades from Texas to Montana, particularly the numerous and obdurate Sioux and Cheyenne. For Sheridan, who had gained a sterling reputation as a fierce and highly proficient commander during the Civil War, killing Indians was not unlike killing Confederates. The only difference was that Indians were something less than human—wild and brutal savages, "miserable wretches" to be subdued. That Sheridan as a young lieutenant once took an Indian mistress while campaigning in the Northwest during the 1850s appears to have blessed him with no particular appreciation for Indian culture.

Although he later disavowed saying it, Sheridan is credited with originating perhaps the most famous epigram of the Indian frontier. At the conclusion of a council with the Comanche chief Toch-a-way, Sheridan heard the chief refer to himself as a good Indian, to which he is said to have snapped: "The only good Indians I ever saw were dead." Adopted with celerity into the public vernacular and particularly popular with western newspaper editors, the remark was soon reduced to: "The only good Indian is a dead Indian."[1]

What an unlikely warrior, this strange little man with abnormally long arms and a ponderous, bullet-shaped head—his forehead so far forward of his ears that it was said he had difficulty keeping a hat on his head. Photographs lend support to this fact if not precisely the cause; rarely does Sheridan appear wearing one, and when he is, the hat is almost invariably tipped to one side. Since he was only five feet, five inches tall, the moniker "Little Phil" bestowed on him by his troops was inescapable. Dark eyes and a drooping mustache gave his face an almost Asiatic appearance (one historian believes he resembled a Mongol emperor), although a staff officer thought him "thick-set & common Irish-looking." Lawyer George Templeton Strong of New York, that keen observer of the Civil War, once invited Sheridan to dine and described him as "a stumpy, quadrangular little man, with a forehead of no promise and hair so short that it looks like a coat of black paint. But his eyes and mouth show force."[2]

Though he was generally congenial and good-natured, these attributes vanished when Sheridan took to the field. One observer characterized him as "mad with lust during an engagement." When he spoke, those of lesser rank paid attention. Obstinate, restless, often irritable and demanding, he did not suffer fools gladly and was given to intense rages when a subordinate failed to live up to expectations, a fact Howard would soon discover. Sheridan held the job that Sher-

ROUTE FROM BIG HOLE TO YELLOWSTONE PARK

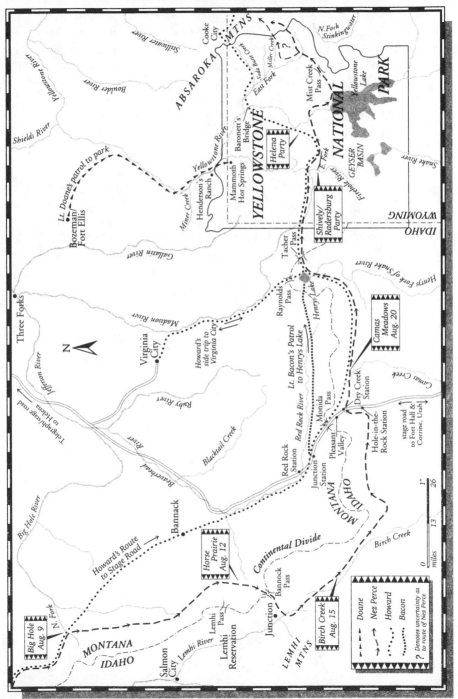

man had earlier occupied before he became General of the Army, a position Sheridan would succeed to upon Sherman's retirement in 1883. Together these two men, who had brought new meaning during the Civil War to the expression "total war," would plan and execute the government's militant response to these "enemies of our race and civilization," as Sherman once described defiant Indians in a letter to Sheridan. They were a foe who had been repeatedly warned not to question the rule of law and now would be bludgeoned into submission, even should it result in their "utter annihilation."[3]

On receiving Gibbon's message sent from the Big Hole on August 13, Sheridan wired General Terry, telling him to cooperate with Howard, "including placing troops as you may have to spare under his command." But any idea of the Nez Perce forming a juncture with the Sioux, now self-exiled in Canada—a possibility suggested by Howard once the Nez Perce reached Montana—was "preposterous," said Sheridan. A few days later, however, he was less confident, telegraphing Terry with advice that would soon seem almost prescient. Sheridan warned Terry to alert Colonel Miles in eastern Montana "to keep scouts out" for the Nez Perce, ready to "clean them out completely" should they head for Yellowstone Park and the Big Horn country beyond. "I have my doubts now if Gen. Howard can overtake them."[4]

The same day that Sheridan sent his first message to Terry, General Howard again commenced the chase, now fully three traveling days behind the Nez Perce. Colonel Gibbon detailed some fifty men to accompany the command as far as Bannack, Montana, and with a forward detachment numbering 310 men, Howard set off south on the wide trail, deeply furrowed by travois poles burdened with the bands' wounded. Within a week his infantry, left near Lolo Pass to catch up as best they could, would overtake the command.

Shortly after Howard marched away, the Bitterroot volunteers turned for home, and Gibbon began moving his wounded to Deer Lodge. The journey over rolling prairie covered with sagebrush was excruciating for the injured men. Meanwhile, citizens in Deer Lodge, Butte, and Helena, upon receiving Gibbon's message, assembled wagons and ambulances loaded with sumptuous food—mutton and chicken, cans of strawberries, peaches, oysters, and sardines—muslin for bandages, medicine, "four gals. brandy," and "2 gal. whiskey" and started for the Big Hole. The two parties met fifteen miles from the battlefield. When they arrived three days later in Deer Lodge, citizens lined the main street and cheered.[5]

The soldiers' wounds were frightful, declared Montana newspapers, delivered by an adversary whose every warrior equaled at least three Sioux warriors. Private George Maurer, Company F, had received a bullet through his jaw, "carrying away cheek, roof of mouth and front teeth," but the writer blithely noted that enough teeth were left on one side of the man's mouth "to help him wonderfully in getting through the world." Another man had his "left arm shattered," suggesting certain amputation. Lieutenant Charles Coolidge was shot in both thighs and also through the hand, this last wound "carrying away the knuckles of four fingers," leaving his fingers permanently extended. Even more tragic was an unidentified officer (probably Captain Constant Williams) who had a bullet strike him "square in the breast," follow a rib around to his back and lodge against the spine. "He will not die," concluded the writer, "but may be disabled for life."[6]

Most of the men wounded or killed had been married. Volunteer Myron Lockwood, with a wife, five children, and a pilfered homestead awaiting him in the Bitterroot Valley, had been "shot through both thighs; ugly wounds, but both balls have been extracted." In a few days, General Sherman himself would arrive in Deer Lodge and pronounce that a depressed and despondent Lockwood would be a cripple for life. His brother, Amos, who had also fought in the battle was dead.[7]

Married only a few weeks before, Lieutenant William English's wife was on hand to meet him when the wounded arrived in Deer Lodge. She had been told ahead of time her husband's stomach wound was probably mortal but that she must be as encouraging as possible. Climbing into the wagon and embracing him, she said in a cheerful voice, "How are you, Willie?" Lieutenant English lived three days before succumbing to peritonitis.[8]

Exactly how Howard viewed the battle is unknown. Any blame or praise the general might have had for Gibbon's effort is conspicuously absent from his official report. Thomas Sutherland, however, probably reflected the general's true feelings when he wrote that had Gibbon "not been quite so anxious to cover himself with glory, the result would have been very different." Passing through the Bitterroot Valley, Howard had been acutely aware of adverse press relentlessly dogging him, this time from Montana editors. Near Corvallis, he found time to write a message to Governor Potts complaining of newspapers "filled" with the "grossest falsehoods." The effect had created distrust "on the part of your people," groused Howard, with whom he desired the "heartiest" cooperation.[9]

When Potts passed along the general's message, Montana editors, still smarting over Fort Fizzle, reacted predictably. Howard "can put down adverse criticism better with his sabre than he can with his pen," crowed the *Missoulian.* The general as an Indian fighter and impresario of this chase "is a dead failure," declared the *New North-West,* "and the sooner he goes home the sooner effective work will be done."[10]

For Gibbon, oddly enough, the regional press at first had little but praise. "The country owes a debt of gratitude to Gen. Gibbon and his brave handful of regulars and volunteers," exclaimed James Mills, "for the telling and terrible blow struck on the Big Hole." Howard fights his battles in newspapers while Gibbon fights Indians. "Blessed be Gibbon," wrote Mills alongside a headline that read "Another Thirty Good Indians." Such accolades lessened somewhat during subsequent weeks when it became apparent that the Nez Perce not only had failed to slow their retreat after the battle but in fact seemed more determined than ever to reach the buffalo country. "Gibbon broke one of the hind legs of the hostiles at Big Hole," Mills observed, "but it must be confessed they travel well on what remains."[11]

If the public failed to find Gibbon's effort entirely laudable, never did its mood turn sour. Perhaps the harshest criticism was this droll verse entitled "Big Hole" that appeared in the *Missoulian* two months after the battle:

> *Col. Gibbon to Gov. Potts:*
> We've had a hard fight

and I'm sorry to say
They've whipped us out quite
And the devil's to pay.

I wait at Big Hole
For an answer from you,
And confess on my soul,
I don't know what to do.

Gov. Potts to Col. Gibbon:
Licked again? Your command
Nearly turned inside out?
Did Chief Joseph take a hand,
Or was Howard about?

Your dispatch, trusty soul,
I answer this minute:
If you're near a big hole,
You'd better crawl in it.[12]

On the afternoon following the battle, Nez Perce survivors loaded their wounded on horses and started up the Big Hole Valley. Those who could not ride were placed in travois. That night, they camped about twelve miles from the battlefield, throwing up rock fortifications against pursuing soldiers. The traveling had been unbearably painful for the wounded, and many had died and been hastily buried along the trail. Others were left behind because of age or the severity of their wounds and their tendency to slow the fleeing bands. Montana newspapers berated this behavior, seizing on it to bolster their accusations of the "barbarism" of Indians against even their own kind.

Most, if not all the badly wounded, however, asked to be left behind. Such altruism was common among individuals who valued the survival of the family above personal welfare. Or they simply may have wished to die. In following days, a white scout, John (J. W.) Redington, discovered one of these Nez Perce lying on a buffalo robe along the trail. When the aged man wanly smiled and pointed to his head, Redington understood that he was inviting him to end his misery. The scout refused, much to the distress of the man who "seemed quite disappointed." He would find others. Later he happened on an elderly woman who requested in broken English that he kill her. Then she began chanting her death song, a sound described by Redington as "wild and weird." When the scout declined and began riding away, the woman suddenly launched into a rendition of "Nearer My God to Thee." Some historians distrust Redington's account of the war, thought to be imaginative and windy, but these particular instances have the ring of truth. Howard's Bannock scouts were more obliging; any live Nez Perce found along the trail was shot, scalped, stripped, and left as carrion for coyotes, wolves, and vultures.[13]

At camp that evening, as on the trail throughout the afternoon, there had been much crying and wailing for the dead. Nearly everyone had lost a friend or family member. One of those to die during the night was Ai-Hits-Palo-Jam (Fair Land), a wife of Ollokot. At either this camp or the next, Yellow Wolf, having caught up with the bands, witnessed another woman lying "on a buffalo robe, moaning, with many around her. Badly shot through the stomach at the last battle. They told me she could not live. Next morning the woman on the robe was dead."[14] Exactly how many died in those first days is unknown, and even today many Nez Perce revere the trail through Idaho, Montana, and Wyoming as sacred ground, scattered with the bones of their ancestors. One of Howard's scouts later remarked that he had little trouble finding the Nez Perce trail after the battle, marked as it was so frequently by Indian graves.

During the three days following the battle, the bands made no more than sixty miles as they headed south up and out of the Big Hole Valley. At the head of the valley, instead of trailing directly east through a low pass that would have taken them close by the settlement of Bannack, the bands pushed south over a narrow, forested drainage.

About this time Looking Glass is said to have lost his position as leader, the inference being that having placed so much trust in the word of Bitterroot settlers and failing to keep watch over the back trail, he was replaced. Lean Elk or Poker Joe, joining the bands in the Bitterroot Valley and intimately familiar with the trails of Montana, now ascended over the disgraced chief. However attractive this idea appeared to whites anxious to simplify Indian leadership roles, it is improbable. While Poker Joe did become a kind of trail boss, deciding the bands' daily direction and schedule, Looking Glass was far from finished. He continued to take an active part in councils and decision making, although it does seem likely that his prestige had been dealt a blow. Soon the camp fell into a routine, rising early each morning and traveling until about ten o'clock. Then Poker Joe would order a halt to breakfast and allow the horses to graze. About two o'clock, the camp would start up again, traveling until nearly ten o'clock each night. In this manner, by gaining an hour or two each day over their pursuers, the Nez Perce hoped to maintain their lead.

As the bands entered the rich, grassy valley known as Horse Prairie, they ascended the headwaters of the Beaverhead River. From here they crossed west over the Continental Divide into Idaho's Lemhi River Valley, whose river is a tributary of the Salmon River. Exactly why this route was chosen is unclear, and here the record grows sparse. By now scouts along the back trail knew that Howard was trying to close on the bands. The fastest and shortest route to the plains lay in the opposite direction, east from Horse Prairie across the main stage and telegraph line connecting Montana and Utah, then up the Red Rock River Valley to Henrys Lake in eastern Idaho. From there several trails led to the buffalo country.

Instead, the Nez Perce headed back into Idaho in what was first thought to be an effort to return to their homeland. But settlers in the area doubted such a move. The only reasonable southern passage—the Old Nez Perce Trail—leading through the rugged Salmon River Mountains of central Idaho commenced back in the Bitterroot Valley, a locale few thought the bands would attempt to pass through again. Others feared they were planning to enlist the northern Shoshoni band led by Chief Tendoy, then residing along the Lemhi River and known to have been friendly with the Nez Perce in the past. But none of these theories proved correct. Both Wottolen and Yellow Wolf maintain that once the decision had been made in the Bitterroot, the bands' intention to escape to the buffalo country never faltered. It appears they simply chose this circuitous route in an attempt to avoid more numerous white settlements in southwestern Montana, and possibly to confuse and elude their pursuers.

Before leaving Horse Prairie, the Nez Perce encountered their first settlers since departing the Bitterroot. Most residents in the area had been forewarned of their approach and had taken refuge in the barricaded second story of the new brick courthouse in Bannack. Food and water had been stored in the building and featherbeds piled against the windows. For area ranchers, the arrival of the Nez Perce could not have been more inopportune, since haying season was underway. Several daring souls sent their families to Bannack but refused to abandon their homes or fields. Thomas Flynn and W. L. Montague were at the Montague-Winters ranch on August 12 when some fifty or sixty warriors rode up to the house. Flynn, described as an "impetuous, hot-tempered man," had earlier declared he would "settle with the damned Injuns" if they put in an appearance. He was found later lying face down in a pool of blood in the kitchen with four bullet holes in his body; his double-barreled shotgun loaded with buckshot had been discharged. Smeared over the walls of the room was the bloody imprint of a hand. Whether it was Flynn's hand or that of an Indian was never determined.[15]

Montague was found dead in the bedroom, his feet protruding from under a mattress, shot six times. Although the house had not been burned, the inside—furniture, dishes, carpets, and clothing— was a shambles, everything upset and broken, with feathers from ripped mattresses ankle-deep in nearly every room. In addition, all fabric that could be used for bandages had been carried away. A short distance from the house, two more bodies were discovered. One man had been shot five times, leaving behind a widow and eight children; another was found with multiple wounds, covered with a quilt, two hundred dollars untouched in his pocket. Three other farmhands escaped, having hidden in nearby willows along the creek. These men arrived in Bannack footsore but alive the following day, having lost their loose cowhide boots in quicksand in their rush to avoid pursuing Indians.

In another incident, four men dove into the brush along the creek when warriors suddenly appeared. Calling to the whites to come out, they claimed they were friendly. One man dropped his gun and ammunition and surrendered. When the other three refused to follow, the warriors shot and killed him. Also missing when settlers ventured back to their homes were some 100 to 150 horses.

Two days afterward, a large concourse of citizens gathered to bury the dead at the cemetery in Bannack. The procession through town had just gotten underway when a man suddenly appeared, shouting that a Nez Perce war party was advancing on the town. Down went the caskets, men running to get their guns and horses while women and children scurried to the court house. Their fears were soon allayed, however, when a lieutenant and two white scouts came riding into town, sent ahead by Howard to purchase supplies and obtain fresh horses.

The greeting Howard's command received upon his arrival the next morning was nothing short of glorious. "These people were so happy to see us, so pleasant in their manner and speech," exclaimed the general. Smiling faces. Welcome words. So different from Bitterroot residents who "had stoutly blamed us for chasing the Indians to their neighborhood."[16]

Here the men rested while Howard composed a long, plaintive telegram to McDowell, for the first time expressing doubt that his command could catch the Nez Perce. Was it realistic to continue on without the help of General Sheridan's division? "We have made extraordinary marches, and with prompt and energetic cooperation from these eastern departments, may yet stop and destroy this most enterprising band of Indians. Without this cooperation, the result will be, as it has been, doubtful. If Gibbon had 100 more men the work would have been complete. Surely he might have had more from all this Territory, three times as many."[17]

Three days later these words would elicit a stinging rebuke from McDowell, now thoroughly disgusted with Howard's failure to bring this supreme humiliation to an end. Neither man seemed to understand each other's problems. There was simply no other force in the immediate area to lend Howard a hand, and his early glowing reports had given McDowell confidence none would be needed. But at the same time, McDowell had no idea how the long chase over some of the most formidable and uninhabited country in the West had worn down Howard's command and how desperately he needed assistance.[18]

Another week would pass before McDowell's reply would catch up with Howard, for the next day the general was preparing again to take up the bands' trail. His plan, as he wired McDowell, was to descend Horse Prairie eastward to the stage road near Red Rock River, then cross back into Idaho and intercept the Nez Perce as they swung east toward Montana's plains. If instead they headed back to western Idaho, he would drive them between himself and Major Green, still on the Clearwater River, where they would be trapped.

Although Howard thought the Bannack citizens' reception grand, not so Major Mason, who found their welcome a little too friendly. People "filled our camp all afternoon," complained Mason, "all full of advice as to what should be done, and giving their opinions in an offensive manner." Soon even Howard was overwhelmed, amazed how quickly well-wishers began calling "me to account for the way I did things in the military line." Two volunteer companies of about sixty men from Butte and Deer Lodge had overtaken the command. Now their two leaders, William Clark and Thomas Stuart, suggested Howard drop his wagons and with his cavalry push on into the Lemhi Valley as quickly as possible. To which the general responded, said the two men, with a "less than cordial feeling."[19]

Still, the advice was difficult to ignore. The Nez Perce had crossed back into Idaho by way of Bannock Pass. A few miles north was Lemhi Pass, the one used by Lewis and Clark during their journey west in 1805. If Howard hurried over this low pass, the citizens claimed, he would be able to entrap the Indians between his cavalry and a group of Idaho volunteers reported to be forted up and in imminent danger at Junction, Idaho, near the bottom of the two passes.

Contrary to this suggestion was word from two of his Nez Perce horse herders, Old George and "Captain" John. They assured Howard the bands had every intention of traveling to the buffalo country and that their present movement "was only a feint to get me hopelessly in the rear." The general also feared a trap not of his own making, calling Lemhi Pass "an ugly gap" pregnant with the possibility of ambush. As Howard debated what to do, a messenger rode in from Idaho saying the bands had already arrived in the Lemhi Valley, done little harm, and were headed "eastward as fast as they could." Now Howard was free to pursue his former plan, setting off for Red Rock River and the stage road, "hoping almost against hope to catch the Indians" as they headed for Montana's plains.[20]

The next day the command moved down Horse Prairie with Clark and Stuart's volunteers scouting along the southern flank several miles distant. Before long, a courier arrived informing Howard that the volunteers had veered off, intending to attack the Nez Perce before they reached the stage line near Beaver Creek. Howard immediately sent aide Lieutenant C. E. S. Wood after the men to inform them that such a foray would destroy his chances of interception and to order them to return to a position nearer his right flank. The volunteers complied, but that night they gave up in disgust and started back to Butte and Deer Lodge. In a letter they wrote to editor James Mills, the men said they had found Howard "kind, courteous and gentlemanly," but they had little faith that he would ever overtake the Indians.[21]

In Thomas Sutherland's view, Montana volunteers had proved no better than those of Idaho, a class of men he had regarded before this war as "courageous as lions." It seemed that in almost every town the command passed near, out would come volunteer companies "in a cloud of dust, thirsting for gore, and on finding that . . . they were getting unpleasantly near the Indians, would suddenly recollect business at home and leave us." With few exceptions, concluded the disgruntled correspondent, citizen volunteers were a "miserable failure."[22]

Twenty determined but nervous Idaho volunteers armed and waiting in the log stockade at Junction in the Lemhi Valley on August 13 seemed to have had a higher opinion of themselves. Near midmorning about sixty Nez Perce led by Looking Glass and White Bird approached the stockade, telling the whites they had nothing to fear and that the bands wished to pass through the valley in peace. As they were talking, Chief Tendoy and a number of Lemhi Valley Indians rode up. The three chiefs went into a council that lasted well into the afternoon. Exactly what transpired is uncertain, but if the

Nez Perce ever thought Tendoy might join them, they were soon dissuaded. The chief had no intention of going against valley whites, and furthermore, he informed Looking Glass and White Bird that his friend, "Colonel" George Shoup, and a group of volunteers were on their way from Salmon City. Following the meeting the Nez Perce quickly repacked their camp and, to the relief of whites behind the barricade, headed south out of the valley.

Much has been made of Tendoy's refusal to aid the Nez Perce. Indignant war buffs sympathetic to the plight of the Nez Perce claim that Tendoy, like the Flatheads, betrayed the bands, and probably not a few have taken grim satisfaction in the Lemhis' subsequent fate. But such proscriptions seem heavy-handed, for the relationship enjoyed by the two tribes was never much more than one of mutual convenience. Although this mixed band of some nine hundred northern Shoshonis and Bannocks were on agreeable terms with both Flatheads and the more distant Nez Perce, all occasionally joining in defense against their mutual enemy, the militant Blackfeet of Montana and Canada, relations were better with their Bitterroot neighbors to the north. Besides, Bannocks of southwestern Idaho had long intermarried with northern Shoshonis and by 1877 were culturally integrated (although somewhat less so linguistically), even to the extent that most whites of the period simply lumped together all southeastern Idaho Indians as Bannocks (today they are known as the Shoshoni-Bannock Confederated Tribe). Tendoy himself was said to have descended from Bannock stock, surely no small factor in the eyes of traditional Nez Perce who remembered a time before Lewis and Clark when Bannocks were mortal enemies.

For whites, Tendoy's actions confirmed the long-standing friendship the Lemhi Valley Indians had demonstrated ever since the first explorers. Their former chief, Cameahwait, had been instrumental in aiding Lewis and Clark on their trip west when they stumbled on the Lemhis and, in a stroke of incredible good fortune, learned that their guide Sacagawea was Cameahwait's long-lost sister. As with most other Indian tribes who had managed to avoid armed conflict with whites, the credit can usually be traced to a powerful headman dedicated to a nonviolent response to white encroachment. Like the Flatheads' Charlot, Tendoy fulfilled this seemingly impossible role.

Unlike the Flathead chief, Tendoy appears to have had help from a very influential—however improbable—white man, "Colonel" George L. Shoup.

Sand Creek, Colorado. November 29, 1864. Shoup was the second-in-command under Colonel John Chivington, that Methodist minister turned soldier, a man of imposing girth with violent, obsidian eyes, rabid to punish Indians—any Indians. During a dawn raid, Chivington's seven hundred troops thundered into the camp of Black Kettle, a Cheyenne chief who earlier had surrendered to the U.S. Army. Thinking there had been a mistake, Black Kettle raised both a white and American flag outside his tipi, counseling his people not to resist. The result was some 150 to 200 slaughtered Indians, two-thirds of whom were women and children. The congressional investigation afterward revealed a level of barbarity heretofore unequaled on the frontier, described by one veteran army officer as far exceeding any Indian injustices he had ever known. Almost all the victims had been scalped and mutilated, some allegedly while they were yet alive. In one instance, thirty or forty women took refuge in a ravine, sending out a small girl with a white flag. The child was immediately cut down. One witness testified he saw a pregnant woman sliced open, her disemboweled fetus lying by her side. Another that a three-year-old child had been jokingly used for target practice. Afterward, citizens cheered as both Cheyenne scalps and genitals stretched over saddle pommels or adorning hats were displayed in Denver, the *Rocky Mountain News* exulting that ' 'Colorado soldiers have again covered themselves with glory.'"[23]

It is difficult to ascertain what role Colonel Shoup played in this heinous affair. In testimony afterward he claimed to have seen no atrocities, a surprising admission for a man who was second-in-command and must have witnessed much of the fight. It appears more than one officer objected at the onset of the attack, to which Chivington reputedly reacted with derision, exclaiming, "Scalps are what we are after. . . . I long to be wading in gore!" By the end of the investigation, the contemptuous Chivington seemed to attract the brunt of the eastern public's condemnation of the massacre (although he was never convicted), most participants having distanced themselves from any personal culpability. One year later, in a successful bid for lieutenant governor of Colorado, Shoup accepted his party's nomination with a speech calling the "chastisement" of Indians at Sand Creek "justly merited."[24]

If Colonel Shoup ever loathed Indians, either at Sand Creek or later after moving to Idaho, it was not apparent in his dealings with Tendoy. In 1874, when the chief was pressing for a separate reservation for his people, it was Shoup who wrote territorial delegate John Hailey, claiming that the Lemhis under Tendoy "had always been friendly to the whites, and that the white settlers wished them to remain there for they acted as a protection to the settlers against other Indians who were not good." Hailey wrote back bewildered. He had only assumed that he was doing constituents a favor by removing the Lemhi Indians. "You must certainly have a much better set of Indians in your county than we have in my county or you would be ancious to git rid of them." The next year, about the same time that he was rescinding Joseph's Wallowa reservation, President Grant approved Tendoy's request, establishing the 160-square-mile Lemhi reservation.[25]

Now, two years later, Tendoy was not about to risk his new reservation or his good relations with valley settlers for a hopeless alliance with the Nez Perce. Although Tendoy probably had little effect on the relatively peaceful passage of the bands through the valley, Salmon City's *Idaho Recorder* claimed that "without his allegiance and diplomacy, the entire Salmon and Lemhi Valleys would have been laid waste, and their inhabitants put to the tomahawk."[26]

With the Nez Perce, however, also went white gratitude. In years to come, the Lemhis suffered at the hands of a number of singularly unscrupulous Indian agents who stole or withheld government food allotments so frequently that the tribe bordered on starvation. Later not even Shoup himself, serving first as Idaho's governor and then as U.S. senator, could thwart a cost-cutting attempt by the government to close the reservation and move its inhabitants to Fort Hall.

In 1907, after forty-four years as head chief and suffering from rheumatism and partial paralysis, Tendoy fell off his horse into a stream and died, drunk from whiskey given to him by a white man. Two years later the reservation closed. In a scene remarkably similar to the eviction of the Flatheads eighteen years earlier, the wife of a

Lemhi Valley rancher said that as the Shoshonis packed their meager belongings and started on their final journey out of the valley, citizens lined the road to bid them farewell. As they passed by, nearly all the Indians were crying. What was so startling, the woman recalled, was that some of the whites were crying too.[27]

The day after the Nez Perce left Tendoy and the settlers' stockade and departed Lemhi Valley, "Colonel" Shoup and twenty-six men rode into Junction from Salmon City. Here he found all "safe and sound," the only loss some cattle "killed for subsistence and some horses taken." The men rode on, joined by a party of Lemhis led by Tendoy, for Shoup was concerned about a large freight train he knew was somewhere on the road from Corrine, Utah. The train consisted of eight covered wagons pulled by some thirty mules, carrying food and merchandise valued at over one thousand dollars for his store in Salmon City, along with supplies for other merchants, ten thousand rounds of ammunition, and ten barrels of whiskey. Just beyond Junction, the riders came upon two Chinese men who related a tale that made Shoup fear not only for his property but also for the lives of the train's drivers and passengers. Some forty-five miles farther along on Birch Creek, they found what was left—the smoldering and twisted wreckage of the burned wagons and five murdered men.[28]

Precisely what happened will never be known, for both Nez Perce and white accounts are garbled, but during the following weeks after three survivors turned up, this story unfolded. The train driven by Albert Green, James Hayden, and Daniel Coombs also contained four passengers—the two Chinese and two passengers of unknown identity—and two dogs belonging to Green and Coombs. While the men were resting on August 15 along Birch Creek near a bend in the road, Albert Lyons, who had been out searching for some stray stock, happened on the train and stopped to visit. Suddenly fifty or sixty warriors rode up. When several warriors cocked their rifles, a half-breed who spoke English, possibly Tom Hill or Poker Joe, raised his hand and said, "Don't shoot. We fight soldiers, not citizens."[29]

No doubt realizing the seriousness of their predicament, the teamsters offered some food. Then the warriors demanded the train continue on with them to the Nez Perce camp a few miles away. Here the men were introduced to Looking Glass, White Bird, and Joseph. Some Nez Perce wanted to buy flour and paid $2 each for several sacks. When another man offered to buy ten sacks for $1.50 each, after some parlaying, Albert Green agreed. Angered by this transaction, one of his previous customers grabbed Green by his whiskers and pushed him around "somewhat roughly." Soon the whiskey was discovered, and with the exception of the chiefs and several others, an unknown number of warriors "drank to excess." From here, things went rapidly downhill.

Lyons, seizing an opportunity to move away from the throng, wandered off toward the creek and hid in the brush. After dark he escaped into the hills where he became lost, going without food or water for the next four days. A week later he was discovered, hungry, dehydrated, a "wreck of his former self [and] completely unnerved."[30]

The other whites were not so lucky. One account claims the Chinese were required to get down on all fours and run around like horses. When warriors tried to force the whites to do the same, they refused. According to the Chinese, near sunset the five white men were placed on horses without saddles and several warriors accompanied them out of camp. Soon afterward, a drunken man grabbed one of the Chinese and, despite his pleadings, pulled the man's head back and started to cut his throat when another warrior stopped him. Escorted to the edge of the camp, they were released. Yellow Wolf, who was not drinking, said, "They cried, and were left to go see their grandmother!" As the men scrambled away, they heard shots and saw warriors return with the horses the whites had ridden earlier. Several days later, the two Chinese men encountered Colonel Shoup and his party near Junction, where Shoup reported them unhurt but badly scared.[31]

The bodies of the five whites were found one-half mile from the wagons. Albert Green lay in Birch Creek, stabbed in the right side, his pockets emptied. Nearby were Hayden and Coombs. Hayden had been shot several times, the broken and bloody stock of a gun underneath his body, the barrel by his side, his face beaten to a gelatinous blob. Coombs also had several bullet wounds, his neck stabbed, an ugly wound where one arm had been sliced open by a knife, his hand tightly clenched around the severed handle of a "blacksnake" mule whip. Loaded with lead shot, the whip butt was covered with blood and hair "which showed that he had done some work with it." The corpses of the two passengers had multiple wounds. One appears to have almost escaped, his body found nearly a mile away, shot through the back, the bullet ranging upward as though he had been riding leaning far forward when struck. The only survivors were the dogs; Green's was lying under the axle of a partially burned wagon, and Coombs's was found near his body, chewing on a bone he had carried up from the wreckage, "keeping watch over his dead master."[32]

Whites were not the only casualties in this encounter. Soon after the killings, Peopeo Tholekt and Yellow Wolf, at the direction of the chiefs, dumped the remaining liquor on the ground. A brawl immediately commenced. Ketalkpoosmin, who had helped capture the howitzer at the Big Hole, was shot in the back while attempting to help dispose of the whiskey. Two or three days later, he asked to be left alongside the trail, where he died shortly after. Perhaps one or two more men were shot or stabbed, but apparently they recovered. Ketalkpoosmin's killer later died in the final battle at the Bear Paw Mountains. After taking what they wanted from the wagons, the Nez Perce burned the rest, leaving a pile of debris that could be seen by travelers passing along the road for years.

From Birch Creek the bands continued south for several miles, then turned abruptly east. Traveling along the edge of the mountains on the Snake River Plain—a dry volcanic prairie filled with sparse sagebrush and grass, stretching south to the Snake River—they encountered no settlements for about forty miles until reaching Hole-in-the-Rock on Beaver Creek, one of several stage stations below Monida Pass. Several miles north near Dry Creek Station on August 16, they crossed the stage road and telegraph line connecting Montana communities with the Union Pacific railhead terminus at Corrine, Utah, the same road that Howard had hoped to reach ahead of them. Warned of the bands' progress over the wire, the stationmaster and several other men hid in a nearby lava cave. The Nez Perce passed after cutting the telegraph wire and destroying some grain and twenty sets of harness. Farther south along the road, nervous freighters abandoned their wagons when they heard Indians were ahead, leaving unattended one carrying metallic cartridges and another loaded with black powder. Neither wagon was discovered.

After crossing the stage road, the bands continued east. Here they entered the high, rolling country known as Camas Meadows, bordered on the north by Montana's Centennial Mountains, with abundant grass along south-flowing creeks, the drainages interspersed with rugged lava outcroppings and islands of quaking aspen. Some forty miles farther on lay the headwaters of the Snake River, Henrys Lake, and two major passes, one leading directly into Montana and another toward Yellowstone National Park.

The day the Nez Perce reached Hole-in-the-Rock, General Howard's command camped at Red Rock Station, about sixty-five miles north on the stage road in Montana. By the following night, the soldiers had considerably shortened that distance, traveling up Red Rock Creek to Junction Station, the next stage stop. Here the command was joined by fifty-odd volunteers from Virginia City under "Captain" James E. Callaway.

That evening, unaware the Nez Perce were only about twenty-five miles away near Dry Creek, Howard deliberated about what direction to take. From Junction Station, the road continued south over Monida Pass and down into Idaho to the next stage stations, Pleasant Valley, Dry Creek, and finally Hole-in-the-Rock. The general suspected that the Nez Perce were headed for Henrys Lake; therefore, his shortest and most direct route from Junction Station was not on the southern road but east up Red Rock Creek and Montana's Centennial Valley, then across a low pass to the lake. Still, he was unsure whether the Indians had yet crossed the stage road. If not, another hard day of riding south on the road might place the command directly in their path.

Finally, he decided to send a reconnaissance patrol of some forty picked cavalrymen led by Lieutenant George R. Bacon, along with guide "Rube" Robbins and several Bannock scouts, toward Henrys Lake via Centennial Valley. According to Howard, Bacon's instructions were to set out at midnight, proceed to Henrys Lake "with a view of intercepting and hindering the Indians should they come in that direction, or of procuring and transmitting to me early informa-tion of value."[33]

A few hours before or after Bacon departed—the exact time is unclear—Howard received word from the stage agent that the Nez Perce had been seen beyond the Dry Creek Station. Soon he dis-patched several citizen scouts along with Buffalo Horn and one or two other Bannocks south "to watch the enemy." Additional word came later that night confirming that the bands had indeed crossed the road south of Pleasant Valley, indicating they had once again taken the lead.

Now a strange thing happened.

Instead of striking off after Bacon once he learned the Nez Perce were ahead, Howard continued to equivocate, unsure what to do. Later he maintained that the stage operators "thronged" him, advis-ing that although the stage road appeared more circuitous than the "straight line" trail through Centennial Valley, its well-maintained surface made it quicker in the long run. The next morning, however, he chose neither and instead ordered his men and horses to remain in camp for several hours, "hoping to give the animals rest and grazing." It was true that both horses and men were bone weary. The day before, Major Mason had written to his wife that "our cavalry horses have traveled up to today over 1000 miles and are broken down. . . . If we are to continue the pursuit we must buy new horses for the cavalry and also mount our infantry."[34]

While the command lingered, an impatient Howard decided to see for himself what was happening on the southern stage road. Taking a wagon, a driver, one other officer, and a "well-armed" civilian riding a horse, the four men set off toward Pleasant Valley. The general had requested that the volunteers from Virginia City provide an escort, but he left before the men could pack their camp. Some eighteen miles later, one of the scouts sent out the night before met Howard's wagon and delivered the news that the Nez Perce were in force near Dry Creek Station, less than a dozen miles ahead. When Howard also learned that a trail east to Henrys Lake passed near there, he sent back word to Mason to bring up the command as quickly as possible. The column arrived at Dry Creek late that night, only to find they had missed what probably had been either a raiding party or the bands' rear guard, the main group having crossed the road the day before.

The news was not all bad for the command. Earlier, Buffalo Horn had sighted the Nez Perce camp only fifteen miles east at Camas Meadows, even exchanging a few shots with their rear guard. Once again Howard was behind, but this time, claimed the general, there was a difference: Bacon was ahead and the Indians trapped between. "How confident I then felt!" he exclaimed. "He can annoy and stop them, if he cannot do more!"[35]

Precisely why Howard thought fewer than fifty men could stop some seven hundred determined Indians is anyone's guess. With each successive version written by the general after the war, Bacon's mission grows and grows until one is left with the distinct impression that the lieutenant's inability to locate and close on the Nez Perce is the prime cause of the army's failure.

After leaving Junction Station at 1 o'clock that morning, Bacon and his men rode the sixty miles to Henrys Lake, arriving early the next day. The picturesque lake, situated in a seven-mile-wide grassy basin surrounded by mountains, lies at the bottom of two major passes: Raynolds Pass, leading north down the Madison River Valley toward Fort Ellis at Bozeman, and Tacher (now Targhee) Pass, a narrow and forested passage heading east toward Yellowstone National Park. When the men saw stock grazing on the flats surrounding the lake, they cautiously approached until they discovered the herd of horses and cattle belonged not to Indians but a Montana rancher. Upon learning about the proximity of the Nez Perce, the owner left "with all possible speed." Bacon and his men then searched the valley for sign of Indians for another day and, finding none, started back to Junction Station.[36]

Writing years later in *My Life and Experiences Among Our Hostile Indians,* Howard impaled the lieutenant with his pen:

Bacon was to move rapidly away from the Indian trails and strike Henry[s] Lake in the vicinity of Tacher Pass, a gateway to the National Park. He was to head off the Indians and detain them by his fire till we could come upon them from the rear. Bacon got into position soon enough, but did not have the heart to fight the Indians on account of their number. . . . [Joseph] went straight toward the National Park, where Lieutenant Bacon let him go by and pass through the narrow gateway without firing a shot.[37]

A muffed opportunity. A bungled trap. All due to a subordinate's cowardice.

Howard's account played well to a public still looking for scapegoats long after the war, and for nearly a century no one questioned his explanation. After all, he gave Bacon the orders. Fortunately for historiography—less so for Howard's version—Chief of Staff Major Mason retained a copy of the lieutenant's orders, serendipitously discovered by historian Stanley Davison in 1959. The last sentence reads: "Should you not at the expiration of 48 hours discover any trace of the hostiles, you will return to this camp by easy marches, sending a courier in advance." One of the civilian scouts with Bacon confirmed these instructions a few days later, telling the editor of the Virginia City *Madisonian* that Bacon was "under strict orders to return within 48 hours if no enemy was visible." Good soldier that he was, Bacon did exactly as ordered, missing the Nez Perce, and quite possibly an early grave, by a single day.[38]

On June 19, the command traveled from Dry Creek Station to Camas Meadows, halting near where Buffalo Horn had observed the bands' camp the evening before. Here the horses grazed on plentiful grass while the men set up camp near the confluence of two creeks, augmenting their field rations with immense, freshly caught trout. Called by Nez Perce Wewaltolkit Pah, meaning a creek that flows some distance and then dries up, Camas Creek disappeared beneath the surface not far to the south. From Camas Meadows "curious lava-knolls" stretched for miles, observed Howard, "each knoll so much like another, that you cannot fix your whereabouts by the distinct and diverse features around you. Should you drive to pasture five horses over these wave-like knolls for a mile, and then leave them for an hour to graze, it would be next to impossible to find them."[39]

With Indians nearby, the men took special precautions. Major Mason ringed the camp perimeter with extra guards, and although the horses were usually allowed to freely graze throughout most nights, that evening they were rounded up and hobbled or picketed close by. The 150 to 200 pack mules, however, were allowed to roam over the meadow. After sunset the sky clouded over, intermittent rain fell, "and intense darkness prevailed." An "unusual feeling of security prevaded the camp," recalled Howard. For the first time in many nights, Lieutenant C. E. S. Wood ventured to sleep without his pants and boots on, and others did likewise. The general's son, Lieutenant Guy Howard, declared, "I've loaned my pistol to a scout for tonight, so think likely the Indians will come back."[40]

He was right.

About eighteen miles away, Nez Perce scouts returned to their camp bringing word of the soldiers' location. The night before, said Vottolen, a wounded warrior named Black Hair dreamed a vision. The man had seen warriors go back over the trail in the darkness and "bring away the soldiers' horses." That night in council they decided "to make an attack and try capturing all the horses and pack mules of the enemies just as Black Hair had seen and foretold." Exactly how many Nez Perce started back over the trail and who led them is disputed. Some sources claim every available warrior participated in the raid; others say as few as twenty-eight went. Joseph is credited by whites with leading the raiders, but it was more likely Toohoolhoolzote and Ollokot.[41]

Sharing his tent with a private that night, Sergeant H. J. Davis was "in a state of innocuous desuetude" when near 4 A.M. "we were awakened by a disconcerting concert of demoniacal yells and a cracking of rifles, while the whizzing of bullets could be heard well overhead. Every one was out in a minute, and all we could see was a magnified imitation of a swarm of fireflies flittering in the alders as the rifles spoke, while the tramping of hundreds of hoofs added to the din."[42]

The Nez Perce, said Yellow Wolf, hoped to steal the horse herd before anyone sounded the alarm. When an alert picket challenged the approaching horsemen in the dark, an overeager warrior began shooting. Some warriors quickly joined in, while others attempted to stampede the herd. Camped between the two creeks, "Captain" Callaway's volunteers stumbled from their blankets only to plunge into waist-deep water. The panic was so great as the volunteers attempted to dress that one man recalled seeing Callaway himself mistake his hat for a boot, punching out the crown with his naked foot before realizing his error. "I heard them cry like babies," declared Yellow Wolf. "They were bad scared."[43]

Minutes later, before some men were even out of their tents, the raiders disappeared. Only one soldier had been slightly wounded. But gone was the entire herd of pack mules valued at nearly ten thousand dollars, as well as some twenty horses belonging mostly to volunteers. During the excitement, the soldiers' picketed horses had milled "round and round" until they had twisted themselves into a grotesque puzzle, said Sergeant Davis, but the warriors had failed to capture them. Several miles away when first light began to break, they realized their mistake. "Eeh! Nothing but mules—all mules!" recalled a disappointed Yellow Wolf.[44]

Howard lost no time ordering a pursuit. Soon Major George Sanford with three companies of about 150 men under Captains Jackson, Carr, and Norwood galloped after the Nez Perce. After organizing the remaining infantry and cavalry into a defense of the camp, General Howard sat down to breakfast. Soon a messenger from Sanford rode up and reported that several of the mules had been recaptured. Before Howard had finished his meal, another courier arrived announcing that the warriors had returned in force and were flanking the major's command. Howard immediately set out with reinforcements. Several miles to the northeast they came over a sagebrush-covered rise and met Major Sanford returning with Carr and Jackson's companies. There were so many Indians, said Sanford, that he had decided to "draw back a little."

"But where is Norwood?" asked the general.

"That is what I am trying to find out," answered the major.[45]

A little farther on they came upon Norwood's company with seven wounded men, the warriors having broken off the fight and departed.

What happened here? It appears from the patching together of various accounts that some six miles from the soldiers' camp the warriors turned on their pursuers. When they got uncomfortably close, Sanford ordered a retreat. Both Carr and Jackson quickly withdrew. Norwood, located in the center of the skirmish, at first "declined to obey," claiming to do so would have unnecessarily exposed his men, although a short time later he fell back several hundred yards to a lava knoll covered with scrubby aspens where he determined to make a stand. There Indians "entirely surrounded his company and kept up a continuous sharp fire" for four long hours, according to an unidentified eyewitness's account in the Virginia City *Madisonian.* How Sanford "lost" Norwood's men has never been satisfactorily explained. Did the men retreat so far that no one could hear the sound of the ongoing battle? Howard is mum in his report. The only grumblings left to posterity were those in the *Madisonian,* saying "much bitterness was expressed concerning the action of the other companies in not going to Norwood's assistance, and the belief was general that had he been vigorously supported a decisive victory would have been obtained."[46]

Some of the men of Norwood's command had reason to wish they had retreated with the others. Having left their horses several hundred yards in the rear, the detachment engaged the Nez Perce on foot. No sooner had Carr and Jackson's men withdrawn, however, than sharpshooters began pouring a raking fire on their flanks.

One man pinned down under the zipping bullets was a very determined officer, Lieutenant Henry M. Benson of the Seventh Infantry. Benson had been in poor health on recruiting duty in Baltimore when he learned of the Nez Perce retreat into Montana. Traveling by train to Bismarck, North Dakota, then by steamboat to Fort Benton and wagon to Fort Shaw, he arrived two days after Gibbon had left for the Bitterroot. Losing his way in a snow storm, this young hotspur missed covering himself in glory at the Big Hole. When Gibbon and his wounded arrived in Deer Lodge, Benson was there, begging for an assignment to Howard's command. Now as he lay next to Sergeant Davis, the lieutenant found glory scant cover when a bullet "entered at the hip-pocket and went out at the other, having passed entirely through both buttocks." About the time the men realized they were being flanked, they heard their bugler blowing "recall" some five hundred yards in an aspen thicket to the rear. Despite his painful wound, Benson and the others quickly got up and started running.[47]

"The race to the thicket was something never to be forgotten," recalled Sergeant Davis, "for a cavalryman is not trained for a five hundred yard sprint. Luck was with us, however, and no man was hit in that mad race for safety. I had a horse's nose-bag slung over my shoulder containing extra cartridges, and a bullet cut the strap and let it fall to the ground. A hero would have stopped, gone back and recovered that bag, but not I."[48]

Here, on a small knoll, the men threw up rock cairns (still visible today) and made their stand. One man received a huge hole in his shoulder from exploding lead, the others a head wound, a knee wound, and one man had a bullet tear through his foot. Private Harry Trevor was blasted in the back by a warrior at fifteen feet, the bullet passing through a lung. Twenty-six-year-old blacksmith Samuel Glass took a bullet through the urinary bladder. Glass lived two days, Trevor six weeks. Catching up with Private Trevor as he lay dying in Virginia City were some government documents he had been long awaiting. His discharge papers had been issued that June, but because he had been constantly in the field since the outbreak of the war, they had failed to reach him. Another wounded man was Corporal Henry Garland. A bullet hit Garland's cartridge belt and drove two cartridges "from it clear through his body." His wound never healed, said Davis, and he "blew out his brains a few years later."[49]

Inspecting the battlefield afterward, survivors found three dead Nez Perce horses and "some pools of blood" but no dead or wounded Indians. Yellow Wolf claimed later only two warriors were slightly wounded. Wottolen was one of those injured when either a ricochet or spent bullet hit him in the ribs. The injury knocked the breath out of him, but when he looked, only "a black spot came as large as a good-sized apple."[50]

The only soldier killed outright was twenty-one-year-old Bernard Brooks, Captain Jackson's well-liked orderly and company bugler. Shot out of his saddle early in the fight, Sergeant Davis watched as Brooks tried "at once to spring up on to his feet again, but only succeeded in getting to his knees. His horse, a very intelligent animal, went back to his fallen master, nickered, and edged up alongside of him. Brooks caught the stirrup strap and tried to lift himself back in the saddle, but just then death came. The horse whinnied and champed and stood around Brooks, plainly urging him to remount. It was a snapshot scene that did not last long, but was quite pitiful while it was passing." Jackson himself recovered the body under fire, for which he was awarded the Medal of Honor.[51]

That afternoon the command assembled on a small knoll near where Howard's tent had been pitched the night before. The incongruity and strangeness of Brooks's death here in the middle of nowhere, in the center of this vast and desolate land, claimed Howard, was unsettling. "He was tenderly prepared for burial. The grave was dug by his comrades; Mason read the touching Episcopal service beside it, while officers and men stood around with solemn and often tear-moistened faces. The farewell volleys were given, and the remains of young Brooks were left to rest there in loneliness till the resurrection."[52]

10

That cloudy August morning in that vast and desolate land seemed to end badly for everyone. The Nez Perce in particular were piqued not to have stolen the cavalry's horses. Mules were not only valued less than a good cayuse, but the raiders were feeling more than a little chagrined over their failure to distinguish the animals in the dark. It was not until later in the day when scouts reported soldiers still camped at Camas Meadows that they began to realize they had struck a telling blow. As one officer admitted, an army expedition was like a dog fastened by a chain—"within the length of chain irresistible, beyond it powerless. The chain was its wagon train and supplies." With the command's wagons still between Junction Station and Pleasant Valley transporting infantry, Howard's fetter had been the pack mules.[1]

Thomas Sutherland thought there was another reason why the general halted his pursuit within striking distance of the Nez Perce. The dog had never proved formidable, chain or no chain. "I candidly think Joseph could whip our cavalry, and cannot blame General Howard for not giving him battle with that battalion at Camas Meadows." Sutherland claimed he had been told by a man who spoke Nez

Perce that in the predawn raid a warrior had cried, " 'Go ahead, you have only cavalrymen against you!' showing, as it were, a species of contempt for our horsemen."[2]

The ever-eager Montana newspapers were filled with ridicule when they learned of the debacle. The *Fort Benton Record* ventured that some of the mules had actually been laden with critical news reports that Howard had been collecting ever since the start of the war. The Indians, mused the paper, would have gotten away without a fight if they had not stopped to read the voluminous accounts.

Late that evening, Captain Marcus Miller and 280 infantry arrived in the wagons, traveling an astonishing forty-six miles since hearing of the fight. The next morning the column again started on the Nez Perce trail, camping not far from where warriors had launched their raid. Here Henry Buck noted that Indians had dug over acres of the meadow for roots of a flowering plant. Nearby, small pine trees had been stripped of their outer bark so that the nutritious layer of cambium could be reached. "These maneuvers led us to believe that their provisions were running low."[3]

Before sunrise on August 22, fifty Bannock warriors rode into camp, having traveled 150 miles from Fort Hall to join the command's other Bannock scouts still under the leadership of Buffalo Horn. Sutherland thought them the most "gorgeous set of warriors" he had ever laid eyes upon. Some carried coup poles trimmed with eagle feathers that "whirled about in the breeze like toy windmills," while others were adorned for war with "dangling scalps." Many had their hair dyed green, some red, others a combination of red, green, and yellow. Their horses' manes and tails were also green, "decorated with bunches of different colored feathers and jingling sleigh bells." The warriors wore buckskin, beautifully ornamented with bead work, and were wrapped in their brightest blankets. As a reward for their efforts, the scouts were promised all the Nez Perce horses they could capture. "This created much excitement among them," remarked Sutherland, "and under their dashing chief, Buffalo Horn, they began almost immediately to plan some way of cutting off the hostiles' immense herd of nearly three thousand head."[4]

Nearly as impressive as the Bannocks was the white scout who had accompanied them from Fort Hall, Stanton (S. G.) Fisher. At first there appeared little remarkable about the man. Howard described him as a tall, pale frontiersman of fair proportions, slightly deaf but possessing extraordinary sharpness of sight. "Yet of all the scouts in our Indian campaign," said the general, none came to equal Fisher. "Night and day, with guides and without, with force and without, Fisher fearlessly hung upon the skirts of the enemy. The accuracy, carefulness, and fullness of his reports . . . were a delight." Such praise is singular when one considers the numerous scouts employed during the war. Howard must have realized he had an unusually capable individual when the next day he ordered a rest halt, sending a signal indicating "war or trouble" to Fisher on the trail ahead. When the scout learned he had been called back for no particular reason, he was livid, informing the general that "I was no 'Injin!' Howard asked me my meaning, whereupon I told him I was a white man and could read writing, and when he had orders or anything of the kind to send them in writing." According to Fisher, Howard apologized and told the scout he could do as he liked as long as he kept the command informed.[5]

That night the column camped beside the Henrys Fork of the Snake River, and Buffalo Horn's scouts performed a war dance. As the painted Bannocks cavorted, their shadows twisting and writhing in the firelight like some phantasmagoria from Dante's *Inferno*, Howard felt apprehension rising among onlooking soldiers, a feeling akin almost to "panic." This is understandable—most men must have sensed that these "friendly" Indians had more in common with those waiting beyond the darkness than themselves. Not everyone saw it that way, however. Henry Buck recalled feeling quite at ease, saying that "we all enjoyed it very much."[6]

Near midnight, the general could take no more and called a halt to the dancing. Soon after, Buffalo Horn and "a thick-set, semi-savage half-breed" named Charley Rainey approached Howard and asked to kill the command's three Nez Perce herders, "Captain" John, Old George, and another man. Rainey claimed the men, two of whom had enlisted because they had daughters traveling with the bands, were traitors. Because "they had rejoiced openly at Joseph's success in surprising our mule herd," they ought to die. The general brought Old George forward to face his accusers. "He was so frank, and evidently so honest, that the story against him was not for a moment believed," said Howard, "and Buffalo Horn was denied the small favor of killing the three. He was very angry in consequence, and never quite forgave me for this refusal."[7]

Buffalo Horn was so aggravated, in fact, that he quit and rode off alone to Fort Hall several days later. Even before this, the chief had shown his disgust when Howard refused to promptly pursue the Nez Perce after the battle at Camas Meadows. Asked later what he thought of Howard, he is said to have replied, "Howard he no good; he walk-walk-walk. No catchem Indian walk!" Buffalo Horn's only surviving photograph supports this view of a haughty individual: a fierce, scowling face with a piercing stare, long chestnut-brown hair swept back over his left ear, a bandolier of ammunition strung over one shoulder, and seven mottled eagle feathers fanning out behind his head. Before another year would pass, Buffalo Horn would lead his people in a futile war over broken treaty promises and white encroachment not unlike those suffered by the Nez Perce, and Howard's forces would hunt him down and kill him.[8]

Due to the excitement stirred up by the war dance, Howard ordered "boots and saddles" at two o'clock the next morning and off went the command again. Seven hours later they arrived at the southern end of Henrys Lake. As the men halted to rest, scouts returned saying that the bands had passed through Tacher Pass toward Yellowstone National Park two days before. When they heard the news, "the greatest discouragement seized upon officers and men," said Howard. "It was like a poor dog watching the hole from which the badger had just escaped."[9]

When Howard gave orders to start up again, Chief Surgeon Charles Alexander walked up to him and announced, "You can go no farther." The command was in terrible shape, Alexander argued, and had rations for only five more days. They needed rest and resupply. Others agreed. "Our men are very short of clothing," wrote Major Mason to his wife that night. "Many are without overcoats and blankets; some men have neither; all are ragged, dirty and lousy, not having had opportunity for 23 days to wash or even take off their clothes. . . . I have never known a command to be so hard pushed as this has during the past month." The men had begun the campaign in summer uniforms, and now with ice forming on water pails at night, they were suffering. They had marched nearly continuously for twenty-six days, averaging nearly twenty miles per day. Scout J. W. Redington reported that many of the infantry were wearing cowhide shoes with soles fastened by brass screws, a current War Department experiment. When wet, the screws bored into the men's feet. Some had been forced to make burlap moccasins to avoid going barefoot.[10]

Even Thomas Sutherland, Howard's always-faithful champion, favored a halt. "Our pursuit of Joseph and his nimble followers has been one tiresome jog trot from the rising of the sun to the going down of the same," wrote the correspondent. Occasionally the Indians' "pranks" would inspire the men to give another "spurt" of energy in pursuit, but for the most part "our marches have been tiresome and accomplished only with much fatigue." Because the Nez Perce "have a faculty of stealing fresh horses from the settlers whenever needed, while the pursuers are compelled to bestride the same fagged out animals from beginning to end, it is a wonder that we have ever caught up with them at all."[11]

John FitzGerald was more emphatic. "Everyone, believe me," he wrote Emily, "is sick and tired of a fruitless pursuit of these Indians." FitzGerald held Howard responsible. "Not many officers are in sympathy with him, and a great many think he is guilty of folly of the gravest kind to follow on at the expense of loss in men and animals in a hopeless pursuit."[12]

Besieged on all fronts, Howard ordered the command to make camp while he deliberated. It was a difficult decision, made no easier for his Chief of Staff Major Mason when the general "changed his plans three or four times—making work for me each time." Finally Howard decided to travel to the nearest telegraph office at Virginia City, some seventy miles distant, and wire San Francisco. If McDowell ordered him on, then he could make arrangements there for resupplies. "I am anxious on the men's accounts to have the campaign close," Mason wrote his wife. "But I don't expect it will, for the craving over newspaper applause overrides other considerations."[13]

Late that afternoon, Howard, his son, Guy, and Lieutenant John

Q. Adams, the acting quartermaster, left in a light wagon for Virginia City. The road was full of boulders and sleep was almost impossible in the springless wagon, said Howard, but after riding for past days using the "clothes-pin method," the men welcomed the change. After an all-night ride, they rolled into Virginia City, a mining town "planted . . . in the midst of a wilderness of hills and mountains."[14]

Howard wasted no time dashing off a telegram to General McDowell in San Francisco requesting "to hear from you in answer to telegrams sent" over a week before from Bannack, Montana. Back came a reply from McDowell's adjutant general, Lieutenant Colonel J. C. Kelton, that was dated August 17 but had failed to reach Howard when the Nez Perce cut the telegraph wire near Pleasant Valley. With icy formality, Kelton upbraided Howard, reminding him that on repeated occasions General Sherman himself had directed that he "pay no attention to boundary lines" in his pursuit of the Nez Perce, that he was "to follow them up till they are defeated and surrender, or are driven beyond the United States." If the Indians can find food, Sherman had said, "the troops can also, of course." Then Kelton chided Howard over his earlier insinuation that he had not had "prompt and energetic cooperation" from other departments in heading off the Nez Perce. Everything that could be done had been done. "The General, in all kindness, asks me to suggest to you to be less dependent on what others at a distance may or may not do, and rely more on your own forces and your own plans."[15]

Howard quickly backed down, replying that he was "very sorry to be misunderstood." He had not wanted to complain of lack of cooperation but had only wanted timely assistance from other departments, which now appeared was being rendered. As for continuing the chase, "my duty shall be done fully and to the letter without complaint."[16]

So went Howard's official response—obedient, submissive, soldierly.

When Thomas Sutherland learned of the contents of Kelton's telegram, he penned a ruthless dispatch to the San Francisco *Chronicle* aimed squarely at McDowell:

The hero of Bull Run may possibly know how to waddle around a parlor and toady to San Francisco capitalists, but if he can see a single instance of genuine cooperation that General Howard has received from his brother department commanders . . . then he is even a more wonderful person than he is in his own estimation. . . . If I were a general and should receive only such assistance as this, I would make it a point to tell McDowell, "in all kindness," that he is an ass, should he unjustly taunt me as he has Howard. Another brilliant remark of this fire eater is that where Indians can live, of course we can. This coming from a man whose waistcoat covers the most delicate and expensive viands of the San Francisco market every blessed day, is exceedingly ironical.[17]

Of course, the remark about "living off the country" had been made by Sherman, not McDowell. The rest may have contained some truth. McDowell was rather corpulent, a renowned bon vivant, known more for his lavish parties and support for the arts in the Bay area than his grasp of frontier realities. He was also a rabid prohibitionist. Once, a story goes, his horse reared and fell on him, knocking him unconscious. A surgeon tried to open his mouth to get some brandy in him, but his teeth were clenched too tightly. Later, when told what happened, McDowell said he was glad that even when unconscious liquor could not be forced down him. The reference to Bull Run also hit home. In the Union's opening gambit of the Civil War, it had been McDowell's army that was ignominiously trounced. Two days after the battle, Lincoln went to Arlington to visit McDowell. "I have not lost a particle of confidence in you," said Lincoln, sensitive to his commanding general's defeat. To which McDowell responded, "I don't see why you should, Mr. President." A few days later, Lincoln sacked him.[18]

That Sutherland had drawn blood became evident when an officer passed through San Francisco en route to Montana and wrote Howard that he had found the general in "exceedingly bad humor generally and particularly so at . . . Louis Scribbler" who should be "shut up or kicked out of camp." Later Howard apologized to

McDowell for the article saying, "I did not dream that anything vituperative had been sent." Despite such penance, it is difficult to imagine Howard not taking at least a modicum of delight in Sutherland's broadside.[19]

Howard also exchanged telegrams with General Sherman, just returned from Yellowstone Park and now in Helena. When Howard suggested that his command was "so much worn by overfatigue and jaded animals that I cannot push it much farther," Sherman gently but firmly replied that his force "should pursue the Nez Perces to the death, lead where they may." If Howard was too tired, he should "give the command to some young energetic officer, and let him follow them, go where they may, holding his men well in hand, subsisting them on beef gathered in the country, with coffee, sugar and salt in packs."[20]

If Sherman had in mind his highly successful March to the Sea during the Civil War, the man who had led his right wing of that epic tramp was acutely aware of the difference as he pondered the general's answer. No enemy had preceded Sherman, absconding with stock and food in its wake. Besides, this was the wild West, not Georgia, and they were about to enter one of the most isolated and uninhabited areas in the country, one that Sherman himself had just visited. Within a few weeks Sherman would attempt overland travel by horse and wagon between Missoula and Portland, later admitting in his annual report: "I recognize the full measure of the labors, exposure, fatigue, and fighting of General Howard and his command, having personally seen much of the route over which he passed, and knowing the great difficulty in procuring food for men and horses in that mountain region." But for now, although couched in language less severe than Kelton's, he offered little sympathy.

Howard replied with characteristic resolve. When his command was ready to resume the pursuit within a few days, he wired Sherman:

You misunderstood me. I never flag. It was the command, including the most energetic young officers, that were worn out and weary by a most extraordinary march. You need not fear for the campaign. Neither you nor General McDowell can doubt my pluck and energy. My Indian scouts are on the heels of the enemy. My supplies have just come in and we will move in the morning and will continue to the end.

To which Sherman responded:

Glad to find you so plucky. Have every faith in your intense energy, but thought it probable you were worn out, and I think sometimes men of less age and rank are best for Indian warfare. They have more to make. . . .

This final message sounds supportive, but in truth, Sherman had lost faith in Howard's ability. In less than a week, unknown to Howard, the general of the army would move to replace him as the campaign's commanding officer. Using the excuse of wishing to confer with Howard during his trip to the Department of the Columbia, Sherman ordered Lieutenant Colonel Charles C. Gilbert from Camp Baker east of Helena to overtake Howard's command and, provided Howard agreed to take Sherman's "advice," relieve him. Sherman also wired Sheridan: "I don't think Howard's troops will catch Joseph, but they will follow, trusting to your troops heading them off when they come out on the east of the mountains."

Over a week before Sheridan had anticipated this turn of events. Now he was amassing, throughout Montana and Wyoming, over one thousand of the army's most experienced soldiers in Indian warfare to "clean out" the beleaguered Nez Perce as they exited from the Yellowstone country. The only problem was that since no one knew the exact route by which the Indians might leave the park, all exits had to be covered. Ordered to Camp Brown in central Wyoming, the Fifth Cavalry's Colonel Wesley Merritt was assembling six companies, preparing to head off the bands should they break out southeast of the park. Nearby in the Bighorn Mountains, Major Verling Hart with another battalion of Fifth Cavalry was ordered by Sheridan to cover the eastern boundary. Near the northeast entrance, Colonel Samuel Sturgis waited impatiently with six companies of the recently refurbished Seventh Cavalry, anxious to atone for the Little Bighorn. And in eastern Montana at his district of the Yellowstone headquarters on the Tongue River, restlessly watching these unfolding events, was the most eager Indian fighter with "more to make" than all the others, Colonel Nelson Miles.

When he left the telegraph office that morning, Howard quickly began buying nearly everything that Virginia City could furnish in the way of provisions, clothing, and fresh stock. Over two hundred horses and mules were purchased from "the shrewdest of jockeys," who claimed the animals were well broken. Later, Howard discovered that their "pitching and plunging, hooting and yelling, running and falling, made one think of danger ahead from something beside Indians!" That evening, leaving the supplies to be freighted to camp, the general and his son climbed into the wagon and started back to Henrys Lake, arriving the following morning. Not long afterward, Howard dispatched three companies under Captain Harry Cushing to Fort Ellis to obtain additional provisions and reinforcements, then to circle around via the Yellowstone River. There Cushing was to link up with Sturgis, who Howard had learned by telegraph in Virginia City was in the best position to try to trap the Nez Perce as they exited the park.[21]

During Howard's absence at Henrys Lake, the men had relaxed, swimming, washing and mending their clothes, and hunting and fishing. Sutherland had watched as some of the men dragged a seine through the lake, loading a boat with numerous huge trout. "Swans, geese, ducks and snipe are very abundant, while on the prairies nearby antelope and deer are very plentiful."[22]

When the men learned of McDowell's orders, Howard claimed they were ready, to a man, to go to the "death." Putting the best face on the dressing-down he had received at Virginia City, he said that it was worthwhile "to bear a little chagrin in order to awaken such a loyal spirit." It appears true that after their initial grumblings and a four-day rest, most of the men, although far from happy about it, accepted their fate. Major Mason believed by now the Nez Perce were "two or three hundred miles away," and he looked forward to seeing the world's premier national park. "I shall be glad to see these wonderful places," the lonely officer wrote his wife, "but one hour at home would be worth it all."[23]

. . .

The same evening that Howard's weary men settled in at Henrys Lake for their well-earned reprieve from chasing Indians, some thirty-five miles away in Yellowstone National Park prospector John Shively was sitting near his campfire eating supper. About fifty-five years old, Shively was on the final leg of a long and fruitless journey in search of gold that had begun months before in Wyoming's Bighorn Mountains, taken him around Yellowstone Lake, and finally into the Lower Geyser Basin of the Firehole River. The day before he had befriended a party of nine tourists from Radersburg, Montana, who were just completing their vacation, intending to start home the next day via the Madison River trail. Shively planned to accompany them and was camped in the Lower Geyser Basin near the East Fork of the Firehole (now known as Nez Perce Creek) about a mile away.

Three Indians with rifles suddenly appeared in the tall grass in front of him. Shively jumped up, turned around, reaching for his gun leaning against a nearby tree, but found himself surrounded, staring into the rifles of thirty or forty warriors. He asked who they were. Sioux, answered one who could speak English. "No, you're not Sioux," the prospector said. Then the warrior admitted they were Nez Perce, and several "flourished their pistols" close to his head. Folding his arms, Shively determined to die "game," telling them to kill him "at once, that he was not afraid to die."[24]

The warriors talked to each other for several moments; then one stepped forward, placed his hand over Shively's heart, and said, "Hyas skukum tum tum." The prospector knew enough pidgin Chinook to realize the warrior was declaring that he had a strong heart. The men then put him on a horse and led him down the river a short distance to their camp. There he was placed in the center of a council circle of chiefs and asked if he would guide the bands to Crow country. He would be "very glad" to do so, he replied, finding such a task "very much preferable to being shot."

So began John Shively's nine or ten days of captivity by the Nez Perce, a detailed account of which he gave a few weeks later to editor James Mills of the *New North-West*. Mills vouched for the prospector, declaring him "a gentleman of strict veracity and high character," and Shively even certified Mills's published version. Despite such ringing endorsement there are problems with this recollection: confusion over dates, his estimate of the total number of warriors, and more than a little doubt about how much the Nez Perce actually relied on Shively as a guide. Suspicion increases when, as in so much frontier eyewitness narrative, the author immodestly places himself on center stage. As one of the Indians who captured Shively, Yellow Wolf gave a version substantially less dramatic, mentioning nothing about the prospector's self-congratulatory courage and denying he guided the bands more than briefly. But no matter. What is important is that Shively became one of few whites to travel for an extended period with the Nez Perce, view the daily rhythms of camp life during their journey through Yellowstone Park and, most of all, live to tell about it.

"There are from 600 to 800 Nez Perces in the band," he observed quite accurately, the actual number thought to be about 700 after their losses at the Big Hole. "Of these, 250 are warriors, but all will fight that can carry a gun. They have almost 2,000 head of good average horses. Every lodge drives its own horses in front of it when traveling, each lodge keeping its band separate." Their horses looked in fair condition. One-sixth appeared to be disabled, lame, or sore-backed, but enough remained for riders to change frequently and "still hold all the best horses in reserve." The Nez Perce were well armed and may have had "more ammunition than they want." They seemed anxious about the soldiers overtaking them at first and had "no intimation any troops were trying to intercept them in front."

So far as Shively could tell, no particular chief appeared in command. His statement that "all matters were decided in council of several chiefs" arrived too late to quell the blossoming myth of Joseph. Looking Glass wore a white feather and Joseph a single feather of an eagle. The latter always seemed in a pleasant mood, the miner said, meeting him each time with a "nod and smile." The Indians said they had "lost 43 warriors altogether, of these 6 or 7 were killed in Norwood's fight near Camas Meadow[s], the remainder at the Big Hole, where they lost many women and children." Ten or twelve were seriously injured and at least one died during his stay. They said they would fight soldiers but did not want to fight citizens. They claimed to have been "robbed and swindled" in Idaho and now they were "going to make a new home in the Crow country, and would be joined by a thousand or more lodges, including Crows, when they reached that country."

Shively told Mills he was put in the care of Joe Hale (Poker Joe), who admonished him that he "would be his friend, but that he must not try to escape or the Nez Perces would be heap mad. Mr. S. says he assented. A feeling of desperation had possessed him. He would keep his own counsel, take what [might] come, escape when he got a chance or die if he had to, and with this philosophic conclusion, slept soundly all the night."

Sleeping not so serenely only a mile away at the Radersburg tourist camp was twenty-three-year-old Emma Cowan. While some of the male members of her party have been accused of offering inaccurate and exaggerated accounts of events that were about to transpire, Emma's appears the least pretentious and for that reason, the most trustworthy. Photographs show her to be a striking woman, slim with high cheek bones, her long hair rolled into a bun with a pompadour. Only a few days before, General Sherman's party, with an escort of only four soldiers, had ridden up and announced the Nez Perce might be near. "No one seemed to know just where they were going," declared Emma. "The scout who was with the General's party assured us we would be perfectly safe if we would remain in the Basin, as the Indians would never come into the Park."[25]

Then she watched them ride away, noting that Sherman's party "preferred being elsewhere, as they left the Basin that same night."[26]

Cowan's group had been warned of the outbreak on leaving Radersburg on August 6 but thought it nothing more than "an old-time Indian scare." Now they were growing apprehensive. That evening, Albert "Al" Oldham and Emma's twenty-seven-year-old brother, Frank Carpenter, "in order to enliven us somewhat, sang songs, told jokes, and finally dressed up as brigands, with pistols, knives and guns strapped on them. Al Oldham, with his swart complexion, wearing a broad sombrero, looked a typical one, showing off to good advantage before the glaring camp fire. They made the woods ring with their nonsense and merriment for some time."

The others were all family or friends—her thirty-five-year-old husband, George Cowan, a lawyer with a long sweeping mustache, receding hairline, and alert eyes; Ida Carpenter, Emma's thirteen-year-old sister; William Dingee; Charles Mann; A. J. Arnold; and D. L. Meyers. Outfitted with a double-seated carriage, baggage wagon, and four saddle horses, they also had a dog, guns, fishing rods, a violin, and a guitar. The following day, August 24, was Emma and George's second wedding anniversary.

At first light, Dingee and Arnold rose and built a campfire. Taking a pail and coffeepot to the nearby stream, Dingee was startled when he looked up and saw three Indians sitting quietly on horses. He nodded and they nodded back. Then they followed him back to camp. From inside the tent she was sharing with her husband and sister, Emma heard voices, sure they were those of Indians even before she looked through the flap of the tent.

Yellow Wolf was one of the warriors. Having observed their campfire the night before, he was in favor of killing them. Another man suggested letting the chiefs decide their fate. As they approached the camp, "a fine looking man"—probably Arnold or Oldham—stood up and shook hands with the warriors, an action, said Yellow Wolf, that "put me in mind not to kill him."[27] Soon all were awake and after talking, the whites decided "to break camp at once and attempt to move out as though nothing unusual was at hand. No one cared for breakfast save the Indians, who quickly devoured everything that was prepared." By now twenty or thirty warriors had arrived, with more coming every moment. "The woods," recalled Emma, "seemed full of them."

While the men packed up camp, Arnold stood in the wagon and began giving away sugar, flour, and bacon. When he observed this, Emma's husband, George, walked up and, brandishing his rifle, "ordered the Indians away, not very mildly either. Naturally they resented it, and I think this materially lessened his chances of escape."

As they headed down the trail toward the Madison River, the warriors rode with them. They had not gone far when forty or fifty additional men joined them. "Every Indian carried splendid guns, with belts full of cartridges. As the morning sunshine glinted on the polished surface of the gun barrels, a regiment of soldiers could not have looked more formidable." There was a brief discussion, then one of the warriors ordered them to turn around and start after the bands, already on the trail up East Fork Creek toward the Yellowstone River. George Cowan loudly protested but finally concluded they had no choice. "The Indians pretended all this while to be our very good friends," said Emma, "saying that if they should let us go, bad Indians, as they termed them, would kill us."

Two miles farther the trail narrowed, and with much fallen timber ahead, they were forced to unhitch their wagons and mount horses. "It gave us no pleasure to see our wagons overhauled, ransacked and destroyed." Emma watched as spokes were cut from the buggy wheels to use as whip handles. "One young chap dashed past us with several yards of pink mosquito bar tied to his horse's tail." Another "ugly old Indian" appropriated a piece of swansdown Emma had found earlier and wrapped it around his head turban fashion, an act that "did not please me either."

As they moved through the dense timber, she could scarcely believe how the Nez Perce drove their horses. While whites would have stopped to cut away fallen trees, they pressed on relentlessly. Whenever a pack horse got wedged between trees, "an old squaw would pound them on the head until they backed out. And such yelling."

Some ten miles beyond near Mary Mountain, the bands stopped to rest. Poker Joe approached and, speaking "good English," told them he wanted to "trade" for their horses and saddles, that afterward they were free to go. A few moments later they were left with one saddle, several worn-out horses, and a mule with a fresh bullet hole in its shoulder. During the exchange, Dingee and Arnold managed to slip into the dense timber and escape. Then Poker Joe told Emma and the others to "go quick."

One-half mile back down the trail to the Lower Geyser Basin, Emma turned around to see a group of twenty or thirty warriors riding hard to catch up with them. "Their gaiety of the morning was lacking," she said, finding their somber faces ominous. The warriors rode silently alongside for a few minutes, then

suddenly, without warning, shots rang out. Two Indians came dashing down the trail in front of us. My husband was getting off his horse, I wondered for what reason. I soon knew, for he fell as soon as he reached the ground—fell headlong down the hill. Shots followed and Indian yells, and all was confusion. In less time than it takes me to tell it, I was off my horse and by my husband's side, where he lay against a fallen pine tree. I heard my sister's screams and called to her. She came and crouched by me, as I knelt by his side. I saw he was wounded in the leg above the knee, and by the way the blood spurted out I feared an artery had been severed. He asked for water. I dared not leave him to get it, even had it been near. I think we both glanced up the hill at the same moment, for he said, "Keep quiet. It won't last long." That thought had flashed through my mind also. Every gun of the whole party of Indians was leveled on us three. I shall never forget the picture, which left an impress that years cannot efface. The holes in those gun barrels looked as big as saucers.

As Emma clung to her husband, a warrior wrenched her away while another stepped close and brandishing "an immense navy pistol," pointed the gun directly at George Cowan's forehead. The gun fired, "my husband's head fell back, and a red stream trickled down his face from beneath his hat." The last thing Emma saw before she fainted was a warrior pounding her husband's head with a rock.

Screaming, Ida Carpenter started to run away, but a warrior "caught me by the throat and choked me." When her assailant loosened his hold, the scrappy teenager bit his fingers.[28]

Her brother, Frank, claimed he instinctively crossed himself as an Indian prepared to shoot him, whereupon the man appeared to change his mind and led him away from the others. The warrior, Red Scout, later emphatically denied the sign had anything to do with saving Carpenter's life, accusing Christians of being "the cause of most of these troubles." He had simply taken "pity on the women, seeing their tears."[29] Moments later, Poker Joe came riding up and ordered the three whites placed on horses. Surrounded by warriors, the group started up the trail after the bands. Neither Emma, Frank, nor Ida had seen what happened to the other three men.

Why the tourists were attacked after Poker Joe first released them is unclear, but indications are that none of the chiefs realized that some warriors had turned back. Asked earlier that morning by one of the whites if the Nez Perce planned to kill them, Yellow Wolf had replied, "They are double minded," implying that not everyone agreed with the decision to free them. Some no doubt feared that the fleeing tourists would meet Howard and tell him of their location. After the Big Hole most Nez Perce considered all whites bitter enemies. When the chiefs learned the warriors were missing, they sent Poker Joe to protect the whites, but he arrived just after Cowan had been shot.[30]

That night the bands camped in Hayden Valley a few miles west of the Yellowstone River. Frank and Emma were held in Joseph's camp, Ida with Poker Joe. Food was offered, but Emma had no appetite, scarcely able to believe the fate that had befallen them. As Joseph sat by the campfire, she observed that he was "sombre and silent," personifying a more perfect image of "the noble red man" than any she had ever seen. "Grave and dignified," she said, "he looked a chief."

Frank Carpenter recalled that when Joseph heard about the attack on the whites, "with a motion of disgust [he] got up and went over where his squaw and . . . daughter were. He was evidently displeased with the actions of the Indians, in the shooting of our party."[31] Sitting near the fire, Joseph's wife smiled at Emma. When she was given the child to hold, "I glanced at the chief and saw the glimmer of a smile on his face, showing that he had heart beneath the stony exterior." When Emma began crying, the woman asked Frank Carpenter the reason for her tears. "He told her my husband had been killed that day. She replied, 'She heartsick.' I was indeed."

Emma's misery evoked little pity from Poker Joe. Striding up, the warrior lifted "his dirty old shirt and showed us a bullet wound through his chest and back—just a small hole in front and an ugly ragged one in the back. How he escaped blood-poisoning, I cannot say. There was no dressing on the wound, and all that covered it was his shirt, but it seemed to be healing in spite of the dirt and lack of care. How he could harangue the camp, so to speak, with such an injury, was a wonder to us. He could be heard for half-a-mile." Other accounts claim Poker Joe had not been wounded at the Big

Hole or Camas Meadows. In particular, Shively, who was under the close personal supervision of Poker Joe throughout his capture, fails to mention any injury.

The following day, the bands moved to the Yellowstone River where at noon they crossed some six or seven miles above the lake. On the far side they stopped to rest and eat. Emma watched as a woman prepared cutthroat trout, slicing the largest ones in half and dumping them "into an immense camp kettle filled with water, and boiled to a pulp. The formality of cleaning," she observed uncomfortably, "had not entered into the formula."

Here a council was held. Seven men sat in a circle and passed a long pipe around. "Each took a few whiffs of smoke, and then one by one they arose and spoke." Then Poker Joe told Emma that she and her sister would be released along with James Irwin, a recently discharged soldier traveling through the park whom the Nez Perce had captured that morning. When she protested, refusing to go until they released her brother as well, they agreed to keep Irwin instead. As she prepared to leave, Emma said good-bye to Shively, promising to deliver messages to friends in Philipsburg should they escape. So little did she trust the Nez Perce that she told the prospector she considered his chances of survival better than their own. "No," Shively replied, "something tells me you will get out safely."

Mounting the threesome on "poor" horses, Poker Joe led them back across the river and about a mile down the valley. Here he gave them a little food and some matches, and warned them not to stop until they reached Bozeman, but to travel "all night, all day, no sleep." He also gave them an urgent message. "Me want you to tell'm people in Bozeman me no fight no more now. Me no want to fight Montana citizens. Me no want to fight Montana soldiers. Me want peace." On and on he went about peace until Emma thought he would never stop talking. Then he abruptly spun his horse around and left them alone. As Emma and her brother and sister rode down the river and away from the Indian camp, "it seemed folly to think we could escape."

But they did.

By late afternoon the following day some twelve miles from Mammoth Hot Springs near the northwest entrance of the park, they stumbled on a small scouting detachment from Fort Ellis led by Lieutenant Charles Schofield. Here they encountered Frederic Pfister, a tourist from another party also unlucky enough to have met the Nez Perce. The entire group returned to Mammoth that night, and joined by several other tourists the next day, they started for Bozeman, believing most, if not all, of the remaining members of each tourist party dead.

After escaping into the brush, Dingee and Arnold had headed back toward the Madison River. Four days later, without arms, food, or extra clothing and after making wide detours whenever they happened on Fisher's Bannock scouts whom they mistook for Nez Perce, the two men arrived at Henrys Lake. As they debated whether or not the figures camped on the distant shore were Indians, "we heard a strain of the most beautiful music that I ever heard," said Arnold. "It was a bugle call. We had found the soldiers." Myers and Mann showed up soon afterward, along with another lone prospector who had been camped not far away, all unharmed except for Mann who arrived with "a ball hole" through his hat.[32]

On August 29, as Howard's command struck the Madison River wagon road near the park's west entrance, they discovered Al Oldham. Major Mason recorded he had been shot through the face and "was almost dead from hunger and cold."[33] At the same time warriors had converged on George Cowan, a man riding just uphill of Oldham had turned and shot him in the left cheek, the ball penetrating downward, knocking out two teeth, partly severing the root of his tongue and passing through the bottom of his jaw. Tumbling off his horse but holding on to his rifle, he rolled down a ravine. When Oldham looked up, his assailant was coming down after him. He raised up the gun to shoot and the warrior ran back up the hill. As he pulled the trigger, the gun misfired. Choking on blood pouring down his throat, Oldham escaped into the brush. By the time soldiers found him, his blood-encrusted tongue was so swollen he could barely swallow or breathe. When asked what had happened, he grunted and motioned for pencil and paper.

Back near Hayden Valley not far from where Oldham and the others had escaped lay George Cowan, his clothes soaked in blood but still alive. Regaining consciousness, he cleared the matt of blood and hair from his eyes and discovered he had been shot in the forehead. When he probed the wounds on the back of his head where a warrior had beaten him with a rock, "I then thought the ball had passed entirely through my head in some way. Feeling my leg, I found it completely benumbed, but there were no bones broken." Cowan raised up, using a small tree for support. Then he saw an Indian close by sitting on a horse watching him. "As I was hobbling away, I glanced backward and saw him on one knee aiming his gun at me. Then followed a twinging sensation in my left side, and the report of the gun and I dropped forward on my face. The ball had struck me on the side above the hip and came out in front of the abdomen." He lay motionless, expecting the coup de grace at any moment. Twenty minutes later he was still waiting, the warrior inexplicably having disappeared.[34]

Now Cowan's ordeal began.

With both legs paralyzed, he started crawling the ten or so miles back to his party's last camp in the Lower Geyser Basin. Nights were so cold, he claimed, that moving was the only way to keep warm. At the remains of the abandoned wagons, he discovered his dog, who bounded out to meet him. Five days after being wounded he crawled into the old camp, having eaten no food along the way. There he found twelve matches and a handful of coffee. He managed to build a fire and heat water in a discarded can; the coffee, he reported later, "refreshed me greatly." The next day he crawled down the trail, dragging himself through East Fork Creek to the bank of the Firehole River. Exhausted and unable to go farther, Cowan collapsed, giving "myself up for dead." Two hours later, J. W. Redington and another man who were carrying rations ahead to Fisher's scouts found him beside the trail. The men built a fire, placed Cowan close by, and gave him some hardtack and a blanket, then rode on after saying the command would be along shortly. Later that night, according to some accounts, Cowan awoke to find his clothes on fire, forcing him to crawl into the nearby Firehole River to escape the flames. With the knowledge of the army's approach, however, soon "my desire for life returned, and it seems the spirit of revenge took complete possession of me. I knew that I would live, and I took a solemn vow that I would devote the rest of my days killing Indians, especially Nez Perces."[35] There is no evidence that this man ever made good his oath, but by the time he had recovered, others were fast fulfilling his wish.

If Howard had any doubts that Cowan's cantankerous nature had kept him alive when the command found him propped up against a tree the next day, they were soon dispelled. Instead of gratitude, the lawyer had nothing but contempt for the general and his staff who he claimed went off "picknicking" in the geyser basin while he lay dying. It seems nearly everyone in the command found the man disagreeable. When A. J. Arnold, who had accompanied the soldiers from Henrys Lake in hope of finding survivors, finally located and returned with Surgeon FitzGerald, Cowan accused FitzGerald of "probing my wounds in anything but a gentle manner." Using forceps, the surgeon removed the flattened ball embedded in his skull, the damp powder in the cartridge apparently having failed to fully ignite. Then FitzGerald stalked off, refusing to dress his remaining wounds.[36]

The day the army rescued him, Cowan learned Emma had survived. "His joy when told of the safety of his wife was most touching," recalled Major Mason, although he admitted Cowan's "whole tale sounds like a romance."[37] A few days later in Radersburg, wearing a black mourning dress, an astonished Emma Cowan answered a knock at the door and learned that her husband was alive. After an arduous and painful journey over the Mount Washburn trail in the same springless wagon in which Howard had spent a sleepless night the week before, Cowan—cared for only by Arnold the entire way— was finally reunited with his wife at a ranch outside the park exactly one month after being shot.

His troubles were far from over, however. During the journey from the ranch back to Radersburg, several miles outside of Bozeman the wagon broke and flipped over, depositing Cowan in the road just before it plunged over a steep hill. Hours later, after managing to secure another wagon, Emma and Arnold finally placed Cowan in a hotel bed. As they redressed his suppurating wounds, the bedstead suddenly gave way and crashed to the floor with "a fearful jolt." Cowan looked up, said Arnold, and suggested that "if we couldn't kill him any other way, to turn the artillery loose on him." A week later, Cowan arrived home in Radersburg where he finally recovered. Apparently no worse for wear and as irascible as ever, he lived until 1926, dying at the age of eighty-four.[38]

Another party of tourists was less fortunate. On the day the Nez Perce crossed the Yellowstone River, ten men from Helena— Charles Kenck, Andrew Weikert, John Stewart, Frederic Pfister, Richard Dietrich, Joseph Roberts, August Foller, Leonard Duncan, Leslie Wilkie, and a black cook named Ben Stone—observed the bands in the distance, mistaking them for an elk herd or a large party of tourists. An investigation soon revealed both unshod horse prints and moccasin tracks, and the men wisely decided to vacate the area. For some reason, however, that evening they camped at Otter Creek, a mile or two above the Upper Falls of the Yellowstone and only six miles away from where the Nez Perce had crossed the river. Although they passed nearby that afternoon, Emma, Frank, and Ida failed to see any sign of the Helena party. After a nervous and mostly sleepless night, in the morning Weikert and Wilkie returned upriver to reconnoiter while the others remained in camp. At noon Ben Stone began to prepare lunch and Pfister went to gather firewood.

Suddenly Indians began firing from the edge of the trees. Roberts and Foller escaped into the forest where three days later, footsore and hungry, they met Howard's command coming up the Madison River. Pfister also ran into the heavy timber and later encountered Lieutenant Schofield's detachment about the same time as did Emma Cowen and her brother and sister. Ben Stone ran toward the creek, turning "three somersaults" down a slope. Fifteen or twenty yards away a warrior fired at him but missed, and Stone rolled into the creek, pretending to be dead. "I lay there three hours while the Indians plundered the camp. The creek was very cold and I was soon chilled through." When he started shaking uncontrollably and fearing the warriors would discover he was alive, Stone crawled out and started for Mammoth Hot Springs.[39]

Stewart was asleep when the Nez Perce attacked. He and Kenck began running across the meadow toward the timber when Stewart fell, shot in the leg and hip. As two warriors ran past, Stewart heard Kenck shout, "Oh, my God!" Two shots rang out and he heard, "I'm murdered!" Then one of the warriors returned and leveled a gun in

Stewart's face. "I instinctively threw up my hands and begged for my life." The warrior asked him if he had any money. Reaching into Stewart's pocket, he came away with $263 and a silver watch. When the other warrior came up, presumably having stopped to strip Kenck, "they opened my roll of money and had a great laugh over it, seeming very much elated at getting so much. Then they examined my wound which, at the time, was bleeding profusely, told me they would not kill me, and walked off."

After the Nez Perce looted the camp and stole the men's horses, Stewart tried to make his way up the hill to see whether Kenck was dead or alive, but "I was too weak and had to abandon the trip. I then called to him at the top of my voice but could receive no answer." Using a stick for a crutch and filling his pockets with food and matches, he started on the trail down the valley. He had gone only a short distance when he discovered his horse, which somehow had managed to break away from the raiders. A little farther on Stewart ran into Ben Stone, and soon after that, Weikert and Wilkie rode up.

These two men had traveled up the river, discovered the bands had moved on to Yellowstone Lake, and had started back when they ran into an ambush. As they wheeled their horses around and began riding away, leaning far forward in the saddle, a bullet creased Weikert's shoulder blade, leaving a four-inch gash but not breaking the bone. When another bullet shattered the stock of his rifle, "I then began hugging my horse a little closer." Suddenly his horse tripped and fell, and he sprawled in front of the animal. The horse regained its feet, and shooting once at the Indians, Weikert leaped back into the saddle and caught up with Wilkie. The pair returned to Otter Creek to find the camp destroyed and had started down the trail when they discovered Stone and Stewart. After riding all night, the four men arrived safely at Mammoth Hot Springs where they found Lieutenant Schofield's detachment, Emma Cowan, her brother and sister, Pfister, and another small party of frightened tourists. Not long afterward, Duncan and Dietrich arrived.

The next day, Schofield's detail and all the tourists except for Stone, Dietrich, and Weikert started for Bozeman. Dietrich, a music teacher, was particularly concerned about the missing twenty-year-old Joe Roberts, telling the others that he had persuaded Roberts's parents to allow him to come on the journey and he could not return to Helena without knowing his fate. Weikert and the proprietor of the Mammoth "hotel," James McCartney, volunteered to ride back to Otter Creek and search for survivors. That left Stone, Dietrich, and an employee of McCartney's named Jake Stoner at Mammoth. As Weikert and McCartney started to leave, McCartney turned to Dietrich, telling him "to look out for his hair." Dietrich replied that he would try to, then, addressing Andrew Weikert, cheerfully said, "Andy, you will give me a decent burial, won't you?"

"I told him jestingly that I would," said Weikert, "never thinking that I would be called on to perform the reality so soon."

Everyone seemed convinced that the bands, last seen near Yellowstone Lake, were headed away from the lower river toward the eastern edge of the park. For the most part this was true, although at least three separate Nez Perce scouting parties were at that moment exploring the lower Yellowstone River below the falls. On August 31, warriors slipped several miles below Mammoth Hot Springs to Bart Henderson's ranch along the river. After a brief fight, Henderson's son and four others escaped uninjured across the river in a boat and watched as the Nez Perce burned the ranch.

Not long afterward, at McCartney's hotel, a breathless Jake Stoner returned from hunting grouse and announced that a party of ten Indians was rapidly approaching. Dietrich had gone out to picket a horse. Stoner and Stone quickly decided to hide. Stone climbed up a nearby forested gulch, but a warrior saw him and started after him. Hearing the crash and breaking of twigs close behind and knowing running was useless, Stone grabbed a low branch and hoisted himself up a tree. "I had no more than got into the tree," he said, "before an Indian on horseback dashed under it, gazing in every direction for me."

After nightfall Stone started for Henderson's ranch, but had not gone far when an Indian brandishing a rifle suddenly stepped out of the darkness. Stone threw up his hands and his captor motioned him forward with the rifle barrel. A few terrifying moments passed before he found himself standing in front of Lieutenant Gustavus C. Doane. In his haste to escape, Stone had stumbled into an army camp, the detachment having just arrived from Fort Ellis and consisting of officers and friendly Crow scouts, one of whom had discovered him. From Doane he learned that a detail under Lieutenant Hugh Scott had reached the hotel that afternoon, surprised Nez Perce raiders who, after a brief chase, had rapidly departed. Stoner had escaped. The soldiers had found Richard Dietrich lying in the doorway, his body still warm, shot twice, one bullet, claimed Scott, "going the entire length of his body."[40]

Yellow Wolf was a member of the scouting party who killed Dietrich. When he and his six or seven companions rode up and saw Dietrich standing in the doorway, they discussed what to do. Chuslum Hahlap Kanoot (Naked-Footed Bull) claimed the man was no different than those who had murdered his sister and three younger brothers at the Big Hole. "Chuslum Hahlap Kanoot then fired and clipped his arm. As he made to run, another warrior, Yettahtapnat Alwum [Shooting Thunder] shot him through the belly."[41]

Soon after Stone arrived, Weikert and McCartney walked into Doane's camp with their own tale to tell. They had discovered Charles Kenck's body a few hundred yards from the Otter Creek camp, shot in the stomach and back of the head, the bullet passing out just to the side of his nose. After burying Kenck and finding no sign of Roberts and Foller, the two men headed back, riding most of the night. The next morning, not far from Mammoth, they ran into a party of eighteen Nez Perce. During a running fight, Weikert's horse went down with a bullet and McCartney's bucked him off when the saddle slid back on the animal's haunches. Both men dove into nearby brush and the warriors soon withdrew. Late that night they arrived at the hotel and found Dietrich's body, then walked on until they discovered the soldiers' camp. The next morning, the men returned to the hotel and buried Dietrich in the only makeshift casket they could find—"an old bathtub." Six weeks later Weikert came back in a wagon, exhumed both bodies, and returned with them to Helena. "This was about as lonely a ride as I ever took," he said. "Two dead men in a wagon . . . for over two hundred miles."

The killings were far from over. The following day, Lieutenant Scott's detail rode up the Yellowstone River. Here they met two scouts who had been sent by Colonel Sturgis to explore the headwaters of the Clarks Fork for sign of the Nez Perce. John Groff and J. S. Leonard, described by Sturgis as "very bright and intelligent mountain men," along with an unidentified Indian boy whom Groff had raised from an infant, had been ambushed not far from where Weikert and McCartney had run for their lives, possibly by the same raiding party. The boy fell at the first volley, and Groff was wounded in the neck. When the two men retreated to a rock outcrop, the warriors abandoned the fight. After telling Scott what happened and despairing that the boy could have survived, the two men traveled on to Fort Ellis. Scout Jack Baronett later looked for the body and found where the youth had recovered consciousness and dragged himself for nearly half a mile. Near a creek Baronett lost the bloody trail, and no further trace of the boy was ever found. Groff and Leonard arrived at Fort Ellis, were given dispatches for Sturgis, and soon started back up the Yellowstone River. Neither man was ever seen again.[42]

The same afternoon that the Nez Perce crossed the upper Yellowstone River and released Emma Cowan and her brother and sister, the bands moved upriver about four miles, camping just below the lake. The next day, August 26, they crossed Pelican Creek and camped near the lake's north shore. A day later, they moved only four miles up the creek. Compared to their earlier haste, they were obviously in no hurry and, according to Shively, had ceased sending out a rear guard after crossing the Yellowstone River. Although they had clashed with tourists since entering the park, they had seen no soldiers and, by the time they reached the river, were probably aware that Howard had yet to leave Henrys Lake.

Not far behind, however, were S. G. Fisher and his scouts, including J. W. Redington. Riding into one of the abandoned camps along the river, Redington discovered an aged Nez Perce woman. "She laid on a few ragged robes, and suddenly closed her eyes as if expecting a bullet but not wanting to see it come. She seemed rather disappointed when instead of shooting her I refilled her water bottle." The woman made signs that she wished to die. Redington refused and rode on, but a few minutes down the trail he heard shots and knew that "one of our wild Bannock scouts acceded to her wishes and put her out of her misery." When Howard learned that no one had interrogated the woman before shooting her, he was outraged, ordering that all prisoners be brought back unharmed into camp. The order, admitted Redington, was never obeyed.[43]

From Yellowstone Lake, the bands had three choices leading to Montana's Crow country: north to Mammoth Hot Springs and down the Yellowstone River, northeast over the Absaroka Mountains to the Clarks Fork, or east via the Stinking Water (Shoshone) River. Until now, their swiftness and path through the park indicated they were headed for the Stinking Water. From where the river debouched from the mountains near present-day Cody, Wyoming, the most obvious route skirted north near this point to the lower Clarks Fork River and beyond to Crow country. It appears the Nez Perce had never used this eastern route through the park in the past, but they must have been aware of its existence, if not its precise location. Colonel Sturgis in particular could not shake the belief that they would exit the mountains on or near the Stinking Water, claiming that the last communication he received from Howard said that he should expect the bands some one hundred miles southeast of the Crow agency. Four days after he had telegraphed this message to Sturgis, Howard was poised to enter the park, and receiving word from Fisher that the Nez Perce were last seen on the northeast shore of Yellowstone Lake, had little reason to believe otherwise.

But if the army should have learned one thing up to now, it was that nothing in the behavior of these Indians could be termed predictable. With Howard far behind and apparently no knowledge that any resistance was being organized to block their passage back into Montana, the bands stopped. For one week, between August 28 and September 4, they remained in the high mountains east of Yellowstone Lake, only moving occasionally to recamp and find new pasture for their horses. Here in one of the most remote and inaccessible areas of the park, which has experienced little change over the century following the bands' passage (until the catastrophic 1988 fires), historians and war buffs alike have scrambled to explain why the Nez Perce halted and, once they started again, where they went.

Shively was convinced they were lost. While camped at Yellowstone Lake, the prospector said he pointed out the trail to the Stinking Water, but instead the Nez Perce chose as a guide a "Snake chief" who had joined the bands and supposedly knew the route. Early the next morning, Shively observed that "they got on the wrong trail and were returning to the Yellowstone," but he said nothing. Both Irwin and he were kept busy chopping out the trail—the hardest work he had ever done "on an empty stomach, for [I] had nothing for two days but a little meat."

It appears this day the bands traveled over a relatively low divide above the lake, not into the Stinking Water drainage but toward the upper East Fork of the Yellowstone (Lamar River). Here Shively claims they wandered about for two days until he was reinstated as guide. Since their location on the East Fork meant the bands would have had to backtrack to find the Stinking Water, Shively showed them a shorter, northeastern route over the Absaroka Mountains in the direction of the Clarks Fork River. Soon afterward, both he and Irwin managed to escape, Irwin on September 1 and Shively some thirty-six hours later. The prospector never saw Howard's command, slipping away after darkness and eventually making his way down the Yellowstone River to Mammoth Hot Springs and finally back to Bozeman. Irwin was discovered by Fisher the same day he escaped. When he met up with the command the following day, Irwin brought Howard news that the Nez Perce were "uncertain of their exact whereabouts and rather bewildered," thus corroborating Shively's story that they were lost.[44]

Not so, say the Nez Perce. But they offer no explanation for the delay nor why they eschewed the easier route down the Stinking Water. Howard believed they had received word that soldiers under Colonel Wesley Merritt were approaching from Wyoming's Camp Brown, but these troops were nearly two hundred miles away and did not even begin their march north until September 9, arriving well after the bands had departed the mountains. The same was also true of Major Verling Hart's battalion, which failed to arrive on the Stinking Water until after mid-September. Some historians believe the Nez Perce sent out couriers to the Crows after crossing the Yellowstone River on August 25, and the rebuff they brought back discouraged the bands from joining them. This seems highly improbable since even Indians familiar with the route would have had severe difficulty making the three-hundred-mile round-trip to the Crow agency through some of the most rugged mountains in North America in only a few days.

Still others suggest that since deer, elk, forbs, and grass were plentiful in the mountains and the soldiers were far behind, the Nez Perce simply halted to fatten their horses and rest. Yellow Wolf admitted that Shively guided the bands during some of this time in the park, but said it was only for half a day when they were attempting to find their way from the Lower Geyser Basin to Yellowstone Lake. Yellow Wolf, however, was a member of one of the raiding parties down the Yellowstone River about this time and probably did not rejoin the bands before the night of August 31, the same day Shively claims he pointed out the Clarks Fork route. Yellow Wolf was hardly in a position to know exactly what transpired in his absence.

Adding to the confusion, Lieutenant Hugh Scott maintained long after the war that Joseph told him the bands had planned to travel down the Yellowstone Valley until returning scouts warned of soldiers near Mammoth Hot Springs. Scott even claimed Joseph later signed a statement to that effect, although it has never been found. If true, this decision must have come much later, while the bands were wandering around the upper East Fork. For in all probability, had the Nez Perce early on intended to travel down the Yellowstone River, they would have chosen either a more direct route over the Mount Washburn trail or even earlier a traditional Bannock trail leading from near the west entrance directly to Mammoth Hot Springs and the lower river.

Lost or not, exactly where the bands traveled before they reappeared near Crandall Creek in the Clarks Fork drainage about September 6 or 7 is an even greater mystery. Nez Perce accounts offer no answer. The only surviving descriptions by Shively, who escaped about September 2, and Fisher, who tracked the bands until September 4, are vague and imprecise. Because the only maps of this time were crude and none but the largest drainages were named, their descriptions of the terrain can be variously interpreted. Piecing together these versions, it appears that the bands traveled down the East Fork for an undetermined distance, then struck up one of the major drainages leading east, possibly Miller Creek or the upper

East Fork. Once they crested the Absaroka divide, they moved down Crandall Creek toward the Clarks Fork River. There is also evidence that the bands may have separated during this period, pursuing more than one route until reuniting on Crandall Creek, thus adding even more complexity to the puzzle.[45]

Whatever route they chose, it seems certain that much of it was littered with severe deadfall and steep talus slopes, obstacles that make their insouciance concerning the passage of seven hundred people and two thousand animals even more remarkable. At one point, just after leaving the lake and heading east, Fisher could hardly believe the Nez Perce had traveled down "the roughest canyon I ever undertook to pass through. About every foot of it was obstructed with dead and fallen timber and huge blocks of granite which had fallen from its sides. We found plenty of dead and crippled horses that had been left by the enemy. They evidently had a hard time getting through this place for the trees and logs were smeared with blood from their horses."[46]

On September 4, from his camp on the East Fork, Fisher discovered at least a portion of the bands moving east up an unknown creek toward the Absaroka divide. One of his Bannocks called the drainage "the trap" and told the head scout that "there is no way of getting out of it except at each end and that is about fifteen miles long." Although most of Fisher's scouts had grown weary of the chase and headed back to Fort Hall days before, several stumbled into forty rear guardsmen in the canyon and a brief skirmish ensued. The men reported that the Nez Perce could not make out who was firing on them, calling to their attackers: "We don't want to fight you, for if you are Crows, Bannocks or Snakes [Shoshonis] you are our friends." But the scouts, said Fisher, "knew their game too well and told them they would talk with their guns."[47]

As the Nez Perce moved up the canyon toward the divide, Fisher's men broke off the fight and retreated. A day later, when his courier failed to find Howard's command at Yellowstone Lake, Fisher suspected correctly that the general had taken the Mount Washburn trail from Hayden Valley down to the Yellowstone River at Baronett's Bridge. The next day, Fisher and his handful of men continued down the East Fork over "an exceedingly rough trail" to

Soda Butte Creek, struck Howard's trail, and finally reunited with the command on September 7 near the northeast corner of the park.

"I have been thinking of wife and little Maud all day and am becoming tired of trying to get the soldiers and the hostiles together," wrote the discouraged scout in his journal. "Uncle Sam's boys are too slow for this business."[48]

11

As twilight faded into darkness on a restless world this final
day of August 1877, there was more than enough despair to
go around. Russia and Turkey were again clutching at each other's
throats in a blood-drenching Crimean war. Two days before, in Salt
Lake City, Brigham Young had died, leaving behind seventeen
wives, fifty-six children, and a grieving flock of Latter-day Saints. In
his tent, not far from Yellowstone Park's Lower Geyser Basin, and
unaware the bands had paused in their flight, a discouraged General
Howard had concluded that nothing short of divine intervention
would allow him to overtake the Nez Perce.

Unknown to Howard, camped less than forty miles away at Henderson's smoldering ranch near Mammoth Hot Springs was the man
who might have shown him the way. No other person had such
extensive military experience and knew Yellowstone Park so well as
Lieutenant Gustavus C. Doane. A bear of a man with a striking
handlebar mustache, Doane looked every bit the frontiersman, with
long black hair sweeping to his shoulders in a most unmilitary fashion. He is said to have commanded rapt attention when he spoke, his
voice deep and sonorous. Thomas Leforge, a former white scout
during the Little Bighorn campaign who had been adopted into the

Crow tribe, said that he had never known the lieutenant to show "any feeling of fear under any circumstances, so the soldiers adored him."[1] Only seven years before, Doane had escorted the most famous of the early park explorations, known as the Washburn-Doane expedition, and as a result he had intimate knowledge of the park's trails and terrain.

The lieutenant's present assignment, however, could hardly have been more awkward. In the aftermath of the Big Hole, he had been ordered to recruit a large force of Crow Indians to watch the lower Yellowstone country and intercept the Nez Perce should they break through into central Montana. As an officer in the Second Cavalry, Doane was stationed at Fort Ellis near Bozeman under the command of Colonel Gibbon's District of Montana. Because of the shortage of troops that summer, Colonel Nelson Miles, commanding the adjacent District of the Yellowstone in eastern Montana, had detailed a small company of Sturgis's Seventh Cavalry led by Lieutenant Charles DeRudio to Doane's command.[2]

Although as senior officer Doane headed this detachment along with about thirty volunteers, his mixed force was subject to orders from both Gibbon and Sturgis, a situation that had already caused him extreme vexation. Only a week before he had received orders from Sturgis to remain near Fort Ellis and watch for the Nez Perce should they boldly travel down the Yellowstone River, in which case he was to send word immediately so that Sturgis's Seventh could sweep up from the Crow agency. If the bands broke out east of the park, Doane was to hurry down the Yellowstone to Sturgis's aid. The success of this strategy depended on the lieutenant's location. If Doane scouted too far up the Yellowstone, reasoned Sturgis, he would be unable to form a timely juncture should the colonel need him.

A cautious and unambitious man might have remained close to Fort Ellis, but Doane was neither. When Colonel Gibbon suggested he scout farther up the Yellowstone, the lieutenant lost no time complying. Writing years later, Lieutenant Hugh Scott maintained that "Doane had told us where the Nez Perces were going to go a month and a half before they actually went. He knew that country and the habits of the Indians so well that he could predict everything they did."[3]

ROUTE FROM YELLOWSTONE PARK TO BEAR PAW MTNS

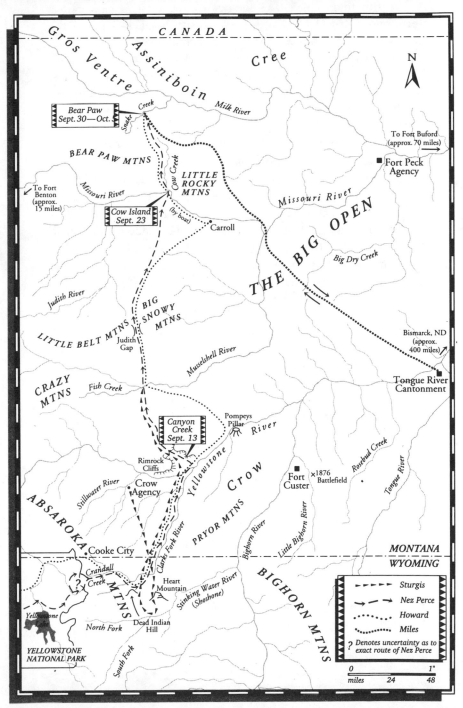

The trip to the park had not been easy. First, a tremendous storm pummeled Doane and his scouts with baseball-size hail, destroying a nearby Crow village and killing over one thousand horses, leaving those people who had managed to cover themselves with buffalo robes nursing blackened and bruised bodies. Then along the way most of Doane's Crow scouts had deserted, unwilling to fight against their former ally. Doane first pleaded then cajoled, recalled Scott, but the scouts said that "the Nez Perce heart was Crow, and the Crow heart was Nez Perce." Frank Carpenter, who joined the command briefly in hopes of learning the fate of his party's companions after delivering his sisters safely in Bozeman, witnessed the scouts' withdrawal. The last Carpenter saw of them, a furious Lieutenant Doane "was addressing them in language that was remarkable for its force rather than its grace." Now only forty-two Crow scouts remained.[4]

From his camp at Henderson's ranch just outside the park, Doane was confident that the Nez Perce were east of the upper Yellowstone River. His shortest route from the ranch lay up the valley to Baronett's Bridge and the East Fork, then up Soda Butte Creek to the small mining camp near present-day Cooke City. From there a rough trail used by miners led down the Clarks Fork and north to Crow country. A rapid advance might allow the remainder of his force to get ahead of the Nez Perce or at least link up with Howard and nip closely at their heels. Late that night, however, a dispatch arrived from Fort Ellis that laid to waste Doane's hopes. In it the lieutenant found a message from Lieutenant Colonel Charles Gilbert announcing that after conferring with General Sherman in Helena, he was on his way up the Yellowstone to assume command of Howard's pursuit.

In the morning, Doane sent a courier to find Howard and deliver this message, biding his time until Gilbert arrived. The next day, September 2, the lieutenant colonel and a company of cavalry rode into Doane's camp. According to Lieutenant Scott, "Doane begged him with tears in his eyes" to proceed up the Yellowstone after the Indians, but Gilbert stubbornly refused, "saying that he was only trying to reach Howard and did not want to be delayed by a fight and miss him."[5]

His mind made up, Gilbert ordered Doane and his men to back-track down the Yellowstone River, then up and over a pass leading to the upper Gallatin River. From there the detachment trailed to the Madison River and on to the Lower Geyser Basin, arriving days later and hopelessly behind Howard. Scott's later complaint that Gilbert had "no idea of marching cavalry" seems benignly understated, for the command ended up circumnavigating almost 120 miles only to arrive at Baronett's Bridge and Howard's cold trail, a mere 24 miles up the Yellowstone Valley from Henderson's ranch. Two weeks later near the Crow agency, Gilbert finally gave up and returned to Fort Ellis, his men and horses so jaded from the nearly three-hundred-mile journey that only twenty men (including Doane and Scott) remained out of a force that had numbered well over a hundred at the start. The rest had all fallen by the wayside and eventually straggled back to Fort Ellis.

As he pushed on toward the upper Yellowstone River, Howard had no idea what was conspiring at Henderson's Ranch. Doane's messenger failed to find the command and Howard only learned of Gilbert's intentions long after he had left the park and there was no chance the lieutenant colonel could overtake him. There seems little doubt that had he succeeded, Howard would have relinquished leadership of the campaign. In his possession, Gilbert carried a letter for Howard from the general of the army that, despite Sherman's earlier words of encouragement, contained a sentence that rang of an unmistakable command:

> I don't want to order you back to Oregon, but I do say that you can, with perfect propriety, return to your command, leaving the troops to continue till the Nez Perces have been destroyed or captured, and I authorize you to transfer to him, Lieutenant Colonel Gilbert, your command in the field and to overtake me en route, or in your department. . . .

I am, with great respect
Your friend
W. T. SHERMAN
General[6]

Howard later took umbrage that Sherman, after first proposing to replace him with a younger man, had sent instead "an officer much older than I" and of lower rank. He was glad Gilbert never reached him, saying that "it would have been a great hardship to me personally to have stopped short of success," giving the "lying" press even greater reason to "disgrace me." Scoffing at the entire debacle, Thomas Sutherland wrote that Gilbert "now is rendering us invaluable service by widening our trail and picking up such little things as we may have lost in our hurry." Always the pragmatist, Sherman himself seemed to agree for he made no further attempt to meddle with corralling the Nez Perce. Too many heads, the general ruefully concluded, had proven to be worse than one.[7]

The day that Doane attempted to send on Gilbert's ill-fated dispatch to Howard, the command's cavalry reached the Yellowstone River above the Upper Falls not far from where the Helena tourists had been attacked at Otter Creek. The rough trail from the Lower Geyser Basin had proven exasperatingly difficult for the wagons. In fact, Captain Spurgin's "skillets" were still cutting a trail through the deadfall, a task that took nearly three days to go the same number of miles. The open trail across Hayden Valley proved easier, but as they approached the river, a four-hundred-foot descent gave them pause again. Someone suggested sliding the wagons down to the river, Henry Buck recalled, the sparsely timbered slope being "as steep as the roof of an ordinary house." Using a hundred-foot rope, the men took several turns around a nearby tree, skidding the wagons down the hill, tying them off when they reached the end of the rope, then repeating the procedure until they made the bottom. The spot was aptly christened Spurgin's Beaver Slide, and over a century later rope burns were still plainly visible on at least one of the surviving trees.[8]

From this experience Howard concluded that continued use of wagons was impractical, and he ordered the command's provisions moved to the pack animals he had procured in Virginia City. Spurgin was left to cut a wagon trail over Mount Washburn and return with his teamsters to Fort Ellis. Two weeks later the weary men, including Henry Buck, rolled into Bozeman and were finally discharged.

At this same camp Howard was beset by a problem with his Bannock scouts. Fed up with the slowness of the troops, most of the Bannocks had quit Fisher's detachment and headed back to Fort Hall, but not before stealing about forty horses belonging to some volunteers. When Howard discovered the theft, he sent soldiers after them and arrested ten scouts, informing the others they could gain their companions' release by returning the missing horses. A day later, half the horses had been found. Howard held out for the remainder, telling an elderly headman that his men would be freed when he brought back all of the animals. "The old chief himself mounted, grunted, and with a shrug of the shoulders, departed." That night the remaining twenty horses were returned, and all but one of the prisoners released.[9]

Meanwhile, the command took advantage of nearby hot springs, bathing and washing clothes. When one bashful trooper refused to strip past his red flannel underwear, fellow soldiers first threw him into the water, then tore off his long johns, exclaiming that his "seam squirrels needed an airing."[10]

If Howard had any doubts about whether or not to follow the Nez Perce around Yellowstone Lake and into the rugged upper East Fork drainage, they were soon dispelled when James Irwin arrived in camp. The ex-captive encouraged the general to take the trail over Mount Washburn, down to Baronett's Bridge and then up Soda Butte Creek to the Clarks Fork. The advice proved invaluable, claimed Howard, shortening the army's route by some one hundred miles. Of course, what it really saved was the entire campaign wallowing in the morass of deadfall and precipitous mountains the Nez Perce had encountered east of Yellowstone Lake, country that Howard's force would have found hopelessly impenetrable. Besides this news, Irwin also passed on an incisive observation of Indian camp life, which Sutherland mentioned briefly in one of his dispatches. Irwin, wrote the journalist almost in disbelief, claims that Chief Joseph plays virtually no leadership role, "never speaking and apparently very much oppressed in mind."[11]

On their way around the canyon, the men stopped briefly to view Yellowstone Falls, "truly the grandest scenery in America," wrote Major Mason. The day was marred for the chief of staff, however, when late in the afternoon after they had halted to make camp, Howard suddenly ordered that the command make a short march, "just long enough to make trouble for everybody." In a rare reproof, Mason grumbled that "the General has very little idea of how troops should be marched, and manages to make double the trouble necessary. I could gain the same results with about half the worry and labor to the troops, but he commands, and I don't."[12]

On September 5, the cavalry arrived at Baronett's Bridge to find the eastern end of the corduroy log crossing partially burned by a Nez Perce scouting party. Several hours later, they had propped up the swaying structure enough to scramble safely across. Their relief inspired Howard of a biblical metaphor, imparting "something of the feeling of the Israelites when they had reached the other shore of the Red Sea and looked back." Beyond the bridge, the journey up Soda Butte Creek was relatively easy. Two days later found the command at the park's northeast boundary. Thomas Sutherland paused momentarily at the pass, looked back over the spectacular view of Yellowstone Park, and reflected, "I seriously doubt if there is a place in all the world in which Nature is at once so mighty and so beautiful." Then the troops began their descent into the Clarks Fork, and soon were overtaken by Fisher and his handful of remaining scouts.[13]

Not far down the trail, Howard received his first news about Sturgis from three of the colonel's scouts. Sturgis had sent the men to warn the miners in the upper Clarks Fork of approaching Indians since he had no idea of Howard's location. From them Howard learned Sturgis's six companies of the Seventh Cavalry were waiting at the bottom of the Absaroka Mountains, camped between the mouth of Clarks Fork Canyon and Heart Mountain, less than thirty or forty miles away. At last it was about to happen. For the first time since the campaign had begun, the Nez Perce faced a substantial force both in front and behind. It was just a matter of closing the jaws of the trap. Howard quickly sent the couriers back to inform Sturgis of his approach, then as the command made camp along the river he penned an optimistic message to McDowell. "Hostile Indians are between my command and that of Colonel Sturgis, and one day in advance of me; seems hardly possible that they can escape this time." After raining most of the day, the skies cleared that night, the temperature dropped, and by morning the men awoke to find their water pails frozen solid.[14]

The following day at Crandall Creek, Fisher discovered the Nez Perce trail. "They are two days ahead of us, judging from the signs," the scout recorded in his journal. The next morning, September 9, Fisher and his men followed the trail along the southern rim of Clarks Fork Canyon, while a local miner guided the command over a shorter route up Lodgepole Creek and down to the base of Dead Indian Hill. Scattered along the trail Howard observed "nicely peeled" lodge poles that had been hastily discarded years before by a band of Crows in their effort to escape pursuing Sioux raiders.[15]

At the bottom of Dead Indian Hill, the scouts learned that the Nez Perce trail left the increasingly precipitous canyon rim and ascended two thousand feet straight up the steep hill, the last obstacle before descending to the lower Clarks Fork and Crow country. Here Fisher called a halt for the night. As he was dismounting, a scout named Charles Sumner rode past him up the creek, suddenly shouted, and a moment later three shots rang out. "I sprang into my saddle and got to him just in time to see a Nez Perce breathe his last. He had been wounded in the hip and left by his comrades to his fate. Sumner said that as he was riding past, near where the hostile lay, he saw the Indian raise to a sitting posture and he at once pulled out his pistol and shot, the bullet passing through the chest. The Indian fell back, but Sumner gave him two more shots to make sure of him." While the men stood around and watched, a white scout walked up and scalped the dead man. When Howard unexpectedly appeared, Fisher momentarily distracted the general while another scout "got his toe against the stick upon which the scalp was hung, and kicked it down into the tall rye grass out of sight." Not long afterward, a disgusted Thomas Sutherland observed that the man had "the capillary adornment of the defunct aborigine dangling to his horse's tail."[16]

Late that evening, scouts arrived saying that they had spotted warriors on the hillside a mile or two above camp. With Colonel Sturgis waiting beyond the hill no more than ten miles away and the Nez Perce trapped between, Howard told Fisher to expect a fight tomorrow. "We have a steep hill to go up in the morning and must pass through a narrow cut at its summit," wrote the scout that night. "The boys are apprehensive that we will get a game there."[17]

The solemn and sober man who waited at the bottom of the Absaroka Mountains to bring overdue glory to the Seventh Cavalry would have hardly described his efforts so jauntily. Sporting a shock of wavy gray hair and a dangling goatee that looks strangely out of place on such a rotund face, Samuel D. Sturgis appears in fading photographs more like an aging choirboy than the commander of the famous Seventh. Until 1877, the plump, fifty-five-year-old colonel had experienced a career that seemed to match those cherub features. It had started well enough: West Point, acceptable performance in the Mexican War. In the 1850s, Sturgis saw active duty all over the West, campaigning against the Apache, Cheyenne, Comanche, and Kiowa. During the Civil War he served at South Mountain, Antietam, and Fredericksburg, but at Brice's Cross Roads it began to fall apart. Confederate General Nathan Bedford Forrest surprised him, capturing his supply train and sixteen of his eighteen artillery pieces, even though he commanded more than twice as many soldiers as Forrest did. A board of inquiry later found no cause to reprimand Sturgis, but its suggestion of impropriety did little to instill confidence in the colonel's ability.

The years he spent following the war as commander of the Seventh Cavalry were equally lackluster. In 1876, General Sheridan tapped Sturgis's subordinate, George Armstrong Custer, to lead the Seventh against the Sioux and Cheyenne, while the colonel held down a desk as temporary head of the Mounted Recruiting Service in St. Louis. When the smoke cleared to reveal over two hundred stripped and glistening corpses on that Montana hillside, Sturgis was incensed, likening Custer to a thief shot during a robbery, a fool who deserved and received a fool's death. He had never liked the egotistical upstart, but he was particularly embittered that Custer had led his young son, Lieutenant Jack Sturgis—who shortly before the battle had requested assignment to his father's regiment—to his death that day. His body was never discovered but was assumed to be among those mutilated beyond recognition. The only trace ever found was Jack's blood-soaked underwear, a fact that the colonel somehow managed to keep from his distraught wife for the remainder of her days.[18]

Now Sturgis was again in the field and commanding green troops (thanks to what Custer had done to his regiment), probably for the last time, eager to redeem an altogether undistinguished career and avenge his son's demise (the Seventh had assumed the nickname "Custer's Avengers"). To say Sturgis was anxious for a fight does poor justice to his state of mind. As events were about to prove, the man simply could not wait to strike a blow.

From the beginning, on August 12, when Colonel Miles ordered him to take 360 men and march to Judith Gap in central Montana to block the Nez Perce should they break away from Howard, Sturgis was plagued with problems. First, his supplies sent by steamboat failed to catch up with him at the mouth of the Little Bighorn because the boat ran aground. Subsisting on short rations, his men with hardly any food for days at a time, Sturgis moved south to the Crow agency on Stillwater Creek when he heard the Nez Perce were moving toward Yellowstone Park. There he lingered several days waiting to find out from Lieutenant Doane if the Nez Perce were coming down the Yellowstone River. He also attempted to procure Crow scouts at the agency, but like Doane, he had difficulty convincing more than a handful of men to scout against their former allies. On August 26, he received his only communication from Howard, which suggested the bands would likely exit east of the park. A few days later, a courier arrived from Miles telling him to "please move farther south" closer to the Stinking Water. On the last day of August, while Doane was awaiting Gilbert at Henderson's ranch, Howard was starting from the Lower Geyser Basin toward the upper Yellowstone River, and the Nez Perce were wandering about the mountains of the East Fork, Sturgis began marching toward the park's east boundary.[19]

A few days later he arrived at the mouth of Clarks Fork Canyon. Here at the abrupt edge of the Absaroka Mountains, with abundant grass for his horses, he camped and debated his next move. Stretching up the canyon was what appeared to be an inviting thoroughfare leading west into the mountains and Yellowstone Park. Several miles upriver near Dead Indian Hill, however, the valley narrows into a steep, rugged gorge with sheer walls that rise in places as much as eight hundred feet. In the belief that "no trail could possibly lead through it," Sturgis moved several miles farther south near the base of Heart Mountain, a large promontory just beyond the bulk of the Absarokas about halfway between the Clarks Fork and the Stinking Water. From there he had a sweeping, panoramic view of the open ridges and foothills leading some ten miles up to the summit of Dead Indian Hill. It was the perfect location to send out scouts and watch for Indians.[20]

Descending the upper Clarks Fork toward the opposite side of Dead Indian Hill and just beyond Sturgis's probing eyes, the Nez Perce thought likewise. There is no evidence that they suspected soldiers were waiting at the bottom of the mountains for them, but the numerous miners they had encountered along the river, some employed as observers for Sturgis, had made them extremely wary. The bands sent out scouts to learn what might lie ahead. On September 7, Yellow Wolf and several warriors stumbled on two of Sturgis's scouts somewhere in the foothills southwest of Heart Mountain.

The two men quickly sprang on their horses and began riding away. The warriors fired and one man fell, his arm shattered. The other, "a tall fellow, wearing a buckskin suit," was pursued by Yellow Wolf and Otskai. Soon Otskai shouted to Yellow Wolf that his horse was giving out, encouraging him to catch the white man.

I kept running my horse to his best. But just beyond my reach, this fellow jumped to the ground. His horse knocked him over, and I, going fast, passed him a few steps. I was off my horse as the man regained his feet. We both drew up rifles and fired. I did not know if I hit him. His bullet glanced my head, shaving through my hair. I was brought to my knees, blinded. Nearly knocked out, but did not know I was hit. I was partly out of sense. The enemy was trying to work his gun when Otskai killed him. Then was seen why his gun would not work. The hammer had been knocked off by a bullet—my bullet, for the other warriors were a good distance away. Had this not been done, he must have killed some of us. He was a brave man.[21]

The next day, September 8, Lieutenant Luther Hare and twenty men discovered the dead man, one imaginative account claiming the body was "stripped and bristling with arrows." Near the men's camp, they found the other scout, covered with blood and seriously wounded but still alive. Unknown to the soldiers, Yellow Wolf and his companions observed their movements and hurried back to warn the Nez Perce camp that troops were ahead of them. Later that afternoon as Hare was making his report to Sturgis, another scouting party rode into the cavalry camp saying they had seen "what appeared to be the hostiles moving on the Stinking River trail, and that they had disappeared behind a range of mountains, going in the direction of the Stinking River."[22]

Restless, impatient, and as impetuous as the man he so despised only a year before, Sturgis could wait no longer. The circumstantial evidence, he claimed later, was irrefutable. Tents were quickly struck, horses saddled, and leaving no observers behind on Heart Mountain in case he was mistaken, Sturgis and his command departed immediately for the Stinking Water less than twenty miles away.

The following morning dawned cold and clear, the kind of autumn morning in the Rocky Mountains when the air is dense and still and clarity is at its greatest. If there had been anyone on Heart Mountain scanning the distant ridges, they would have seen the seven hundred people with their immense herd of two thousand horses emerging from the pass just below Dead Indian Hill, making their way slowly and deliberately down the ridge, spilling out into the Clarks Fork Valley below.

Riding ahead of Howard's command over Dead Indian Hill the next day, S. G. Fisher paused when he saw the Nez Perce trail strike off toward the southeast, a "direction my Indians told me would take them onto the Stinking Water, to the south of Heart Mountain, which [is] in plain sight from the top of the divide we passed over this morning." Two miles farther on, Fisher realized something was wrong when the trail suddenly became confused, as if the Nez Perce

257

had "milled" their horses around in every direction. Spreading out, the scout discovered their trail bore off the side of the long open ridge leading east down the mountain, passing along the edge of the timbered north slope. After leaving the protection of the trees, the trail descended a narrow and steep drainage to the mouth of Clarks Fork Canyon, not far from the location of Sturgis's camp the day before.[23]

When he arrived at the pass, Howard could hardly believe his bad luck. His signal men waved flags "furiously toward Heart Mountain and watched with strained eyes, with telescope and field-glass for some return signal. But it was all in vain." Fearing the worst, the command continued down the ridge, descending the steep and rugged drainage the bands had taken in order to remain concealed as long as possible, one so narrow, Thomas Sutherland recalled, "that it almost met in places at the top, resembling an irregular tunnel." Others were so impressed that the Nez Perce had traveled through the nearly impassable couloir that they named it the "devil's doorway." Two miles from the Clarks Fork, out on the open plain leading north to Crow country and Canada beyond, Howard called a halt for the night. The Indian trail was unmistakable, sweeping down the valley, and not a soul was in sight.[24]

Later that evening, Major Mason could see his frosty breath as he huddled over a candle and wrote a letter to his wife. Despite the wonders he had witnessed in the park, the "magnificent" view from their camp at the mouth of the towering canyon was the "grandest mountain scenery" he had ever seen. But his thoughts were on Sturgis's failure that day, one he found "disgusting in the extreme." The entire chase had turned into "a perfect farce," the major fumed, with the Nez Perce moving "35 and 40 miles a day while we are dragging our worn-out horses and leg-weary men" less than half that distance. "When will this campaign end? I have not the least idea!"[25]

Weariness and discouragement seemed to grip the entire command, for the next day they moved only a few miles down the valley. That evening, a large group of cavalry was seen approaching from the direction of the Stinking Water. Howard and several staff officers rode out to meet them. Thomas Sutherland was there to witness a "deeply chagrined" Sturgis and record his entirely believable words: "Poor as I am I would give $1,000 if I had not left this place!"[26]

By the time they met, Howard had vented any ire he might have harbored over Sturgis's performance, even going so far as to empathize with the colonel's humiliation. It was little satisfaction, but he doubtlessly realized that no longer would he alone have to bear criticism for the army's failure. Afterward Howard blamed Sturgis's Indian scouts, saying that he had been "probably misled by some treacherous Crows," but this is specious reasoning since the most trusted scouts were always white. The three men whom Howard had met on the upper Clarks Fork and had sent back to Sturgis had failed to find him, either the result of the colonel's untimely departure or interception by the Nez Perce.[27]

Precisely where Sturgis's scouts claimed to have seen Indians three days before, how many there were, or their actual direction of travel has never been satisfactorily explained. Sturgis's report is the only detailed account of the affair, one so full of niggling excuses, inflated distances, and bitter accusations that the entire document resonates with suspicion. Had his men mistook a scouting party for the entire Nez Perce camp? Or did they witness the bands' short feint toward the Stinking Water that momentarily confused Fisher? Most authorities believe the bands climbed Dead Indian Hill the day after the Seventh departed, their false trail made to foil Howard, not Sturgis. On the other hand, if this ruse occurred one day earlier and was observed by Sturgis's scouts, it worked magnificently. Whatever the truth, the bands' delayed departure from Yellowstone Park, intentioned or not, seems only to have confirmed Sturgis's unwavering conviction that they would appear on the Stinking Water trail. Realizing his blunder, the colonel came hurrying back over the foothills, found the tracks of Howard's troops superimposed over those of the Nez Perce near Dead Indian Hill, descended through the "devil's doorway," and finally caught up.

Down but not out, the colonel told Howard he wanted to attempt to overtake the Indians. Although Sturgis's horses were nearly played out, Howard readily agreed, noting that even in their exhausted state, the animals displayed an "elastic tread" and could "in a very few minutes walk away from ours." Once Howard had returned to his own camp, Seventh Cavalry Private Theodore Goldin observed that Sturgis was "hopping mad that the savages had outwitted him, and as we returned to camp we heard the old veteran, with many an explosive adjective, declare that he would overtake those Indians before they crossed the Missouri River if he had to go afoot and alone." Early the next morning before daylight, in rain mixed with snow, Sturgis's men, along with fifty of Major Sanford's First Cavalry riding the least jaded of the command's horses and with Lieutenant Otis's two howitzers packed on mules, rode off in pursuit.[28]

Since leaving the mountains two days before, the Nez Perce lost no time moving down the broad Clarks Fork Valley toward the lower Yellowstone River. If there had been confusion about their route during past weeks, there was now none as the bands moved swiftly into open prairie country they knew nearly as well as their own. Still, the pursuit of nearly one thousand miles in the last three months was taking its toll, particularly on the elderly and young, sick and wounded. Trailing behind the bands as a rear guard after leaving the mountains, Yellow Bull recalled that somewhere along the Clarks Fork they had to leave "an old man, whose medicine was working in him, but we had no time to make a singing, and we left him in a shelter to die. We had not gone far when, looking back, we saw a few soldiers and some Indian scouts come up to the camping place. A soldier rode round the wickiup and shot twice."[29]

Along the way, Yellow Wolf and several other warriors surprised a group of six Scandinavian miners headed back to the safety of the Crow agency, among them Sturgis's wounded scout who earlier had been rescued by soldiers near Heart Mountain after being left for dead by the Nez Perce. Yellow Wolf recognized the man, observing that this time he was not so fortunate. He also claimed another man was shot from his horse and killed, but the remaining four got away. Whites remembered it differently. Two separate accounts state the wounded miner later turned up alive at the Crow Agency, but that three or four other corpses were found, one man with a miner's pick driven through his neck into the ground. After so long, it is impossible to know exactly what happened. What does seem certain is that more than a few luckless men known to have been in the area at the time were never heard from again. Howard continued to receive inquiries about missing miners for years afterward. "Every white man in those mountains," said Yellow Wolf, "could be counted our enemy."[30]

Humans were not the only danger lurking along the brushy banks of the river. After scouting all night, Yellow Wolf had taken several horses down to the river to drink when he fell asleep on the bank.

I must not have been full awake when I heard, as dreaming, "Look out for *hohots!* Look out for *hohots!*"

Still I was sleeping. I did not understand with good sense. I heard again, away off like dreaming, "Look out for *hohots! Hohots* coming close to you!"

I was partly awake now. I turned my head where was a noise. *Eeh!* I saw it—a big *hohots* [grizzly bear]. My rifle was in my hand. I sprang up as I threw back the hammer. That *hohots* made for me, a bad sound coming from his mouth. As he stood up, I held my rifle ready. That bear came stepping to the muzzle of the gun. Just touched it when I pulled the trigger. He fell, and I finished him with my war club. Struck him on the ear.

You ask if I was afraid? No, I was not scared. The bear had no gun. Did my heart travel fast after it was all over? No! I could not save myself by running. I must hold my ground. Must stand face to face with that *hohots*. After I had killed him, why, I thought about it. I had been close to death.[31]

Sometime before the bands reached the Yellowstone River, the Nez Perce finally encountered the Crows. The exact location of this meeting is unknown but was likely somewhere along the lower Clarks Fork. Yellow Bull said that "a Crow chief, son of Double Pipe, came and talked to Looking Glass, telling him that the Crows who were with the soldiers would not shoot at us with the intention of hitting us, but they would aim over our heads. Later, however, one of them shot a Nez Perce, and then we regarded them as enemies, the same as the soldiers, and knew it was useless to expect help from them."[32]

Put so dispassionately years afterward, Yellow Bull's words belie little of the supreme disappointment the Crows' icy welcome must have brought the Nez Perce. Or perhaps they had given up hope of ever receiving any assistance from former allies. Certainly by now they realized that the U.S. Army would never allow them refuge anywhere within the country's borders. Still, of all their fellow Plains Indians they seemed to have expected more from these people they called *E-sue-gha*. Some Nez Perce preferred the nickname *Tsaplishtake*, or Pasted On, referring to the Crow custom of increasing their hair length by attaching strands of hair with adhesive. The Crows' own name for themselves was *Absaroka*, probably originally pronounced *Absanokee*. Lieutenant James Bradley, who knew them well before he breathed his last at the Big Hole, insisted that the correct spelling was "up-sah-ro-ku." By the time anyone got around to asking, no one in the tribe could remember exactly what the word meant. Some tribal elders thought it referred to a large bird not seen anymore, since it is believed their ancestors migrated sometime in the seventeenth century from somewhere east or south of present-day Montana. In sign language the people made a bird symbol with upraised hands touching palm to palm, which French explorers apparently mistranslated into "gens de corbeaux" or simply "crow."[33]

That the Crows had memory of a recent time in a warmer climate was revealed to Colonel John Gibbon, when on the banks of the Yellowstone River only a year before, he watched as two Crow warriors covered themselves in red paint before attempting to swim the river. "I had the curiosity to inquire the object of this, and was surprised to learn that it was to protect them against the attack of alligators. As the alligator is an animal unknown to the waters of this region, the fact referred to is a curious evidence of the southern origin of the Crows."[34]

By 1877, the Crows had carved out a domain along the Yellowstone River between their most bitter enemies, the Sioux and Cheyenne to the east and the Blackfeet to the north. A large number of Mountain Crows lived on their reservation south of the Yellowstone River while a smaller clan of River Crows frequently ranged as far north as the Judith River Basin. Their relations with whites, like the Nez Perce's until this summer, were exceptionally good. Admired for their long, beautiful hair and light-colored skin, they were "very handsome" and "extremely good-natured," declared one army officer, their language musical with a lilt "not unlike Spanish." The painter George Catlin was particularly impressed with several warriors whose magnificent long black hair swept the ground when they walked, "giving exceeding grace and beauty to their movements." William Clark never saw the Crows on his return journey down the Yellowstone in 1806, but his camp likely received a visit late one night, the men waking the next morning to find their horses gone. For what a Crow warrior loved more than anything was to pilfer horses, pursuing the act with such mastery that it might have approached art if it had not been larceny.[35]

Exactly how long the Crows and Nez Perce had been allies is unclear, but by 1874 they were so close, claimed Thomas Leforge, that individuals of each tribe were difficult to distinguish to the unfamiliar eye, with mixed marriage and "sweethearts" quite common. That same year the two tribes formed an alliance of over two thousand warriors and routed an even greater number of Sioux near Pryor Creek along the Yellowstone River. Leforge recalled that Looking Glass's voice could be heard above the din, urging his men to battle, not unlike how he must have sounded at the Big Hole three years later. "The Crows accorded great credit to Looking Glass and his followers for their aid in repulsing the Sioux," said the old scout. "They remembered this too, when Looking Glass and his people came through here with Chief Joseph in 1877."[36] Leforge seems to be speaking for the majority of Crows who, while refusing to give succor to the Nez Perce, at least declined to assist the army. But the tribe was large, individual independence was stubbornly embraced, and not all Crows viewed the Nez Perce as compatriots. Finally there was that ponderous herd of horses, a temptation so great for some that any memory of past friendship soon paled. Like their cognomen, these Crows would simply be unable to resist joining in the pursuit of a fleeing and wounded prey.

Throughout the day as Sturgis pushed down the Clarks Fork after the bands, it continued to rain. At 9 P.M., the weary command halted near Rock Creek for the night, having made some fifty miles in fifteen hours. Surgeon John FitzGerald, who accompanied Sturgis's troops and complained in a letter to Emily that he went to bed entirely soaked and "with but little to eat," felt the first pangs of a lung inflammation that had begun to fester in an old Civil War wound, one that eventually took his life two years later. At daybreak the camp awoke, everyone "stiff and tired," wrote Private Goldin, with rations scarce and "men not in the best of humor." Saddling their horses, they swam the Yellowstone River below the mouth of the Clarks Fork.[37]

Here a discouraged Sturgis halted and called for a courier to send on the dispatch that had just arrived from Howard for Colonel Nelson Miles at the Tongue River Cantonment some 160 miles down the Yellowstone. In it Howard told Miles that the Nez Perce had gotten around Sturgis and that it appeared they would now "make all haste" toward Canada, possibly joining Sitting Bull's exiled Sioux. "Earnestly request you to make every effort in your power to prevent the escape of this hostile band," wrote Howard, "and at least hold them in check until I can overtake them." Sturgis sent this message in duplicate to increase the chances of delivery. Then, as the sun broke through the damp morning, the colonel ordered his men to unsaddle their horses and make camp.[38]

"So the chase was over," concluded Goldin, "the Colonel had given up." Suddenly Goldin looked up to see a scout "coming down the valley at a wild gallop, yelling 'Indians! Indians!'" at the top of his lungs. Downriver, he could see a huge column of smoke rising skyward and hear the pop of distant gunfire. "In an instant all was excitement." Officers and men were on their feet, horses saddled, and a few moments later off dashed the command.[39]

That morning raiders had attacked several homesteads along the river, killing two men near present-day Billings, burning haystacks and several houses. At one ranch, the Helena stagecoach carrying mail and some half dozen passengers was warned just before the Nez Perce struck. Abandoning the stagecoach, most of the passengers escaped upriver, but station owner Ed Forrest and Portland passenger Fanny Clark, described as a "popular entertainer in mining towns," hid in nearby willows. According to scout J. W. Redington, who came on the pair soon afterward, two dogs had accompanied them into the brush and began barking when warriors rode up. Unable to silence the animals, Forrest plunged a knife into one of them and was attempting to sever the throat of the other when the dog escaped. "Nursing the cut," observed the scout, "kept the dog too busy to bark any more." Then several whooping warriors jumped on the stage and, tying their horses in the rear, began riding "in great style" after the rest of the Nez Perce camp. Later Redington discovered mail and baggage strewn across the prairie, one curious piece of luggage the gripsack of a dentist, his "store teeth and tools of torture" scattered in the wake of the stage.[40]

Coming over a rise five or six miles north of the river, Redington, Fisher, and the other scouts stumbled on the entire Nez Perce procession spread out over the broad valley for nearly a mile and heading up nearby Canyon Creek. Here for some eight miles, yellow-gray sandstone rimrock parallels the Yellowstone, severely limiting access to the open and rolling prairie north of the river. Canyon Creek cuts a narrow passage through the rimrock, and it was up this drainage that the bands hurried. Bringing up the rear of the Indian column was the plundered stagecoach, its riders and horses festooned with apparel belonging to the former passengers. "When these hostiles saw us, they quickly unhitched the horses, mounted their cayuses and dashed into the skirmish line flanking their outfit," said Redington, abandoning the vehicle in the sagebrush.

As soon as the whites were spotted, Nez Perce sharpshooters began firing, although the distance was too great for much accuracy. Fisher's men charged but quickly fell back when bullets began landing uncomfortably close. A few moments later, behind them on the bluff, two hundred cavalry led by Major Lewis Merrill appeared, rapidly dismounted, and began returning fire from some five hundred yards away. Caught between the gunfire, Fisher's men lost no time retreating to the cavalry line.

Neither Fisher nor Redington could believe that instead of charging, Merrill had chosen to engage the Nez Perce in long-range combat or that only half of the command had joined the fight. "When the cavalry finally appeared above us on the bluffs," said Redington, "we all thought there would be a charge of the [four hundred men] right there that would wind up the Nez Perce war. That seemed the proper procedure. But there was no charge." Instead of taking an active role in the battle, Colonel Sturgis watched the entire fight through binoculars from the relative safety of a small rise. Redington believed Sturgis was "too cautious on account of losing a son by Custer's intrepidity the year before," but there was another reason. As his command approached Canyon Creek, Sturgis had mistaken a band of approaching Crow warriors for Nez Perce. Fearing for his supply line approaching from the river, he held back the other two hundred troops under Captain Frederick Benteen.

Meanwhile, the Nez Perce took advantage of the delay, herding their horses, women, and children toward the narrow passage leading up to the prairie above the canyon. Redington recalled one particularly troublesome warrior sequestered behind a point of rocks who single-handedly held their entire force at bay for over ten minutes. When the position was finally taken, "I counted forty empty shells on the ground where he had been crouching." Not long after, the scout was wounded when a bullet went through his horse and lodged in his knee. "One of my fellow Boy Scouts took his mouthful of tobacco and slapped it onto the wound, making it stay put with a strip of his shirt. It smarted some, but caused hurry-up healing, and the few days' stiffness did not hinder horse-riding."

Realizing his mistake and seeing that the bands were about to escape, Sturgis ordered Captain Benteen to try to cut off the Nez Perce before they reached the protection of the canyon. A moment later, he directed Major Merrill to mount his troops and protect the captain's right flank. The entire effort ground to a halt, however, when the men holding Merrill's horses fell too far to the rear and, in the confusion, failed to bring up the horses until after Benteen had charged. Fisher watched as Benteen's single company managed to cross the creek but with no protection on their flank, they soon fell back.

At one point, Fisher tried to help Lieutenant Otis position a howitzer to shell the passage, now thoroughly protected by Indian sharpshooters firing from behind boulders and trees. But Otis "was very much excited" and insisted on running the gun down into the ravine "where he could not even see the bluffs on either side," recalled the scout, "so I left him in disgust."[41] Also overwrought with excitement was Howard's son, Lieutenant Guy Howard. Private

Goldin could scarcely believe his eyes when the lieutenant attempted to fire one of the howitzers loaded on the back of a mule, nearly flattening the unsuspecting animal with the recoil. When Howard attempted a second shot, Goldin wryly noted that the mule braced itself by crouching low and splaying all four legs in opposite directions.

By this time, the Nez Perce had reached the canyon and were herding the last of their horses and families up to the prairie, while warriors held off the soldiers below. The desultory shooting continued until sundown with soldiers probing Indian positions, but the men were unable to dislodge them. The "reds" were so thick in the rocks above, recalled Fisher, "that we could not raise our head to shoot without a dozen shots being fired at us. I drawed lots of shots from them by raising my hat on the muzzle of my gun above the bank, dodging it down whenever they fired a volley at it." The great distance between the two forces was not helped by the wind "blowing nearly a gale," he complained, making it almost "impossible to do good shooting. The ground also was wet, and it was very seldom that we could see where our balls struck."

Two of Fisher's scouts, Charley Rainey (the mixed-blood who had offered to scalp Howard's Nez Perce scouts near Henrys Lake) and Baptise Ouvrier, described by Fisher as "a little Frenchman," got too far ahead at one point, drawing fire from a passing company of soldiers who mistook them for Nez Perce. With bullets "cutting feathers out of Charley's bonnet, shooting several holes through their clothing and tearing up the brush and dirt on all sides of them," Ouvrier jumped up and yelled, "You damn fools! Can't you tell white men from Indians yet?"

At dark, Sturgis's trumpeter sounded "recall," and the men set up camp on the battlefield. The losses, recorded the colonel, were three soldiers dead and eleven wounded, with sixteen Indians killed and some one thousand horses captured. Others disagreed. Surgeon FitzGerald maintained that two soldiers were killed outright, eight wounded, two mortally. "Many ponies were captured and it is said that 6 or 8 Indians were killed. I have seen only two, and I made some effort to see all of them." Thomas Sutherland counted six dead warriors, one hundred horses captured, and six hundred more after the chase by the Crows the following day. Fisher, whose scouts combed the battlefield looking for bodies, believed these reports greatly exaggerated. "I do not think a single dead Indian was found dead on the battle ground. . . ."

In their accounts after the war, Nez Perce survivors hardly mentioned the Canyon Creek fight, remembering more the treachery of the Crows in the days following the battle. Yellow Wolf maintained no warriors died and only three were wounded in the fight, with some thirty or forty horses captured the next day. Where the truth lies is anyone's guess. What seems certain, however, is that Sturgis's estimates of Indian dead were grossly inflated, and he encouraged subordinate officers to follow suit. Captain Benteen later wrote in a letter to Private Goldin that the colonel "wanted me to make a 'hullabaloo' of a report; but I couldn't."[42]

Less disputed was the suffering of those soldiers alive after the battle. There was little to eat, and the only water available was stagnant rain that had collected in alkaline buffalo wallows. Despite orders not to drink it, many did, and were soon visited by acute dysentery. On returning to camp after dark, Fisher found that the Crows, whose arrival had earlier derailed Sturgis's attack, had lifted all of his pack animals, clothing, and bedding. "The Crows took no part in the fight, but staid in the rear and stole everything they could get their hands on."

Just before daybreak on September 14, some two hundred additional Crows joined the soldiers' camp. With all the "shouting and singing," recalled Private Goldin, "sleep was an impossibility, as between the beating of their tom-toms, their shrill war whoops as they danced their war dances, pandemonium raged, but at the first peep of dawn they were off, vowing to overtake and annihilate the enemy." Upon reaching the passage through the rimrock, the soldiers found it abandoned, obstructed with rocks and brush the Nez Perce had hastily cast behind as they escaped during the night. "The farther we advanced," said Goldin, "the more clearly we realized that it would have been utterly impossible for us to have forced our way through here against even fifty well-armed Indians." At the top, the men faced the empty prairie stretching away for miles. As at the Clarks Fork, there was not an Indian to be seen.[43]

Late that afternoon and nearly forty miles farther north, Sturgis's tired and hungry command met Crows returning with what Goldin termed "a considerable number of ponies" stolen from the Nez Perce. Yellow Wolf recalled his feelings that day upon discovering that after successfully evading soldiers, their former allies were now in pursuit. "I rode closer, Eeh! Crows! A new tribe fighting Chief Joseph. Many snows the Crows had been our friends. But now, like the Bitterroot Salish, turned enemies. My heart was just like fire." A major fight, however, never developed, the Crows instead sniping at the rear guard of the fleeing bands and stealing horses whenever they could. In the running pursuit that day, three Nez Perce died and an undetermined number of horses were stolen. When the Nez Perce captured the young Crow warrior they named The-Boy-That-Grabs, they put him on a broken-down horse, quirted him about the head, and sent him back to his people with the message that "the Crows were old women who would not fight and were only fit to stay at home."[44]

Not all Crows wished the bands ill. Somewhere along the trail, a pregnant Nez Perce went into labor and, finding herself unable to keep up with the bands, hid in some brush where she delivered her baby alone. Soon afterward, the woman and her daughter were befriended by a Crow woman. Three or four years passed before they were discovered by white authorities, who promptly had them arrested and sent into exile in Indian Territory.

That night the weary men of Sturgis's command, spread out over some ten miles and with one-third of them on foot leading their horses, arrived in camp with nothing to eat. It was not long before the men began eyeing several lame animals that had escaped from the Nez Perce herd, remembered Private Goldin. "A visit to a neighboring ravine, two or three muffled shots, a rush of soldiers, and fifteen minutes later hundreds of tiny camp-fires were blazing along the banks, and the men with much joking and laughter were making themselves acquainted with good grass-fed pony steaks and rib roast. Terrible! Well, perhaps it would seem so now, but at that time we thought we had never tasted sweeter meat."[45]

The following morning in a downpour, Fisher and the men of Howard's detachment who had traveled with Sturgis since Clarks

Fork Canyon started back to rejoin the general's command now at the Canyon Creek battlefield. Sturgis sent a message to Howard saying that he would push the Indians "until they drop their whole herd, or we drop. . . ." By that night on the banks of the Mussel-shell River, Sturgis dropped first, totally exhausted after living for days on nothing but horsemeat "straight." Here he waited for Howard to catch up. In the past eight days, his men had ridden well over two hundred difficult miles, lost the Nez Perce, found them, then lost them again. Doubtless it was enough to make the colonel wish he had never left his St. Louis recruiting desk.

Surgeon FitzGerald—taciturn, pragmatic, and until now unwavering in his belief in the militant response of his government toward Indians—sent a revealing letter to Emily. "Poor Nez Perces!" he wrote. "There are not more than perhaps 140 or 150 [warriors], while we had about 400 soldiers and nearly as many Crow Indians. I am actually beginning to admire their bravery and endurance in the face of so many well-equipped enemies."[46]

12

When the Nez Perce crossed Montana's Musselshell River that rainy and cold autumn day, they entered the last stronghold of the Plains Indian. A little more than one hundred miles north lay their only remaining natural obstacle, the Missouri River. Another hundred miles beyond was the Canadian border and freedom. Much of this country, particularly that just east of the Musselshell, was a no-man's-land, a vast hunting ground periodically inhabited by a potpourri of nomadic tribes—Sioux, Blackfeet, Cheyenne, Assiniboine, Gros Ventre, Cree, Flathead, Bannock, Shoshoni, and Crow, as well as Nez Perce—but owned by none. Pioneers called it the Big Open, a dry land of sparse settlement, wire grass, and rolling high plains, surrounded by small, scattered mountain ranges and punctuated with solitary buttes that even today seem somehow larger than they truly are when viewed against the backdrop of such spacious vistas. Roaming over this landscape like the people who pursued it was the greatest migratory animal that ever graced the earth in human memory, the North American bison.

During the early nineteenth century, some forty million buffalo inhabited the plains country stretching from Texas into Canada. By

1850, the number had dropped to twenty million; by 1865, to fifteen million. Even in the face of this declining population, pioneers strained to find words worthy of the immense herds: "teeming myriads," "inconceivable numbers," "the world looked like a robe." In October 1868, a writer traveling west of Kansas City reported the animals roaming as far as he could see. "In estimating the number, the only fitting word was 'innumerable.' One hundred thousand was too small a number, a million would be more correct. Besides, who could tell how many miles those herds, or the herd, extended beyond the visible horizon?" That same autumn, General Phil Sheridan witnessed a gargantuan buffalo herd in north Texas possessing "a front of from 50 to 60 miles in extent, and a depth of from five to ten miles."[1]

Twenty years later, the animal that had helped Plains Indian culture evolve for thousands of years had almost vanished, extinguished like a match. Gone was not only a rich cultural tradition but the lives of many who had depended on endless numbers of the great shaggy-headed beasts.

As early as 1850, cries of pending extirpation fell on deaf ears. Every protection bill introduced in Congress to save the vast herds met with either defeat or presidential veto. To most officials, the buffalo, inseparable as it was from the nomadic life of Plains Indians, deserved to disappear. In 1871, Secretary of Interior Columbus Delano blatantly told Congress that "I would not seriously regret the total disappearance of the buffalo from our western prairies, in its effect upon the Indians. I would regard it rather as a means of hastening their sense of dependence upon the products of the soil and their own labors."[2]

The U.S. Army agreed—an unusual accord since both the departments of War and Interior bickered constantly over which one could best administer Indian affairs. General Sheridan himself purportedly addressed a joint meeting of the 1875 Texas legislature, which was considering a bill to protect remaining buffalo:

[Buffalo hunters] have done in the last two years and will do more in the next year to settle the vexed Indian question, than the entire regular army has done in the last thirty years. They are destroying the Indian's commissary, and it is a well-known fact that an army losing its base of supplies is placed at a great disadvantage. Send them powder and lead, if you will; for the sake of a lasting peace, let them kill, skin and sell until the buffalo are exterminated.[3]

By 1877, buffalo had disappeared from the southern plains and the animals were becoming increasingly scarce in Montana, the heart of their last refuge. The autumn before the Nez Perce fled their homeland, one-half million animals were reported within a 150-mile radius of the army's Tongue River Cantonment on the Yellowstone River. Five years later, two hundred thousand hides were shipped from Montana and the western Dakotas. During the spring of that year a single herd estimated at seventy-five thousand animals crossed the Yellowstone above Miles City, holding up a steamer for hours. From the boat, the passengers shot animals in the water until, according to an observer, the river ran red with blood. The army issued free ammunition—they did not want the herd to reach Sitting Bull's Sioux in Canada. Word spread quickly and armed men came running. Fewer than three hundred buffalo escaped the line of gunners that were waiting in camps to the north. Unable to salvage most of the carcasses, white gunners left thousands upon thousands to rot. By 1883, only forty thousand hides were shipped from the West; one year later, a mere three hundred. In 1886, William T. Hornaday made a search for surviving specimens for the National Museum. He left Miles City and was gone two months. When he returned, he had collected only twenty-four animals.

No one believed it could have happened so quickly. Because Indians perceived no pattern to herd migrations, they were convinced that buffalo were simply elsewhere and would eventually return. Many believed that each spring the animals poured forth from caves leading deep beneath the earth's surface. When succeeding years brought fewer and fewer, Indians cast about for the reason. Some lyrically attributed their disappearance to a "death wind." Others were more prosaic. The Blackfeet accused the Canadian Crees; the Crees, the Flatheads and Sioux; the Flatheads and Sioux, the Crows. Soon they knew the truth.[4]

273

Pretty Shield, a Crow medicine woman, interviewed near the turn of the century, had no doubt who was responsible:

Ahh, my heart fell down when I began to see dead buffalo scattered all over our beautiful country, killed and skinned, and left to rot by white men. . . . The first I saw of this was in the Judith Basin. The whole country there smelled of rotting meat. Even the flowers could not put down the bad smell. Our hearts were like stones. And yet nobody believed, even then, that the white man could kill all the buffalo. Since the beginning of things there had been so many! Even the Lakota, bad as their hearts were for us, would not do such a thing as this; nor the Cheyenne, nor the Arapahoe, nor the Pecunnie; and yet the white man did this, even when he did not want the meat.[5]

This unimaginable yet impending doom was not in evidence as the Nez Perce crossed the Musselshell in mid-September and headed north into the Judith River Basin. Throughout their journey, small but frequent herds of buffalo dotted the prairie, although the bands tarried long enough to secure only the barest subsistence. The grueling pursuit was becoming increasingly costly as more Nez Perce fell out from the column each day, awaiting their end at the hands of trailing army scouts.

Before leaving the basin, they stumbled on a band of River Crows led by Chief Dumb Bull. Under no illusions about their former friends, the Nez Perce stole horses and a large supply of dried buffalo meat the Crows had been gathering for the coming winter. A few days later at the basin's only trading post, J. W. Redington discovered Dumb Bull "feeling pretty sore about the way the hostiles had cleaned him out of all his horses. But still he declined the invitation to come along with the scouts and get some sweet revenge."[6]

Back near the Yellowstone River, Howard's straggling force was once again united. On September 16, the same day that Fisher and the detachment temporarily assigned to Sturgis's command limped back to the Canyon Creek battlefield, many of the men footsore and leading worn mounts, Captain Harry Cushing arrived with limited supplies from Fort Ellis. After leaving the command at Henrys Lake and under instructions from Howard, Cushing had wasted no time obtaining supplies at Bozeman. His orders were to rendezvous with the command as it exited Yellowstone Park. The captain, however, had not counted on running afoul of Lieutenant Colonel Gilbert, then on his way to Fort Ellis and the upper Yellowstone River to assume command of the pursuit. Countermanding Howard's orders, despite Cushing's objections, Gilbert absorbed some of Cushing's men into his own command and brusquely ordered the captain to remain at the fort on post duty. Almost a week later, after Gilbert had departed on his futile chase, Cushing decided to "act on my own responsibility" and carry out General Howard's original wishes. When Howard learned his order had been canceled, he was incensed, stating that Gilbert was not only a buffoon, but had nearly brought Howard's command "to the verge of starvation," jeopardizing his entire effort.[7]

For his part, S. G. Fisher had had enough. The scout was convinced that the soldiers had no chance of catching the Nez Perce, and later that day, his enlistment period over, Fisher departed for Idaho with his remaining Bannocks. Other scouts filled their place, one named "Liver-eating" Johnson, who was a living caricature of legendary frontiersmen. Johnson—a giant of a man with a wild, unkempt shock of black hair and full beard reaching far down his chest —purportedly had once killed twenty Crow warriors in retaliation for the murder of his Indian wife, cutting out their livers and eating them raw. Although Lieutenant Hugh Scott remained suitably skeptical of this tale, he found the scout an accomplished raconteur, with language so "quaint" that he enthralled listeners late into each night.[8]

On September 17, Howard's command started after Sturgis, detouring first down the Yellowstone River to pick up additional supplies from Fort Custer, a small army post under construction on the Bighorn River, then up an established trail to the Musselshell River. Four days later when he arrived in camp, a message was waiting from Colonel Miles. After receiving Howard's earlier note, the colonel had departed the following day from his headquarters on the lower Yellowstone River in pursuit of the Nez Perce. His command was moving as rapidly as possible toward Carroll, a steamboat landing on the Missouri River, hoping to cut off the bands before they reached Canada. "I fear your information reaches me too late to intercept them," wrote Miles, "but I will do the best I can."[9]

Now Howard slowed his march, having learned that whenever he fell a day or two behind, the Nez Perce slowed their pace as well. In the bitter acrimony following the final battle, as both commanders vied for the glory and fame of capturing the bands, Miles derided this tactic, saying that if it truly occurred, it had little bearing on the final outcome. But in a dispatch sent to the San Francisco *Chronicle* about this time, Thomas Sutherland supports Howard's assertion. "The Indians camped at Judith Gap two days ago. We do not push them much, hoping to give General Miles a chance to get ahead of them on the Missouri River: then to attack them simultaneously."[10]

Such may have been Howard's intentions, but within a few days it became apparent that the Nez Perce were so far ahead that his weary and bedraggled command would never catch them. Time and again he had given up hope, only to come tantalizingly close. But now with the season rapidly deteriorating, the command short of supplies, and the bands just days away from Canada, the only remote chance of capture seemed to lie with Miles. Once they were across the Missouri, no one in the command believed they could be stopped. Howard would continue the pursuit to the border as Sherman wished, but he would do it with a skeleton force composed mostly of Sturgis's men. To this end, he prepared to disband all but one company of his own cavalry to return to the railhead at Corrine, Utah, then on to their far-flung posts before the onset of winter. At the same time, he sent most of his remaining civilian volunteers and packers overland back to Idaho. Then, with a fervent prayer to God to stop the Nez Perce before they crossed the border "even at the expense of another's receiving the credit of the expedition," the general plodded on toward the Missouri River.[11]

On September 27, two couriers arrived with news that days earlier the bands had crossed the Missouri at Cow Island, about forty miles upstream from the steamboat landing at Carroll and at least seventy miles ahead of Howard's forces. The general also learned Miles had crossed the Missouri near the mouth of the Musselshell and was still in pursuit. "This information settled the question in regard to following the Indian trail," Major Mason wrote his wife, "as of course that was no longer necessary."[12] Four days later, on October 1, the command arrived at Carroll. Leaving Sturgis bivouacked at the landing with the majority of remaining troops, Howard and a few staff, along with his Nez Perce interpreters, "Captain" John and Old George, and some one hundred men, boarded the steamboat *Benton* and started upriver for Cow Island. There Howard hoped against hope to receive a message that Miles had succeeded in halting the Nez Perce before they reached Canada.

Nothing could be more impossible, Surgeon Charles Alexander told the general. "There isn't one chance in a million for Miles."[13]

The Nez Perce, in fact, knew nothing of Miles's effort but had lost little time under Poker Joe's leadership in distancing themselves from Howard and Sturgis's pursuit after crossing the Musselshell River. In less than thirty-six hours, they had traveled some seventy-five miles from the lone trading post at the head of Judith Basin near where they had intercepted Dumb Bull's Crow band to the traditional Missouri crossing at Cow Island. Only a few short trails existed along this stretch of the river due to the difficult surrounding landscape—known as the Missouri Breaks or Badlands—rising as much as eight hundred feet in places, with broken and rugged country extending six or more miles back along both sides of the river. Here, some 130-odd miles downstream from the booming frontier community of Fort Benton, was the end of the steamboat line during the river's low-water seasons of late summer and fall. Goods and supplies for upstream destinations were stored temporarily in an open-air depot under a bluff on the north side of the river, then transported up Cow Creek and south of the Bear Paw Mountains to Fort Benton via oxen-driven wagons, locally known as "bull trains." This combination of conveyance along the Missouri was in no regard small-scale. Shipping prices of over one hundred dollars per ton gave rise to a fleet of more than forty steamboats along the upper river, with some two thousand freight wagons powered by over thirty thousand oxen transporting supplies throughout western Montana.

Steamboat passengers frequently passed through Cow Island as well. In a near repeat of General Sherman's close shave with the

Nez Perce in Yellowstone Park, a party consisting of General Alfred Terry, several officers, and a number of officials—known as the Sitting Bull Commission—decided at the last minute against traveling via the Missouri River and chose instead the longer but safer railroad route to Corrine, Utah. From there they traveled by stage to Fort Benton and on to Canada in an unsuccessful attempt to convince the truculent chief and his followers to return to the United States. As it was, Terry's party arrived at Fort Benton only a few days after the Nez Perce crossed the river at Cow Island.

On the morning of the day the Indians reached the crossing, a bull train consisting of fifteen wagons driven by eight men and hauling thirty-five tons of freight left the landing and started for Fort Benton. The ascent up Cow Creek was arduous, adjacent bluffs requiring no less than thirty-two crossings of the narrow, willow-choked stream. Because the bull train was ponderously slow, eleven river passengers who had also landed at Cow Island rode several miles ahead, leaving their baggage to be brought up by the teamsters.

Guarding the freight at Cow Island when the bands suddenly appeared on the south shore of the river later that day was a group of a dozen soldiers, led by Sergeant William Moelchert, and four citizens who worked for the steamboat line. Ordinarily no soldiers guarded freight at the depot, but several had been detailed to watch over government supplies belonging to a small detachment of troops attempting to clear a channel at Dauphin Rapids, a bothersome navigation obstacle several miles upriver. Moelchert and a few men had been sent down that very day to retrieve additional rations, traveling in a flat-bottom boat, one man riding a horse along the shore that would be used to pull the boat back upstream. No sooner had the men beached the boat at the tent depot than the Nez Perce appeared on the opposite shore.

After some deliberation among themselves, two warriors on horseback crossed the river and speaking "English as well as anyone could," according to Moelchert, asked to meet with the man in charge. Taking the advice of one of his men, the sergeant ventured out unarmed. The Nez Perce (one of whom was probably Poker Joe) walked up, shook Moelchert's hand, and pointing to the fifty-odd tons of freight and supplies piled under the bluff, asked for food. Their women and children were hungry, having had nothing to eat but dried buffalo obtained from the raid on the Crows two days before. With stunning if not farcical boldness, Moelchert simply said no; it was not his freight to give away. The warriors turned to go but a few moments later came back, offering to pay for food in gold or silver. Again, the sergeant shook his head. Moelchert said that one of the Indians, returning a third time, "pleaded with me for something to eat so then I went back to the breastworks and put a side of bacon in a sack filled about half full with hardtack, took it out to them and they very kindly thanked me for the same."[14]

How few mouths this hollow gesture might have fed Moelchert did not have long to contemplate, for, at sundown, after crossing their families and heading up Cow Creek, the warriors attacked. Throughout the night and well into the next morning, claimed the sergeant, some one hundred warriors waged a fierce battle to dislodge his men, charging and being repulsed at least seven times. Probably more likely was Yellow Wolf's account that after finding that the whites' barricade could not be overrun without significant loss and with darkness upon them, the Nez Perce kept up a desultory and sporadic fire throughout the night. Moreover, the freight—piled as high as a house—was easily reached by the warriors under cover of a nearby ravine. After taking flour, bacon, ham, sugar, coffee, and beans, along with pots and pans for cooking, warriors torched the rest, the huge grease-fed blaze casting a luminous glow on the bluff overlooking the river and making those who showed themselves an easy target. If bullets grew infrequent, words did not. The Nez Perce taunted the whites with English obscenities (since their own language had none); the defenders remarked later that their pronunciation was as proficient and eloquent as that of any frontier bushwhacker.

By morning, the warriors were gone. Two whites had received minor wounds, and not far away Moelchert discovered the body of the unlucky soldier who had ridden the horse down from Dauphin Rapids. The men found no dead Indians, and Yellow Wolf said later only one warrior had been slightly wounded. Freight or no freight, the exhilarated survivors were thankful to be alive, as they well

279

might have been considering what had happened to others during past months who had behaved far less foolishly. The ebullient company clerk, Michael Foley, wrote this tongue-in-cheek message to his supervisor, "Colonel" George Clendenin:

RIFLE PIT, AT COW ISLAND
September 23, 1877, 10 A.M.

Col:—Chief Joseph is here, and says he will surrender for two hundred bags of sugar. I told him to surrender without the sugar. He took the sugar and will not surrender. What shall I do?

Michael Foley[15]

Late that evening at dusk, the defenders were startled when a Seventh Infantry major with the unlikely name of Guido Ilges, leading a detachment of about fifty men, most of them volunteer citizens, hailed from across the river. Days before, Ilges had received word at Fort Benton that the Nez Perce were attempting to reach Canada, their movement a potential threat to river commerce. Striking out with some of his men in a small boat and others on horseback, the major arrived just in time to witness the last billowing plumes of smoke from the burning freight. After crossing with his men over to the depot, and fearing the bull train traveling up Cow Creek would soon meet an identical fate, Ilges and some thirty-six mounted volunteers rode off the next morning in pursuit of the Indians.

The major's concern proved to be well-founded. Some ten miles up Cow Creek the day following the skirmish at the landing, the Nez Perce overtook the fifteen wagons and eight drivers. When they rode up, one of the men and part-owner of the outfit, O. G. Cooper, said he expected to be attacked, but "they offered us no violence," the lead warriors milling around the wagons in an unthreatening manner. Soon the main body of Nez Perce came up, passed by, and went into camp not far away. A few warriors drifted back, examining the goods in the wagons. "They all wanted food," claimed Cooper, "one young buck who staid around the wagons asked us repeatedly, in good English, when we were going to have dinner. I told him the men were afraid to go after wood as they thought the Indians would kill them. He replied, 'Oh hell, they won't touch them.' "[16]

By nightfall, the warriors returned to their own camp, but the teamsters took no chances, sleeping well away from the wagons. After breakfast the next morning, the men were gathering their grazing oxen when a group of warriors suddenly appeared and began stripping the canvas coverings and setting fire to the wagons. "We knew then that war was declared," said Cooper, "and without stopping for further information, we jumped down a cut bank and made for the hills."[17]

Coming upon this scene at this precise moment less than a mile away were Ilges and his volunteers. It is unclear whether the Nez Perce attacked the bull train on discovering the approach of the major's party or if the two events happened coincidentally. Regardless, warriors lost no time charging Ilges's men, who rapidly sought cover in a nearby ravine. After either a two- or five-hour fight—depending on which account is believed—much of it beyond a thousand yards and devoid of accuracy, the Nez Perce withdrew without any injuries. One volunteer was killed. Another stopped a bullet with his belt buckle, leaving him dazed and with a painful black-and-blue abdomen. Some had their hats and clothing perforated by bullets but were otherwise uninjured. Less lucky was one of the freight drivers who was shot in the back and killed. Later, Ilges found the body of a prospector while traveling back to Fort Benton along the southern edge of the Bear Paw Mountains. A week after that, the decomposed remains of the man's partner were found as well. Altogether, the Missouri River crossing had cost the lives of five men and at least eighty-five tons of freight. More fortunate were the eleven passengers—four women, a North-West Mounted Policeman, a U.S. Army surgeon, and five enlisted men—who had started out ahead of Cooper's bull train and arrived in Fort Benton, bereft of their luggage and unaware until days later that they nearly had parted with their lives as well.

After abandoning Ilges, the bands made their way along upper Cow Creek for several miles, then ascended the broad grassy prairie leading north between the Bear Paw and Little Rocky mountains, two relatively low ranges whose northern edges drain into the Milk River, thence into the Missouri. In four days, the Nez Perce traveled no more than fifty miles, and on September 29, in rain mixed with snow, they made camp on a minor tributary known as Snake Creek. They had had no tipis since the Big Hole, using only buffalo robes or scraps of canvas stolen along the way to form temporary wickiups during inclement weather. Less than ten miles north was the Milk River and thirty miles beyond lay Canada.[18]

Why they dallied so close to the border has been the subject of endless speculation. Some authorities believe they may have hesitated in the face of an uncertain welcome from their old antagonists the Sioux, but no direct supporting evidence exists. Others have ventured that they thought themselves in Canada, although the Nez Perce later roundly refuted this theory, saying they knew the boundary's exact location. It seems the bands were aware that Howard had yet to cross the Missouri and harbored no suspicions that any other force might be close. The skirmishes on Cow Creek appeared more the work of citizens defending their property than of soldiers attempting to apprehend them. Their people were weary. Buffalo were abundant on this high prairie, and with winter fast approaching, some wanted to stop long enough to put up a supply of meat before crossing into Canada where herds were known to be less plentiful.

But perhaps the most important reason during these critical few days after crossing the Missouri River was that daily leadership of the bands changed. Many Wounds reported that "Looking Glass upbraided Poker Joe for his hurrying; for causing the old people weariness; told him that he was no chief, that he himself was chief and that he would be the leader." Indian oral history supports this view, saying that once Canada was nearly in view and with soldiers far behind, most Nez Perce no longer saw a reason for a nonchief to continue as trail leader, no matter how brilliant had been his guidance since the Big Hole. With a warning that delay risked death, Poker Joe reluctantly acceded and Looking Glass again began directing the bands' daily movement.[19]

If the Nez Perce were vacillating over who would be leader, the soldiers of the U.S. Fifth Infantry were not.

Their commander, thirty-eight-year-old Nelson A. Miles, could hardly have been more determined. Outside of Crook and Custer, perhaps no single officer ever attained greater fame on the frontier than this six-foot colonel with gray-blue eyes. When it came to fighting Indians, no one doubted he was superb. The only problem, complained Sherman, was that Miles wanted everyone to know it. "I have told him plainly," the exasperated general of the army wrote Sheridan after Miles had repeatedly demanded promotion, "that I know of no way to satisfy his ambitions but to surrender to him absolute power over the whole Army with President and Congress thrown in."[20]

Miles had been ambitious from the start. A self-educated dry-goods clerk when the Civil War broke out, he had risen quickly, attaining brevet major general of volunteers by war's end at the age of twenty-seven. Four times he was wounded, once when a spent minié ball pierced his neck, again when a bullet at Chancellorsville blew away part of his stomach—a wound that by all rights should have killed him. A few weeks later he was back at the front, prompting a fellow officer to remark to General Howard, for whom Miles was an aide-de-camp, "that officer will get promoted or get killed."[21]

No doubt Miles preferred promotion, yet he displayed little hesitation once he discovered putting his life on the line was the quickest avenue to advancement. A list of the campaigns he fought reads like a summary of the entire Civil War, for which he received a Medal of Honor, a reputation for battlefield excellence, as well as an egomaniacal desire for recognition he was never to lose.

After the war, Miles's career almost foundered when he was placed in charge of guarding Jefferson Davis. Supporters of the Confederacy's ex-president accused him of prisoner maltreatment, and Davis himself despised Miles, calling him a "miserable ass." Miles reciprocated with equal contempt before requesting another position. Howard liked him enough to offer employment in the Freedman's Bureau, but after a short stint, Miles returned to the regular army as a full colonel. He thought he deserved greater rank and did not hesitate to say so. Soon he married General Sherman's niece, a relationship he and his wife never ceased to exploit.[22]

When Miles met Custer in 1869, the two men instantly liked one another. They had much in common. Both loved horses and hunting dogs, and when Custer attacked and wiped out Black Kettle on the Washita (along with nearly a hundred women, children, and elderly men), no one was more eager than Miles to emulate him. Here their similarities parted company. While each was fearless, confident, tireless, and obnoxiously self-promoting in his pursuit of frontier glory, Miles was rarely cavalier on the battlefield. Neither did his impatience extend to Indians, with whom he often attempted conciliation before resorting to combat. The more he fought them, the more they held his admiration. Indians possessed "courage, skill, sagacity, endurance, fortitude and self-sacrifice" of the highest order, all qualities which "we could copy to our advantage." But like so many others, he saw the wave of western expansion as "irresistible" and Indians as "a doomed race."[23]

In 1876, Miles requested duty in Montana after Custer's untimely demise. During that winter, he doggedly pursued both Sitting Bull and Crazy Horse until the former fled to Canada and the latter gave up. All this he did with fewer than five hundred infantrymen, often in subzero temperatures and on short rations, pushing them so relentlessly that during one bleak battle his outnumbered men attacked out of pure hunger, knowing dried buffalo meat awaited them in the village below. The Sioux hardly knew how to react, so used were they to summer campaigns. By the time of the Nez Perce outbreak six months later, after twelve hundred miles, three major fights, and some eight skirmishes, over four thousand disaffected Sioux and Cheyenne had agreed to return to the agencies.[24]

With each success that winter, Miles continued to ballyhoo his exploits, demanding promotion while at the same time finding fault with virtually every peer. For Crook, Gibbon, Sturgis, and eventually Howard, he voiced little but derision. Given his own department and fifteen hundred men, "I could clean this country entirely in four months," he boasted to Sheridan. To his wife, he was perhaps a little more candid but no less confident: "I have my hands full and have Indians on the brain."[25]

Now he was about to demonstrate how true this was.

Miles was watching the sun set on the evening of September 17 as Howard's lone courier completed his four-day ride down the Yellowstone River from the Clarks Fork. Stopping on the shore across from the Tongue River Cantonment, he hailed a ferry. Miles's men had built the temporary cottonwood log and sod buildings during the previous autumn and winter, roofing them with poles and chinking them with mud. That spring the roofs had leaked and mud had dripped on the troops below, making for miserable conditions. Construction had already started that summer on Fort Keogh, a more permanent structure a short distance away.

Miles had headquartered his men—a mixture of scouts and assorted detachments, including several companies of the Second Cavalry, three companies held over from Sturgis's Seventh, and Miles's own battle-hardened Fifth Infantry—in the cantonment throughout the stifling months of July and August, with occasional forays north against the Sioux. His eye that summer had been on Sitting Bull, sequestered in Canada but periodically raiding across the border and rumored to be preparing for an all-out war against Montana settlers. So focused was Miles on capturing this Indian who was credited with toppling Custer that he had threatened to ignore the international border and march into Canada after him and probably would have if Sherman, more sensitive to the political folly of such impudence, had not repeatedly warned him off. Unwilling to give up on the Sioux, Miles had sent Sturgis to aid Howard's pursuit of the Nez Perce rather than responding himself. Now with autumn rapidly approaching and the chance for an encounter with Sitting Bull less likely, Miles opened the courier's envelope and read Howard's message "wishing I would take some action to intercept them."[26]

Twelve hours later, after a sleepless night in hurried preparation, his men were mounted and ready to ride.

The distance was prodigious, even for troops used to Miles's unrelenting pace—at least 120 miles to the Missouri River, then an equal distance to the border. Four days out, four companies of cavalry who had been on their way to Fort Benton to escort General Terry's Sitting Bull Commission to Canada, and now redirected by Miles to help apprehend the Nez Perce, caught up with the command near the Musselshell River. This brought Miles's total force to eleven companies of some 350 men, in addition to thirty Sioux and Cheyenne scouts whom Miles had fought and subdued the winter before and who were now eager to strike a blow against their traditional enemies. The following day, September 23, as the Nez Perce were crossing the Missouri at Cow Island, the command arrived some eighty miles downstream at the mouth of the Musselshell, having traveled the final fifty-four miles in just twenty-four hours. Here Miles had the uncanny good fortune of encountering the steamboat *Fontenelle,* the same vessel that had recently dropped passengers and freight at Cow Island, missing the Nez Perce by mere hours.

Miles commandeered the boat to ferry part of his force across the Missouri the next day. He planned for the remainder of his men, pack mules, and forty supply wagons to proceed along the southern shore to the crossing at Cow Island, for he doubted the Nez Perce had yet reached the river. Splitting his force provided insurance in case the Indians somehow managed to get ahead of him, since he might not have another opportunity to make a safe crossing of the deep river until Cow Island. The next morning, however, he realized his mistake when three men in a rowboat appeared floating down the river, two of whom were civilians wounded in the Cow Island fight and were attempting to reach Fort Peck, an outpost another day downstream. From these men, Miles learned the bands had already crossed the Missouri and were last seen heading north. Meanwhile, the *Fontenelle* had steamed off about a mile downriver. Miles quickly ordered the howitzer loaded and a shot fired across the boat's bow. On board was Miles's trusted adjutant, Captain Frank Baldwin, who had recently become ill and was returning to the cantonment. Baldwin sensed something was amiss, ordered the boat back upriver, and the entire command crossed later that afternoon.

As the jubilant men took up their march again, Seventh Cavalry Surgeon Henry Tilton depicted the scene:

It is evening. One battalion marches out of the valley, over the hills, the men singing as they go. With the camp fires, the scattered animals, the rumble of the moving train, the crack of the drivers' whips, the occasional scream of the steamer's whistle and the song of the cavalrymen as they march off, the scene is intensely interesting, and it is difficult to realize that we are in the wilderness.[27]

The next day, the command reached the high prairie grassland above the Missouri River, the Little Rocky and Bear Paw mountains plainly visible to the north and west. Although buffalo and antelope were almost always in constant view—Tilton calling it a "hunter's paradise"—Miles prohibited any shooting, fearing the Nez Perce might take alarm should they see a stampeding herd coming across the prairie. On September 29, the same rainy day that the bands halted on Snake Creek, Miles's force skirted around the north side of the Little Rockies and crossed the fifteen-mile-wide valley between the two ranges, much of the time obscured from view by low-lying clouds and fog—another stroke of luck since no one watching from a distance could witness their approach. The men spent a disagreeable night below a prominent butte along the eastern edge of the Bear Paw Mountains far up a tributary of Cow Creek. After midnight the clouds briefly lifted, the moon and stars appeared, the temperature fell, and the damp ground began to freeze.

Reveille came at 2 A.M. and just after daylight, as the command stopped briefly to rest beside a small stream, a lone wolf howled. Soon Cheyenne and Sioux scouts discovered the wide trail of the Nez Perce heading north. A short time later, the scouts gave brief chase to several Indians thought to be Nez Perce watching the back trail for just such a force following the bands. Then word came that the Indian camp had been spotted along a creek only seven miles away. Without hesitation the scouts quickly stripped for battle, painting their faces and bodies and mounting fresh horses each had kept in reserve. Rifles in hand, the troops trotted forward until within two or three miles of the camp. Miles gave the command and the men began galloping. "To be astride a good horse, on the open prairie, rifle in hand . . . galloping on a hot trail," exclaimed Surgeon Tilton, "sends a thrill through the body which is seldom experienced."[28]

The frozen ground, many said later, shook and rumbled like distant thunder as the four hundred horsemen charged across the prairie toward the Nez Perce camp.

13

hile the men of Miles's command were spending an uncomfortable night, in the Nez Perce camp several miles away Wottolen was also having difficulty sleeping. In a recurring dream, the warrior distinctly recognized the village on Snake Creek, the ragged bits of canvas used as shelters stretching along the brushy stream. Immediately to the east and south of the village were thirty- to forty-foot-high bluffs, steeply incised with coulees and ravines leading up to the rolling, undulating prairie. Where the prairie to the west sloped gently down toward the creek, the horse herd grazed. Everything seemed as it should. Then Wottolen had a strong vision. Above the camp, thick smoke from battle hung in the air. When he looked into the stream, the water had turned red with the blood of both soldiers and Indians. Near dawn he awoke with a start, knowing the camp would soon be attacked.

No one believed Wottolen's vision. Hunting parties had gone out the day before. There had been no warnings, no alarms. The soldiers were known to be days behind.

After the weather cleared and turned cold during the night, morning brought a hazy, overcast sky. A stiff west wind blew frost-yellowed leaves from the willows along the creek. By nightfall there would be snow. After eating a morning meal, the camp prepared to move.

Some had already caught their horses and were packing when two scouts came galloping into camp from the south. As they drew near, Yellow Wolf heard one of the men, Tom Hill, yelling, "Stampeding buffaloes! Soldiers! Soldiers!"[1]

Still there was incredulity. Most thought the animals were being chased by Nez Perce hunters. So much did Looking Glass disbelieve soldiers could be the cause, said Yellow Wolf, that the chief mounted his horse and rode about the camp cautioning against panic, telling people to take their time preparing to leave.

Not long afterward, Yellow Wolf looked up to see another scout riding hard from the south. The man rode to a nearby high bluff, and as he circled about the top, he fired his gun and waved a blanket: "Enemies right on us! Soon the attack!"[2] Then came the great rumbling roar of pounding hoofs.

The camp erupted.

Yellow Wolf heard Chief Joseph's voice above the noise, "Horses! Horses! Save the horses!"[3]

All across the creek bottom men, women, and children scattered as soldiers, splitting their forces in an attempt to surround the village, streamed over the prairie from the south. Between one hundred and two hundred people, many only partially dressed and with few or no possessions, managed to reach the horse herd just as the troops appeared. These quickly mounted and fled north. The remainder took up positions at the top of the bluffs south and east of camp to face the oncoming attack.

One of those who ran toward the horse herd was Eelahweemah, the same fourteen-year-old boy who along with his brother had watched as their mother and five other women had been slain while taking shelter in the creek at the Big Hole. Warned by his father "to skip for my life," Eelahweemah caught his horse and tried to mount, but the terrified animal kept rearing and turning in tight circles. Just as the first soldiers led by Cheyenne warriors began charging through the herd, the boy managed to climb on the horse and gallop away. A half mile later, he remembered his younger brother still in camp and, turning around, rode back through the stampeding herd until he found him. Mounting double, with his brother's arms tightly clasped around his waist, Eelahweemah started after the herd. Both Cheyennes and soldiers aimed their rifles at them, one bullet cleanly parting a braid of hair close to Eelahweemah's brother's ear. Just ahead, the boys saw a Cheyenne riding a spotted horse catch up with a woman and, despite her pleadings, shoot her. Two Moons, seeing two soldiers about to catch the youths from behind, charged the men and drove them back. The boys rode on, Eelahweemah surviving to eventually succeed Joseph as chief of the Wallowa band. Their father was killed in the attack.[4]

Another youth who escaped was White Bird, the chief's ten-year-old nephew, who had lost his thumb at the Big Hole and whose wounded mother had submerged him under water while appealing to the mercy of Gibbon's soldiers. Barefoot and clothed only in a shirt, he again jumped into the creek to avoid the attackers. Cold, wet, and shivering in the autumn air, he was pulled up behind a woman as she passed by on a horse and they galloped after the stampeding herd.

At least one Nez Perce warrior tried to reason with a Cheyenne scout who led the attack. From a distance, Yellow Wolf observed Heyoom Iklakit (Grizzly Bear Lying Down) talking in signs to the scout, reminding him that he had "red skin, red blood. You must be crazy! You are fighting your friends. We are Indians. We are humans. Do not help the whites!" The scout signed that he would only shoot in the air. Mollified, Heyoom Iklakit turned to meet the soldiers and was instantly killed. The Cheyenne, witnessing the man's death, quickly grabbed the bridle of a nearby horse ridden by a Nez Perce woman, pulled out his pistol, and shot her dead.[5]

Some reached the herd in time to escape but then chose not to. Giving his twelve-year-old daughter Kapkap Ponmi (Noise of Running Feet) a rope and telling her to catch a horse and follow the others, Chief Joseph mounted a horse and started back to the camp where his younger wife and three-month-old daughter remained. Resolving "to go to them or die," he charged back unarmed as soldiers began shooting at him. "It seemed to me that there were guns on every side, before and behind me. My clothes were cut to pieces and my horse was wounded, but I was not hurt. As I reached the door of my lodge, my wife handed me my rifle, saying, 'Here's your gun. Fight!' "[6]

Tom Hill, who had raised the first warning, had "a wife whom I loved more than anything else. I took a horse and tied her to it, and told her to go fast." Then the warrior hurried back to the bluffs to meet the soldiers.[7]

Those who reached the herd too late were forced to turn back. Six-year-old Josiah Red Wolf, whose mother and sister had been killed at the Big Hole while he hid under a buffalo robe, was running back to the bluffs holding the hand of his grandmother when he saw an elderly woman ahead suddenly collapse after being shot. " 'She's dead!' my grandmother hollered running with me. But when we got up to her she got up and went on. She wasn't dead, she laid down just as if she was dead. The bullet went through her dress and right between her legs."[8]

Watching the attack from a hill just south of the village, Miles realized that although directed to charge the camp, the Second Cavalry instead was pursuing the stampeding horse herd. Several miles north along Snake Creek, a group of some sixty retreating warriors stopped long enough to countercharge, forcing the troops to dismount and allowing their women and children to gain a significant lead. Most would not stop until they reached Canada. Led by Toohoolhoolzote, five or six warriors took refuge on an exposed rocky bluff overlooking the creek. Caught between soldiers on each side, all were soon killed.

Immediately in front of Miles, the news was not good. Here three companies of the Seventh, originally detailed as a backup force, had finally charged the southern edge of the village when it appeared the Second had struck off after the horse herd. In those precious few moments, warriors had taken up defensive positions at the top of the bluffs. As the 115 cavalrymen, riding by columns of fours with drawn pistols but encumbered by heavy winter coats they had not stopped to remove, charged within two hundred yards of their defenses, warriors suddenly stood up and began firing. In the murderous shower of bullets, men tumbled from their saddles, wounded and screaming horses fell, and the charge ground to a halt. Those still mounted who managed to reach portions of the bluff found the slope too steep to descend.

Rallying his men and inclining to the right, Captain Owen Hale led Company K along the eastern edge of the bluffs. Moments later, Companies A and D, commanded by Captains Myles Moylan and Edward Godfrey, followed. The officers—both veterans of Custer's fights at the Washita and Little Bighorn—had ridden only a few steps when Godfrey looked up to see a warrior not more than seventy-five yards away taking aim at him. The rifle cracked and Godfrey's horse fell dead, the momentum pitching him forward. Falling hard on his head and shoulder, Godfrey turned a complete somersault and landed on his feet. Still holding his revolver, he attempted to shoot his assailant but found he could not lift his injured arm. As the warrior took aim again, Trumpeter Thomas Herwood, seeing Godfrey's danger, quickly rode between the two men. For his trouble, Herwood received a bullet through his left lung. Later, after the young recruit was helped back to the rear, a surgeon made a hasty examination and, noting that Herwood had lost a massive amount of blood, announced, "He can't live; take in those who have a chance to recover." Visiting the wounded the next day, the surgeon was surprised to find Herwood not only alive but more than a little riled. "I am the man you left on the ridge to die! If you are going to probe my wound with a finger, as you did [yesterday], please cut the nail off!"[9]

Meanwhile, Godfrey recovered sufficiently to mount a blood-spattered horse belonging to a sergeant who had been fatally shot. Again, Moylan, Godfrey, and their men began moving to the relief of Hale's company, then hotly engaged in hand-to-hand combat with the Nez Perce a few hundred yards away. They had not gone far when another warrior just over the edge of the bluff dropped to his knee and fired at Godfrey. "I felt a shock," said the captain, "as if hit by a stone or club on my left side." Moments later "I felt my body swaying forward and a stinging pain in my side and body. I was powerless to prevent going over my horse's neck. My horse stopped, stood perfectly quiet and then, as if knowing the situation, partly lowered his head and I slid to mother earth!"[10]

Looking up, Godfrey saw the warrior take several steps toward him, then stop and run back over the bluff, evidently satisfied he was no longer a threat. Momentarily out of danger, the captain thought it strange that although obviously wounded he was not bleeding. "In order to investigate I loosened my belt and the instant I did I felt the warm blood running down my body. So I 'cinched up' again as quick as I could." With assistance, he eventually made it back to the make-shift hospital set up in a swale a quarter mile south of the bluffs. Soon afterward Godfrey saw Moylan ride in, shot in the thigh, a bright red streak of blood trailing down his leg.

Moylan and his men had made it to Company K's position but arrived too late. Only minutes before, Captain Hale had ordered his men to dismount. While leading their horses, alternately firing and advancing along the top of the bluff toward the village, they had been surprised when warriors suddenly rushed up from ravines along their flanks. Fighting hand to hand, Hale's men had fallen back several hundred yards and formed a defensive line but not before leaving numerous dead and wounded. At least one injured man seen trying to retreat, Hale's second in command, Lieutenant Jonathan Biddle, was caught in the intense crossfire that followed. Later, when surgeons examined his perforated body, they were un-able to determine exactly which of the many bullets had killed him.

As the soldiers regrouped, Miles's adjutant, Lieutenant George Baird, rode up with orders for Captain Hale. Hale had hardly been sanguine about the fight from the start. Describing him as a man with "a gay and cheerful temperment," a wife of one of the officers at the cantonment had felt apprehension two weeks before when the "bold, dashing, dauntless" captain morosely bid her good-bye, say-ing, "Pray for me, for I am never coming back!" Captain Godfrey echoed similar sentiments when just before the charge he had heard Hale remark, "My God! Have I got to be killed this cold morning?" Hale's words, said Godfrey, began facetiously, "but when he ended he was serious and his remark was received in silence." Now Lieu-tenant Baird dismounted behind the line and began searching for Hale among the prone men firing at the Nez Perce. Finding him, Baird saluted and began the customary opening: "The General's compliments and he directs. . . ." The lieutenant stopped. Hale lay motionless before him, a hole just under his Adam's apple, a bullet having passed through his neck, killing him instantly.[11]

All told, in less than one hour of fighting, nearly half of the men in the three companies had been either killed or wounded. All three first sergeants were dead, and only one rookie officer, Lieutenant Edwin Eckerson, was left on the line. Soon afterward, as the fight turned into long-range sniping, Eckerson—covered with blood but himself unwounded—reported to Miles, his first words revealing his shock at what the attack had cost the battalion: "I am the only damned man of the Seventh Cavalry who wears shoulder straps, alive!"[12]

Not exactly. Moylan and Godfrey would recover. But the lieutenant himself would not wear straps for long. In less than a year, despite a petition attesting to his bravery signed by some ninety-six fellow officers and enlisted men, Eckerson would be dishonorably discharged after becoming drunk and assaulting and attempting to arrest a post sutler who had displeased him. The lieutenant's fondness for the bottle was hardly a singular affliction in the Seventh. Liquor was soon to bring down those dark stars of the Little Bighorn, Marcus Reno and Frederick Benteen, as well.

With the Seventh repulsed, Miles ordered his Fifth Infantry to hold Company A and D's previous position south of the village while he considered his options. The surprise charge, a tactic that had worked so well that winter against the Sioux and Cheyenne, had ignominiously failed against the Nez Perce. Trenchantly described by Thomas Sutherland, Miles had descended like a "wolf on the fold, but the fold was a den of tigers."[13] Now Miles decided to try a head-on attack. Dispatching Lieutenant Henry Romeyn to take command of the leaderless Seventh, he devised a simultaneous charge with his remaining troops from both the south and east.

When all was ready, Romeyn rode forward on his horse waving his hat to signal the start of the attack but fell almost immediately. His horse twice shot, the lieutenant also had his field glass case blown away, his pistol belt severed, as well as a bullet through his right lung, a wound that nearly killed him. Just behind Romeyn, many of the cheering men managed only a few steps toward the bluffs before collapsing, so precise was the fire of the warriors. Carrying orders from Miles to the fallen Romeyn, Lieutenant Baird had his left forearm shattered and a good portion of one ear carried away by a bullet. The casualties were not all on the soldiers' side, however. Seventh Cavalryman Albert Davis observed a shooting match between an unidentified corporal and a Nez Perce sharpshooter in which the warrior was killed. The corporal, claimed Davis, "wormed over to him, scalped him and dragged back his fixings, also his gun, and this during hot action."[14]

"Hot" seems an inadequate description of the scene Surgeon Henry Tilton observed as he ministered to the wounded just behind the firing line. "The bullets hum all the notes of the gamut, fit music for the dance of death; zip, zip, zip, thud, thud; the dirt is thrown up here and there, while others go singing overhead; riderless horses are galloping over the hills; others are stretched lifeless upon the field; men are being struck on every side, and some so full of life a few moments before have no need of the surgeon's aid."[15]

The luck of soldiers charging from the south was little better. Ten or twelve men descended the bluffs and reached the most southern edge of the village where Chief Joseph's band was located. In an intense hand-to-hand fight in which three warriors died, the Nez Perce forced the soldiers back, leaving nearly a third either dead or wounded.

His second attempt having ended in failure, Miles by that evening was fast running out of men. Twenty-three soldiers lay dead and over forty wounded, nearly twenty percent of his entire command hors de combat. The price the Nez Perce paid was as steep, twenty-two dead and about forty wounded. Among those who died that day besides Toohoolhoolzote were Joseph's brother, Ollokot, and Poker Joe, the last, along with three other warriors, accidentally killed by one of his own people who mistook him for a Cheyenne. In relative terms, their loss was much more devastating than that of the soldiers, considering fewer than eighty warriors had borne the brunt of the battle that day.

"You have seen hail, sometimes leveling the grass," said Yellow Wolf describing the battle. "Indians were so leveled by the bullet hail. Most of our few warriors left from the Big Hole had been swept as leaves before the storm. . . . When I saw our remaining warriors gone, my heart grew choked and heavy. Yet the warriors and no-fighting men killed were not all. I looked around. Some were burying their dead. A young warrior, wounded, lay on a buffalo robe dying without complaint. Children crying with cold. No fire. There could be no light. Everywhere the crying, the death wail." Despite their successful defense, the young warrior had no doubt what the attack portended. "I felt the coming end. All for which we had suffered lost!"[16]

As daylight faded across the battlefield, Miles was not sure he had won anything at all. In a hasty message to General Terry, he scrawled that the Nez Perce "fight with more desperation than any Indians I have ever met." They had been brought to bay and had no easy means of escape, their horses either captured or stampeded, but the two attacks had failed at great cost; Miles could not afford another. The only alternative was a siege. He would simply wait them out until help arrived. Adding to the colonel's discomfort, however, was the realization that Canada was close by, so close that Sitting Bull's forces, thought by Miles to number over two thousand warriors, could easily come to the aid of the besieged Nez Perce should a messenger manage to reach them. To thwart such an attempt, Miles ordered pickets to surround the village and prevent anyone from escaping. Then he called for a courier to ride back to the Missouri River at Carroll. Addressing a message to either Howard or Sturgis, he briefly described the situation, ending the note with the urgent postscript: "Please move forward with caution and rapidity."[17]

Not long after the courier departed, darkness settled over the prairie, a raw wind continued to blow, and soon snow began falling. Soldiers dug rifle pits and tried to fortify their positions, believing a desperate attack by the Nez Perce might occur at any moment. Few slept, bundled in overcoats and lying prone, alert to any sound or movement that instantly drew blind gunfire.

Because the command's wagons failed to catch up until the following day, surgeons had no tents and little medicine for the wounded. Captain Godfrey received a stiff concoction of brandy laced with opium, but for the forty or so men who lay exposed in the deepening snow, recalled Surgeon Tilton, it was a night of "ceaseless agony." For the dead—the exact day of burial is disputed—a long trench was dug and the corpses placed side by side. No effort was made to remove clothing, belts, or spurs. According to one gravedigger, many of the men had been literally shot to pieces. After covering them with a few inches of soil, an officer briefly read from the Bible and a single salute was fired over the mass grave.

Only a few hundred yards away, fearing attack as well, warriors piled up boulders and scraped out rifle pits. Under cover of darkness, some searched bodies of fallen soldiers for weapons and ammunition. By most accounts, wounded soldiers were left unharmed. At least one warrior, hearing a soldier beg for water, filled an empty can and returned to place it by the injured man. Throughout that night in the village, women and children—using trowel bayonets captured at the Big Hole along with pots and pans obtained at Cow Island—excavated shallow pits or caves. There was little to eat, but water was available in the creek at the edge of camp. Once sheltered from sight inside the pits, women collected bison dung to start small fires, for no other fuel was available save scattered willows along the creek. Appropriately, Nez Perce survivors remembered the woodless prairie camp as Ali-Kos-Pah or Place of Manure Fires, although the area had this name long before Miles's attack.

Sometime during the night, a number of Nez Perce managed to slip through the pickets and escape, eventually joining those who had gotten away that morning. Precisely how many succeeded altogether in reaching Canada is widely disputed, estimates ranging from over 300 to less than half that number. Black Eagle recorded that 233 survivors (140 men and boys, and 93 women and girls) ultimately joined the Sioux across the border. Later in October, Inspector James M. Walsh of the North-West Mounted Police in Saskatchewan estimated 290 Nez Perce (90 men, 200 women and children) in the Sioux camp, although he admitted having no firsthand knowledge of their numbers. Duncan McDonald, who visited the camp the following summer, recorded only about 120, but by then, some had already tried to make their way back to Idaho while others were living nearby in scattered groups. After so long a time, the exact number is impossible to determine.[18]

What does seem certain was that not all who fled the battlefield found their way to Canada—more than a few died making their escape. Lieutenant Hugh Scott, having returned to Fort Ellis after participating in Lieutenant Colonel Gilbert's ill-fated attempt to find Howard, was escorting a mule train from Fort Benton a few days after the battle when he stumbled on five freshly dead and scalped Indians near the Milk River. Traveling on, he soon encountered an Assiniboine village whose inhabitants told him the bodies were those of Nez Perce. Without hesitation, they described how the refugees had arrived hungry and without clothing during a snowstorm. They had fed them a huge meal, allowed them to ride off, then followed and slaughtered every one. If at first Scott was leery of this tale, he lost all doubt when he saw five fresh scalps "hanging on a pole to dry in the wind." Soon afterward, Scott joined up with a detachment from Miles's command sent to round up fugitives before they crossed the border. In a Cree camp they discovered some forty-five Nez Perce whom they promptly arrested, eventually returning them to Miles. The journey was completed in bitter cold, recalled the lieutenant. Along the way the scantily clad children cried so pitifully that the soldiers were forced to stop and shoot several buffalo, wrapping them in the raw hides for warmth.[19]

Just how many Nez Perce died at the hands of Assiniboine and nearby Gros Ventre Indians is unknown. At least one report claims as many as thirty-four. That such behavior was encouraged by the army is evidenced in a letter Miles sent his wife two weeks after the battle. "The Assiniboines are killing the Nez Perces," wrote the colonel, "as I sent them word that they could fight any that escaped and take their arms and ponies."[20]

Not all Nez Perce who encountered those of other tribes were ill-treated. After escaping alone that morning, ten-year-old Suhm-Keen halted at the Milk River for the night, his horse too tired to continue. "I had no food, no blankets except the one I used for the horse's saddle-blanket. Along came an Indian, and when we 'threw the signs,' I discovered he was a friendly Cree. He was kind and generous, for he gave me a pair of moccasins and some food."[21]

Others reported receiving similar treatment from Crees. Father J. B. Genin, a Catholic missionary who was living in a nearby Cree village, was startled one stormy night when the camp suddenly filled with refugees. He had heard the booming of a cannon the day before but had no idea there was a battle going on less than fifteen miles away. While hurrying about caring for the sick and wounded, he looked up to see a man on horseback possessing no feet and only a single hand. So great was the determination of the Nez Perce to avoid capture, concluded the priest, that the man "had cut off the other [hand] and both his feet to free himself from his chains." Notwithstanding such a creative explanation, history records that Seeskoomkee, the limbless ex-slave who first raised the alarm at White Bird Canyon and was last seen hobbling and crawling away at the Big Hole, survived to reach Canada where he lived out his life with the Sioux.[22]

For most Nez Perce the journey was made without assistance in winterlike conditions. During the four to ten days it took to reach Canada, many walked the entire way, suffering from hunger and frostbite, their swollen and cracked feet wrapped with strips of blanket. Father Genin reported one group arrived in a nearby Cree camp "weeping and yelling terribly." In running away from soldiers, they had placed some of their small children on the backs of horses and traveled throughout the dark night, only to find in the morning that the children were missing. "The desolation of the mothers was great," said the priest, but "to go back was to find sure death."[23]

Some of the refugees had been wounded during the initial attack. When Inspector James Walsh arrived at Sitting Bull's camp on October 8 in time to view the last stragglers from the battlefield, he reported them in a "pitiable condition." One woman had been "shot in the breast and the ball had turned upward passing through the side of her head. Despite her condition she valiantly rode a small pony with a child strapped on her back."[24]

Penahwenonmi, the lone surviving wife of Ollokot, was one of those who escaped after her husband's death, with only the clothing she wore, too fearful of pursuing soldiers to build warming fires along the way. Interviewed by Lucullus Virgil McWhorter after the war, she expressed her reasons for escaping: "You know how you feel when you lose kindred and friends through sickness-death. You do not care if you die. With us it was worse. Strong men, well women, and little children killed and buried. They had not done wrong to be so killed. We had only asked to be left in our own homes, the homes of our ancestors. Our going was with heavy hearts, broken spirits. But we would be free."[25]

Morning dawned the second day on the battlefield, with a stiff wind blowing from the north and freezing rain mixed with snow. Soon several soldiers pointed toward two long lines of mounted Indians approaching on the horizon. For a few breathless moments, Miles believed that his worst fear had come true until an officer with binoculars determined the distant figures were not Sioux coming to the aid of the Nez Perce but two herds of buffalo. Tensions eased but with little good reason. As Miles had suspected, some of the people who managed to slip through the cordon the night before had been carrying a request for assistance to Sitting Bull. Eventually these messengers made contact with this charismatic Hunkpapa Sioux mystic who arguably possessed more vile hatred of whites than any living Plains Indian leader. According to white accounts, upon hearing of the ongoing battle, the chief—estimated to have some two thousand followers seventy miles from the battlefield—wasted no time moving his camp as far away as possible, anxious to distance himself from Miles, his bête noire the winter before.

Some Nez Perce tell it differently. Survivors say the first couriers to reach the Sioux had difficulty communicating the location of the battle in sign language, confusing the word *stream*—meaning Snake Creek—with *river*—meaning Missouri. Under threat of losing Canadian sanctuary if his warriors were caught raiding below the border, Sitting Bull was reluctant to follow so deeply into the United States. When other escapees soon arrived, the correct location was determined and Sitting Bull, with "many hundreds" of warriors painted and stripped for war, started south. Near the Milk River they happened on the last refugees fleeing north the day after the final surrender. Upon learning he was too late, Sitting Bull purportedly dismounted and led his men in wailing for the Nez Perce and the treatment they had received at the hands of whites. Inspector Walsh, however, claimed that on October 7 he visited Sitting Bull at his camp in Canada, making unlikely the chief's role in this affair. Nevertheless, Father Genin reported that a large contingent of Sioux warriors passed near his Cree village shortly after the battle. If true, it is tempting to conclude that one or two days in this cold autumn of 1877 may have been all that separated the relatively obscure Snake Creek battlefield from the Little Bighorn, Miles from Custer, and success from defeat for the Nez Perce.[26]

If soldiers were restless that morning about Sitting Bull's antici-pated arrival, no less so were the Nez Perce. According to Yellow Wolf, the anxiety proved too great for Looking Glass when, from his position in a rifle pit on the bluff, he spied a lone Indian horseman in the distance. Believing the man a Sioux courier bringing news from Sitting Bull, Looking Glass stood up to get a better look. Almost instantly, an army sharpshooter's bullet struck the left side of his forehead, his skull exploded, and the chief fell back dead. The horse-man, it turned out, was a Nez Perce attempting to rejoin the bands.[27]

Not long into this day, a truce flag went up. Who first displayed it depends upon the source—soldiers claim the Nez Perce; they say the soldiers. Surgeon Tilton recorded that the Indians were hailed, then a white flag appeared on their side, implying that Miles sug-gested a meeting and the Nez Perce complied. Regardless how it began, because he spoke English, Tom Hill was sent to Miles's camp and soon returned, saying the colonel wanted to talk with Joseph. Hill claimed he informed Miles of the deaths of most of the other headmen, but even had they been alive, Miles likely would have asked for Joseph anyway. Under the assumption promulgated months earlier by Howard and now accepted by most whites, the colonel had little reason to believe the Nez Perce had any other leader.

The meeting, presumably to discuss surrender, was fiercely de-bated in the Indian camp. Although they were suffering greatly, a number of warriors were not ready to capitulate, particularly if Sit-ting Bull was on his way. White Bird, the only other original headman still alive besides Joseph and Huishuis Kute, was opposed to any such talk. Mistrustful of whites, he believed he would be hung if taken alive since primarily members of his band had committed the murders in Idaho. Despite this opposition, before long Joseph stood up and, accompanied by several warriors, walked across the battle line into Miles's camp. After five long months and some twelve hundred difficult miles since the council with Howard at Lapwai in May, Joseph once again found himself the bands' spokesman—albeit a reluctant and somewhat tenuous one, his sudden ascendancy due to the simple fact that most other Nez Perce leaders were dead.

As he watched the chief approach, a wounded Captain Romeyn could not believe that Joseph's clothes could be filled with so many bullet holes while the man inhabiting them remained unscathed. Elaborating on this scene, Surgeon Henry Tilton said the chief "is a man of splendid physique, dignified bearing and handsome features. His usual expression was serious, but occasionally a smile would light up his face, which impressed us very favorably. . . . He was inclined to surrender, but did not have control of the entire camp."[28]

Miles demanded unconditional surrender, including relinquishment of all weapons. Serving as interpreter, Tom Hill said that Joseph refused, maintaining that because they were destitute and had little or no food to begin the winter, his people needed at least half their weapons for hunting. Miles was adamant. If the colonel's official version is to be believed, after a trip or two back and forth to explain the terms to fellow warriors, Joseph and a handful of men agreed to surrender, but the majority of Nez Perce still refused. Other accounts say the talks stalemated over Miles's insistence that all guns and ammunition be surrendered.

In any event, when Joseph turned to go back to the camp for the last time, Miles suddenly ordered him arrested. It was a rash and uncharacteristic move, considering that Miles had declined to seize Indian negotiators during a similar truce with the Sioux the very winter before—a behavior, he once wrote his wife, that only exacerbated Indian mistrust of whites.

No sooner had he taken Joseph prisoner, however, than he regretted it. Dispatching Lieutenant Lovell Jerome "to ascertain what was being done in the Indian village," Miles claimed the fearless and daring young lieutenant wandered too close to the line.[29] Sensing something was wrong when Joseph did not return, several warriors reciprocated by seizing Jerome; quid pro quo. Miles's official report is mum, but by most accounts, he was furious at Jerome's carelessness. Although Jerome was never officially reprimanded, when Miles drew up a lengthy list of officers to receive the Medal of Honor for the battle, his name was absent. Jerome might have received an inkling of his superior's wrath that evening when soldiers suddenly recommenced shooting at the Indian camp, lieutenant or not. Jerome actually had little to fear. The Nez Perce placed him in one of their underground excavations, allowed him to keep his pistol, fed him, and gave him water and a blanket, guarding him against those few discontented warriors who were anxious to avenge Miles's treachery.

According to Yellow Wolf, Joseph's accommodations were hardly so hospitable: he was first hobbled by being rolled in a blanket, then left lying outside all night in the snow near the command's pack mules. Wottolen, among others, claimed the chief's hands were manacled behind him, and his feet drawn up and tied to the cuffs. Later, C. E. S. Wood, who was not present for this incident but arrived a few days later, refuted that Miles ever bound Joseph. Miles himself shed no light on Joseph's treatment in his official report and in fact never even admitted holding the chief against his will. Writing to his wife the following day, the colonel only conceded that "I had Joseph in my camp one night and I believe he was acting in good faith, but unfortunately Lieutenant Jerome got detained in their camp, White Bird was disposed to fight it out, and Joseph had to be exchanged for Jerome."[30]

Whatever the circumstances, the next morning each side learned the other's captive was alive. Later, as snow continued to fall, the two hostages were exchanged, Jerome stopping to shake Joseph's hand before returning to the soldiers' line. Then the fighting resumed, although by now both warriors and soldiers were well protected in rifle pits and the battle settled down into a long-range sniping duel. Only occasional shots came from the Nez Perce, so carefully did they husband their ammunition in case the soldiers charged. The following day, with the raw weather showing no sign of abatement, Fifth Infantry Captain Simon Snyder recorded in his diary the thought that must have been poised in every soldier's mind: "All hope of their surrender is gone & I suppose we will have to starve them out. To charge them would be madness."[31]

As the battle lapsed into a waiting game by the morning of October 3, less than fifty miles away at Cow Island the steamboat *Benton* was discharging its passengers—General Howard and his retinue of a little over a hundred soldiers. Here the general met a messenger sent by Miles when he had been trailing the Nez Perce near the Little Rockies. Believing that the Indians must be by now either captured or hopelessly beyond the border, Howard sent Major Mason and his soldiers back to Carroll to rejoin Sturgis. Meanwhile, Howard and aides Guy Howard and C. E. S. Wood, his two Nez Perce herders, "Captain" John and Old George, interpreter Ad Chapman, and several scouts—some seventeen men in all—struck off toward the Bear Paw Mountains. For the sake of history, leaving Major Mason behind was an unfortunate choice, given that his assiduous pen would not be present to record the critical final events that were about to unfold on the battlefield. Mason returned to Carroll that same evening, only to find Sturgis crossing the Missouri, having just received the urgent message sent by Miles the first day of the battle. The following morning, Mason, Sturgis, and the remainder of the command started north toward the battlefield, although when faced with leaving the comforts of the steamboat, Mason admitted in a letter to his wife that "I confess a disinclination to go out and sleep on the ground again and live on bacon and hardtack." They would never get there. Within a day or two of Snake Creek, a message arrived saying to wait until Howard joined them, then return to the Missouri and head for home: the war was over, the Nez Perce had surrendered.

The journey to Snake Creek was most unpleasant for Howard's party. Snow, wind, and cold plagued the poorly clad men, and the alkali water they were forced to drink along the way gave everyone acute dysentery, making for both sudden and frequent halts. Howard claimed he survived the ride only because Thomas Sutherland, who apparently stayed behind, had loaned him his enormous overcoat. Just after sunset on October 4, Howard heard shooting and soon saw muzzle flashes in the darkness ahead. Alerted to their arrival, Miles and several officers rode out to meet them. Later that night in Miles's tent, Howard claimed that he and the colonel had "a long consultation," with the general assuring Miles that "I had no desire to assume immediate command of the field, but would be glad to have him finish the work he had so well begun."[32]

According to C. E. S. Wood, Miles, who up to then had been coolly reserved, quickly became more genial, so apprehensive had he been that Howard would absorb his command—which was his privilege due to his seniority and General Sherman's earlier orders placing him in charge of the chase regardless of administrative boundaries. When Miles related the story of the failed truce, Howard suggested they try again in the morning, this time using "Captain" John and Old George, both of whom had daughters traveling with the bands and had followed hoping to persuade the women to surrender.

The next morning, firing along the line suddenly ceased, and just before noon the two Nez Perce approached the village. What they found after five days of siege were a people living in wretched conditions—cold, wet, and hungry. What little dried meat they had was gone, the last handfuls given to children the day before. Some people had gone at least three days without eating, many of the warriors squatting shoulder to shoulder in rifle pits, briefly sleeping while leaning on their rifles. Days before, the soldiers' single twelve-pound field cannon had been brought to bear on the camp. Due to the elevated nature of the terrain surrounding the village, the artillery crew was forced to depress the tongue of the carriage, lofting the barrel and lobbing shells like a true modern-day howitzer. The cannon's resulting inaccuracy coupled with limited ammunition rendered it relatively ineffective, particularly when its intended victims were so well sheltered. On the morning of the day Howard arrived, however, an explosive shell landed directly on one of the shelters, burying alive four women, a small boy, and a girl about twelve years old. Rescuers armed with pots, pans, and entrenching tools dug frantically, but they were too late to save the young girl and her grandmother from suffocation. Still, Nez Perce fortifications were so secure that after the heavy casualties resulting from the first day's attack, only Looking Glass and these two victims were killed during the entire five-day siege.

Negotiations began almost immediately, with the two Nez Perce herders coming and going between camps, relaying messages for nearly four hours. What was discussed is purely conjectural, but clearly the knowledge that Howard's remaining force was only a day or two away contributed greatly to the Indians' willingness to consider surrender. The very length of the talks, nevertheless, suggests the terms were not unconditional.

It was midafternoon, recalled Lieutenant C. E. S. Wood, when "Captain" John returned with Joseph's final reply. As the old man's "lips quivered and his eyes filled with tears," the lieutenant took out his notebook and recorded one of the most celebrated speeches ever attributed to an American Indian:

> Tell General Howard I know his heart. What he told me before I have in my heart. I am tired of fighting. Our chiefs are killed. Looking Glass is dead. Toohoolhoolzote is dead. The old men are all dead. It is the young men who say yes or no. He who led on the young men is dead. It is cold and we have no blankets. The little children are freezing to death. My people, some of them, have run away to the hills, and have no blankets, no food; no one knows where they are—perhaps freezing to death. I want to have time to look for my children and see how many of them I can find. Maybe I shall find them among the dead. Hear me, my chiefs. I am tired; my heart is sick and sad. From where the sun now stands I will fight no more forever.[33]

In the years since Wood took down these words, some historians have come to doubt if they were the actual ones spoken by the chief. The messenger apparently related them from memory, meaning Wood heard the words thirdhand since he asserts Ad Chapman interpreted. Wood did not help his case years later when he disavowed that they had come by messenger but claimed Joseph had delivered them himself upon surrender. Still, there is a resonance to the speech that closely resembles other declarations attributed to Joseph. If not his explicit words, Wood—probably with some literary polish—seems to have captured their gist.[34]

Less dramatic but of far more lasting significance were the words describing the actual terms of surrender—words apparently lost almost as soon as they were spoken. Exactly what those terms were neither Miles nor Howard ever chose to reveal, a critical omission that would soon bring untold anguish and a lasting sense of betrayal to the Nez Perce. For his part, Joseph did not insist on any documentation, possibly by now suitably mistrustful of the worth of written agreements between his people and the government. Probably of greater import, however, was the ingenuousness of frontier Indians to nearly all agreements: they were satisfied with oral commitment, putting great stock in the integrity of their personal word and that of the government's representative. Although there is no direct evidence, much of the four hours of negotiation was probably used by the Nez Perce in attempting to determine if Howard and Miles really meant what they promised, whatever that may have been.

At least one major point and the most important to the Nez Perce—return to the reservation in Idaho—was never in dispute as far as they tell it. From the beginning, Howard had been under orders from both McDowell and Sherman to return them to his department once they were apprehended. There seems little doubt that was what both sides truly believed would happen. Later, both Howard and Miles qualified their understanding of these orders, Miles saying that "we could only assure them that as long as they were under our control they would be treated justly and fairly and that we believed they would be sent back to the country whence they came. This was the only assurance that we could guarantee. They were distinctly told that whatever the authorities at Washington directed would have to be carried out."[35]

Because no record of either the final parley or surrender terms exists, whether this last proviso was explained adequately or even at all to the Nez Perce in the heat of the negotiations is entirely unknown. To Joseph, it was simple. "General Miles had promised that we might return to our country with what stock we had left. . . . I believed General Miles, or I never would have surrendered."[36]

The only other window on this tenebrous affair came many years later from Lieutenant Wood. Because of the standing order to return the Nez Perce to the Department of Columbia, said the lieutenant, the point was not considered worthy of discussion. Thus, later, when both Miles and Howard stated that the terms of surrender were contingent upon approval of higher authority, they were in principle correct. But Wood had regrets. "We stood on a technicality with an unlettered simple people not allowed to state their own side and broke the real spirit of the surrender," he said, "which was that we all expected fully that Joseph would be returned to Idaho."[37]

After Joseph's final message of surrender that afternoon, in a touch of melodrama not lost on those who witnessed the scene, the clouds parted and the sun broke through. About 4 P.M., Howard, Miles, and a small group of staff assembled near the hospital tent south of the village. Soon Joseph was seen slowly riding up the hill, three or four men walking alongside his horse, their hands touching both Joseph and the horse, talking in earnest but low voices as if imploring the chief to reconsider his decision. As they approached, Lieutenant Wood recalled that all were bareheaded. Joseph's hair hung in two braids, one on each side of his face, his waist and shoulders wrapped in a blanket, gray with a black stripe. Across his pommel balanced a rifle. "When he dismounted," said Wood, "he picked up the rifle, pulled his blanket closer around him and walked to General Howard and offered him the rifle. Howard waved him toward Miles. He then walked to Miles and handed him the rifle."[38]

Soon others arrived, laying down their weapons in a pile while the officers looked on. As they moved past, Howard could scarcely believe their appearance. "They were covered with dirt, their clothing was torn, and their ponies, such as they were, were thin and lame." Still, they possessed a "dignified bearing." One woman even carried a baby born during the siege. It was remarkable, the general said, that given their condition they managed to resist as long as they had.[39]

By sunset most of the people had come over to the soldiers' line, and Miles ordered them fed and extra blankets given them for the night. Not all surrendered, however. Exercising his autonomy in typical Indian fashion and still fearful of retribution, White Bird had earlier sent a message to Miles and Howard saying, "What Joseph does is all right; I have nothing to say."[40]

Either later that night or one or two nights before—the record is ambiguous—White Bird and a contingent of followers (numbered by Howard at fourteen, while others say as many as one hundred) escaped, eventually arriving in Canada. Asked later why more did not attempt flight, Joseph replied, "We could have escaped from Bear Paw Mountain if we had left our wounded, old women, and children behind. We were unwilling to do this. We had never heard of a wounded Indian recovering while in the hands of white men."[41]

The following day before dawn, Yellow Wolf also slipped away, perhaps the last to escape the battlefield. According to the warrior, Joseph had told him to go out on the prairie and try to find his daughter and Yellow Wolf's mother, both of whom escaped during the first day of battle. Yellow Wolf found them with the Sioux in Canada, but neither the warrior nor the women chose to return.

The evening of the surrender, Miles prepared a message to be sent immediately by courier to General Terry at Fort Benton. According to Lieutenant Wood, Howard read over the dispatch without objection, and after some delay, the courier rode off. Within a day, news of the surrender was telegraphed throughout the country; the following day it made front-page headlines in national newspapers from coast to coast.

The cost of the war in lives, property, and suffering on both sides had been enormous. Some 123 soldiers and 55 civilians had died with nearly an equal number wounded. Total Nez Perce casualties are less certain, but probably at least 155 died (perhaps as many as 200 if high estimates of those who lost their lives fleeing to Canada are included) and some 90 were wounded—a casualty rate exceeding thirty percent. Perhaps as many as one-third of the Nez Perce dead and wounded were women and children. The cost to the government was calculated by the Secretary of War to be $931,329.02 (less than one-tenth today's value), but this absurdly precise figure fails to include destroyed property or stolen stock.[42]

No one tried to put a price on what the war cost the Nez Perce bands who before this struggle had been some of the wealthiest Indian people in the Northwest. Gone forever was their land, their animals, their way of life. Now they had little more than the clothes they were wearing.

14

*F*or several weeks following their surrender, the Nez Perce became the subject of intense national curiosity. They had fought for a cause—deemed however hopeless in the face of an expanding nation—that had struck an empathic chord in nearly all Americans: a love of home and a fierce determination to keep it. Now that their defeat was a fait accompli, the country could afford to be generous with encomiums. Surprisingly, the U.S. Army led the way. General Sherman called it "one of the most extraordinary Indian wars of which there is any record. The Indians throughout displayed a courage and skill that elicited universal praise; they abstained from scalping, let captive women go free, did not commit indiscriminate murder of peaceful families which is usual, and fought with almost scientific skill, using advance and rear guards, skirmish-lines and field-fortifications." Miles was no less laudatory, saying the Nez Perce were "the boldest men and best marksmen of any Indians I have ever encountered, and Chief Joseph is a man of more sagacity and intelligence than any Indian I have ever met."[1]

This glow, however, soon faded. The wounds incurred by settlers since they had first begun wresting frontier land from its aboriginal inhabitants were simply too fresh, the disparity between cultures too great, the threat of still more violence to come too real. Not long after their capture, the *New York Times* ventured to place the struggle of the Nez Perce into a larger perspective, observing that America had little of which to be proud. More than any other Indian war this one "was in its origin and motive nothing short of a gigantic blunder and a crime."[2] But few people were listening. That the country was not yet willing to grapple with the troubling moral dilemma posed by Indian dispossession was never more evident than five days after the surrender when thousands of fervent admirers flocked to the military academy at West Point, where the bones of George Armstrong Custer were finally laid to rest.

As public regard for the plight of the Nez Perce waned, the reputation of the U.S. Army began a meteoric rise, particularly that of Nelson Miles. This could not have suited the colonel or his unquenchable desire for approbation more, nor could it have proven more frustrating for General Howard who fully believed he deserved equal credit for the capture. In fact, glory—or more specifically the relentless pursuit of it—was soon to becloud the entire issue concerning the terms of surrender.

After resting for two days, Miles started his troops and some 430 prisoners back toward the Yellowstone. At the same time, Howard gathered up Mason, Sturgis, and the remainder of his command and prepared to return them to their respective posts before the onset of winter. The journey back to the Tongue River Cantonment for Miles was slow, the wounded loaded into wagons packed with brush and grass to cushion their pain. An unknown number of both Nez Perce and soldiers succumbed to their wounds en route. The two commands met at the Missouri near the mouth of the Musselshell on October 13, and after shuttling Miles's column across the river and conferring briefly with the colonel, Howard and his men boarded the *Benton* and started down the Missouri toward Omaha. From there they would return to their duty stations throughout the West.

Before leaving the battlefield, Howard had issued an order to Miles stating that due to the lateness of the season and the cost of transporting the prisoners by rail, they were to be retained by him until the following spring, when "unless you receive instructions from higher authority, you are hereby directed to have them sent, under proper guard, to my department, where I will take charge of them and carry out the instructions I have already received." Howard admitted both men feared that without a full explanation, General Sheridan, far removed from the realities of the conflict and surrender, might refuse to send the Nez Perce back to the Northwest. Therefore they agreed that before Howard departed for Oregon, he should "go through to Chicago and see General Sheridan."[3]

On October 21, about thirty-five miles above Bismarck, Dakota Territory, the *Benton* anchored for the night and several officers from Fort Abraham Lincoln came aboard bearing copies of Chicago newspapers with first accounts of the final battle. Howard could not believe his eyes when he saw Miles's name splashed in bold headlines at the top of nearly every column. There was little or no mention of Howard or his command, the long and arduous pursuit, or his participation in the surrender. Reading on, he came across a copy of Miles's message sent to General Terry just after the surrender, which Terry had telegraphed on to General Sheridan. It read in part:

Dear General: We have had our usual success. We made a very direct and rapid march across the country and after severe engagement and being kept under fire for three days (3) the hostile camp of Nez Perces under Chief Joseph surrendered at two o'clock today.[4]

Howard, reported Lieutenant Wood, "was absolutely brokenhearted over this; he could not understand it." Wood was certain that the message Miles had briefly shown Howard the evening of the surrender was not the same one he had sent Terry. The following day Miles submitted a more detailed report, but by then the damage had been done. Newspapers seized on the first words of surrender. Miles was catapulted into the headlines and universally praised for decisive action, his promotion to a coveted brigadiership guaranteed. Howard felt particularly betrayed since not only had he deferred the honor of the surrender to Miles, but earlier that year at the colonel's behest, Howard had written General Sherman recommending him for promotion, saying that "for gallantry, persistency & ability as an officer, few if any could exceed Miles."[5]

Lieutenant Wood believed this unwelcome news began to grate on Howard, for late that evening, unwilling to wait until the following day, the general—along with Wood and Guy Howard, a few staff officers, and four privates to man the oars—set off in a small boat downriver for Bismarck. They arrived before daylight the next morning and boarded the train for Chicago several hours later. Along the way, Wood secured Howard's permission to write a "true account of the surrender." Three days later, on October 25, an article appeared in the Chicago *Tribune* based on an interview with an officer who had been an eyewitness to the surrender—unquestionably Lieutenant Wood. Howard's official report to Sheridan, written while he was aboard the *Benton* nearly a week before and generously crediting all who had participated in the conflict, also appeared in the paper. "Colonel Miles and his command," wrote Howard, "have and deserve the great honor of the final battle and surrender, while appreciation and gratitude are due our officers and men who engaged the hostiles with success in Idaho, have cheerfully made forced marches for 1,600 miles [*sic*], were part of the last operating force north of the Missouri, and were represented by their commander at the surrender."[6]

The same day this article appeared, Howard, along with son Guy and Lieutenant Wood, called on General Sheridan at his headquarters in Chicago. The three men had barely entered the building when Sheridan exploded, his rage so great that after a short but fiery exchange they promptly departed. Whether the general's snit was precipitated by Wood's release of Howard's report, or he was simply peeved that Howard was claiming some of the credit for a victory that took place within his bailiwick, is unclear. Certainly hubris—with which so many officers were abundantly endowed throughout this campaign—played no small part in the outburst.

Later that afternoon, Howard sent an apology to the general saying that his only intention in releasing the report to the press had been "with the view of placing before the public the facts of the campaign," and that "I am sorry to have compromised you in any way." Not good enough, Little Phil fumed in a note to Sherman. "I do not feel much compromised. It seems to me that General Howard compromised himself." Resurrecting an antiquated Civil War order, Sheridan circulated a memo making it a court-martial offense to disclose either official reports or their substance "without proper authority."[7]

This proved a rather insipid attempt to bolster his position, since official army orders frequently appeared after the fact in newspapers and continued to do so long after Sheridan's pronouncement. General Terry even joined in when he returned from Canada, bitterly complaining in a letter that found its way to the adjutant general in Washington that Howard, an officer of another division, had improperly issued orders to Miles at the surrender concerning the disposition of prisoners. Endorsing and forwarding this complaint to Howard, the adjutant general agreed that Howard was "clearly" in the wrong and requested that he promptly "disclaim any intended discourtesy to General Terry."[8]

This final slam was too much. Citing General Sherman's early instructions giving him jurisdiction over troops outside his department, Howard defended his actions, claiming he had "endeavored to exercise the functions of such commander with all possible courtesy to the Department Commanders within whose limits I was forced to go."[9] Finally, Sherman put a halt to the backbiting, granting equal credit for the capture to both Howard and Miles and demanding that the squabble cease. The unofficial grumblings went on for some time, however, with both Miles and Gibbon refuting press reports attributing battlefield success to Howard's forces, reports they charged had been circulated by Howard himself. Miles and Howard's friendship never did recover. Despite their formal association as high-ranking officers during ensuing years, the two men barely remained civil to one another.

Writing later, Howard discounted the quarrel by saying that "such jealous disputations" would soon be forgotten. "Accomplished results are the things that, in the main, concern a general, an army, a historian, a man."[10] Or perhaps a defeated enemy. Considering Sheridan's reputation for ironhandedness when it came to punishing rebellious Indians as well as events that were occurring beyond the ken of either man, the outcome might have been no different had the two generals talked that day in Chicago. But any chance Howard had to persuade Sheridan to support the surrender terms agreed to on the battlefield was now irrevocably lost.

Meanwhile, Miles—the creator of this imbroglio—continued with his prisoners back to the Yellowstone River, arriving at the cantonment on the cold but clear day of October 23. As the column of soldiers, Indians, and wounded in wagons trailed down the bluffs, a cannon boomed in welcome, and flatboats began shuttling people across the river. From the opposite shore, the Fifth Infantry band struck up "Hail to the Chief" as Miles started across with Joseph in the first boat, then broke into the then popular song, "Not for Joe, oh no, no, not for Joseph!" Soon a nearby campsite was selected for the prisoners, rations were issued along with canvas for shelters, and they began preparing for a winter in detention before returning to Howard's Department of the Columbia the following spring.[11]

The surrender agreement lasted exactly six more days.

On October 29, an order signed by General Terry (but originating from Sheridan's headquarters) arrived stating that due to the cost of maintaining such a large number of prisoners at a distant post, they should be moved downriver to Bismarck's Fort Abraham Lincoln where the cost of supply would be less. Miles apologized to Joseph but said he had no choice; the matter had been decided by higher authority. If he did not carry out the order, someone else would.

With winter rapidly advancing, two days later Miles began moving the prisoners toward Bismarck, some four hundred river miles away. By now steamboats had ceased traveling on both the Missouri and Yellowstone due to low water and approaching winter, and the only available river craft was a small fleet of flatboats. About 200 people—mostly the wounded, women, children, and elderly—were crowded aboard fourteen boats, while the remaining 230 or so prisoners were loaded into wagons for transport overland. Remaining behind at the cantonment were the most valuable possessions the Nez Perce had retained: their horses and saddles. The exact number of these is disputed, Miles reporting that after rewarding his Cheyenne scouts 150 horses, and with the demise of over 100 during the journey back to the Yellowstone River, only 425 horses survived.

Many of these, said Miles, "were broken down & worn out and subsequently died."[12] Joseph later claimed 1,100 horses and 100 saddles were confiscated on the battlefield. What became of these animals is unknown, but the Nez Perce never saw any of them again. Miles reported not long afterward that all Indian saddles and an undetermined amount of personal items were burned in a cantonment fire.

The trip by water took a little over two weeks, by land a few days longer. Soon after those traveling in wagons reached the Missouri River, they made camp at Fort Berthold, the agency headquarters of the Arikara, Hidatsa, and Mandan tribes. That afternoon Joseph addressed nearly 1,500 Indians who had gathered to view the procession. Using sign language and without uttering a single word, he related the entire war from beginning to end. According to Lieutenant Hugh Scott, who was part of the military escort and witnessed the event, "he was completely understood by all that vast concourse." The weeks spent traveling with the chief made a profound impression on the young lieutenant, who would go on to become one of the most decorated generals of World War I. The Nez Perce, maintained Scott, "were among the finest Indians America produced," and their treatment "a black page in our history."[13]

Others were similarly impressed during the journey to Fort Lincoln. Fred Bond, who captained one of the flatboats and left a compelling record of the journey, recalled that by the time they reached the Missouri, ice was forming in the river and dodging the huge floes made travel particularly hazardous. Although no other accounts mention losses, Bond claimed that one boat broached in a rapid, disappearing with all on board. As the days passed, Bond grew close to his twenty-two passengers, trusting them with his rifle to supply game each evening and depending on them to help steer the boat. But as they progressed downriver, the Nez Perce grew more despondent about the fate that awaited them. On reaching Bismarck's Fort Lincoln and the western terminus of the Northern Pacific Railroad, they were startled to hear the near simultaneous blast of a train whistle, a burst of steam from a locomotive, and a welcoming salvo from the fort cannon. Many of the people, who for almost four months had either defeated or outmaneuvered the world's most modern army, had never before seen a train. Prostrating themselves in the bottom of the boat, "they became so helpless," said Bond, "I had to work the boat across the river all alone to the Fort Landing." While Bond crossed the river, his passengers began singing, a deep, moaning sound that the riverman identified unmistakably as "their death chant."[14]

Their reception in Bismarck, however, was anything but funereal. When Miles arrived with the overland contingent (his troops' pockets turned inside out to protest Congress's failure to pass an appropriations bill), the entire town filled the streets while a band played the "Star Spangled Banner," its cheering crowds offering food of every kind to the Nez Perce. All this from the same frontier community who only eighteen months earlier cheered as Custer's Seventh rode out of Fort Lincoln and on to immortal glory and whose bellicose voice, the Bismarck *Tri-Weekly Tribune,* had demanded total war against the Sioux and Cheyenne, one that would force "them on to their ultimate destiny—extinction."[15] If the Nez Perce had any doubt about the town's hospitality, they were soon convinced otherwise when city leaders extended an invitation to Joseph and several other warriors to attend a formal dinner in their honor later that day.

This brief respite was shattered when Miles informed Joseph that he had just received new orders from General Sheridan to move the prisoners to Fort Leavenworth in Kansas. Standing nearby when the chief received this unwelcome news was a *Tri-Weekly Tribune* reporter who said Joseph's "head dropped and he murmured in his mother tongue, 'When will those white chiefs begin to tell the truth.' "[16]

Two days later, on November 23, the Nez Perce boarded eleven railway coaches to begin their eight-hundred-mile journey to Fort Leavenworth. At the station with a large crowd of well-wishers was Fred Bond. Just before the train started, Chief Joseph appeared on the platform of the rear coach. Suddenly a young white woman ran up, kissed the chief on the cheek, then disappeared back into the crowd. The last Bond saw as the train pulled away was Joseph standing alone on the rear platform waving good-bye.

Unknown to either Miles or the Nez Perce during these last weeks since the surrender, government officials more senior than General Sheridan had been debating the Indians' fate. In early November, President Hayes asked for a recommendation from the Secretary of War, who in turn sent the request on to General Sherman. Despite his admiration for the fighting ability of the Nez Perce, Sherman was inclined to deal firmly with them. Incarcerate the prisoners at Fort Leavenworth for the winter, he suggested, then come spring turn them over to the Department of Interior for permanent relocation in Indian Territory. These Indians, he declared, "should never again be allowed to return to Oregon or to Lapwai."[17]

Whether Miles knew of Sherman's intentions when he placed his captives on the Leavenworth train before returning to Montana is uncertain, but at the very least he must have suspected something was amiss for he wired Sheridan for permission to send a delegation of Nez Perce to Washington to plead their case. The general disapproved this request, then sent a copy of Miles's telegram on to Sherman, the Secretaries of War and Interior, and Commissioner of Indian Affairs Ezra Hayt, all of whom concurred with Sheridan's rejection. By now the decision of what to do with the Nez Perce had been made at the highest level of government. According to Lieutenant C. E. S. Wood, who visited Washington in late November and in a meeting with Secretary of Interior Carl Schurz suggested that they be returned to Idaho, Schurz's opinion was "that these Nez Perces should go to the Indian Territory."[18]

Miles did not give up. Although he continued to declare publicly that the Nez Perce were never actually promised they would be returned to the Northwest, the colonel became increasingly uneasy about the entire affair. Writing Howard, he reminded him that "every assurance and promise made them by you or myself has been disregarded." They had been "stripped of everything but their clothing and banished to a far distant country." Miles believed that the recent fate of Old George, one of Howard's loyal Indian messengers at the Bear Paw battle, was symbolic of what was now happening to the Nez Perce. Finding his daughter among those who surrendered, the herder had been rewarded for his service by being allowed to return with her to Lapwai. Somewhere along the Missouri River white men discovered their camp, shooting Old George, beating and repeatedly raping his daughter, leaving them both for dead. "Such is the fate of a doomed race," Miles reflected, "and such the evilness of our progress."[19]

Howard did not respond to Miles's letter. A few weeks earlier, Sherman had written Howard, brushing off Miles's concerns, saying that the Nez Perce had lost the war and "must now submit to whatever fate is allowed them, thankful that their lives are spared."[20] Soon Howard sank from view over the matter, unwilling to challenge Sherman's decision. When he resurfaced later that year, he demonstrated how little he had learned about the independent nature of Indian leadership when he lamely asserted that the surrender terms had been abrogated when White Bird failed to give himself up on the battlefield. By then Howard was staunchly in favor of never returning the Nez Perce to the Northwest.

As harsh as General Sherman's pronouncement would ultimately prove to the Nez Perce, he appears to have undergone a tempering change, possibly due to the influence of Miles and the Interior's Schurz and Hayt. During late August when the outcome of the chase was still in doubt, Sherman had written Sheridan suggesting that upon capture Nez Perce leaders "should be executed." And a few days after their surrender, he wrote the adjutant general that punishment should be meted out with "extreme severity, else other tribes alike situated may imitate their example."[21]

Sherman was not alone in his desire for retribution, although opinions varied about the methods. Northwest Indian Inspector Erwin Watkins—Howard's friend and confidant at the beginning of the war—claimed he spoke for most Idaho settlers when he wrote the Commissioner of Indian Affairs that he feared "the white people living in the vicinity would kill any and all Indian prisoners if set at liberty, and thus begin another war." Watkins had repeatedly promised reservation Nez Perce that their wayward relatives would be severely punished and never allowed to come home. Now fearing a loss of prestige should they be sent back to Idaho, he told Hayt to send them "so far away that they can never return."[22]

Still others clamored for blood. Soon after their surrender in October, the First District Court of Idaho indicted thirty-one Nez Perce for murders committed at the outbreak of the war. In late December, the U.S. Attorney General received word from the Idaho Attorney General that "the people of North Idaho are very anxious that those Indians who are known to have been engaged in the murders should be brought here and tried." By the time this message was passed on to General Sherman, he had cooled down, returning the letter with the recommendation that Idaho's request be denied, saying he now doubted "the wisdom of proceeding against these Nez Perce prisoners. I do not suppose they are exempt from prosecution by the terms of their surrender in battle, but their understanding was that they were. As a tribe they have been severely punished."[23]

Not enough, however, to keep them out of Leavenworth.

Although Sherman had authorized placing the prisoners there for the winter, the idea originated with General Sheridan. When the commander of the Department of the Missouri, General John Pope, heard of the decision, he wrote Sheridan suggesting he could provide better facilities for the prisoners at Kansas's Fort Riley. Sheridan, who detested Pope's increasing sympathy for Indians, turned down the offer, telling Sherman that Pope's reason for recommending Fort Riley over Leavenworth "was the abundance of comfortable quarters for them there."[24]

On November 27, 418 prisoners (87 men, 184 women, and 147 children) arrived at Fort Leavenworth—13 people fewer than the 431 Nez Perce acknowledged by General Sheridan in a communication dated three days earlier. What happened to these additional people—death, escape, or simply a miscount—is unknown. After detraining, the prisoners were marched under guard two miles above the fort where a winter camp was established for them in a low-lying marshy area close to the Missouri River. Of all potential locations, reported Commissioner Hayt, it proved to be "the worst possible place that could have been selected."[25]

Another observer who visited the Nez Perce camp that winter was more explicit:

In fact it would seem as if this spot had been selected for the express purpose of putting an end to Chief Joseph and his band. We found the Indians in just the condition which might be expected from the location of the camp. It was simply horrible. The 400 miserable, helpless, emaciated specimens of humanity, subjected for months to the malarial atmosphere of the river bottoms, presented a picture which brought to my mind the horrors of Andersonville. One-half were sick, principally women and children. All were filled with the poisonous malaria of the camp.[26]

The Nez Perce did not meekly submit to this treatment. In December, eight tribal leaders including Joseph petitioned the post commander to fulfill the surrender terms and return their people to Idaho. A sympathetic officer, Captain George Randall, had the temerity to endorse the petition and send it on to General Sherman. The petition soon returned, Sherman writing "disapproved" across it and reprimanding Randall for meddling in the affair. Later that winter, Commissioner Hayt—who now believed the government had made a mistake—petitioned Secretary of Interior Schurz to investigate the possibility of sending the Nez Perce back to Idaho. By now, however, most officials were convinced that returning them to the Northwest would only result in additional bloodshed, so vengeful did settlers there appear to be. When Schurz solicited General Sherman's opinion on the matter, he responded that after canvassing Sheridan, McDowell, Howard, and Miles, only Miles was in favor of returning the Nez Perce. Rebuffed, Schurz quietly withdrew, concluding that repatriating the Nez Perce to Idaho at this time was "unadvisable."[27]

Joseph was nonplussed. "I cannot understand how the government sends a man out to fight us, as it did General Miles, and then breaks his word," said the chief. "Such a government has something wrong about it." For his part, Miles never did give up, subsequently petitioning the president and encouraging him to intercede on behalf of the Nez Perce. In a speech that December, President Hayes admitted that "many if not most of our Indian wars have had their origin in broken promises and acts of injustice upon our part," and that "the faithful performance of our promises is the first condition of a good understanding with the Indians." But apparently this insightful reflection did not extend beyond the lectern.[28]

In May 1878, Congress appropriated twenty thousand dollars for permanent settlement of the Nez Perce in Indian Territory. Surprisingly, opposition in the Senate came not only from those who wanted the Nez Perce returned to Idaho because they sympathized with their plight, but from those senators who represented states bordering Indian Territory and saw any expansion of its existing Indian population as a threat to their repeated efforts to open up the territory to white settlement (efforts that eventually succeeded). These opposing senators lost by only three votes.

By midsummer, the U.S. Army was finally rid of its charges. On July 21, in sweltering heat and after a two-day delay during which the Nez Perce were forced to wait without food or shelter at the depot, the prisoners boarded a train for Indian Territory's Quapaw agency in the northeast corner of present-day Oklahoma. At the conclusion of their eight-month stay at Fort Leavenworth, twenty-one people were dead and more than two hundred were ill. During the few days it took to travel to that portion of the reservation set aside for them, three more children died. After their arrival and before shelter was arranged, rain squalls swept the camp. By October, the deadly effects of the preceding winter became more manifest, with "260 out of 410" prisoners sick, reported Commissioner Hayt. By year's end, the Nez Perce had "lost by death more than one-quarter of their entire number." A little care in the selection of a wholesome location near Fort Leavenworth, concluded the indignant commissioner, "would have saved much sickness and many lives."[29]

None of the survivors were pleased with the Quapaw agency or its similarity to the climate in which they had suffered the previous winter. They found the heat and humidity oppressive compared to that of the Northwest, calling the country Eeikish Pah (Hot Place). That October, Joseph told a visiting joint congressional committee, "I think very little of this country. It is like a poor man; it amounts to nothing." Commissioner Hayt was sufficiently concerned about their discontent to visit them that same month. Joseph, said Hayt, proved "to be one of the most gentlemenly and well-behaved Indians that I ever met. He is bright and intelligent, and is anxious for the welfare of his people."[30]

Hayt convinced Joseph and Huishuis Kute to accompany him some two hundred miles west to central Oklahoma's Ponca Reservation. After an exhaustive search, the commissioner found acreage near the junction of the Salt Fork of the Arkansas and Chikaskia River, as "fertile, well-timbered and attractive country as Oklahoma had to offer." Joseph liked it better than Quapaw. But it was still "not a healthy land. There are no mountains and rivers. The water is warm. It is not a good country for stock. I do not believe my people can live there. I am afraid they will all die. The Indians who occupy that country are dying off." Nonetheless, Hayt returned to Washington to garner support for the move.[31]

About the same time that summer that the Nez Perce departed Leavenworth for Indian Territory, Colonel Miles sent a small delegation headed by Lieutenant George Baird, including several captured warriors, to Canada in hopes of convincing White Bird and the remaining fugitives to return to the United States. When they met, Baird informed the chief that Joseph would not be sent back to Idaho as long as he and his followers remained in Canada. Far from falling for this ruse, White Bird replied that he would surrender only upon hearing that Joseph had returned to Idaho and not before. The talks stalemated, and Baird eventually gave up.

Later that summer, small groups of Nez Perce returning from Canada to Idaho caused a brief panic when several miners were killed near Philipsburg, Montana, doubtless the work of war survivors filled with enmity toward all whites. During this year and those immediately following, at least eighty Nez Perce—including Yellow Wolf—grown weary of a fugitive existence and the increasing scarcity of buffalo, eventually made their way back to Idaho or nearby reservations only to be apprehended and sent to join their tribesmen in Indian Territory. Others either remained in Canada or decided to return there after finding no refuge in the United States. For reasons that remain obscure, one who was not sent to Oklahoma when she was discovered in Idaho during the summer of 1878 was Joseph's oldest daughter, twelve-year-old Kapkap Ponmi, now known as Sarah Moses by whites. She died a few years later, childless, without seeing her father again.

White Bird's fate was equally dire. The following summer, Montana's Flathead Reservation Agent Peter Ronan reported the aging chief arrived at his agency "utterly broken in spirit and health and . . . perfectly blind. White Bird and his family have not a horse left and the blind chief is being led thither on foot." The chief, Ronan wrote Commissioner Hayt, had asked for "a home where our children can grow . . . a place to stop for good," but lacking government permission, the agent refused and White Bird returned to Canada. Ronan's account may be wrong, for new evidence indicates the chief never left Canada, where he was axed to death in 1892 by one of his own people when his shamanistic powers failed to heal two sick children and the distraught father sought revenge.[32]

In January 1879, the hope of survivors in Indian Territory began to brighten. With the help of Commissioner Hayt and others, Joseph, Yellow Bull, and interpreter Ad Chapman traveled to Washington to plead their case, even briefly meeting President Hayes. Addressing a large gathering of Cabinet members, Congress members, diplomats, and business leaders in Lincoln Hall, Joseph delivered a two-hour jeremiad in which he vividly and passionately described the wrongs done his people and their present unhappiness in Oklahoma. When he was done, the crowd gave him a standing ovation. Washington newspapers praised the speech and several philanthropic organizations, including the Indian Rights Association and, strangely enough, the Presbyterian church, began to show an interest in the exiles.

That March, Joseph returned to Washington to confer with Hayt, and a month later a lengthy article, purported to be the words of Chief Joseph, was published in the well-respected *North American Review*. In the years since this appeared, critics have suggested that both the periodical's editor and Joseph's interpreter, Ad Chapman, had reason to embellish the chief's words—the first to make better copy and the second to enhance his rather low prestige among the Nez Perce.[33] Moreover, as a participant throughout the war, Chapman had his own understanding of events and is suspected of altering certain facts. Doubtless this assessment is true to some degree, yet portions of the article possess an eloquence not unlike that attributed to Joseph before the war.

If the white man wants to live in peace with the Indian he can live in peace. There need be no trouble. Treat all men alike. Give them all the same law. Give them all an even chance to live and grow. All men were made by the same Great Spirit Chief. They are all brothers. The earth is the mother of all people, and all people should have equal rights upon it. You might as well expect the rivers to run backward as that any man who was born a free man should be contented penned up and denied liberty to go where he pleases. . . .

When I think of our condition my heart is heavy. I see men of my race treated as outlaws and driven from country to country, or shot down like animals. I know that my race must change. We cannot hold our own with the white men as we are. We only ask an even chance to live as other men live. We ask to be recognized as men. We ask that the same law shall work alike on all men. . . .

Whenever the white man treats the Indian as they treat each other, then we shall have no more wars. We shall be all alike—brothers of one father and one mother, with one sky above us and one country around us, and one government for all. Then the Great Spirit Chief who rules above will smile upon this land, and send rain to wash out the bloody spots made by brothers' hands upon the face of the earth. For this time the Indian race are waiting and praying. I hope that no more groans of wounded men and women will ever go to the ear of the Great Spirit Chief above, and that all people may be one people.[34]

Despite growing congressional support for returning the Nez Perce to the Northwest after this article appeared, western legislators balked, and in early June the Nez Perce were moved to the Ponca Reservation. During the nine-day journey, two more people died. Upon arriving, they once again found no preparations had been made. Although promised houses, stoves, plows, horses, and cattle, they had received nothing by year's end, their only shelter canvas so rotten "as to be no longer capable of keeping out the rain," reported their agent. They now totaled about 370 people, having been joined by most of the 80-odd fugitives captured and sent to Indian Territory as they returned to the United States from Canada. All told, approximately 130 people had lost their lives since the Nez Perce first boarded the train for Leavenworth nearly two years before—almost as many as had perished during their four-month flight. Among the dead was Joseph's youngest daughter who had been born the day the war began and had repeatedly survived attacking soldiers, only to fall victim to malaria.[35]

When A. B. Meacham, a former Superintendent of Indian Affairs in Oregon, visited the Nez Perce in July, he found Chief Joseph despondent. "You come to see me as you would a man upon his death-bed," Joseph told him. "The Great Spirit above has left me and my people to their fate. The white men forget us, and death comes almost every day for some of my people. He will come for all of us. A few months more and we will be in the ground." Echoing General Miles's words to Howard two years before, he concluded, "We are a doomed people."[36]

During the winter of 1879–1880, three Nez Perce arrived from Lapwai to assist those in exile, among them James Reuben, Howard's former scout and interpreter until he was wounded following the Clearwater battle. Although the others found the climate oppressive and soon returned to Idaho, Reuben stayed on, opening a school to teach his fellow tribespeople English as well as attempting to convert them to Christianity. In June 1880, enlisting Reuben as scribe, Joseph sent a long, supplicating letter to General Howard informing him that 153 of his people had now died in the years since the war, beseeching him to honor the words "you told me at the time of surrender" and to exert whatever influence Howard had to send his people back to Idaho. "I know religion is good," wrote Joseph. "It makes all feel kind toward each other. I want you to know now I am going to be Christian man."[37]

Howard wrote back that he was glad Joseph was trying to become "a real Christian," but the chief must know that he had never actually promised his people would be returned to Idaho. He had only told Joseph that he had been ordered "to dispose of all the prisoners somewhere *within* my Department." Had the Nez Perce been returned as originally ordered, said Howard, "I should have tried to have put you all at some place far removed from Mount Idaho and Lewiston." He regretted that so many had sickened and died, but now Joseph must be content in Oklahoma. "Make a garden of the land," advised the general, and "you Joseph will show yourself a truly great man, and your people can never be blotted out."[38]

That summer, some Nez Perce successfully raised gardens, and one hundred cattle promised the year before finally arrived. Their agent reported that they "seem to be natural herders, and show more judgment in the management of their stock than any Indians I ever saw." The following year, however, drought descended on Oklahoma, and the Nez Perce were reduced to total dependency on government rations. Only eighteen families were housed in small wooden shacks, the remainder still living in tents and tipis. By now hopelessness and despair were widespread. Almost all of the Nez Perce, claimed Yellow Wolf, were lonely for their former homes. "All the newborn babies died, and many of the old people too. It was the climate. Everything so different from our old homes. No mountains, no springs, no clear running rivers."[39]

In August 1881, a man named John Bull was digging a grave for a recently deceased friend when he shot himself in the stomach, dying the following day. Agent Thomas Jordan attributed the suicide—the third that year—to the fact that Bull "was very homesick for Idaho," admitting that his charges "are all unhappy, discontented and homesick." John Bull, said the agent, believed that "all his friends were dying—that the government only kept them here so that the climate would kill them—so he thought he might as well anticipate matters a little."[40]

In his annual report, Jordan cautioned that the death rate among the Nez Perce was so high that "the tribe, unless something is done for them, will soon be extinct." The agent recommended that if all of them could not be relocated to Idaho, then at least some of the women should be sent back. The next year, the Commissioner of Indian Affairs agreed. "The deep-rooted love for the 'old home' can never be eradicated and any longer delay . . . is in my judgment

328

futile and unnecessary." Then he declared that at least some Nez Perce should be returned to Idaho the following spring.[41]

In 1883, James Reuben closed his day school and started back to Idaho with twenty-nine people—two elderly men, the rest widows and orphans. Although authorizing the move, Congress failed to appropriate funds in time for the journey and the Nez Perce were forced to raise the necessary money by selling handicrafts and what few possessions they owned. Since they fell short, Reuben made up the balance out of his own pocket, for which he was later reimbursed.

With this breakthrough, congressional resistance began to crumble. By May 1884, Congress had received no less than fourteen petitions from citizen groups from Kansas to Connecticut. C. E. S. Wood, having retired his army commission and increasingly critical of the government's treatment of Indians, began a letter campaign.[42] Another petition from Cleveland, Ohio, contained five hundred signatures, the most notable that of the widow of James Garfield, who before becoming president had played no small part in attempting to remove Montana's Flatheads from the Bitterroot Valley. During that spring session, scarcely a day passed without some member of congress taking the floor to denounce the treatment of the Nez Perce and urge their repatriation to the Northwest. On July 4, 1884, with virtually no debate, Congress finally amended the Indian appropriations bill, allowing the Secretary of Interior to remove the Nez Perce from Indian Territory.

When they heard the news, the Nez Perce greeted the announcement with a joyous celebration, even purchasing clothing and provisions for the anticipated journey home. Yet despite official permission, the Department of Interior hesitated. There were still outstanding warrants in Idaho for warriors identified in the initial murders, one newspaper calling their proposed return a "shameless outrage." There was little reason to believe the attitude of Idaho settlers had changed since Lewiston *Teller* editor Alonzo Leland had earlier declared: "But let them send these Indians back among the friends of the murdered men, women and children, if they think it best for them. We won't be responsible for their lives 24 hours after their arrival."[43]

329

Opposition began to mount. In August, a Presbyterian missionary at Lapwai, G. L. Deffenbaugh, wrote a letter to the Commissioner of Indian Affairs opposing relocation. It was a mistake to return to Idaho the Indians who had committed crimes, wrote the missionary, for "it is difficult for men and women to forgive and forget such hellish treatment as they were subjected to when their houses were burned, their property destroyed, their husbands and children murdered, and their wives ravished." Converting and maintaining order among the treaty Nez Perce was hard enough, declared Deffenbaugh, for both he and Agent Charles Monteith were still contending with "conjugal infidelity and gambling in horse racing."[44]

But that autumn, John Scott, the new Ponca Reservation agent, rose to their defense. The Nez Perce were extremely anxious to return to their own country, Scott wrote the commissioner. "They regard themselves as exiles. The climate does not seem to agree with them, many of them have died, and there is a tinge of melancholy in their bearing and conversation that is truly pathetic. I think they should be sent back, as it seems clear they will never take root in this particular locality."[45]

Torn between these arguments, the commissioner presented the problem to the Nez Perce, encouraging them to consider dividing into two bands, one to be sent to Lapwai, the other to a safer location somewhere in the Northwest. At first they adamantly refused, particularly when they learned that Joseph would have to join the latter group and would not be allowed to return to Lapwai. Exactly why Joseph was singled out is unclear, but by now the myth of his leadership and military prowess during the war was firmly rooted. Sometime that winter, faced with the alternative of never being able to leave Indian Territory, they relented, agreeing to separate. In spring of 1885, the commissioner finally issued the order to return the Nez Perce to the Northwest.

Shortly before dawn on May 21, the 268 survivors left the Ponca Reservation in a pouring rain. With the sick, elderly, and lame riding in wagons, the remainder began walking in the rain and mud thirty miles to the rail depot at Arkansas City, Kansas. The next day, under the supervision of W. H. Faulkner, a doctor appointed to accompany them on the journey, they boarded the train, some having walked the entire night to reach the depot in time for departure. Early that afternoon, the train pulled away from the station, leaving behind a trail of unmarked graves strewn across thousands of miles, the remains of nearly half of the eight hundred men, women, and children who had fled their homeland eight years before.[46]

The journey passed uneventfully until they reached Pocatello, Idaho. Here Faulkner was told by train officials that they had received word to separate the Nez Perce, sending some north through Montana while the others continued on to Wallula Junction in Washington Territory. Faulkner grew suspicious and wired the Commissioner of Indian Affairs for confirmation, but before he received an answer, he encountered a member of General Miles's staff bearing alarming news. A U.S. marshal from Montana carrying an order to arrest Chief Joseph and several other Nez Perce was due to arrive in Pocatello that morning. Exactly how Faulkner managed to convince train officials not to hold them until the marshal arrived is unknown, but they were all soon on their way to Wallula, although both the doctor and the Nez Perce lived in constant fear the train would be ambushed by vigilantes.

On May 27, the train arrived at Wallula Junction on the Columbia River and here they were divided, with the official blessing of the federal government. However, the terms of separation had apparently been left until now. According to Yellow Wolf, they were given an ultimatum, to either go to Lapwai and become Christians or be sent to the Colville Indian Reservation some two hundred miles away in northeastern Washington. The only person who was not allowed a choice was Joseph. He would have to go to Colville.

The following day, 118 Nez Perce under the leadership of Huishuis Kute were placed in the custody of Agent Monteith, who supervised their journey to Lapwai. There they received an exuberant welcome from fellow tribespeople and displayed none of the belligerent or rebellious behavior agent Monteith or the missionaries had feared. In fact, the former exiles appeared "very much broken in spirit," Monteith wrote the commissioner, providing a good lesson "for the more restless members of the tribe who are not disposed to settle down and enter upon civilized pursuits." G. L. Deffenbaugh agreed, noting that within a month after their arrival, eighty of the exiles had joined reservation churches. The decision to send those who refused to be subdued somewhere "remote from the scenes of their dastardly deeds and wanton depredations," declared the missionary, had been the "very proper thing" to do.[47]

Besides the 150 Nez Perce who accompanied Joseph to the Colville Reservation, at least one white man took issue with this assessment, although for far different reasons than the Nez Perce. The Colville Indian agent was upset that the government was relocating them anywhere in the Northwest, convinced they had only been returned "on account of the sickly sentiment expressed in the East." They were unwelcome and had arrived "against the wishes of the people of the Territories."[48] As a result, he withheld rations of food and clothing, and not until the following spring were the exiles issued full subsistence allowances. The agent was not the only one unhappy about the relocation. The reservation was home to a variety of tribes—Columbias, Nespelems, San Poils, Lakes, Okanogans, Colvilles, and others. When most of the Nez Perce, including Joseph, selected land near the small reservation community of Nespelem, some five hundred Indians already living there objected. Finally, soldiers were brought in to maintain the peace, and by 1887 the Nez Perce were permanently settled in Nespelem.

By 1890, however, only a few Nez Perce were farming and the government was still providing nearly full subsistence. A year later, the Dawes Act, which forced Indians to take up land in severalty, was finally implemented at Colville. Also known as the General Allotment Act, this federal legislation was intended to hasten assimilation by extinguishing collective tribal ownership, breaking up reservation land into individual Indian family-sized farms—a proposal that proved ultimately devastating to those people like Joseph's band who were attempting to hold on to their traditional culture.[49]

Under the act, Yellow Bull and his family moved back to Lapwai. Although given the same opportunity, Joseph and the remaining Nez Perce refused. Why not return? They had every reason to: unsympathetic and incompetent agents, poor medical services, few educational opportunities, and a colder climate than Lapwai. But the fact was, thirteen years after the war, they still feared hostility. The Colville Reservation, said Yellow Wolf, "was better than Idaho, where all

332

Christian Nez Perces and whites were against us."[50] Perhaps more important, however, was the anticipation that eventually they would be allowed to return to Oregon's Wallowa Valley. The Wallowa was still relatively sparsely settled by whites, and given Joseph's popular support in the East, they believed they had reason to be hopeful. At Colville many Nez Perce still considered themselves prisoners of war, exiles in detention. Selecting land on the Nez Perce Reservation would forever end any chance they might have for repatriation.

By 1896, whites were beginning to settle on the Colville Reservation, which was now land thrown open to homesteading under the Dawes Act. The Nez Perce, reported Agent George Newman, were the only Indians there who still resisted becoming self-supporting farmers. They refused "citizens' dress," preferred living in tipis, and depended almost entirely on limited government food rations. With "encroachment of the whites upon all sides, the scarcity of game, the almost utter lack of employment," he proclaimed, it was a "wonder how they managed to live." All in all, the situation was "a fine field for missionary work," concluded the agent.[51] He could not have been more correct. Only a few years before in 1892, it had become an offense punishable by imprisonment to follow the practices of medicine men, perform religious dances, and openly advocate Indian beliefs—all constitutionally protected freedoms for American citizens. Indians were not considered citizens, and thus these rights did not apply.

As prospectors moved into the area and whites settled nearby Nespelem, Joseph became increasingly alarmed that what had occurred years before in Idaho was about to happen again at Colville. In 1897, he traveled to Washington, D.C., in another attempt to secure a homeland in the Wallowa Valley. A personal guest of General Miles—who by now had risen to the military's highest position as general of the army—Joseph met with President William McKinley. He also participated in the dedication of Grant's tomb in New York, the same president whose change of heart had resulted in his initial loss of the Wallowas.

While in New York, Joseph stayed at the prestigious Astor House and, according to a *New York Sun* reporter, when the chief appeared in full regalia cum eagle-feathered headdress, shortened "the breath of the less *outré* guests." Later, Joseph visited an Indian exhibition in south Brooklyn. Soon after arriving he was approached by a young woman who, the reporter recalled, "was dressed to impress and had a store of slated questions to ask. 'Did you ever scalp anybody?' she inquired. Chief Joseph pondered a moment and then turned to the interpreter. 'Tell her,' he said, pointing at the combination aviary and garden on her head, 'that I have nothing in my collection as fine as that.' "[52]

During this trip, government officials promised to look into Joseph's appeal to relocate his band in the Wallowas, but it was three more years before Indian Inspector James McLaughlin finally arrived at Colville. In McLaughlin, Joseph could not have found a more determined adversary. Described by one historian as "ambitious, vain and petty," the inspector was largely responsible for the breakup and dismemberment of the Sioux Reservation. Ten years earlier, McLaughlin had played a prominent role in the arrest of Sitting Bull, an action that resulted in his murder and contributed greatly to the Wounded Knee Massacre, the century's last violent Plains Indian uprising in which some 150 Sioux men, women, and children perished.[53]

In the summer of 1900, Joseph and McLaughlin traveled to the Wallowa to investigate the possibility of relocating Joseph's band to the valley. There, declared McLaughlin, Joseph returned twenty-three years after he had fled his homeland to find that the "desert" of his youth had been developed by settlers into "a rich and bountiful country." Towns and villages stood "where the pony-herds of the Nez Perces were wont to graze on the scant grass; orchards grew where the sage-brush had been, and Joseph knew not his old home." Traveling on, they came upon the grave of Joseph's father, the surrounding ground now owned by a white man. "With a spirit too rare among his kind," admitted McLaughlin, the owner had enclosed and maintained the grounds around it. As the two men stood before the grave, the agent said he looked up to see Joseph's eyes filled with tears.[54]

Although Joseph was received politely by valley residents, his request for a reservation was refused. Then the chief offered to purchase a small parcel of land, and that too was rejected. McLaughlin concurred, recommending that Joseph's band remain permanently at Colville. "It is enough that the white man has turned the desert into a garden," reasoned the inspector, "that he should enjoy the profit of his enterprise."[55]

Despite this official rejection, Joseph did not give up trying to relocate to the Wallowa, a desire that only intensified when, a year after his trip, he ran afoul of the new Colville agent, Albert Anderson. Plump, balding, and brimming enmity from every pore, Anderson was incensed at Joseph and his people's refusal to adopt white culture. "He, with his handful of unworthy followers, prefers the traditional tepee, living on the generosity of the Government and passing away their time in a filthy and licentious way of living. . . ." History had been too kind to Joseph "in chronicling his atrocious acts," claimed the agent. "The appalling wrongs done by him are crying from the bloodstained soil of Idaho for restitution."[56]

In an attempt to hasten assimilation by forcing the Nez Perce to send their children away to boarding school at Fort Spokane, Anderson cut off all government subsistence to them in 1901. Joseph fought the move, demanding a school in Nespelem instead, but eventually relented when his people began to suffer. His protestations were not unfounded. At the Fort Spokane school, as at most Indian boarding schools at the turn of the century, traditional Indian dress and customs were replaced by uniforms and strict adherence to white standards. In more rigorous institutions like Fort Spokane, children caught speaking their own language were frequently beaten.

In 1903, now well into his sixties, Joseph traveled to the nation's capital for the last time. Gold had been discovered at Colville, giving the Nez Perce even more concern over their future. Once again General Miles was the chief's host, arranging a buffalo dinner with President Theodore Roosevelt. Although considered one of America's more reform-minded presidents, Roosevelt was not sympathetic to Indians. During a New York lecture in 1886, he had declared, "I don't go so far as to think that the only good Indians are the dead Indians, but I believe nine out of every ten are, and I shouldn't like to inquire too closely into the case of the tenth."[57] Still, according to Joseph, Roosevelt promised to send a committee to Colville to investigate encroachment by miners; the chief claimed one never arrived.

In November, Joseph visited Seattle, where he spoke to several hundred people, making his final public plea to be returned to the Wallowa Valley:

My White Friends:
I am pleased to meet you all this evening, old and young. I feel very thankful for such a kind and hearty reception in your city. I have a kind feeling in my heart for you all. I am getting old and for some years past, have made several efforts to be returned to my old home in Wallowa Valley, but without success. The Government at Washington has always given me many flattering promises but up to the present time has utterly failed to fulfill any of its promises to me. But I am not surprised as much of my life has been filled with broken promises. I have but few years to live and would like to die in my old home. My father is buried there, my children are buried there and I would like to rest by their side when I die. I have fought bravely and honorably in defending my inheritance from [the Creative Power]—the land and houses of my forefathers. I will fight no more and hope you will all help me to return to the home of my childhood where my relatives and friends are resting. Please assist me. I am thankful for your kind attention. That is all.[58]

A year later, on September 21, 1904, one of Joseph's wives discovered him slumped over in his tipi, dead, probably the victim of a heart attack. The agency doctor, who knew Joseph but was not present at his death, said that he believed the chief had died of a broken heart. The next day, because many Nez Perce were away from the reservation serving as seasonal farm laborers, Joseph was buried without ceremony. With him died forever the last hope of exiled Nez Perce for repatriation to the Wallowa Valley.

The following summer on June 20, with a few hundred Nez Perce and whites in attendance, three white admirers—including photographer E. S. Curtis—exhumed the body and several Nez Perce men reburied it beneath a modest granite memorial in the Nespelem cemetery, under the shadow of the steepled reservation church. Then, after a traditional Indian potlatch, all of Joseph's possessions were placed in a pile to be given away the following day to friends and relatives: a few worn buffalo robes; several rifles, including the one Joseph had used during the war; a leather trunk containing bundles of letters received from whites over the years; a single tintype picture of his long-dead eldest daughter. Inscribed on the back of the picture were the words: "For Chief Joseph from your loving Daughter Sarah Moses."

Soon after the potlatch, Yellow Bull appeared—aged and nearly blind, the father of one of the three young men whose murders sparked the war twenty-seven years before, now the oldest living Nez Perce warrior. Riding Joseph's favorite horse, he was dressed in a regal red robe trimmed with ermine, and over his left arm he carried a white wolf cape. In both hands Yellow Bull held Joseph's peace pipe. On his head he wore the chief's eagle-feathered headdress, filled with hundreds of black-tipped feathers trailing nearly to the ground.

Three times the old man slowly circled the crowd of onlookers as he spoke of Joseph, the struggle that had consumed both his life and the lives of his people, and the universality of grief at his death. So moving were his words that women were said to have covered their faces with their hair and wept as he passed.

Notes

Due to the autonomous nature of tribal bands within Nez Perce society, orthography of their language varies considerably. Thus *Ollokot, Ollicut,* or *Allokut; wyakin* or *way-a-kin.* Not only do some names and words have multiple spellings, but they may also possess more than one meaning. *Hillal* is known as "the season of rivers rising due to melting snow in the mountains" by Nez Perce residing along the Clearwater River at Kamiah, Idaho; while some downriver people may know *hillal* or *tie'yalh'* as "the time of spawning salmon." Unless otherwise noted, this text reflects spellings and definitions as first recorded by historian Lucullus Virgil McWhorter or, more recently, Nez Perce tribal historian Allen Slickpoo, Sr.

Sources provided in notes are in shortened form; see Bibliography (pages 375–89) for full citations.

CHAPTER 1 (pages 1–17)

1. McWhorter, *Hear Me,* 125. McWhorter recorded twenty-eight Nez Perce deaths at the hands of whites prior to 1877, with only one man brought to trial and sentenced to hang for killing a Nez Perce woman and attempting to kill her husband. McWhorter claimed the accused was never executed.

2. Ibid., 189–90.

3. John B. Monteith to E. Smith, letter, 4 June 1874. Actually, traditional Nez Perce believe in an omniscient creator called *Hunyawat*. (W. Halfmoon to author, 27 December 1991.)

4. McDonald, "Nez Perces" (3 May 1878). After the final battle of the war, Lieutenant C. E. S. Wood asked Joseph why he had refused to surrender the murderers. He answered, "That was unthinkable. I would no longer be a Nez Perce, much less a Chief. That is never done by Indians. No, I had to stay with my people." Wood believed that the independent nature of Nez Perce society gave a chief little power over individuals. "After those savage killings by the young Indians," the lieutenant concluded, "it would have been perfectly useless to have attempted to appease the public wrath against the Indians by surrendering the culprits." (C. E. S. Wood to E. Lyman, 17 January 1939, Wood Papers.)

5. McDermott, *Forlorn Hope*, 16. McDermott's comprehensive work is the primary source for events leading to war.

6. *New North-West*, 6 December 1878.

7. Ibid.; McDermott, *Forlorn Hope*, 105–106; McWhorter, *Hear Me*, 216–17. In an article published long after the war, Brice's story continued to grow, reaching epic proportions. The author, Charles Moody, claims Brice assured the Nez Perce that he would return to let the warriors "work their will upon him" if only they allowed him to remove Maggie to safety. Brice returns as promised but the warriors, so impressed by his courage, refuse to kill him. Brice enjoyed the adulation and made no effort to set the record straight. (Moody, "Bravest Deed," 783–84.)

8. *An Illustrated History*, 55.

9. McDermott, *Forlorn Hope*, 158–60. Duncan McDonald claimed that Jennet Manuel hid upstairs in the loft of the house, and the first warriors knew of her presence were her screams coming from the burning building. According to McDonald, the warriors tried to put out the fire by filling their hats at the creek and running back to the house, but the woman and child both perished in the flames.

In July 1877, the *Teller* printed: "Squaws still report that Mrs. Manual is living and a prisoner." Years later, demanding that his words not be published until after his death, Yellow Bull revealed that Jennet Manuel recovered and was held captive for a month until the Nez Perce had fled over Lolo Pass into Montana. One night, said Yellow Bull, she was killed and her body hidden in the brush. In 1935, when Peopeo Tholekt was asked to describe the trophies in his cabin, he picked up a human scalp and hairlock.

"Hair of white woman, Mrs. Manuel," he declared. Taken prisoner, she had become sick and soon died. The Nez Perce buried her under some rocks along the Lolo Trail.

Historian Lucullus Virgil McWhorter believed that one of the raiders, Red Wolf, captured Jennet and made her ride behind him on his horse until she grabbed the knife from his belt and attempted to kill him. Red Wolf struck her and she fell to the ground, later dying from the fall. One white account repeated in Montana newspapers claimed that as the Nez Perce traveled over Lolo Pass, a young white woman was seen among them. (Lewiston *Teller*, 28 July 1877; McDermott, *Forlorn Hope*, 159; McWhorter, *Hear Me*, 215–16; Buck, "The Story of the Nez Perce" [manuscript].)

10. McDermott, *Forlorn Hope*, 20–22. All quotations attributed to Helen Walsh are from this source.

11. Lewiston *Teller*, 13 April 1878.

12. McDermott, *Forlorn Hope*, 29.

13. San Francisco *Chronicle*, 20 July 1877.

14. Adkison, *Nez Perce Indian War*, 39.

15. Greenburg, "Victim of the Nez Perce," 8.

16. Wilfong, *Following the Nez Perce Trail*, 73; San Francisco *Chronicle*, 20 July 1877.

17. McWhorter, *Hear Me*, 220; Lewiston *Teller*, 13 April 1878.

18. Lewiston *Teller*, 2 June 1877.

19. McDermott, *Forlorn Hope*, 41.

20. Lewiston *Teller*, 13 April 1878.

21. Adkison, *Nez Perce Indian War*, 25.

22. Rowton, "Tribute," 2.

CHAPTER 2 (pages 19–37)

1. The population of pre-Columbus North America is a topic of unending scholarly debate. Perhaps the best recent treatment is Russell Thornton's *American Indian Holocaust and Survival: A Population History Since 1492*. Thornton estimates that from 5 million, the population of Native Americans decreased to 600,000 by 1800, then to 250,000 by 1890. Between 1800 and 1890, when Indian populations were approaching their nadir, the non-Indian population of the United States grew from 5 million to over 63 million.

2. Koch and Peden, *Selected Writings*, 33.

3. Josephy, *Nez Perce Indians*, 3. Josephy's work is the best description of Nez Perce culture from early contact to the beginning of the war. See also

David Lavender's *Let Me Be Free,* although Lavender's conjectural work contains several notable errors.

4. Haines, *Nez Perces,* 15; Spinden, "The Nez Perce Indians," 172. Nez Perce were also known as *Tsit-nit-pa-lu,* or People of the Mountains. In this case, the index finger passing up the front of the face designated people of the mountains coming to the plains to hunt. (W. Halfmoon to author, 27 December 1991.)

5. Miller, "Letters," 22; Josephy, *Nez Perce Indians,* 116.

6. Josephy, *Nez Perce Indians,* 29.

7. Ibid., 13–14.

8. McWhorter, *Hear Me,* xix; S. McFarland to author, 2 December 1991; W. Halfmoon to author, 27 December 1991.

9. Lavender, *Way,* 343.

10. Josephy, *Nez Perce Indians,* 74.

11. Ibid., 100–101.

12. Limerick, *Legacy,* 39.

13. Morgan and Harris, *Rocky Mountain Journals,* 235–36.

14. Lee, "Diary," 140.

15. Drury, *Henry Harmon Spalding,* 180.

16. Josephy, *Nez Perce Indians,* 333–34. The actual size of the reservation guaranteed by the 1855 treaty has been variously reported between 5,000 and 12,000 square miles, a discrepancy due to vague treaty language used in describing the boundaries. Most authorities agree that the Nez Perce understood the treaty allowed them the larger area, the eastern boundary extending to the crest of the Bitterroot Mountains dividing present-day Idaho from Montana.

17. Josephy, *Nez Perce Indians,* 392.

18. Limerick, *Legacy,* 192.

19. *An Illustrated History,* 1223.

20. Josephy, *Nez Perce Indians,* 408.

21. Ibid., 410.

22. Report of the Adjutant-General of Oregon, 1865–1866, 18.

23. Ibid.

24. Josephy, *Nez Perce Indians,* 429.

25. In 1941, descendants of Joseph's band filed a suit in the U.S. Court of Claims, arguing that the band had been deprived of the Wallowa Valley without either its consent or compensation. In its decision, the court reasoned that since Old Joseph was a signatory to the 1855 treaty where the tribe had acted as a whole concerning land ownership, he was bound by

subsequent treaties signed by a majority of the tribe regardless of whether he remained a dissenting party. The court denied that Joseph's band ever had exclusive possession of the Wallowa Valley and never questioned Hale's version of what bands constituted a majority. (U.S. 95th Court of Claims, *Joseph's Band*, 1941–1942.)

26. Ruby and Brown, *Dreamer-Prophets*, 32.

27. Joseph, "An Indian's View," 419.

28. Josephy, *Nez Perce Indians*, 448. That Joseph may not have demonstrated such sterling qualities earlier in his life has been alleged in at least one Nez Perce account. Yellow Bull claimed that before whites began encroaching on the Wallowa, Joseph "was a drunken, carousing sort of a fellow in whom the Indians had but little confidence. His father was a better man and much better liked. Ollicut [Ollokot] was better liked than Joseph and he was an abler man." (Yellow Bull interview, 3 February 1915, Camp Interviews.)

29. McWhorter, *Hear Me*, 132–35.

30. Wood, *Status* (gov't doc.) 32.

31. L. Grover to C. Delano, 21 July 1873, Report of Secretary of War, 1875–1876, 130.

32. Josephy, *Nez Perce Indians*, 460–61.

33. Howard, *Nez Perce Joseph*, 28–29. (Throughout Notes section, Oliver O. Howard is referred to as simply Howard; Helen Addison Howard is referred to by her full name.)

CHAPTER 3 (pages 39–55)

1. This sketch of Howard's life is based on: Carpenter, *Sword*; Utley, "Oliver Otis Howard"; Ellis, "The Humanitarian Generals."

2. Carpenter, *Sword*, 25.

3. W. Sherman to O. Howard, 29 November 1873, Howard Papers.

4. Carpenter, *Sword*, 212, 216.

5. Ibid., 333.

6. S. Whipple to O. Howard, 28 August 1875, Report of Secretary of War, 1875–1876, 128–29.

7. Wood, *Status* (gov't doc.), 41–46 passim.

8. Report of Secretary of War, 1875–1876, 126.

9. Josephy, *Nez Perce Indians*, 473–74 passim.

10. Wood, *Supplementary to the Report* (gov't doc.), 2–4.

11. Howard, *Nez Perce Joseph*, 40. Smohalla later obtained an almanac listing eclipses and used it to demonstrate that he could control the darken-

ing of the sun and moon. When after a year or so his astronomic prophecies came to an abrupt end, Smohalla asked Major J. W. MacMurray to "readjust it for eclipses, as it did not work as it had formerly done." MacMurray's inability "to amend the 1882 almanac for use in prognosticating in 1884 cost me much of his respect as a wise man from the East." (Mooney, *Ghost-Dance Religion* [gov't doc.], 718.)

12. Ruby and Brown, *Dreamer-Prophets*, 29.

13. Ibid., 71, 84; Mooney, *Ghost-Dance Religion* (gov't doc.), 711.

14. Report of Commissioner of Indian Affairs, 1876–1877, 608.

15. Ibid., 609.

16. Howard, *My Life*, 240–43.

17. Laufe, ed., *Army Doctor's Wife*, 222; McWhorter, *Hear Me*, 147.

18. Laufe, *Army Doctor's Wife*, 223–24.

19. Wood, minority report to Commissioner of Indian Affairs, 1 December 1876, Records of the U.S. Army, No. 3597; *Army and Navy Journal*, 8 September 1877.

20. Howard, "Nez Perce's Campaign" (7 February 1878): 82; Report of Commissioner of Indian Affairs, 1876–1877, 611.

21. Utley, "Oliver Otis Howard," 61.

22. O. Howard to W. Sherman, 18 January 1877, Howard Papers. Sherman was sympathetic but could not refrain from chiding Howard: "You remember I always opposed your undertaking that office, and my experience has been that it is always unsafe for any army officer undertaking any functions outside his profession. You have already suffered enough for this mistake, and I shall surely try to bring it to an end." (W. Sherman to O. Howard, 20 January 1878, Howard Papers.)

23. Howard, *Nez Perce Joseph*, 15.

24. J. Monteith to J. Smith, 9 February 1877, Records of the U.S. Army, No. 1363–77.

25. Lewiston *Teller*, 19 March 1877.

26. Ibid., 21 April 1877.

27. Howard, *Nez Perce Joseph*, 36, 43.

28. Howard, *Famous Indian Chiefs*, 190.

29. The precise number of nontreaty Nez Perce in spring 1877 is unknown. In 1805, Lewis and Clark put the total population at 6,000. Soon afterward, two smallpox epidemics killed upward of 2,000 people. By 1860, the Indian Bureau estimated 4,000, then 2,800 in 1875. Certainly none of these estimates were particularly accurate, although they indicate that the Nez Perce declined in population after contact, a trend that continued well into the

twentieth century. In 1871, Monteith wrote that the tribe was equally split between factions. Considering there were probably then about 3,000 Nez Perce, this would indicate approximately 1,500 nontreaty followers. In the intervening years before the war, the number of nontreaty Nez Perce continued to decline as Indians took up residency on the reservation due to increasing white encroachment. By May 1877, there were about 2,500 Nez Perce—1,700 living either within the reservation boundary or close by, and 800 others who were represented by the various nontreaty bands at this final council. (Report of Commissioner of Indian Affairs, 1878, 549.)

30. Howard, *Nez Perce Joseph*, 57; McDonald, "Nez Perces" (26 July 1878). Although some authorities believe White Bird was in his seventies in 1877, both Yellow Bull and Duncan McDonald assert he was closer to fifty. (McWhorter, *Hear Me*, 181; interview with Yellow Bull, Camp Interviews.)

31. Howard, "Nez Perce's Campaign" (23 April 1878): 259.

32. Report of Secretary of War, 1876–1877, 593–97; Howard, *Nez Perce Joseph*, 58–59.

33. Howard, *Nez Perce Joseph*, 63, 19.

34. Ibid., 64–66 passim. The exchange between Toohoolhoolzote and Howard is derived from this source.

35. Ibid., 56, 67.

36. Curtis, *North American Indian*, 164.

37. McWhorter, *Yellow Wolf*, 41.

38. O. Howard to Adj. General, 18 May 1877, Records of the U.S. Army, No. 2819–77; Howard, *Nez Perce Joseph*, 74.

CHAPTER 4 (pages 57–80)

1. Howard, *Nez Perce Joseph*, 88.

2. Ibid., 76. One year before, Inspector Watkins played a prominent role in encouraging the government's militant response to the Sioux when he recommended that for the good of "civilization and the common cause of humanity," the army should send troops against the Sioux and "whip them into subjection." General Philip Sheridan lost no time in complying. (Carroll, ed., *General Custer*, 5–7.)

3. Howard, "Nez Perce's Campaign" (20 June 1878): 387.

4. Ibid.

5. Howard, *Nez Perce Joseph*, 95.

6. Ibid., 96.

7. Ibid.

8. New York *Tribune*, 21 June 1877.

9. Laufe, *Army Doctor's Wife*, 259–60.

10. Brown, *Flight*, 118.

11. McDermott, *Forlorn Hope*, 57–58 passim.

12. Howard, "Nez Perce's Campaign" (13 June 1878): 371.

13. Howard, *Nez Perce Joseph*, 90.

14. Howard, "Nez Perce's Campaign" (13 June 1878): 371.

15. McDermott, *Forlorn Hope*, 64–66 passim.

16. Ibid., 60–61, 66–68 passim.

17. *New York Times*, 12 July 1877.

18. Rickey, *Forty Miles*, 249.

19. Mulford, *Fighting Indians*, 79; Connell, *Son*, 150; Utley, *Frontier Regulars*, 23.

20. Rickey, *Forty Miles*, 153–155 passim.

21. Report of Secretary of War, 1876–1877, vii–viii.

22. McCarthy, Diary. All quotations attributed to McCarthy are from this source.

23. Hershler, *Soldier's Handbook* (gov't doc.), 53.

24. Howard, *Nez Perce Joseph*, 107.

25. McDermott, *Forlorn Hope*, 197.

26. McWhorter, *Hear Me*, 235.

27. Ibid., 237.

28. Brady, *Northwestern Fights*, 101.

29. McWhorter, *Hear Me*, 251n; McWhorter, *Yellow Wolf*, 56, 57n. Not long after the White Bird battle, editor Leland's son gave an eyewitness count of the bands' strength at 132 warriors. (Lewiston *Teller*, 7 July 1877.)

30. McWhorter, *Hear Me*, 248–49.

31. The Nez Perce's Edward Lebain claimed that White Bird and Joseph "had given orders to all Indians not to fire unless the soldiers fired first." He also maintained that Chapman fired the first shot. (Interview with Edward Lebain, 30 January 1913, Camp Interviews.)

32. McDermott, *Forlorn Hope*, 200.

33. McWhorter, *Hear Me*, 239–40.

34. Ibid., 241.

35. Beal, *I Will Fight No More*, 64.

36. McWhorter, *Yellow Wolf*, 59.

37. Ibid., 58–59.

38. McCarthy fails to explain why the Nez Perce were not conversing in their own language. According to Lucullus Virgil McWhorter, few Nez Perce spoke Chinook. (McWhorter, *Yellow Wolf*, 214n.)

CHAPTER 5 (pages 81–104)

1. Howard, "Nez Perce's Campaign" (1 August 1878): 483.

2. McDermott, *Forlorn Hope*, 116.

3. Ibid., 117.

4. Laufe, *Army Doctor's Wife*, 287; *New York Times*, 12 July 1877.

5. H. Wood to J. Kelton, 18 June 1877, Records of the U.S. Army, No. 6724–77; Report of Secretary of War, 1876–1877, 602; Howard, *My Life*, 283–85; McWhorter, *Hear Me*, 251n; McWhorter, *Yellow Wolf*, 57n; Laufe, *Army Doctor's Wife*, 265.

6. H. Wood to J. Kelton, 18 June 1877, Records of the U.S. Army, No. 6724–77.

7. Howard, *Nez Perce Joseph*, 127; Laufe, *Army Doctor's Wife*, 265.

8. Howard, "Nez Perce's Campaign" (1 August 1878): 515.

9. Laufe, *Army Doctor's Wife*, 262–64.

10. Howard, *Nez Perce Joseph*, 139.

11. Hutton, *Soldiers West*, 6.

12. McDermott, *Forlorn Hope*, 113; McWhorter, *Hear Me*, 258.

13. General Philip Sheridan understood the public's revulsion to physical savagery by Indians and employed it successfully in garnering support for his policies of brutal retaliation. He claimed that "since 1862 at least 800 men, women and children have been murdered within the limits of my present command, in the most fiendish manner; the men usually scalped and mutilated, their _____ cut off and placed in their mouths; women ravished sometimes fifty and sixty times in succession, then killed and scalped, sticks stuck up their persons, before and after death." Although these atrocities mostly occurred early on and were primarily the work of only a few tribes, Sheridan had no difficulty transposing them to all Indians. (Hutton, *Phil Sheridan*, 194.)

14. McWhorter, *Hear Me*, 257.

15. Forse, "Chief Joseph," 5; Joseph, "An Indian's View," 425.

16. Curtis, *North American Indian*, 165; Report of Secretary of War, 1876–1877, 15.

17. McWhorter, *Hear Me*, 258.

18. McDermott, *Forlorn Hope*, 124.

19. Laufe, *Army Doctor's Wife*, 274. At the time of his death, Theller had a gold watch along with several other items given to him by his father. Since the burial party recovered no personal effects, Delia Theller reasoned the body had been robbed by Indians, and the items might eventually fall into the hands of a white person. After the battle she placed an advertisement in

the *Teller,* describing them and requesting their recovery. In December, the *Teller* reported an undertaker had located Theller's grave with the feet "partly projecting out of the ground. . . . The flesh was nearly all rotted from the bones, leaving the mere skeleton enveloped in the clothing he wore in the battle." Inside a pocket of the pants was the gold watch. The well-preserved timepiece, the undertaker reported, had stopped at precisely nine o'clock. (McDermott, *Forlorn Hope,* 127–28, 164.)

20. Wood, Diary.

21. At least one soldier named C. E. S. Wood as the lieutenant. Sixty-four years later, given an opportunity to rebut the accusation, the elderly Wood wrote in a letter to historian Lucullus Virgil McWhorter: "I was sound asleep in my blankets till awakened by the shot and the ensuing excitement. As I recollect this unfortunate incident, one of the guard, being relieved from picket duty, was approaching the campfire, wrapped in a blanket. An officer, I forget which one, was sitting beside the fire with his rifle across his knees. He had fallen asleep and being suddenly awakened by the steps of an approaching figure, wrapped as he was in his blanket, mistook him for a hostile Indian and half-dazed by sleep, fired instantly, almost automatically." Wood was sure that the officer who had fired the shot was "unaware of what he was doing. I am sorry I can contribute nothing more definite and of more value than my assurance I was not the shooter." The affair was eclipsed in the events of the next few days, and Howard made no mention of it in his official report. (McWhorter, *Hear Me,* 260–61.)

22. Howard, "Nez Perce's Campaign" (5 September 1878): 563; ibid. (19 September 1878): 594.

23. Howard, *Nez Perce Joseph,* 120; Report of Secretary of War, 1876–1877, 603.

24. Lewiston *Teller,* 26 June 1877.

25. Ruby, "First Account," 3; McDonald, "Nez Perces" (22 November 1878).

26. Howard, *Nez Perce Joseph,* 148.

27. McWhorter, *Hear Me,* 264–74 passim.

28. Howard, "Nez Perce's Campaign" (19 September 1878): 594. The total number of warriors is elusive. Joseph maintained 250 warriors fought against Howard at the Clearwater. Forty years after the war, Yellow Bull claimed the bands fielded 270 men. After extensive interviews with survivors, Lucullus Virgil McWhorter suggested these band strengths: Joseph— 60, White Bird—50, Toohoolhoolzote—30, Looking Glass—40, and the Palouse—16 for a total of 196 men. Probably a dozen more later joined the

bands in the Bitterroot Valley, bringing the total to just over 200. Since this estimate included the young as well as the aged, the bands' effective force may have been substantially less, possibly as few as 155 men. Although this account reflects McWhorter's more conservative figures, the actual number may lie somewhere between these estimates. (interview with Yellow Bull, Camp Interviews; Joseph, "An Indian's View," 426; McWhorter, *Hear Me*, 177–86.)

29. Howard, *Nez Perce Joseph*, 146; McWhorter, *Hear Me*, 249.

30. Sutherland, *Howard's Campaign*, 46.

31. Sutherland spent much time defending the general. "General Howard has done everything possible, but he is troubled with a lack of efficient scouts and good horses, to say nothing of a want of as perfect a knowledge of the trails through the mountains as the pursued Indians. He is a man of indomitable energy, as the cadaverous appearance of your correspondent from forced marches will clearly prove. I am very much pleased with General Howard," declared Sutherland. "[He] is a brave man, and is fully determined to punish Joseph for his perfidy." (Portland *Weekly Standard*, 20 July 1877.)

32. E. Mason to F. Mason, 2 July 1877, "Scrapbooks" (manuscript); Brady, *Northwestern Fights*, 128.

33. Brown, *Flight*, 173; McCarthy, Diary.

34. Joseph, "An Indian's View," 426; McDonald, "Nez Perces" (29 November 1878).

35. Sutherland, *Howard's Campaign*, 10.

36. Howard, *Nez Perce Joseph*, 151.

37. McWhorter, *Yellow Wolf*, 73–74.

38. Howard, *Nez Perce Joseph*, 152.

39. Report of Secretary of War, 1876–1877, 603; Adkison, *Nez Perce Indian War*, 62; Portland *Daily Standard*, 20 July 1877.

40. McWhorter, *Yellow Wolf*, 81.

41. Howard, *Nez Perce Joseph*, 153.

42. Lewiston *Teller*, 4 August 1877; Helen Addison Howard, *Saga*, 193; Shearer, "Skirmish," 6–7.

43. McWhorter, *Yellow Wolf*, 83.

44. Lewiston *Teller*, 4 August 1877.

45. General Orders No. 23, 30 November 1877, Records of the U.S. Army, No. 7782–77.

46. B. Keeler to I. McDowell, 15 July 1877, *Senate Executive Documents*,

"Claims," 44; Brown, *Flight*, 182; F. Wheaton to O. Howard, 4 November 1877, Howard Papers.

47. McDermott, *Forlorn Hope*, 145.

48. Ibid., 143.

CHAPTER 6 (pages 105–32)

1. Howard, *My Life*, 287.

2. Brady, *Northwestern Fights*, 129–30.

3. Report of Secretary of War, 1876–1877, 604.

4. Ibid.

5. McCarthy, Diary.

6. Howard, *Nez Perce Joseph*, 155; McConville, "Report to Governor Brayman, August 1877" in *Fifteenth Biennial Report*, 66.

7. Lewiston *Teller*, 4 August 1877.

8. Ibid.

9. San Francisco *Chronicle*, 15 July 1877.

10. New York *Herald*, 10 September 1877.

11. McCarthy, Diary.

12. Brady, *Northwestern Fights*, 162–63.

13. McWhorter, *Hear Me*, 319–20n; Wood, Diary.

14. San Francisco *Chronicle*, 15 July 1877.

15. McWhorter, *Hear Me*, 302n.

16. McWhorter, *Yellow Wolf*, 88–89.

17. Wood, "Chief Joseph," 137; Curtis, *North American Indian*, 166.

18. Sutherland, *Howard's Campaign*, 52.

19. Ibid., 50.

20. McWhorter, *Hear Me*, 304–9 passim.

21. Sternberg, *George Miller Sternberg*, 60.

22. Brady, *Northwestern Fights*, 144–45, 148.

23. San Francisco *Chronicle*, 15 July 1877.

24. Brady, *Northwestern Fights*, 146; Howard, *Nez Perce Joseph*, 164; San Francisco *Chronicle*, 28 July 1877.

25. Curtis, *North American Indian*, 28; McWhorter, *Yellow Wolf*, 96n.

26. McWhorter, *Yellow Wolf*, 96–97.

27. Report of Secretary of War, 1876–1877, 606; Brady, *Northwestern Fights*, 132.

28. Sutherland, *Howard's Campaign*, 13.

29. McWhorter, *Hear Me*, 322.

30. San Francisco *Chronicle*, 28 July 1877; Report of Secretary of War, 1876–1877, 606; Brady, *Northwestern Fights*, 133.

31. Howard, *Nez Perce Joseph*, 166; Portland *Weekly Standard*, 27 July 1877; McCarthy, Diary. Later, when Nez Perce survivors gave their personal account of events, they often did so only in the presence of one or more witnesses. (W. Halfmoon to author, 27 December 1991.)

32. San Francisco *Chronicle*, 27 August 1877.

33. Howard, *Nez Perce Joseph*, 167.

34. E. Mason to F. Mason, 14 July 1877, "Scrapbooks" (manuscript).

35. Howard, *Nez Perce Joseph*, 168–69.

36. Ibid.; San Francisco *Chronicle*, 19 July 1877.

37. Howard, *Nez Perce Joseph*, 169; Wood, "Chief Joseph," 138.

38. Ruby, "First Account," 3; Laufe, *Army Doctor's Wife*, 278; B. Keeler to I. McDowell, 17 July 1877, *Senate Executive Documents*, "Claims," 42.

39. New York *Herald*, 1 August 1877; Portland *Daily Standard*, 21 July 1877.

40. San Francisco *Chronicle*, 20 July 1877; B. Keeler to I. McDowell, 17 July 1877, *Senate Executive Documents*, "Claims," 42.

41. Lewiston *Teller*, 21 July 1877; Laufe, *Army Doctor's Wife*, 288–89.

42. Wood, "Chief Joseph," 138. Lieutenant Wood claimed Joseph's words were related to him by an unidentified Indian informant. Unfortunately, doubt surrounding the accuracy of Wood's subsequent recording of Joseph's alleged surrender speech at war's end casts a shadow over the lieutenant's reliability. Consequently, Wood's renderings of Joseph's 'words should be considered only approximations.

43. Curtis, *North American Indian*, 33.

44. E. Mason to F. Mason, 19 July 1877, "Scrapbooks" (manuscript).

45. McWhorter, *Hear Me*, 337; McWhorter, *Yellow Wolf*, 106. A later version of this story has Levi "lying in the grass with a .45 bullet through his lungs." (Wilson, *Hawks and Doves*, 13.)

46. McWhorter, *Hear Me*, 338; *Senate Executive Documents*, "Claims," 4.

47. Howard, *Nez Perce Joseph*, 170.

48. O. Howard to Adj. General, 15 July 1877, *Senate Executive Documents*, "Claims," 39.

49. W. Sherman to I. McDowell, 25 June 1877, *Senate Executive Documents*, "Claims," 20–21.

50. Laufe, *Army Doctor's Wife*, 265.

51. Report of Secretary of War, 1876–1877, 607.

52. Brown, *Flight*, 208.

53. Lewiston *Teller*, 14 July 1877.

54. San Francisco *Chronicle*, 15 July 1877.

55. I. McDowell to O. Howard, 17 July 1877, *Senate Executive Documents*, "Claims," 40.

56. Howard, *Nez Perce Joseph*, 141, 3.

57. E. Mason to F. Mason, 2 July 1877, "Scrapbooks" (manuscript); B. Keeler to I. McDowell, 23 July 1877, *Senate Executive Documents*, "Claims," 47; ibid., 18 July 1877, 44; ibid., O. Howard to I. McDowell, 21 July 1877, 48.

58. San Francisco *Chronicle*, 6 August 1877.

59. Portland *Weekly Standard*, 3 August 1877.

60. Sutherland, *Howard's Campaign*, 52.

61. Ibid., 25.

62. O. Howard to Adj. General, 25 July 1877, *Senate Executive Documents*, "Claims," 50; ibid., 31 July 1877, 55.

63. O. Howard to I. McDowell, 25 July 1877 (margin notes by McDowell), Records of the U.S. Army, No. 6724–77; B. Keeler to O. Howard, 27 and 28 July 1877, *Senate Executive Documents*, "Claims," 51; ibid., 29 July 1877, 52.

64. Laufe, *Army Doctor's Wife*, 285.

CHAPTER 7 (pages 133–54)

1. Olson, "Nez Perce" (master's thesis), 52.

2. B. Potts to I. McDowell, 29 June 1877, *Senate Executive Documents*, "Claims," 24; ibid., 1 July 1877, 25; ibid., 3 July 1877, 27.

3. Clark, *Indian Legends*, 61.

4. Harrison, "Chief Charlot's Battle," 30.

5. *The Weekly Missoulian*, 26 April 1876.

6. Charles C. Rawn, "Report to the Assistant Adjutant General," Fort Shaw, 16 July 1877, in John Hakola and H. G. Merriam, *Frontier Omnibus*, 387–88.

7. Olson, "Nez Perce" (master's thesis), 90; *The Weekly Missoulian*, 13 July 1877.

8. P. Ronan to B. Potts, Miscellaneous Letters of the Montana Superintendency, National Archives.

9. Beal, *I Will Fight No More*, 106.

10. Thwaites, ed., *Original Journals*, 3:63–68 passim; Report of Secretary of War, 1876–1877, 10. The precise derivation of the name *Lolo* (called Khoo-say-na-is-kit by Nez Perce) has been lost, but the stories surrounding its

origin are no less daunting than the trail itself. The word probably derived from the Salish pronunciation of the name of a trapper known as Lawrence, pronounced by French-Canadians as "Lora"—the closest Flatheads came was "Loulou," or "Lolo." The trapper purportedly met his demise when a grizzly bear attacked him and his Indian companions. Lawrence was mauled severely. One man attempted to shoot the animal, but his gun misfired, and the bear left "the now lifeless Lolo" and attacked the shooter, the bear and man rolling down a hillside "locked in deadly combat." During the struggle the man dislodged a log, and the bear, "blinded with blood," kept after the log instead of its victim until the others killed it. (McWhorter, *Hear Me*, 343; Space, *Lolo Trail*, 2.)

11. *Senate Executive Documents*, "Claims," 45–46.

12. J. Gibbon to Adj. General, Div. of Missouri, 22 July 1877, Records of the U.S. Army, No. 4392–77.

13. *The Weekly Missoulian*, 3 August 1877; Curtis, *North American Indian*, 33.

14. *New North-West*, 27 July 1877.

15. Ibid.

16. Olson, "Nez Perce" (Master's thesis), 92.

17. *New North-West*, 27 July 1877.

18. Report of Secretary of War, 1876–1877, 500–501.

19. McDonald, "Nez Perces" (27 December 1878); Joseph, "An Indian's View," 426.

20. Curtis, *North American Indian*, 33; *The Weekly Missoulian*, 3 August 1877.

21. *New North-West*, 10 August 1877.

22. Cave, "Indian Battle."

23. McWhorter, *Hear Me*, 355.

24. Helena *Daily Herald*, 30 July 1877; Myers, "Settlers," 24; Hakola and Merriam, *Frontier Omnibus*, 375; Helena *Daily Herald*, 31 July 1877.

25. Helena *Daily Herald*, 1 August 1877; ibid., 4 August 1877.

26. C. Barbour to B. Potts, 3 August 1877, in Hakola and Merriam, *Frontier Omnibus*, 377.

27. *New North-West*, 7 September 1877; *The Weekly Missoulian*, 14 September 1877.

28. J. Mills to B. Potts, 8 July 1877, in Hakola and Merriam, *Frontier Omnibus*, 367; *New North-West*, 7 September 1877.

29. Noyes, "Land," 66.

30. Brown, *Flight*, 228.

31. Cave, "Indian Battle."

32. Ibid.

33. Buck, "Story" (manuscript), 26–35. All text quotations attributed to Buck are derived from this source.

34. *New North-West*, 10 August 1877.

35. Helen Addison Howard, *Saga*, 235–36.

36. McDonald, "Nez Perces" (17 January 1879); McWhorter, *Hear Me*, 361. McWhorter claims three horses were left as payment.

37. Clark, *Indian Legends*, 78–79. The ancient tree still survives, with ribbons and ornaments placed there by present-day Nez Perce and Flathead Indians, but sometime in the early 1890s most of the horn disappeared. Historian Lucullus Virgil McWhorter reported that a small portion was still present inside the tree in 1935. According to the indignant historian, a white vandal cut off the sacred horn for the purpose of adorning the wall of a local saloon. Today, the tree stands close to U.S. Highway 93 and is threatened by a road-widening proposal. (McWhorter, *Hear Me*, 364–65; S. McFarland to author, 2 December 1991.)

38. McWhorter, *Hear Me*, 364; McWhorter, *Yellow Wolf*, 108.

39. McWhorter, *Yellow Wolf*, 110. The definition of Iskumtselalik Pah given by Yellow Wolf is ambiguous. Some present-day Nez Perce maintain the modern spelling of Its-kum-tsi-lah-lik-pah is better translated as "the place of the buffalo calf." (W. Halfmoon to author, 7 December 1991.)

40. Portland *Weekly Standard*, 24 August 1877.

41. Howard, *My Life*, 291; Sutherland, *Howard's Campaign*, 24.

42. Howard, *Nez Perce Joseph*, 178.

43. McDonald, "Nez Perces" (21 June 1878); Portland *Weekly Standard*, 24 August 1877.

44. Portland *Weekly Standard*, 24 August 1877.

45. E. Mason to F. Mason, 3 August 1877, "Scrapbooks" (manuscript); Howard, *Nez Perce Joseph*, 182.

46. Howard, *Nez Perce Joseph*, 181.

47. Sutherland, *Howard's Campaign*, 28; E. Mason to F. Mason, 7 August 1877, "Scrapbooks" (manuscript).

48. Howard, *Nez Perce Joseph*, 182.

49. E. Mason to F. Mason, 7 August 1877, "Scrapbooks" (manuscript); Laufe, *Army Doctor's Wife*, 297.

50. Howard, *Nez Perce Joseph*, 188–89 passim.

CHAPTER 8 (pages 155–83)

1. Koury, *Diaries*, 76.

2. Thrapp, *Encyclopedia*, 2:551; *New North-West*, 17 August 1877.

3. Thrapp, *Encyclopedia*, 2:551. Even in defeat, Custer—Gibbon's former student at West Point—had usurped the laurels to be shared between all the commands at the Little Bighorn. Gibbon knew of Custer's proclivity for glory hunting, reporting that he went so far as to warn him before the battle "against being greedy, and with a gay wave of his hand he called back, 'No, I will not,' and rode off after his command." Instead Gibbon's men helped bury hundreds of the Seventh's best and then dawdled away the remainder of the summer without ever engaging the Sioux and Cheyenne. (Koury, *Gibbon*, 23.) Unless otherwise noted, all text quotations attributed to Gibbon may be found in Gibbon, "Battle."

4. McWhorter, *Hear Me*, 363.

5. Gibbon, "Pursuit," 333.

6. Ibid., 334.

7. Woodruff, "Battle of the Big Hole" in *Contributions*, 7:108.

8. Curtis, *North American Indian*, 38.

9. Brady, *Northwestern Fights*, 174.

10. Woodruff, "Battle of the Big Hole," 109; Cave, "Indian Battle"; Beal, *I Will Fight No More*, 126. Although Gibbon's alleged statement appeared in separately authored publications, the source for it may have been the same man—volunteer Thomas Sherrill. If true, there is no other corroborative proof. (J. Whitworth to author, 27 December 1991.)

11. Ruby, "First Account," 3; Wilfong, *Following the Nez Perce Trail*, 182.

12. Alcorn and Alcorn, "Old Nez Perce," 66.

13. McWhorter, *Hear Me*, 376–77.

14. Ibid.

15. McWhorter, *Yellow Wolf*, 137n, 132. Years later, a remorseful Loynes told McWhorter: "When I think of those terrible scenes, wrongs waged against human beings, I say shame! shame! This great Christian government had power to do differently by those truly patriotic people. It is such remembrances which touch my emotions, and I am led to marvel at the term 'civilization.' " (Ibid., 137n.)

16. McDonald, "Nez Perces" (24 January 1879).

17. Loynes, "Battle," 2.

18. McWhorter, *Yellow Wolf*, 136, 132.

19. C. Loynes to L. McWhorter, 19 June 1926, McWhorter Papers.

20. McDonald, "Nez Perces" (24 January 1879).

21. McWhorter, *Hear Me*, 386.

22. McWhorter, *Yellow Wolf*, 123.

23. Ibid., 133.

24. Bradley's death proved a great personal loss to Gibbon, the young lieutenant having commanded the column's Crow scouts throughout the Yellowstone campaign the summer before. It had been Bradley who first discovered the two-hundred-odd stripped and mutilated bodies of Custer's command. The two men also shared a literary flair, Bradley an amateur historian whose poems and prose often brightened the columns of Montana newspapers. Now the man who had "thrilled thousands" with his stirring account of the dead of the Custer battlefield, lamented the *New North-West*, was himself dead, leaving behind a young wife and baby. (*New North-West*, 24 August 1877.)

25. McWhorter, *Hear Me*, 383.

26. McWhorter, *Yellow Wolf*, 117.

27. McDonald, "Nez Perces" (24 January 1879).

28. Years later, Sherrill, who became the first battlefield caretaker, claimed to have found the girl's grave, showing Buck several "locks of her golden hair." Sherrill, some say, was truth-stretching. Still, such rumors stoked the belief that Jennet Manuel, one of the first Idaho victims, was alive. Certainly, the girl's young age would preclude the possibility of having been the mother of six-year-old Maggie Manuel. Who else she may have been, or even if she existed at all outside the imagination of xenophobic whites who believed white women hostages proved the undeniable perfidy of Indians, will never be known. (Cave, "Indian Battle.")

29. McWhorter, *Yellow Wolf*, 137.

30. Ibid., 129.

31. Ibid., 128; *New North-West*, 24 August 1877.

32. McWhorter, *Yellow Wolf*, 130n.

33. Ibid., 138. Nearly a half-century after the war, several surviving warriors returned with historian Lucullus Virgil McWhorter to the Big Hole battlefield. Their memory of where particular warriors fell has subsequently proven quite accurate. During archaeological investigations conducted by the National Park Service in 1991, mushroomed lead bullets (indicating possible body impact) were uncovered within a few feet of where Pahkatos Owyeen is said to have fallen. (W. Halfmoon to author, 15 December 1991.)

34. Evidence that cartridges were used to cauterize wounds is anecdotal. In the 1960s, archaeologist Aubrey Haines found two unfired .45/70 cartridges

with split cases. A 1991 archaeological investigation of the battlefield revealed two split .45/70 cartridges, but these appear to have resulted from firing the rounds in a .50/70 caliber gun. (S. Buchel to author, 20 January.)

35. Woodruff, "Battle of the Big Hole," 112.

36. Wilfong, *Following the Nez Perce Trail*, 187–88.

37. Loynes, "Battle," 2.

38. Volunteer Fred "Dutch" Heldt, Gibbon's messenger to nearby miners in Idaho, became lost for three days. Asked what he ate during that time, the disgruntled man replied, "Fried elk tracks!" (Cave, "Indian Battle.")

39. Helena *Daily Herald*, 11 August 1877.

40. P. Sheridan to Adj. General, 11 August 1877, Records of the U.S. Army, No. 4928–77.

41. McWhorter, *Yellow Wolf*, 156, 159.

42. Brady, *Northwestern Fights*, 184–85.

43. Lieutenant Bailey was certain that he was selected for this onerous task because he had fallen out of favor with Howard. A year earlier, Bailey had admitted that although he wanted to unreservedly accept Christianity, he was having trouble resolving "difficult questions" posed by a strictly literal interpretation of the Bible. Word leaked back to Howard, and what had been a promising relationship suddenly soured after the general expressed his "disappointment" in Bailey's lack of faith. (H. Bailey to L. McWhorter, 7 December 1930, McWhorter Papers.)

44. Howard, *Nez Perce Joseph*, 198.

45. Ibid., 203.

46. Laufe, *Army Doctor's Wife*, 303–4.

47. Wilfong, *Following the Nez Perce Trail*, 191. Bannock scouts may not have been the only ones interested in scalps. In 1925, Private Joseph Sinsel of Butte, Montana, claimed he possessed a Nez Perce scalp from the battle. Said Sinsel, "Soldiers were not supposed to scalp Indians . . . but more than one Indian lost his scalp-lock which afterward appeared in the possession of a soldier." (*Billings Times*, 30 April 1925.)

48. New York *Herald*, 16 August 1877; Laufe, *Army Doctor's Wife*, 302–3.

49. McWhorter, *Yellow Wolf*, 159; McDonald, "Nez Perces" (24 January 1879); Joseph, "An Indian's View," 427.

50. By avoiding main trails and frequently going without food for days, Wahlitits's cousin, seventeen-year-old Eloosykasit—known to whites as John Pinkham—eventually led five younger children who were also battle refugees back to Idaho. All were sent to Indian Territory. Wahlitits's rifle,

removed from his dead wife's hands, is still in the Pinkham family's possession. (A. Pinkham to author, 18 December 1991.)

51. *The Weekly Missoulian*, 17 August 1877; Report of Secretary of War, 1876–1877, 505.

52. New York *Herald*, 15 August 1877.

53. Connell, *Son*, 132.

54. Howard, *Nez Perce Joseph*, 211; Catlin, "Battle" (manuscript), 14.

55. E. Mason to F. Mason, 13 August 1877, "Scrapbooks" (manuscript); McWhorter, *Hear Me*, 401; Buck, "Story," 51.

56. Lewiston *Teller*, 8 September 1877; *New North-West*, 24 August 1877.

57. Garcia, *Tough Trip*, 276.

58. Ibid.

CHAPTER 9 (pages 185–212)

1. Hutton, *Phil Sheridan*, 180.

2. Connell, *Son*, 180; Nevin, *The Soldiers*, 161.

3. Connell, *Son*, 180; W. Sherman to P. Sheridan, 15 October 1868, *Senate Executive Documents*, 40th Cong. Although their ruthless policies resulted in untold Indian deaths far beyond the battlefield, Sherman and Sheridan have been unfairly accused of advocating genocide of all Native Americans. Both men were pragmatists, convinced there was a place in American soci- ety for Indians who submissively accepted the values of the conquering race. By 1878, when it appeared Indian rebellion had virtually ended, Sher- idan candidly observed: "We took away their country and their means of support, broke up their mode of living, their habits of life, introduced disease and decay among them, and it was for this and against this they made war. Could any one expect less?" This was not a mea culpa; neither man ever doubted the march of white Christian civilization across the fron- tier. (Report of Secretary of War, 1878, 1:36.)

4. P. Sheridan to A. Terry, 13 August 1877, *Senate Executive Documents*, "Claims," 67; ibid., 18 August 1877, 69.

5. *Butte Miner*, 14 August 1877.

6. *New North-West*, 24 August 1877; Helena *Daily Herald*, 19 October 1877.

7. *New North-West*, 24 August 1877.

8. Brown, *Flight*, 270.

9. Portland *Weekly Standard*, 7 September 1877; *New North-West*, 17 Au- gust 1877.

10. *The Weekly Missoulian,* 24 August 1877; *New North-West,* 24 August 1877.

11. *New North-West,* 24 August 1877.

12. *The Weekly Missoulian,* 5 October 1877.

13. Redington, "Scouting," 56. Articles written after the war by Redington —who bore the improbable middle name of "Watermelon"—always appeared under the byline "J. W. Redington." He claimed to be a special correspondent during the war for the *Salt Lake Tribune,* but no articles appear under his name.

14. McWhorter, *Yellow Wolf,* 164.

15. McWhorter, *Hear Me,* 408.

16. Howard, *Nez Perce Joseph,* 214.

17. O. Howard to I. McDowell, 14 August 1877, *Senate Executive Documents,* "Claims," 60–61.

18. Brown, *Flight,* 278.

19. E. Mason to F. Mason, 16 August 1877, "Scrapbooks" (manuscript); Howard, *Nez Perce Joseph,* 215; *New North-West,* 24 August 1877.

20. Howard, *Nez Perce Joseph,* 215–16.

21. *New North-West,* 24 August 1877.

22. Sutherland, *Howard's Campaign,* 53.

23. White, *Hostiles,* 176.

24. Connell, *Son,* 176; White, *Hostiles,* 43.

25. Crowder, *Tendoy,* 52.

26. *Idaho Recorder,* 16 May 1907.

27. Crowder, *Tendoy,* 90.

28. Brown, *Flight,* 282.

29. Ibid., 283.

30. Ibid., 284.

31. McWhorter, *Yellow Wolf,* 165.

32. Brown, *Flight,* 285.

33. Report of Secretary of War, 1876–1877, 610–11.

34. Howard, *Nez Perce Joseph,* 219; E. Mason to F. Mason, 18 August 1877, "Scrapbooks" (manuscript). Howard's ambivalence over whether or not to take citizens' advice plagued his staff throughout the war, revealed Lieutenant Harry Bailey. "In one situation the citizens had caused the General to change his mind or plans often and frequently, so that [a] temporary staff officer was exasperated into saying he was 'acting like a chicken with its head cut off.' The remark got to his ears, and the staff officer was quickly placed under arrest and we friends of the officer were worried."

Bailey failed to identify the man or exactly when this happened, but he revealed that the officer was released a few days later. (H. Bailey to L. McWhorter, 7 December 1930, McWhorter Papers.)

35. Howard, *Nez Perce Joseph,* 221.

36. Brown, *Flight,* 287.

37. Howard, *My Life,* 292–93.

38. Davison, "A Century Ago," 11–12; Virginia City *Madisonian,* 25 August 1877.

39. Howard, *Nez Perce Joseph,* 224.

40. Ibid., 225.

41. McWhorter, *Hear Me,* 417.

42. Brady, *Northwestern Fights,* 194.

43. McWhorter, *Yellow Wolf,* 167.

44. Brady, *Northwestern Fights,* 195; McWhorter, *Yellow Wolf,* 168.

45. Howard, *Nez Perce Joseph,* 226.

46. Virginia City *Madisonian,* 25 August 1877; ibid., 1 September 1877.

47. Brady, *Northwestern Fights,* 195.

48. Ibid., 196.

49. Ibid.

50. McWhorter, *Hear Me,* 424.

51. Brady, *Northwestern Fights,* 200.

52. Howard, *Nez Perce Joseph,* 229.

CHAPTER 10 (pages 213–43)

1. Baird, "Indian Campaigns," 364.

2. San Francisco *Chronicle,* 3 September 1877.

3. Buck, "Story," 64.

4. New York *Herald,* 10 September 1877.

5. Howard, *Nez Perce Joseph,* 231; Fisher, "Journal of S. G. Fisher," 270.

6. Howard, *Nez Perce Joseph,* 232; Buck, "Story," 66.

7. Howard, *Nez Perce Joseph,* 232.

8. Brown, *Flight,* 296. During the 1878 Bannock outbreak, Twelfth Infantryman Emanuel Rogue recalled, "One day a white scout brought in the head of an Indian in a gunny sack; he claimed it was the head of Buffalo Horn, the Indian chief." (Rickey, *Forty Miles,* 315.)

9. Howard, *Nez Perce Joseph,* 234.

10. Ibid.; E. Mason to F. Mason, 26 August 1877, "Scrapbooks" (manuscript); McWhorter, *Hear Me,* 430.

11. New York *Herald,* 23 August 1877.

12. Laufe, *Army Doctor's Wife*, 307.

13. E. Mason to F. Mason, 24 August 1877, "Scrapbooks" (manuscript).

14. Howard, *Nez Perce Joseph*, 235.

15. J. Kelton to O. Howard, 17 August 1877, *Senate Executive Documents,* "Claims," 61.

16. O. Howard to J. Kelton, 24 August 1877, *Senate Executive Documents,* "Claims," 66.

17. Portland *Weekly Standard,* 7 September 1877.

18. Williams, *Lincoln,* 19–23 passim.

19. Brown, *Flight,* 304–5.

20. The entire text of this telegram and the ones immediately following between Sherman, Howard, and Sheridan are from Report of Secretary of War, 1876–1877, 13.

21. Howard, *Nez Perce Joseph,* 236.

22. San Francisco *Chronicle,* 3 September 1877.

23. Howard, *Nez Perce Joseph,* 237; E. Mason to F. Mason, 24 August 1877, "Scrapbooks" (manuscript).

24. *New North-West,* 14 September 1877. All text quotations attributed to Shively are from this source.

25. Cowan, "Trip," 165–87. Unless otherwise noted, all quotations concerning the Radersburg party are from this source. Cowan places this encounter with Sherman on August 23, but the general had returned to Helena by August 18.

26. During his Yellowstone trip, Sherman was accompanied by his son, two other officers, three drivers, one packer, and only four soldiers. The trip held little danger, he had written the Secretary of War at the outset, for "hostile Indians rarely resort to the Park, a poor region for game and to their superstitious mind associated with hell by reason of the geysers and hot springs." This was not the first time Sherman misread the intentions of Indians. In 1871, forgoing an armed escort in Texas, he narrowly escaped death at the hands of one hundred Kiowa warriors waiting in ambush. A spiritual leader had prophesied there would be two parties coming down the road, one of a few soldiers, another of many wagons. The warriors let Sherman's party pass, then attacked and destroyed a wagon train, killing seven of the dozen teamsters. The near-miss with the Nez Perce in Yellowstone prompted historian Francis Haines to quip: "Do you suppose they could have traded him for the Wallowa?" More likely, not knowing Sherman's identity but observing the soldiers, the Nez Perce would have killed the entire party. (Haines, *Red Eagles,* 287.)

27. McWhorter, *Yellow Wolf*, 174.

28. Guie and McWhorter, *Adventures*, 229.

29. Ibid., 317.

30. McWhorter, *Yellow Wolf*, 174.

31. Guie and McWhorter, *Adventures*, 135.

32. Ibid., 221.

33. E. Mason to F. Mason, 28 August 1877, "Scrapbooks" (manuscript).

34. Guie and McWhorter, *Adventures*, 208–209.

35. Ibid., 214.

36. Ibid., 215.

37. E. Mason to F. Mason, 30 August 1877, "Scrapbooks" (manuscript).

38. Guie and McWhorter, *Adventures*, 228.

39. Quotations attributed to the Helena party are derived from the following: Weikert, "Journal," 153–74; Helena *Daily Herald*, 27 and 31 August 1877; Bozeman *Times*, 30 August and 20 September 1877.

40. Scott, *Memories*, 62. Stone was apparently so overcome with relief upon discovering Doane's command that he loudly and repeatedly thanked God for his deliverance, refusing to stop even when soldiers complained they could not sleep. (Bonney and Bonney, *Battle Drums*, 82.)

41. McWhorter, *Yellow Wolf*, 177.

42. Report of Secretary of War, 1876–1877, 508.

43. Redington, "Scouting," 67.

44. Report of Secretary of War, 1876–1877, 620.

45. For a more extensive though speculative discussion of possible Nez Perce routes through Yellowstone Park, see Lang, "Where Did the Nez Perce Go"; and Goodenough, "Lost."

46. Fisher, "Journal," 275.

47. Ibid.

48. Ibid.

CHAPTER 11 (pages 245–70)

1. Marquis, *Memoirs*, 46. Thirty-seven years old in 1877, Doane was a uniquely qualified officer. In 1858, he had been denied a West Point appointment because of his outspoken abolitionist sentiment. Three years later, as valedictorian of the first graduating class of California's University of the Pacific, Doane delivered his valedictory in both English and Latin. After distinguished service during the Civil War, he drew up elaborate plans to explore the Green and Colorado rivers, but due to his low rank, Congress denied his petition. When John Wesley Powell succeeded a few

years later, Doane contended that Powell pirated his plans, winning national recognition that was rightfully his. In the early 1870s, Doane proposed to explore the Nile River and locate its source but never raised the necessary funds (although Henry M. Stanley utilized a similar plan, Doane never accused him of theft). In 1876, it was Doane who devised the litters used to transport the wounded from the Little Bighorn battlefield to the waiting steamboat *Far West*. In 1880, Doane commanded the ill-prepared Howgate Expedition to the Arctic, spending much of his time violently seasick. Promoted to captain four years later, he died of a heart attack in 1892. (Gustavus C. Doane, Doane Papers.)

2. Like Doane, Lieutenant Carlo Camilius DeRudio (a.k.a. Charles C. DeRudio) was no shrinking violet. DeRudio's life up to 1877 had been the stuff of novels. Born a European nobleman, he fell in with revolutionaries. Along with two other men, he was convicted in 1858 of attempting to assassinate Emperor Louis Napoleon. All were sentenced to lose their heads to Dr. Guillotin's invention, but at the last possible moment, due to the pleadings of his wife, DeRudio's sentence was commuted to life imprisonment on Devil's Island in French Guiana. DeRudio escaped, hollowed out a log, sailed to British Guiana, and eventually made his way back to England. There he attempted to earn money lecturing and publishing an account of his adventures, but no one was interested. In 1864, he emigrated to the United States and joined the army, accepting a commission with the Second United States Colored Troops, a position considered beneath most whites. The army found out about his escapades in Paris and discharged him in 1867, but somehow he reappeared two years later in Custer's Seventh. All of DeRudio's Company E perished at the Little Bighorn but the lieutenant, who had been temporarily transferred to Company A, fighting with Reno and Benteen and surviving. Some of his men did not think much of him, ridiculing his claimed ancestry, calling him Count No Account. He may have been somewhat of a dandy. The lieutenant was the only man who wore his sword into that fateful battle, an anachronistic weapon only considered useful on the parade field by virtually all officers. (Mills, *Charles C. DeRudio;* Connell, *Son*, 384–85.)

3. Scott, *Memories*, 60.

4. Ibid.; Guie and McWhorter, *Adventures*, 200.

5. Scott, *Memories*, 68.

6. W. Sherman to O. Howard, 29 August 1877, Howard Papers.

7. Howard, *My Life*, 295; Carpenter, *Sword*, 258; San Francisco *Chronicle*, 3 October 1877.

8. Buck, "Story," 87.

9. Howard, *Nez Perce Joseph*, 24.

10. Wilfong, *Following the Nez Perce Trail*, 248.

11. San Francisco *Chronicle*, 17 September 1877.

12. E. Mason to F. Mason, 3 September 1877, "Scrapbooks" (manuscript).

13. Howard, *Nez Perce Joseph*, 248; San Francisco *Chronicle*, 17 September 1877.

14. Howard, *Nez Perce Joseph*, 253; O. Howard to J. Kelton, 8 September 1877, *Senate Executive Documents*, "Claims," 71.

15. Fisher, "Journal," 276.

16. Ibid., 276–77; Portland *Weekly Standard*, 12 October 1877.

17. Fisher, "Journal," 277.

18. Upon hearing a monument was to be erected to commemorate Custer, Sturgis blasted his dead rival in a letter to the *New York Times:* "If a monument is to be erected to General Custer for God's sake let them hide it in some dark valley, or veil it, or put it anywhere the bleeding hearts of the widows, orphans, fathers and mothers of the men so uselessly sacrificed to Custer's ambition can never be wrung at the sight of it." The New York *Herald* published an article soon afterward ridiculing Sturgis as an aged, corpulent officer hiding behind a desk while the remainder of the Seventh valiantly fought Indians. (Millbrook, "Monument," 18–33.)

19. Report of Secretary of War, 1876–1877, 510.

20. Ibid.

21. McWhorter, *Yellow Wolf*, 182.

22. Brady, *Northwestern Fights*, 208; Report of Secretary of War, 1876–1877, 510.

23. Fisher, "Journal," 277. Today this ridge along the Clarks Fork Canyon is known as Bald Ridge. Until recently, most authorities believed the Nez Perce descended Dead Indian Hill via Dead Indian Gulch, a steep and heavily timbered drainage that drops 3,400 feet before debouching into the Clarks Fork River some five miles above the canyon mouth. However, subsequent investigation by Montana's Stuart Conner and associates showed that the gulch ends abruptly in a cliff above the river, an insurmountable obstacle that is believed to have changed little in intervening years. In addition, S. G. Fisher claimed "we struck Clarks Fork about two miles below where it comes out of the canyon." Perhaps the strongest evidence in favor of the ridge route is the official campaign map drawn in 1877 by Howard's aide, Lieutenant Robert Fletcher, indicating the route was down Bald Ridge, not the canyon. (S. Connor to author, 14 August

1991; a copy of Fisher's original journal resides at the Idaho Historical Society, Boise, Idaho.)

24. Howard, *Nez Perce Joseph*, 255; San Francisco *Chronicle*, 3 October 1877; Brady, *Northwestern Fights*, 213.

25. E. Mason to F. Mason, 11 September 1877, "Scrapbooks" (manuscript).

26. New York *Herald*, 1 October 1877.

27. Howard, *Nez Perce Joseph*, 255.

28. Ibid., 256; Brady, *Northwestern Fights*, 214.

29. Curtis, *North American Indian*, 167.

30. McWhorter, *Yellow Wolf*, 184.

31. Ibid.

32. Curtis, *North American Indian*, 167.

33. W. Halfmoon to author, 27 December 1991; Curtis, *North American Indian*, 163; Bradley, *March*, 84.

34. Koury, *Gibbon*, 20.

35. Connell, *Son*, 100.

36. Marquis, *Memoirs*, 97.

37. Laufe, *Army Doctor's Wife*, 311; Brady, *Northwestern Fights*, 215.

38. O. Howard to N. Miles, 12 September 1877, in Report of Secretary of War, 1876–1877, 623.

39. Brady, *Northwestern Fights*, 215.

40. Redington, "Scouting," 59–61. All text quotations attributed to Redington are from this source.

41. Fisher, "Journal," 279–81. The following text quotations attributed to Fisher are from this source.

42. Carroll, *Letters*, 204.

43. Brady, *Northwestern Fights*, 220.

44. Ibid., 221; McWhorter, *Yellow Wolf*, 187.

45. Brady, *Northwestern Fights*, 221.

46. Laufe, *Army Doctor's Wife*, 312.

CHAPTER 12 (pages 271–87)

1. Thornton, *American Indian Holocaust*, 52; Andrews, "Buffalo Hunt," 453–54; Hutton, *Phil Sheridan*, 120.

2. McHugh, *Time*, 284.

3. Ibid., 285. In 1881, when some congressional legislators proposed protecting what remained of the northern herd, Sheridan objected. "If I could learn that every buffalo in the northern herd were killed I would be glad," he wrote. "The destruction of this herd would do more to keep Indians

quiet than anything else that could happen. Since the destruction of the southern herd, which formerly roamed from Texas to the Platte, the Indians in that section have given us no trouble." (Hutton, *Phil Sheridan*, 246.)

4. Most Americans today believe the bison met its ruin at the hands of unscrupulous white market hunters. In Montana, however, before whites took up hunting in force, Indians themselves led the way. Lieutenant Gustavus Doane investigated the Judith Basin in 1873, predicting that "in five years more, they [buffalo] will probably cease to be the dependence of the Indians for food." The truth, argued the lieutenant, "is that the Indians kill off the cows only for robes," and the resulting disproportionate number of bulls to cows "at once tells the story of who kills the buffalo, it being well known that white hunters shoot cows, bulls and calves indiscriminately." Because Doane estimated that for every three cows killed only one proved a marketable robe, he calculated the number of robes represented an attrition of 135,000 cows each year, most of which were left to rot on the prairie. Doane's prophecy that buffalo would soon cease to be the mainstay of Indian subsistence was remarkably accurate. Before the end of the decade, General Sherman reported that Indians were traveling as far as four hundred miles on buffalo hunting forays, often returning empty-handed. The lieutenant, however, failed to foresee the thousands of white hunters who soon took over the slaughter, rendering irrelevant his argument that Indians themselves would bring about the demise of the great herds. (Doane, "1874 Judith Basin Survey Report," Doane Papers.)

5. Linderman, *Pretty-Shield*, 250.

6. Redington, "Scouting," 62.

7. Report of Secretary of War, 1876–1877, 626.

8. Scott, *Memories*, 80.

9. N. Miles to O. Howard, 17 September 1877, Report of Secretary of War, 1876–1877, 627–28.

10. San Francisco *Chronicle*, 3 October 1877.

11. Howard, *Nez Perce Joseph*, 264.

12. E. Mason to F. Mason, 28 September 1877, "Scrapbooks" (manuscript).

13. Howard, *Nez Perce Joseph*, 264.

14. W. Moelchert to D. Hilger, letter, 13 November 1927 (manuscript).

15. *Fort Benton Record*, 28 September 1877.

16. Ibid., 5 October 1877.

17. Ibid.

18. Some seventy years before, Lewis and Clark had rejected the Hidatsa name for this meandering stream, lyrically translated as "The River That

Scolds at All Others." Instead, these pragmatic Anglos thought it "about the colour of a cup of tea with the admixture of a tablespoon of milk." (Lavender, *Way*, 197.)

19. McWhorter, *Hear Me*, 473.

20. Hutton, *Soldiers West*, 222. The sketch of Miles is primarily drawn from Johnson, *Unregimented General*.

21. Johnson, *Unregimented General*, 12.

22. Miles's wife, Mary, was the daughter of Sherman's brother, Senator John Sherman, the influential chairman of the Military Affairs Committee.

23. Miles, *Serving the Republic*, 118, 115, 199.

24. Johnson, *Unregimented General*, 110. In early September 1877, Crazy Horse purportedly met his death due to the Nez Perce War. In a meeting with General Crook, interpreter Frank Grouard translated Crazy Horse's reply to Crook's request to scout against the Nez Perce as he would ride *against the whites*, instead of riding to *assist the whites*. Grouard apparently had a grudge against the Sioux chieftain, or perhaps he legitimately misinterpreted his words. Regardless, Crook had Crazy Horse arrested. During the struggle that ensued, a soldier bayoneted the warrior in the stomach and he died the next day. (Connell, *Son*, 73.)

25. Johnson, *Unregimented General*, 162. After the war, Miles wrote Sherman that "I cannot but regard your unfavorable decision and action [not to grant Miles a department command] the severest injury that has been done me by any official or friend." Sherman shot back a terse reply warning Miles that he was making "a fatal mistake" should he continue to so shamelessly importune for advancement (ibid., 216). Chastened, Miles apologized. Shortly afterward, Miles made headlines by capturing Geronimo, the Chiricahua Apache leader who took up arms when the government closed his people's reservation, the same one Howard had failed to secure in writing in his 1872 verbal treaty with Cochise. In 1889, however, when Miles heard a rumor that President Harrison was passing him over for promotion due to his "troublesome" reputation, he demanded an interview in which he convinced the president he was the best qualified candidate. In 1895, Miles became Commanding General of the Army and six years later was awarded a lieutenant-generalcy, the same rank that only Sherman and Sheridan had held before him. It was not long before he collided with Theodore Roosevelt, who called Miles a "brave peacock" when he objected to Roosevelt's reorganization of the army, replacing the position of commander with a general staff. Miles soon reached mandatory retirement age and quietly left the army, snubbed by Roosevelt, who refused to attend his

retirement ceremony. In 1914, at the age of seventy-five, Miles offered his services for the coming world war, which the Secretary of War politely refused. Miles collapsed and died suddenly in 1925 in Washington, D.C., while attending the Ringling Brothers Circus. He was standing at attention, saluting, as the band played the national anthem.

26. Miles, *Personal Recollections*, 261–62.

27. Remsen (Henry Remsen Tilton), "After the Nez Perces," 403–4. Tilton used his middle name as a byline.

28. Ibid.

CHAPTER 13 (pages 289–310)

1. McWhorter, *Yellow Wolf*, 205.

2. Ibid.

3. Ibid.

4. McWhorter, *Hear Me*, 483–84.

5. McWhorter, *Yellow Wolf*, 207.

6. Joseph, "An Indian's View," 428.

7. Curtis, *North American Indian*, 171.

8. Ruby, "First Account," 3.

9. Mulford, *Fighting Indians*, 122.

10. Godfrey Papers. All text quotations attributed to Godfrey are from this source.

11. Baldwin, *Memoirs*, 191–92; Baird, "Indian Campaigns," 364.

12. Titus, "Last Stand," 149.

13. Portland *Weekly Standard*, 9 November 1877.

14. Rickey, *Forty Miles*, 290.

15. Remsen, "After the Nez Perces," 403–4.

16. McWhorter, *Yellow Wolf*, 211–12 passim. According to one recent source, Poker Joe escaped to Canada. (C. Rankin to author, 29 December 1994.)

17. Report of Secretary of War, 1876–1877, 514–15, 512.

18. Interview with Black Eagle, McWhorter Papers; Walsh in New York *Herald*, 3 December 1877; McDonald in McWhorter, *Hear Me*, 521. Yellow Bull claimed that "when the soldiers charged, about 100 of our people caught horses and got away." Later, they were joined by "about 50" others who managed to escape with White Bird. (Interview with Yellow Bull, Camp Interviews.)

19. Scott, *Memories*, 76–77.

20. Johnson, *Unregimented General*, 207.

21. Alcorn and Alcorn, "Old Nez Perce," 71.

22. Letter of Father J. B. Genin in *Collections of the State*, 1:276.

23. Ibid., 275–76.

24. Turner, *Northwest Mounted Police*, 340–41.

25. McWhorter, *Hear Me*, 511.

26. Ibid., 513–14.

27. Some Nez Perce accounts claim Looking Glass died the first day of battle (September 30), others the last (October 5). Virtually no two statements precisely agree, but both Tom Hill and Yellow Bull place the chief's death sometime before the first truce. Chronological inconsistencies in this final battle afflicted not only the Nez Perce; white accounts are equally garbled and uncorroborated, by far the worst of any battle of the entire conflict. One can only conclude that after the initial attack, few events occurred during the subsequent five-day siege to distinguish one dreary day from the next.

28. Remsen, "After the Nez Perces," 403–4.

29. Report of Secretary of War, 1876–1877, 528.

30. Johnson, *Unregimented General*, 203.

31. Snyder, Diary, 3 October 1877.

32. Report of Secretary of War, 1876–1877, 630.

33. The exact content of Joseph's imputed speech has been variously reported. This version appeared a month following the final battle in *Harper's Weekly* (17 November 1877), an unattributed article for which C. E. S. Wood is believed to have been the source (Josephy, *Nez Perce Indians*, 630–31n). Howard's official report published in December 1877 contains an identical version (Report of Secretary of War, 1876–1877, 630).

34. In May 1884, Wood wrote an article for *Century Magazine* that echoes Howard's official report, crediting "Captain" John with delivering Joseph's message. Later, Wood claimed the article contained "editing mistakes" and that Joseph actually spoke these words (with minor variation) himself at his surrender. One problem with Wood's revision was that if Joseph gave this speech in person, no one else present saw fit to mention the fact. Nevertheless, this more noble rendering was favored by historians (and enshrined in a famous painting by Frederick Remington) until nearly a century after the war when Mark Brown—in the best tradition of historical sleuthing—discovered a handwritten draft of Howard's official report written in November 1877. The passage in question was authored by none other than his trusted aide Lieutenant Wood. Unfortunately for Wood, the draft matches the report with Joseph's words relayed by "Captain" John, not Joseph himself. This implies that after all others who had participated in the surrender were no longer alive, Wood—who lived into his nineties to become a well-

respected lawyer, poet, supporter of women's suffrage, personal friend of Chief Joseph, and fierce critic of the government's treatment of Indians— altered the circumstances of the surrender, thereby casting both Joseph and himself in more dramatic roles. (Draft of Howard's report in Fort Dalles Collection, FD 869, Wood Papers.)

35. Bailey, *River*, 180.

36. Joseph, "An Indian's View," 429.

37. C. Wood to L. McWhorter, 28 November 1946, Wood Papers.

38. McWhorter, *Hear Me*, 497–98.

39. Howard, *Nez Perce Joseph*, 299.

40. Report of Secretary of War, 1876–1877, 630.

41. Joseph, "An Indian's View," 429. Both Yellow Bull and White Feather claimed that White Bird escaped with no more than fifty followers on the night of October 3, 1877. (Camp Interviews.)

42. *Senate Executive Documents*, 45th Cong., 40.

CHAPTER 14 (pages 311–37)

1. Report of Secretary of War, 1876–1877, 15, 529.

2. The *New York Times*, 15 October 1877.

3. O. Howard to N. Miles, 7 October 1877, in Report of Secretary of War, 1876–1877, 631, 633.

4. N. Miles to A. Terry, 5 October 1877, *Senate Executive Documents*, "Claims," 74–75.

5. C. E. S. Wood, "The Pursuit and Capture of Chief Joseph" in Fee, *Chief Joseph*, 333–34; O. Howard to W. Sherman, 14 March 1877, Howard Papers.

6. Chicago *Tribune*, 25 October 1877. The actual distance was approximately 1,200 miles.

7. O. Howard to P. Sheridan, 25 October 1877, Records of the U.S. Army, No. 7113–77; Chicago *Times*, 26 October 1877.

8. A. Terry to Adj. General, Div. of the Missouri, 14 December 1877, Records of the U.S. Army, No. 8076–77.

9. O. Howard to Adj. General, 28 January 1878, Records of the U.S. Army, No. 1233–78.

10. Howard, *Nez Perce Joseph*, 271.

11. Miles, *Personal Recollections*, 278–79.

12. Nelson Miles, undated note, Records of the U.S. Army, No. 5386–87.

13. Scott, *Memories*, 83–84.

14. Bond, *Flatboating*, 19.

15. Bismarck *Tri-Weekly Tribune,* 17 June 1876.

16. Ibid., 23 November 1877.

17. Report of Secretary of War, 1876–1877, 15.

18. C. Wood to O. Howard, 16 November 1877, Howard Papers.

19. N. Miles to O. Howard, 8 January 1878, Howard Papers. Despite his concern over what had happened to the Nez Perce, Miles could not help inquiring about a rumor concerning Howard's retirement. "Please let me know if there is any prospect of your doing so, as it would undoubtedly be greatly to my advantage at the present time."

20. W. Sherman to O. Howard, 12 December 1877, Howard Papers.

21. W. Sherman to P. Sheridan, 31 August 1877, Records of the U.S. Army, No. 5558–77; W. Sherman to E. Townsend, 10 October 1877, Records of the U.S. Army, No. 6286–77.

22. E. Watkins to J. Smith, 3 September 1877, Records of the U.S. Army, No. 6170–77.

23. J. Huston to C. Devens, 21 December 1877, Records of the U.S. Army, No. 6062–77.

24. P. Sheridan to W. Sherman, 16 November 1877, Records of the U.S. Army, No. 7295–77.

25. Report of Commissioner of Indian Affairs, 1878, 464.

26. *The Council Fire,* August 1878, 125.

27. Report of Secretary of Interior, 1876–1877, vi.

28. Joseph, "An Indian's View," 431; Bozeman *Avant Courier,* 20 December 1877.

29. Report of Commissioner of Indian Affairs, 1878, 464.

30. Ibid., 465.

31. Joseph, "An Indian's View," 431.

32. Fahey, *Flathead Indians,* 203; McWhorter, *Hear Me,* 524; G. Kush to author, 6 June 1994.

33. Chapman was in trouble with both the government and the Nez Perce. After returning from Washington in January, the interpreter convinced the bands he could arrange their return to the Northwest for two hundred dollars. The Nez Perce scraped together what they could—Joseph offered ten dollars and Yellow Bull five—while some sold their blankets and remaining personal possessions to raise the money. Finally, the agent discovered Chapman's ruse and put an end to his lucrative endeavor. (Clark, "Nez Perces," 218–19.)

34. Joseph, "An Indian's View," 432–33. Lucullus Virgil McWhorter doubted some of the facts concerning certain events of the war attributed to Joseph in the article, maintaining that the Nez Perce he knew never

generalized or talked about things in which they were not personally involved. (McWhorter, *Hear Me*, 502–3n.)

35. Report of Commissioner of Indian Affairs, 1880, 207.

36. *Council Fire*, October 1879.

37. Joseph to O. Howard, 30 June 1880, Howard Papers.

38. O. Howard to Joseph, 20 July 1880, Howard Papers.

39. Report of Commissioner of Indian Affairs, 1880, 207; McWhorter, *Yellow Wolf*, 289.

40. Josephy, *Nez Perce Country*, 154.

41. Report of Commissioner of Indian Affairs, 1881, 152; ibid., 1882, 52.

42. Later in life, Wood became a poet of some renown, perhaps best acclaimed for *The Poet in the Desert*. At least one verse of the long experimental work has been interpreted as reflecting Wood's remorse about the Nez Perce war:

> We swept like fire over the smoke-browned tee-pees;
> Their conical tops peering above the willows.
> We frightened the air with crackle of rifles,
> Women's shrieks, children's screams,
> Shrill yells of savages;
> Curses of Christians.
> The rifles chuckled continually.
> A poor people who asked nothing but freedom,
> Butchered in the dark.

43. Lewiston *Teller*, 7 June 1878.

44. Report of Commissioner of Indian Affairs, 1884, 113, 114. John Monteith died in 1879, his position filled in 1882 by his brother Charles, formerly the agency clerk.

45. Ibid., 133.

46. Not included in this estimate are the number of children who died after being born since the Bear Paw surrender. A visiting doctor reported counting the graves of one hundred children at the Ponca Reservation alone. (Beal, *I Will Fight No More*, 320.)

47. Report of Commissioner of Indian Affairs, 1885, 297, 299. Not all exiles who returned to Lapwai became Christians. Huishuis Kute and several others later moved to the Colville Reservation.

48. Report of Commissioner of Indian Affairs, 1886, 185–86.

49. In 1889, Commissioner of Indian Affairs T. J. Morgan began imple-

menting the General Allotment Act of 1887, perhaps the most egregious law ever passed by Congress against Native Americans. Morgan stated that Indians could not escape civilization "and must either conform to it or be crushed by it." In a final effort to coerce them to adapt to "white man's ways," each head of family was given a farmland allotment. Whatever reservation land remained was purchased by the government (at a price it named); most of it then opened to white settlement. In subsequent amendments, allotments were allowed to be sold, resulting in even greater loss as individual Indians—many still unable to speak English and desperately impoverished—sold their only remaining possession. Of the 138 million acres that legally belonged to Indians in 1887, only 51 million acres remained in their possession by 1981.

The Nez Perce in Idaho have suffered more than most. Once the act was implemented, disease and poverty continued to reduce their population until it reached an all-time low of 1,400 in about 1900. Loss of cultural pride and self-esteem contributed to this general dissipation, evidenced by signs in nearby Lewiston store windows announcing "No Dogs or Indians Allowed." During this nadir for the Nez Perce, the government seized 542,000 acres at a token payment of three dollars per acre, opening most of the reservation to settlement and leaving 243,000 acres in Indian hands. Over the years this acreage has dribbled away; today a total of some 2,900 Nez Perce (1,900 residing on the reservation) own about 80,000 acres, only one percent of the land they understood was guaranteed them in 1855. Non-Indians living within the reservation outnumber Nez Perce eight-to-one. (Slickpoo, *Nonn Nee-Me-Poo*, 281; W. Halfmoon to author, 15 December 1991.)

50. McWhorter, *Yellow Wolf*, 290.

51. Report of Commissioner of Indian Affairs, 1897, 289–90.

52. *New York Sun*, 24 September 1904.

53. Johnson, *Unregimented General*, 278. Sitting Bull returned to the United States from Canada on July 20, 1881, most of his original followers having disbanded and drifted back across the border years earlier as buffalo became increasingly scarce. Handing his rifle to his six-year-old son to give to the U.S. Army major who met him near the boundary, the chief purportedly made a short speech, saying that he wished to be remembered as the last of his tribe to surrender his weapon. The government imprisoned him for two years, and after a tour with Buffalo Bill's Wild West Show, he settled on the Sioux Reservation. In 1889, McLaughlin—then head of the Standing Rock agency—successfully engineered an Indian vote to sell a

huge amount of reservation land to whites. He was accused later by Indians of trickery and deceit. Asked how the Sioux felt about the vote, Sitting Bull is said to have bitterly replied, "There are no Indians left now but me." Five years later, McLaughlin began to fear the old Hunkpapa chief was fomenting rebellion and ordered his arrest. On December 15, 1890, Sitting Bull was shot in the chest by tribal police while resisting arrest, one account claiming he was then scalped and his face battered into jelly with a plank. Two weeks later came the slaughter at Wounded Knee. (Rosenberg and Rosenberg, "There Are No Indians," 18–23.)

54. McLaughlin, *My Friend*, 344–46 passim.

55. Ibid., 366.

56. Report of Commissioner of Indian Affairs, 1898, 298; ibid., 1900, 394.

57. Morris, *Rise*, 794.

58. "Joseph Continues His Fight," *Seattle Times*, 20 November 1903; also in Gidley, *Kopet*, 37–38.

Bibliography

MANUSCRIPTS

Blandau, Richard L. "Nez Perces on the Colville Reservation: An Investigation of the Inception and Maintenance of a Socio-Cultural Isolate, 1885–1968." Master's thesis, Department of Anthropology, Washington State University, 1972.

Buck, Henry. "The Story of the Nez Perce Indian Campaign During Summer 1877." Small Collection 492. Montana Historical Society, Helena.

Camp, Walter. Interviews. Brigham Young University, Provo, Utah.

Catlin, John B. "The Battle of the Bighole." Montana Historical Society, Helena.

Cruickshank, Alexander. "The Birch Creek Massacre." Montana Historical Society, Helena.

Doane, Gustavus C. Papers. Montana State University, Bozeman.

Fisher, Stanton G. Journal. Idaho Historical Society, Boise.

Fort Dalles Collection. Documents of the Headquarters of the Department of the Columbia. The Huntington Library, San Marino, California.

Godfrey, Edward Settle. Papers and Correspondence, 1863–1933. Library of Congress, Washington, D.C.

Howard, Oliver Otis. Papers and Correspondence. Bowdoin College, Brunswick, Maine.

McCarthy, Michael. Diary and Papers of Michael McCarthy. Library of Congress, Washington, D.C.

McWhorter, Lucullus Virgil. Papers and Correspondence. Washington State University, Pullman.

Mason, Edwin Cooley. "Scrapbooks, 1877–1878." Microfilm Collection 80. Montana Historical Society, Helena.

Moelchert, William. Letter to David Hilger, 13 November 1927. Montana Historical Society, Helena.

Monteith, John B. Correspondence sent from Lapwai Indian Agency, 1872–1876. Idaho Historical Society Library, Boise.

Olson, Rolf Y. "The Nez Perce, the Montana Press, and the War of 1877." Master's thesis, University of Montana, Missoula, 1964.

Peo-Peo Tahlikt. "Stories About Indians as Told by Chief Peo-Peo Tahlikt to Sam Lott (Many Wounds), February 25, 1935." Washington State University, Pullman.

Sherrill, Thomas. "The Battle of the Big Hole as I Saw It." Montana Historical Society, Helena.

Snyder, Simon. Diary. Little Bighorn Battlefield National Monument, Montana.

Wilmot, Luther P. "Narratives of the Nez Perce War." University of Idaho, Moscow.

Wood, Charles Erskine Scott (C. E. S.). Diary, Journal, and Papers. The Huntington Library, San Marino, California.

GOVERNMENT DOCUMENTS

Annual Report of the Secretary of Interior, 1876–1877, National Archives.

Annual Reports of the Commissioner of Indian Affairs, 1871–1900, National Archives.

Annual Reports of the Secretary of War, 1875–1877, National Archives.

Hershler, N. *The Soldier's Handbook*. Washington, D.C.: Government Printing Office, 1884.

Miscellaneous Letters of the Montana Superintendency, National Archives.

Mooney, James. *The Ghost-Dance Religion*. Bureau of American Ethnology, 14th Annual Report, Washington, D.C., 1896.

Records of the U.S. Army. Adjutant General's File, 1877–1885. Consolidated Correspondence File comprising Record Group No. 94 (3464 AGO 1877). National Archives.

Report of the Adjutant-General of Oregon, 1865–1866. Salem, Oregon: 1866.

Senate Executive Documents. 40th Cong., 3d sess., 1868–1869. No. 18, pt. 1, 5.

Senate Executive Documents. 45th Cong., 2d sess., 1877. No. 14.

Senate Executive Documents. "Claims of the Nez Perce Indians," 56th Cong., 1st sess., 1899–1900. Vol. 25, no. 257.

U.S. Department of Agriculture (Forest Service). *The Nez Perce (Nee-Me-Poo) National Historic Trail Comprehensive Plan*. Washington, D.C.: Government Printing Office, 1990.

U.S. 95th Court of Claims. *Joseph's Band of the Nez Perce Tribe of Indians v. The United States*. Case No. 1096, 1941–1942.

U.S. War Department. *Record of Engagements with Hostile Indians Within the Military Division of the Missouri from 1868 to 1882, Lieutenant General P. H. Sheridan, Commanding*. Chicago: Headquarters Military Division of the Missouri, 1882.

Wood, (Major) Henry Clay. *Status of Young Joseph and His Band of Nez Perce Indians Under the Treaties Between the United States and the Nez Perce Tribe of Indians and the Indian Title to Land*. Portland: Assistant Adjutant General's Office of Headquarters of Department of Columbia, 1876.

―――. *Supplementary to the Report on the Treaty Status of Young Joseph*. Portland: Assistant Adjutant General's Office of Headquarters of Department of Columbia, 1878.

NEWSPAPERS AND PERIODICALS

Army and Navy Journal
Billings Times
Bismarck *Tri-Weekly Tribune*
Bozeman *Avant Courier*
Bozeman Times
Butte Miner
Chicago *Times*
Chicago *Tribune*
Deer Lodge *New North-West*
Denver *Rocky Mountain News*
Fort Benton Record
Helena *Daily and Weekly Herald*
Lewiston Morning Tribune
Lewiston *Teller*
Missoula *Weekly and Sunday Missoulian*
New York *Herald*
New York Sun
New York Times
Portland *Daily and Weekly Standard*
Salmon City *Idaho Recorder*
San Francisco *Chronicle*
Virginia City *Madisonian*
Washington, D.C., *The Council Fire*

Alcorn, Rowena L., and Gordon D. Alcorn. "Old Nez Perce Recalls Tragic Retreat of 1877." *Montana, the Magazine of Western History* (Winter 1963): 66–74.

Andrews, E. N. "A Buffalo Hunt by Rail." *Kansas Magazine* (May 1873): 453–54.

Baird, G. W. "General Miles' Indian Campaigns." *Century Magazine* 42 (July 1891): 351–70.

Bartlett, Grace. "Ollokot and Joseph." *Idaho Yesterdays* (Spring 1977): 22–30.

Brown, Mark H. "Chief Joseph and the 'Lyin' Jack' Syndrome." *Montana, the Magazine of Western History* (October 1972): 72–73.

———. "The Joseph Myth." *Montana, the Magazine of Western History* (January 1972): 2–17.

————. "Yellowstone Tourists and the Nez Perce." *Montana, the Magazine of Western History* (July 1966): 30–43.

Cave, Will. "Most Bitter Indian Battle Near Missoula." *The Sunday Missoulian*, 7 August 1921.

Clark, Stanley J. "The Nez Perces in Exile." *Pacific Northwest Quarterly* 36 (July 1945): 215.

Davison, Stanley R. "A Century Ago: The Tortuous Pursuit." *Montana, the Magazine of Western History* (October 1977): 2–19.

Dippie, Brian W. "This Bold but Wasting Race: Stereotypes and American Indian Policy." *Montana, the Magazine of Western History* (January 1973): 2–13.

Ellis, Richard N. "The Humanitarian Generals." *Western Historical Quarterly* 3 (April 1972): 169–78.

Forse, Albert G. "Chief Joseph as a Commander." *Winners of the West* 13 (November 1936): 3–6.

Garfield, James A. "Diary of a Trip to Montana in 1872." Edited by Oliver W. Holmes. *Frontier and Midland* 15 (1934): 159–68.

Gibbon, John. "The Battle of the Big Hole." Parts 1, 2. *Harper's Weekly* 39 (21, 28 December 1895): 1215–16, 1235–36.

————. "The Pursuit of Joseph." *American Catholic Quarterly Review* 4 (1879): 317–44.

Goodenough, Daniel, Jr. "Lost on Cold Creek." *Montana, the Magazine of Western History* (Fall 1974): 16–29.

Greenburg, D. W. "Victim of the Nez Perce Tells Story of Indian Atrocities." *Winners of the West* 2 (February 1926): 8.

Haines, Aubrey L. "The Bannock Indian Trails of Yellowstone National Park." *Archaeology in Montana* 4 (March 1962): 1–8.

Haines, Francis D. "How the Indian Got His Horse." *American Heritage* (February 1964): 16–22.

Harrison, Michael. "Chief Charlot's Battle with Bureaucracy." *Montana, the Magazine of Western History* (October 1960): 27–33.

Howard, Oliver O. "The Nez Perce's Campaign of 1877." *The Advance* (3 January through 3 October 1878).

————. "True Story of the Wallowa Campaign." *North American Review* (May 1879): 53–64.

Jacobs, Wilbur R. "The Indian and the Frontier in American History: A Need for Revision." *Western Historical Quarterly* 4 (January 1973): 43–56.

———. "Native American History: How It Illuminates Our Past." *American Historical Review* 80 (June 1975): 595–609.

Joseph. "An Indian's View of Indian Affairs." *North American Review* (April 1879): 412–33.

Lang, William. "Where Did the Nez Perce Go in Yellowstone in 1877?" *Montana, the Magazine of Western History* (Winter 1990): 14–29.

Lee, Jason. "Diary of Reverend Jason Lee." *Oregon Historical Quarterly* 17 (1916): 140.

Leonard, Thomas. "The Reluctant Conquerors: How the Generals Viewed the Indians." *American Heritage* (August 1976): 34–40.

Loynes, Charles N. "Battle of the Big Hole." *Winners of the West* (March 1925): 2.

McDonald, Duncan. "The Nez Perces, the History of Their Trouble and the Campaign of 1877." *New North-West* (26 April 1878 through 28 March 1879).

Millbrook, Minnie Dubbs. "A Monument to Custer." *Montana, the Magazine of Western History* (Spring 1974): 18–33.

Miller, Henry. "Letters from the Upper Columbia." *Idaho Yesterdays* (Winter 1960–1961): 18–22.

Moody, Charles Stuart. "The Bravest Deed I Ever Knew." *Century Magazine* 55 (1911): 783–84.

Mueller, Oscar O. "The Nez Perce at Cow Island." *Montana, the Magazine of Western History* (April 1964): 50–53.

Myers, Rex C. "The Settlers and the Nez Perce." *Montana, the Magazine of Western History* (October 1977): 20–29.

Park, Edwards. "Big Hole: Still a Gaping Wound to Nez Perce." *Smithsonian* (May 1978): 92–99.

Redington, J. W. "Scouting in Montana in the 1870's." *The Frontier* 13 (November 1932): 55–68.

Remsen (Henry Remsen Tilton). "After the Nez Perces." *Forest and Stream and Rod and Gun* 9 (December 1877): 403–404.

Rosenberg, Marvin, and Dorothy Rosenberg. "There Are No Indians Left But Me." *American Heritage* (June 1964): 18–23.

Rowton, J. G. "A Tribute to Mrs. Bunker." *Winners of the West* 3 (March 1926): 2.

Ruby, Robert H. "First Account of Nez Perce War by Man Who Went: Josiah Red Wolf." *Inland Empire Magazine* (17 November 1963): 3–4.

Shearer, George M. "The Skirmish at Cottonwood." *Idaho Yesterdays* (Summer 1958): 1–7.

Sutherland, Thomas A. Dispatches dated May through October 1877. Portland *Standard* (weekly and daily), San Francisco *Chronicle,* and New York *Herald,* June through November 1877.

Thompson, Erwin N. "The Summer of '77 at Fort Lapwai." *Idaho Yesterdays* (Summer 1977): 11–15.

Titus, Nelson C. "The Last Stand of the Nez Perces." *Washington Historical Quarterly* 6 (July 1915), 145–53.

Utley, Robert M. "Oliver Otis Howard." *New Mexico Historical Review* 62 (January 1987): 55–63.

Weisel, George F. "Ram's Horn Tree and Other Medicine Trees of the Flathead Indians." *Montana, the Magazine of Western History* 1 (1951): 5–14.

Whalen, Sue. "The Nez Perces' Relationship to Their Land." *The Indian Historian* 4 (Fall 1971): 30–33.

Wood, Charles Erskine Scott. "Chief Joseph, the Nez Perce." *Century Magazine* 6 (May 1884): 135–42.

Woodruff, Thomas M. "We Have Joseph and All His People: A Soldier Writes Home About the Final Battle." *Montana, the Magazine of Western History* (October 1977): 30–33.

BOOKS

Adkison, Norman B. *Nez Perce Indian War and Original Stories.* Grangeville: Idaho County Free Press, 1966.

Athearn, Robert G. *William Tecumseh Sherman and the Settlement of the West.* Norman: University of Oklahoma Press, 1956.

Ault, Nelson. *The Papers of Lucullus Virgil McWhorter.* Pullman: Friends of the Library of Washington State University, 1959.

Bailey, Robert C. *River of No Return.* Lewiston, Idaho: Bailey Publishing Company, 1943.

Baldwin, Alice. *Memoirs of the Late Frank D. Baldwin, Major General, U.S.A.* Los Angeles: Wetzel Publishing Co., 1929.

Beal, Merrill D. *I Will Fight No More Forever.* 1963. Reprint. New York: Ballantine Books, 1971.

Beck, Warren A., and Ynez D. Hasse. *Historical Atlas of the American West.* Norman and London: University of Oklahoma Press, 1989.

Berkhofer, Robert F. *The White Man's Indian: Images of the American Indian from Columbus to the Present.* New York: Random House, 1978.

Bond, Fred. *Flatboating on the Yellowstone.* New York: American Library Association, 1925.

Bonney, Orrin H., and Lorraine Bonney. *Battle Drums and Geysers.* Chicago: Swallow Press, 1972.

Bradley, James H. "Arrapooish." In vol. 9 of *Contributions to the Historical Society of Montana.* Boston: J. S. Canner, 1966.

———. *The March of the Montana Column: A Prelude to the Custer Disaster.* Edited by Edgar Stewart. Norman: University of Oklahoma Press, 1961.

Brady, Cyrus. *Northwestern Fights and Fighters.* 1913. Reprint. Williamstown, Massachusetts: Corner House Publishers, 1974.

Brosnan, Cornelius J. *Jason Lee, Prophet of the New Oregon.* New York: Macmillan Company, 1929.

Brown, Mark H. *The Flight of the Nez Perce.* 1967. Reprint. Lincoln: University of Nebraska Press, 1971.

Capps, Walter Holden. *Seeing with a Native Eye: Essays on Native American Religion.* New York: Harper & Row, 1976.

Carpenter, John A. *Sword and Olive Branch: Oliver Otis Howard.* Pittsburgh: University of Pittsburgh Press, 1964.

Carroll, John M., ed. *General Custer and the Battle of the Little Big Horn: The Federal View.* New Brunswick, New Jersey: Garry Owen Press, 1976.

———. *The Benteen-Goldin Letters on Custer and His Last Battle.* New York: Liveright, 1974.

Catlin, George. *Letters and Notes on the Manners, Customs, and Condition of the North American Indians.* 2 vols. New York: 1842.

Chittenden, Hiram M. *The Yellowstone National Park.* Edited by Richard A. Bartlett. Norman: University of Oklahoma Press, 1964.

Chittenden, Hiram M., and Alfred T. Richardson. *Life, Letters and Travels of Father Pierre-Jean DeSmet, S. J., 1801–1873.* 4 vols. New York: Francis P. Harper, 1905.

Clark, Ella E. *Indian Legends from the Northern Rockies.* Norman: University of Oklahoma Press, 1966.

Coleman, Michael C. *Presbyterian Missionary Attitudes toward American Indians, 1837–1893.* Jackson and London: University Press of Mississippi, 1985.

Collections of the State Historical Society of North Dakota. Vol. 1. Bismarck: 1906.

Connell, Evan S. *Son of the Morning Star.* Berkeley, California: North Point Press, 1984.

Cowan, Emma Carpenter. "A Trip to the National Park in 1877." In vol. 4 of *Contributions to the Historical Society of Montana.* Boston: J. S. Canner, 1966.

Craighead, John J., and Frank C. Craighead, Jr. *A Field Guide to Rocky Mountain Wildflowers.* Boston: Houghton Mifflin, 1963.

Crowder, David L. *Tendoy, Chief of the Lemhis.* Caldwell, Idaho: The Caxton Printers, Ltd., 1969.

Curtis, Edward S. *The North American Indian.* Vol. 8. Seattle: E. S. Curtis, 1911.

Dary, David A. *The Buffalo Book.* Chicago: Avon Books, 1974.

Dobyns, Henry F. *Native American Historical Demography: A Critical Bibliography.* Bloomington: Indiana University Press, 1976.

Drury, Clifford M., ed. *Diaries and Letters of Henry H. Spalding and Asa Bowen Smith Relating to the Nez Perce Mission 1838–1842.* Glendale, California: Arthur H. Clark Co., 1958.

———. *Henry Harmon Spalding.* Caldwell, Idaho: The Caxton Printers, Ltd., 1936.

———. *Marcus Whitman, M.D.* Caldwell, Idaho: The Caxton Printers, Ltd., 1937.

Ege, Robert J. *After the Little Bighorn.* Great Falls, Montana: Fred H. Werner, 1982.

Fahey, John. *The Flathead Indians*. Norman: University of Oklahoma Press, 1974.

Fee, Chester A. *Chief Joseph, The Biography of a Great Indian*. New York: Wilson-Erickson, 1936.

Fisher, S. G. "Journal of S. G. Fisher." In vol. 2 of *Contributions to the Historical Society of Montana*. Boston: J. S. Canner, 1966.

Garcia, Andrew. *Tough Trip Through Paradise*. 1967. Reprint. Sausalito, California: Comstock Editions, Inc., 1986.

Gass, Patrick. *A Journal of the Voyages and Travels of a Corps of Discovery Under the Command of Capt. Lewis and Capt. Clarke . . . 1804, 1805, and 1806*. Pittsburgh: David McKeehan, 1807.

Gidley, Mick. *Kopet: A Documentary Narrative of Chief Joseph's Last Years*. Seattle: University of Washington Press, 1981.

———. *With One Sky Above Us: Life on an Indian Reservation at the Turn of the Century*. New York: Putnam, 1979.

Goldin, Theodore W. *A Bit of the Nez Perce Campaign*. Bryan, Texas: Privately published, 1978.

Gray, William H. *History of Oregon*. Portland: Harris & Holman, 1870.

Guie, Heister D., and Lucullus Virgil McWhorter. *Adventures in Geyserland*. Caldwell, Idaho: The Caxton Printers, Ltd., 1935.

Gulick, Bill. *Chief Joseph Country: Land of the Nez Perce*. Caldwell, Idaho: The Caxton Printers, Ltd., 1985.

Haines, Francis D. *Red Eagles of the Northwest: The Story of Chief Joseph and His People*. Portland: Scholastic Press, 1939.

———. *The Nez Perces*. Norman: University of Oklahoma Press, 1955.

Hakola, John, and H. G. Merriam. *Frontier Omnibus*. Missoula: Montana State University Press and the Montana Historical Society, 1962.

Harris, Edward. *Up the Missouri with Audubon: The Journal of Edward Harris*. Edited by John Francis McDermott. Norman: University of Oklahoma Press, 1951.

Hathaway, Ella C. *Battle of the Big Hole in August, 1877*. Seattle: Shorey Book Store, 1967.

Hedren, Paul L. *The Great Sioux War 1876–77*. Helena: Montana Historical Society Press, 1991.

Hobson, G. C., ed. *The Idaho Digest and Blue Book.* Caldwell, Idaho: The Caxton Printers, Ltd., 1935.

Hornaday, William T. "Extermination of the American Bison." Part 2 of *Annual Report of the Smithsonian Institution 1887.* Washington, D.C.: Smithsonian Institution, 1889.

Howard, Helen Addison. *Saga of Chief Joseph.* 1941. Reprint. Lincoln and London: University of Nebraska Press, 1965.

Howard, Oliver O. *Famous Indian Chiefs I Have Known.* 1908. Reprint. Lincoln: University of Nebraska Press, 1989.

———. *My Life and Experiences Among Our Hostile Indians.* 1907. Reprint. New York: Da Capo Press, 1972.

———. *Nez Perce Joseph.* 1881. Reprint. New York: Da Capo Press, 1972.

Hunter, George. *Reminiscences of an Old Timer.* San Francisco: H. S. Crocker & Co., 1887.

Hutton, Paul Andrew. *Phil Sheridan and His Army.* Lincoln and London: University of Nebraska Press, 1985.

———. *Soldiers West: Biographies from the Military Frontier.* Lincoln and London: University of Nebraska Press, 1987.

An Illustrated History of North Idaho. Spokane, Washington: Western Historical Publishing Co., 1903.

Jocelyn, Stephen Perry. *Mostly Alkali.* Caldwell, Idaho: The Caxton Printers, Ltd., 1953.

Johnson, Virginia W. *The Unregimented General.* Boston: Houghton Mifflin, 1962.

Josephy, Alvin M., Jr. *Nez Perce Country.* Nez Perce National Historical Park, U.S. Department of Interior, Publication No. 121, 1983.

———. *The Nez Perce Indians and the Opening of the Northwest.* New Haven and London: Yale University Press, 1965.

Kirkwood, Charlotte M. *The Nez Perce Indian War Under Chief Joseph and White Bird.* Grangeville: Idaho County Free Press, 1928.

Knight, Oliver. *Following the Indian Wars.* Norman: University of Oklahoma Press, 1960.

Koch, Adrienne, and William Peden. *Selected Writings of Thomas Jefferson.* New York: Modern Library, 1944.

Koury, Michael J. *Diaries of the Little Bighorn*. Bellevue, Nebraska: The Old Army Press, 1968.

———. *Gibbon on the Sioux Campaign of 1876*. Bellevue, Nebraska: The Old Army Press, 1970.

Kvasnicka, Robert M., and Herman J. Viola. *The Commissioners of Indian Affairs, 1824–1977*. Lincoln: University of Nebraska Press, 1979.

Laufe, Abe, ed. *An Army Doctor's Wife on the Frontier*. Pittsburgh: University of Pittsburgh Press, 1962.

Lavender, David. *Let Me Be Free*. New York: HarperCollins, 1992.

———. *The Way to the Western Sea*. New York: Harper & Row, 1988.

Limerick, Patricia Nelson. *The Legacy of Conquest*. New York: W. W. Norton, 1987.

Linderman, Frank Bird. *Pretty-Shield: Medicine Woman of the Crows*. Lincoln: University of Nebraska Press, 1974.

McConville, Edward. "Report to Governor Brayman, August 1877." *Fifteenth Biennial Report*. Boise: Idaho Historical Society, 1936.

McDermott, John D. *Forlorn Hope: The Battle of White Bird Canyon and the Beginning of the Nez Perce War*. Boise: Idaho State Historical Society, 1978.

McFeely, William S. *Yankee Stepfather: General O. O. Howard and the Freedmen*. New Haven: Yale University Press, 1968.

McHugh, Tom. *The Time of the Buffalo*. New York: Knopf, 1972.

McLaughlin, James. *My Friend, The Indian*. Boston: Houghton Mifflin, 1910.

McWhorter, Lucullus Virgil. *Hear Me My Chiefs!* Caldwell, Idaho: The Caxton Printers, Ltd., 1952.

———. *Yellow Wolf: His Own Story*. Caldwell, Idaho: The Caxton Printers, Ltd., 1948.

Malone, Michael P., and Richard B. Roeder. *Montana: A History of Two Centuries*. Seattle and London: University of Washington Press, 1976.

Marquis, Thomas B. *Memoirs of a White Crow Indian*. New York: Century Co., 1928.

Mayer, Frederic. "The Nez Perce War Diary of Frederic Mayer." *Seventeenth Biennial Report*. Boise: Idaho Historical Society, 1940.

Miles, Nelson A. *Personal Recollections and Observations of General Nelson A. Miles.* Chicago: Werner Co., 1897.

———. *Serving the Republic.* New York: Harper and Brothers, 1911.

Mills, Charles K. *Charles C. DeRudio.* Mattituck, New York: 1983.

Morgan, Dale, and Eleanor Harris. *The Rocky Mountain Journals of William Marshall Anderson.* Lincoln: University of Nebraska Press, 1987.

Morris, Edmund. *The Rise of Theodore Roosevelt.* New York: Random House, 1979.

Mulford, Ami Frank. *Fighting Indians in the 7th United States Cavalry.* Corning, New York: Paul Lindsley Mulford, 1879.

Nevin, David. *The Soldiers.* New York: Time-Life Books, 1973.

Noyes, Alva J. *In the Land of Chinook.* Helena, Montana: State Publishing Co., 1917.

Parker, Samuel. *Journal of an Exploring Tour beyond the Rocky Mountains.* Moscow: University of Idaho Press, 1990.

Prucha, Francis Paul. *A Bibliographical Guide to the History of Indian-White Relations in the United States.* Chicago: University of Chicago Press, 1977.

Quaife, M. M., ed. *Yellowstone Kelly: The Memoirs of Luther S. Kelly.* New Haven: Yale University Press, 1926.

Rickey, Don, Jr. *Forty Miles a Day on Beans and Hay.* Norman: University of Oklahoma Press, 1963.

Romeyn, Henry. "The Capture of Chief Joseph and the Nez Perce Indians." In vol. 2 of *Contributions to the Historical Society of Montana.* Boston: J. S. Canner, 1966.

Ruby, Robert H., and John A. Brown. *Dreamer-Prophets of the Columbia Plateau.* Norman: University of Oklahoma Press, 1989.

Scott, Hugh L. *Some Memories of a Soldier.* New York: Century Co., 1928.

Shields, George O. *Battle of the Big Hole.* New York: Rand, McNally & Co., 1889.

Slickpoo, Allen P. *Nonn Nee-Me-Poo (We, the Nez Perces): Culture and History of the Nez Perces.* Lapwai, Idaho: Nez Perce Tribe, 1973.

Space, Ralph S. *The Lolo Trail.* Lewiston, Idaho: Printcraft Printing, Inc., 1970.

Spinden, Herbert J. *The Nez Perce Indians.* Vol. 2 of *Memoirs of the American Anthropological Association.* Lancaster, Pennsylvania: New Era Printing Co., 1908.

Stegner, Wallace. *Beyond the Hundredth Meridian.* Boston: Houghton Mifflin, 1962.

Sternberg, Martha L. *George Miller Sternberg.* Chicago: American Medical Association, 1920.

Sutherland, Thomas A. *Howard's Campaign Against the Nez Perce Indians, 1877.* 1878. Reprint. Fairfield, Washington: Ye Galleon Press, 1980.

Thornton, Russell. *American Indian Holocaust and Survival: A Population History Since 1492.* Norman: University of Oklahoma Press, 1987.

Thrapp, Dan L. *Encyclopedia of Frontier Biography.* Lincoln and London: University of Nebraska Press, 1988.

Thwaites, Reuben G., ed. *Original Journals of the Lewis and Clark Expedition 1804–1806.* New York: Antiquarian Press, 1959.

Trafzer, Cliff. *The Northwestern Tribes in Exile.* Sacramento, California: Sierra Oaks Publishing Co., 1987.

Turner, John P. *The Northwest Mounted Police, 1873–1893.* Ottawa: Edmond Cloutier, 1950.

Utley, Robert M. *The Indian Frontier of the American West 1846–1890.* Albuquerque: University of New Mexico Press, 1984.

———. *Frontier Regulars: The United States Army and the Indian, 1866–1891.* New York: Macmillan, 1973.

Walker, Deward E. *Conflict and Schism in Nez Perce Acculturation: A Study of Religion and Politics.* Pullman: Washington State University Press, 1968.

Warren, Robert Penn. *Chief Joseph of the Nez Perce.* New York: Random House, 1983.

Weikert, Andrew J. "Journal of a Tour through Yellowstone National Park in August and September 1877." In vol. 3 of *Contributions to the Historical Society of Montana.* Boston: J. S. Canner, 1966.

White, Lonnie J. *Hostiles and Horse Soldiers.* Boulder, Colorado: Pruett Publishing Company, 1972.

Wilfong, Cheryl. *Following the Nez Perce Trail.* Corvallis: Oregon State University Press, 1990.

Williams, T. Harry. *Lincoln and His Generals*. New York: Knopf, 1952.

Wilson, Eugene T. *Hawks and Doves in the Nez Perce War*. Helena: Montana Historical Society, 1966.

Wood, Charles Erskine Scott. *The Poet in the Desert*. 1915. Reprint. New York: Vanguard, 1929.

Woodruff, Charles A. "Battle of the Big Hole." In vol. 7 of *Contributions to the Montana Historical Society*. Boston: J. S. Canner, 1966.

Wooster, Robert. *The Military and United States Indian Policy 1865–1903*. New Haven: Yale University Press, 1988.

Acknowledgments

Books are the result of an author's stimulating encounters with other people and their ideas. If this one falls short, it is not the fault of the many generous people who gave me help and encouragement along the way.

Thanks to Geoffrey O'Gara for his careful critique of the manuscript. Wilford Halfmoon (the great-grandson of Pahkatos Owyeen), Allen Pinkham (a relative of Wahlitits), and Sandi McFarland reviewed the manuscript and offered invaluable advice. As Nez Perce knowledgeable about their people's past, Wilford, Allen, and Sandi presented their own opinions, which do not necessarily represent the official position of the tribe. Maps were rendered by the talented artist Anne Austin. My literary agent, Michael Congdon, and editor, John Macrae, offered advice throughout and never lost confidence in the effort to bring this book into print.

Stuart Conner generously contributed new information about the historic route along the Clarks Fork River, a research effort shared by Kenneth Feyhl, Aubrey Haines, Michael Bryant, and Charles William Jones.

Mary Stark and Dr. Fitzgerald Hiestand, Jr., and Barbara Hiestand offered useful information as well as photographs of Dr. John and Emily FitzGerald. Attorney Reb Gregg provided copies of legal documents concerning tribal challenges to the 1863 treaty and critiqued my interpretations. Author Cheryl Wilfong shared advice and enthusiasm for a subject that means much to us both.

Many of the unpublished manuscripts, papers, and correspondence necessary to a complex study of this kind reside in special collections throughout the country. Special thanks to Barbara Oakleaf and the staff of Wyoming's Fremont County Library for their patient assistance with my countless requests for publications.

Also of particular help were Susan Ravdin and the staff of Bowdoin College (O. O. Howard Papers); Peter Blodgett of the Huntington Library (C. E. S. Wood Papers); John Guido, Tina Atkinson Oswald, and José Vargas of the Holland Library, Washington State University (Lucullus Virgil McWhorter Papers); L. L. Baker and the staff of the Harold B. Lee Library, Brigham Young University (Walter Camp Papers); and the staff of Montana State University (Gustavus Doane Papers).

Special appreciation to both Caxton Printers, Ltd., and the Lucullus Virgil McWhorter family for permission to quote extensively from both *Yellow Wolf: His Own Story* and *Hear Me, My Chiefs!*, as well as from McWhorter's nonpareil collection of Nez Perce memorabilia residing in the library of Washington State University.

Some of the West's richest historical material is available in the Montana Historical Society Library and Archives. Special thanks to Robert Clark for permission to quote from the society's archives and to Dave Walters for his untiring efforts in uncovering much valuable material. Also helpful were Marjorie Geier and the staff of the Idaho Historical Society; Nez Perce historian Allen Slickpoo, Sr.; Jock Whitworth of the Big Hole National Battlefield; Jim Dolan of the U.S. Forest Service, project coordinator for the Nez Perce National Historic Trail; Susan Buchel of the Nez Perce National Historic Park; Margie Bachman of the University of Pittsburgh; the staffs of the University of Montana and Central Wyoming College libraries; the Western History Department of the Denver Public Library; the Chicago Historical Society; the Smithsonian Institution; and the National Archives, Library of Congress, and U.S. Military Academy.

I am forever indebted to my parents, Lucia and Keith Hampton, who early on instilled in me an avid interest in the past. My wife, Molly, with her own busy career, always found time to offer helpful critique and read yet another working draft. This book simply would not have been possible without her ceaseless inspiration and support. It is our profound hope that our daughter, Sara, will grow up in a world that comes to value all human cultures for their richness, diversity, and right to self-determination.

Index

Mason, Edwin C.
  and attempted surrender, 120
  at Bannack, 196
  at Big Hole battlefield, 176, 178,
    179, 182
  at Camas Meadows battle, 212
  at Carroll, 277, 305, 312
  on cavalry, 119–20
  at Clarks Fork Canyon, 258
  at Henrys Lake, 216, 217, 222
  on Lolo Trail, 124–26, 152–54
  at Monida Pass, 205, 207
  in Salmon River Mountains, 96
  on volunteers, 129
  in Yellowstone, 231, 233, 251–52
Mason, Harry, 3, 8–9
Maurer, George, 189
Meacham, A. B., 327
Merrill, Lewis, 265, 266
Merritt, Wesley, 221, 240
Meyers, D. L., 226, 231
Miles, Mary, 367n.22
Miles, Nelson, 146, 188, 222, 246,
    255, 264, 277, 327, 371n.19
  answers Howard, 275–76
  at Bear Paw battle, 292–310
  credited with capture, 312–16
  description of, 283–84, 367–
    68n.25
  as patron of Nez Perce, 311,
    318, 319, 320, 322, 324, 331,
    333, 335
  pursues Nez Perce, 285–87
  and Sherman, 283
  and Sitting Bull, 284
  transports prisoners, 316–18
Miller, Henry, 21–22
Miller, Marcus, 115, 132, 214
Mills, James, 143, 144, 145, 190,
    197, 223, 225
Missoula, Montana, 127, 130, 131,
    135, 136, 137, 138, 139, 142,
143, 145, 146, 149, 153, 156,
    178
Missoula *Weekly Missoulian*, 136,
    139, 140, 143, 144, 181, 190
Mitchell, Campbell, 170–71
Modoc Indians, 46, 63, 64, 121, 140
Moelchert, William, 278–79
Montague, W. L., 194
Monteith, Charles, 57, 330, 331,
    372n.44
Monteith, John C., 41, 48, 137
  becomes agent, 33
  death of, 372n.44
  and 1876 Commission, 43–47
  at final meeting, 50
  with Joseph, 36, 37
  on Nez Perce strength, 83
  with Ollokot, 49
  at outbreak, 60
  proposes Wallowa reservation, 35
  on Smohalla, 43, 45
Moore, Joe, 10, 11, 12, 16
Mount Idaho, Idaho, 4, 5, 6, 14, 16,
    58, 60, 62, 70, 71, 77, 84, 85,
    87, 89, 91, 95, 100, 103, 109
Moylan, Myles, 293, 294, 295
Mulford, Frank, 66
Mullan Road, 127, 130, 178

Nesmith, J. W., 30
Nespelem Indians, 332
New York *Christian Advocate and
    Journal*, 25
New York *Herald*, 96, 181, 364n.18
New York Sun, 333–34
New York Times, 83, 312
New York *Tribune*, 61
Newman, George, 333
Nez Perce Indians. *See specific
    topic*
Nez Perce Reservation, 1, 30, 41,
    54, 137, 333, 342n.16, 373n.49

U.S. Military Academy, 39, 156, 254, 312

Victor, 135
Virginia City *Madisonian,* 207, 210
Virginia City, Montana, 171, 204, 205, 211, 217, 218, 222, 250

Wahlitits, 2, 3, 73, 166–67, 172, 357n.50
Wallowa band (Nez Perce), 4, 48, 49, 50, 291
Wallula Indians, 44
Wallula Junction, 331
Walsh, Helen, 8, 9
Walsh, James, 298, 300
Washington, George, 29
Washita, battle of, 284
Watkins, Erwin, 57, 58, 89, 91, 320, 345n.2
Wayakat (Going Across), 118
Weesculatat, 102–3, 113
Weikert, Andrew, 234, 235, 236, 237, 238
Wetatonmi, 172
Wewaltolkit Pah (Camas Creek), 207
Weyahwahtsitskan, 72
Wheaton, Frank, 127, 128, 130, 178
Whipple, Stephen, 41, 52, 91, 92–94, 95, 97–98, 99, 100, 101, 102, 178
White Bird, nephew of, 163
White Bird (Peopeo Hihhih), 30, 53, 92, 120, 121, 140
  advocates fleeing homeland, 146
  at Bear Paw battle, 291, 302, 309, 320
  at Big Hole battle, 167–68
  at Birch Creek, 202
  in Canada, 324–25
  death of, 325
  description of, 51, 345n.30

  at Stevensville, 147–48
  and Tendoy, 197, 198
  at White Bird Canyon battle, 71
White Bird Canyon, battle of, 70–80, 82, 84, 92, 102, 113, 160, 162, 167, 185
White, Elijah, 27
White Feather, 370n.41
Whitman, Perrin, 60
Wilhautyah (Wind Blowing), 43
Wilkie, Leslie, 234, 235
Wilkinson, Melville, 107
Williams, Camille, 71
Williams, Constant, 176, 189
Wilmot, Lew, 10, 16, 69, 100–101, 102, 103, 108, 109
Wilson, Eugene, 125
Winters, Frances, 111
Wood, Charles Erskine Scott (C. E. S.), 121, 340n.4, 351n.42
  at Bear Paw battle, 304, 305, 306
  at Camas Meadows battle, 208
  at Clearwater battle, 111, 112
  at Horse Prairie, 197
  with Howard in Chicago, 313–14
  as poet, 372n.42
  revises surrender, 369–70nn.33, 34
  supports repatriation, 319, 329
  on surrender, 307, 308–9, 310
  at White Bird Canyon battlefield, 90, 348n.21
Wood, H. Clay, 42, 43, 45, 46
Woodbridge, Francis, 137, 138
Woodcock, William, 177–78
Woodruff, Charles, 159, 162, 171, 172, 173, 175, 176
Workman, James, 113
Wottolen, 116, 193, 208, 211, 289, 304